Quantitative Technical Analysis

Quantitative Technical Analysis

An Integrated Approach
to
Trading System Development
and
Trade Management

Howard B. Bandy

Blue Owl Press, Inc.

Copyright © 2015 Howard B. Bandy

All rights reserved.
First edition 2015

No part of this publication may be reproduced, stored in a retrieval system, or transmitted in any form or by any means, electronic, mechanical, photocopying, recording, or otherwise without the prior written permission of the copyright holder, except brief quotations used in a review.

ISBN-13: 978-097918385-0
LCCN: 2013952750

Published by
Blue Owl Press
3220 Crescent Avenue, #65
Eugene, OR 97408

Published 2015
Printed in the United States
18 17 16 15   1 2 3 4 5 6 7 8 9 10

Disclaimer

This book is an educational document. Nothing in this book is intended as, nor should it be construed to be, investment advice.

The views expressed herein are the personal views of Dr. Howard B. Bandy. Neither the author nor the publisher, Blue Owl Press, Inc., have any commercial interest in any of the products mentioned. All of the products described were purchased by the author at regular retail prices.

Investing and trading is risky and can result in loss of principal. Neither this book in its entirety, nor any portion thereof, nor any follow-on discussion or correspondence related to this book, is intended to be a recommendation to invest or trade mutual funds, stocks, commodities, options, or any other financial instrument. Neither the author nor the publisher will accept any responsibility for losses which might result from applications of the ideas expressed in the book or from techniques or trading systems described in the book.

All results shown are from simulations. None are the results from actual trades. Neither past actual performance, nor simulations of performance, assure similar future results, or even profitable future results.

Programs

The programs used as examples have been tested and are believed to be correct. However, errors may still remain. Programs are "as is" and without support beyond correction of errors. It is the reader's responsibility to verify the accuracy and correctness of all programs before using them to trade. Results will depend on the specific data series used, and will vary with changes in settings such commission, slippage, and delay between signal and transaction.

Programs have been written for clarity and educational value. Computational efficiency is not a consideration. Each and every method, technique, and program has many possible options and alternative implementations. No effort has been made to consider all of them, or to provide computer code to anticipate or accommodate them.

In an effort to maintain ease of understanding the basic concepts illustrated by the programs, code for detecting and gracefully handling run-time errors has been omitted.

Algorithms and programs are not guaranteed to be either without error or suitable for use. Do careful and complete testing and validation of all methods, techniques, and programs on your own computer using your own data before using any in live trading.

Program code that has a "Figure" or "Listing" number can be downloaded from the book's website:
    http://www.QuantitativeTechnicalAnalysis.com/Programs.html

When copying and pasting any program code, be aware of two common causes of introduced errors:
- line wrap
- quotation marks

Errata

If you find an error, please report it in an e-mail to:
    support@BlueOwlPress.com

Corrections will be posted to the errata file:
    http://www.QuantitativeTechnicalAnalysis.com/Errata.html

Questions, comments, discussion

Post questions and comments, share ideas and results, and participate in a discussion of concepts and techniques at the Blue Owl Press blog site:
    http://www.BlueOwlPress.com/WordPress/

Contents

1	Introduction	15
	The Goal	16
	Major Changes	16
	The Process	16
	Premises of Technical Analysis	17
	Two Components of Trading	17
	Position Sizing	19
	Development	21
	System = Model + Data	21
	The Model	21
	The Data	22
	Primary data	22
	Auxiliary data	23
	Assume nothing about distribution	23
	Distributions	23
	Reality	24
	List of trades, in time sequence	24
	List of trades	24
	Distribution of trades	24
	Four moments	24
	Mean and Standard Deviation	25
	Mean	25
	Direct	25
	Stay High on the List	25
	Patterns	26
	Non-stationary	26
	Synchronization	26
	Signal and Noise	27
	Data Series are Not Interchangeable	27

    Learning 27
    Subjectivity and Objective Functions 28
        Rank Alternative Systems 29
        Estimate Distributions of Performance 29
        Trader Psychology 30
    Trading Management 31
        Risk Tolerance 31
        Why Traders Stop Trading 31
            Results are too good 32
            Results are not worth the effort 32
            Results are not worth the stress 32
            She has enough money 32
            There is a serious drawdown 32
        Confidence 33
        Decisions and Uncertainty 35
    Why This is So Hard 35
        Low signal to noise ratio 35
        Nonstationary 35
        Time Series is Different 36
        Feedback 36
        Trend Following 36
        Limited Profit Potential 36
        Different Systems, Same Trades 36
        Very Large Search Space 37
        Out-of-sample Results Matter 37
        Financial Rewards 37
        Competition 37
    Summary 38

2   Risk and Risk Tolerance 39
    Measurement and Management 39
    Drawdown Defined 40
    Frequency of Action 41
        Minimum Holding Period 42
        Trade Exits 42
        Maximum Adverse Excursion (MAE) 43
            MAE for a single day 43
            MAE for a two-day trade 44
            MAE for a multi-day trade 45
            Intra-day prices are visible 45
            Intra-day prices are invisible 45
            MAE for a series of trades 46
    Maximum Favorable Excursion 48
    Accumulated MAE 48
    Bad Stuff Can Happen 49
        Management and measurement should coincide 49
        Does intra-trade drawdown matter? 49

  Mark-to-Market Equivalence 51
  Risk Tolerance 52
   Statement of Risk Tolerance 52
   Account Size 52
   Forecast Horizon 53
   Maximum Drawdown 53
   Degree of Certainty 53
   A Chart Illustrating Risk Tolerance 53
   Tail Risk and Black Swans 55
   Producing the CDF for Estimate of Risk 55
   Backtest Equity Curve 56
   Trade at Full Fraction 57
   Position Size — safe-f 58
   Using Final Equity as a Metric 62
   Evaluating Mark-to-Market Equivalence 64
   No Guarantee 66
   Technique for Risk Management 67
  Trade Quality 67
   Example System 67
  Summary 74
  Program Listing 75

3 Programming Environments 77
  Trading System Development Platform 78
   Default Database 80
   Database Setup — End-of-Day 81
   Free Database using AmiQuote 82
   Data Updates 85
   Sources of Free Data 85
   ASCII Import 85
   Yahoo Historical Data Download 87
   ASCII Import Wizard 87
   ASCII Import 88
   Subscription Data Providers 88
  Data Science and Machine Learning 90
  Python 90
   Environments 91
   Enthought Canopy 93
   Spyder 101
   Google 104
   Tutorials 106

4 Data 107
  Simulated Data 108
  Fundamental Data 108
  Over-the-counter Data 110
  Data Sources 111

  Read and Write Data Files 114
   AmiBroker 114
    Read data seres from disk 114
    Write data series to disk 114
    Write trades to disk 116
   Python 117
    Read end-of-day history from Yahoo Finance 117
    Canopy IDE 118
    Spyder IDE 118
    Read end-of-day data from Google Finance 119
    Read intra-day data from Google Finance 119
    Write csv file to disk 122
    Read csv file from disk 122

5 Issue Selection 123
  Market Research 123
  Risk and Profit Potential 124
   Simulation Outline 125
   Sidebar — Calculating CAR 127
   Drawdown as a Function of Holding Period 129
   Profit Potential 131
   Risk in Being Short 132
   What the Prospector Found 134
   Which Issues are "Best?" 138
   Universal Objective Function 138
   Holding Longer 138
   Long and Short 143
   Portfolios 143
  Summary 145
  Estimating Profit Potential —
   A Monte Carlo Simulation Program 146
  Program Listing 148

6 Model Development — Preliminaries 153
  Introduction 153
   A Mining Analogy 154
   The Past and the Future 155
  Two Processes to be Modeled 155
  Aspects of Model Development 156
  Goal 157
  Pattern Recognition 158
   Signals to Patterns 158
   Sea of Noise 158
  Data 159
   Bar Types 159
   Daily Bars 159
   Intra-day Bars 160

Trend Following	160
Indicators	161
Ideal Indicator	161
Fuzzy Indicator	162
Realistic Indicator	163
Entries and Exits	165
Perfect Bottoms and Tops	165
Trading Signals	168
Impulse Signals	168
State Signals	168
Finer control	169
Reduced distortion	169
Filters	170
200 Day Moving Average	170
Repainting	174
Order Placement	175
Anticipate Signals	175
Model Constraints	176
Comparison of Two Moving Average Systems	176
Restricted Model	177
Unrestricted Model	180
Fitting and Overfitting	182
Fitting a Trading Model	183
Objective Function	184
What is "Best?"	184
Objective Function for Trading	185
Metrics for Trading	186
Backtesting	187
Optimization	189
Dimensions in a Search Space	189
Global Optimum	191
Exhaustive Search	191
Non-exhaustive Search	191
Things to Watch For	192
Stationarity and Synchronization	193
In-sample and Out-of-sample	193
Stationarity	193
In-sample Data Length	194
Out-of-sample Data Length	195
In General	196
Number of Data Points	196
Validation	197
Midterm Exam	197
Walk Forward Testing	197
Some Other Way	200
Model Airplanes are Fun	200
Next Chapters	201

7	Model Development — Indicator-Based	203
	Indicator-based Development	203
	Program Template	203
	Objective Function	205
	Indicators	212
	What the Data Tells Us	212
	System Overview	212
	Indicator Selection	213
	Examples	215
	RSI - Relative Strength Indicator	215
	Z-score	217
	Position in range	219
	Detrended price oscillator	222
	Diffusion index	224
	Chart Patterns	228
	Comments	229
	Doubling Down or Pyramiding	229
	Entries	230
	Time	230
	Price	230
	Exits	231
	Logic	232
	Profit target	232
	Holding period	235
	Trailing exit	237
	Maximum loss exit	243
	Single statement exits	246
	Backtesting	246
	Optimization	248
	In-sample	249
	Out-of-sample	249
	Walk Forward	251
	Discovering Tradable Systems	255
	Validated Systems	256
	Summary	260
	Anticipating Signals	261
8	Model Development — Machine Learning	267
	Python as a Development Platform	267
	Data and Date Ranges	268
	Evaluation of Signals	272
	Translation to Python	274
	Convert Impulse Signals to State Signals	283
	Machine Learning — Generalities	290
	Supervised Learning	290
	Classification	292

Machine Learning—Examples using Iris	293
Sidebar—Python file directories	294
Cross Validation	302
Cross Validation Recommendations	304
Confusion Matrix	306
Overview with Diagrams	309
Train / Test Split	310
Model Fitting	310
Model Prediction	311
Model Evaluation	312
Stratified Shuffle Split	312
Data Preparation	314
Time and date alignment	315
Missing data	315
Outliers	315
Target definition	316
Transformations	316
Standardization	316
Normalization	317
Examples of Learning Algorithms	319
Ada boost	320
Decision tree	322
Gradient boost	324
Linear discriminant analysis	326
Logistic regression	328
Naive Bayes — Gaussian	330
Naive Bayes — multinomial	332
Nearest neighbor	334
Passive aggressive	336
Perceptron	338
Quadratic discriminant analysis	340
Random forests	342
Support vector machine with linear kernel	344
Support vector machine with polynomial kernel	346
Support vector machine with radial basis kernel	348
Balancing Class Membership	350
Adjusting Misclassification Costs	350
A Confusion Matrix for AmiBroker	351
In-sample Out-of-sample	354
Machine Learning—Trading	355
Dealing with Dimensionality	357
Setting Dates and Test Period Lengths	359
Stationarity and Validation	359
Validation	360
Perturb the data	360
Perturb the parameters	360

	Test other data	361
	Portfolios	361
	Walk forward	361
	Pipeline	361
	Save the Model — Pickle and Joblib	362
	Save Best Estimate	362
	Toxic Trades—Two Modeling Phases	363
	Example Trading System in Python	365
	Train / Test / Validate	373
	Caution	382
	Coordination with a TSDP	382
	Transition to Trading	383
	Summary—Calibrate Your Expectations	384
9	Trading Management	385
	Sidebar—Bet Sequencing	388
	Martingale	389
	Anti-Martingale	390
	Two Systems	391
	Trading System	393
	Trading Management Systems	394
	Part 1	395
	Best Estimate and Weights	396
	Part 2	398
	Algorithms and Programs	400
	Data	400
	Robustness	406
	Statement of risk tolerance	406
	Outliers	406
	Sensitivity	407
	How many equity curves?	408
	Action thresholds	411
	Data structure	411
	Listing	411
	Output	416
	Almost Ready	418
	Your Own Genie	418
10	Summary and Random Thoughts	419
A	Bibliography	425
B	Program Listings	431
	Index	435

Chapter 1
Introduction

This book is about trading using quantitative techniques together with technical analysis. The techniques apply to any of the commonly traded financial issues—stocks, bonds, mutual funds, exchange traded funds, futures, currencies, FOREX, commodities. They are based on analysis of the price and volume of previous transactions made in open markets.

As the subtitle says, this book describes an integrated approach to trading system development and trading management.

As every engineer will tell you, in order to design and develop a product, you must know how it will be used; in order to design and develop a process, you must know how it will be measured and managed.

Our product will be a profitable trading system. Our process will be designing and verifying the system, then monitoring its performance and determining the maximum safe position size. Our metrics will be account growth, normalized for risk.

The purpose of this book is to outline a few relatively simple, but not necessarily simplistic, ideas that will assist readers in their system trading. This book is not intended to be encyclopedic. Our attention will be focused toward developing and managing systems that provide a good trade-off between reward and risk.

Chapter 1 begins with the statement of a goal, briefly discusses a number of topics that provide some background for the development and trading of quantitative systems, and concludes with some reasons why this is so hard.

The Goal

The goal is for the trader to have confidence that the signals generated by the trading system precede trades that provide rewards adequate to compensate for the risk.

The key word is confidence.

The primary limitation is risk.

Major Changes

Some major changes are taking place in trading system development and trading management. This book discusses each, hopefully helping readers understand and prepare.

Broadly—Galileo to Hubble	Frequentist to Bayesian
Charts to Equations	Idea driven to Data driven
Subjective to Objective	Profit oriented to Risk oriented
TSDP to Machine learning	Deterministic to Probabilistic
Indicators to Patterns	Reaction to Prediction
Stationary to Dynamic	Decision tree to Non-linear
Position size into Trading mgmt	p-value to Confusion matrix
Single backtest to Monte Carlo	Equity curve to Distribution

The Process

This is a classical example of fitting a model to a set of data, intending to use the model for prediction.

In order to have a system that generates signals that we have confidence in, that is profitable, and that has acceptable risk, we need several things:
- Data series that have enough variation so that buying and selling produces profit in excess of risk-free alternative uses of the money.
- Those same data series must not have so much volatility that the resulting system has risk of drawdown that exceeds the trader's personal risk tolerance.
- Existence of patterns in the data that precede profitable trading opportunities.
- Existence of a set of rules and parameters, call it a model, that recognizes the patterns and issues trading signals.
- Our ability to discover the model and verify that it works for historical data, creating a trading system.

- Our ability to monitor the performance of the trades generated by the system over time to verify that the system has learned to recognize the patterns and that the patterns continue.
- Our ability to compute the correct position size for each trade so that we maximize account growth while holding drawdown within personal limits of risk tolerance.
- Our ability to recognize system breakdown and take the system offline before excessive loss of trading capital.

One paragraph to describe the goal. 2000 pages and counting (this is the fifth book in the series) to describe the process. We begin with some review.

Premises of Technical Analysis

The underlying assumptions of technical analysis are:
- The markets are not completely efficient.
- There is information—*patterns*—in the historical price series that can be used to identify profitable trading opportunities.
- Trading systems can be designed to recognize the patterns and give buy and sell signals.
- Patterns similar to those found in the historical data will continue to be found in future data.

Two Components of Trading

I assume that readers want to actually trade—to buy and sell some financial assets. The money is made or lost by trading, based on signals to buy and to sell that come from the system. There are two distinct components:
- Developing the system that generates the signals.
- Managing the business of buying and selling.

The flowchart in Figure 1.1 illustrates those two components, the subtasks, the sequence in which they are performed, and the interrelationships.

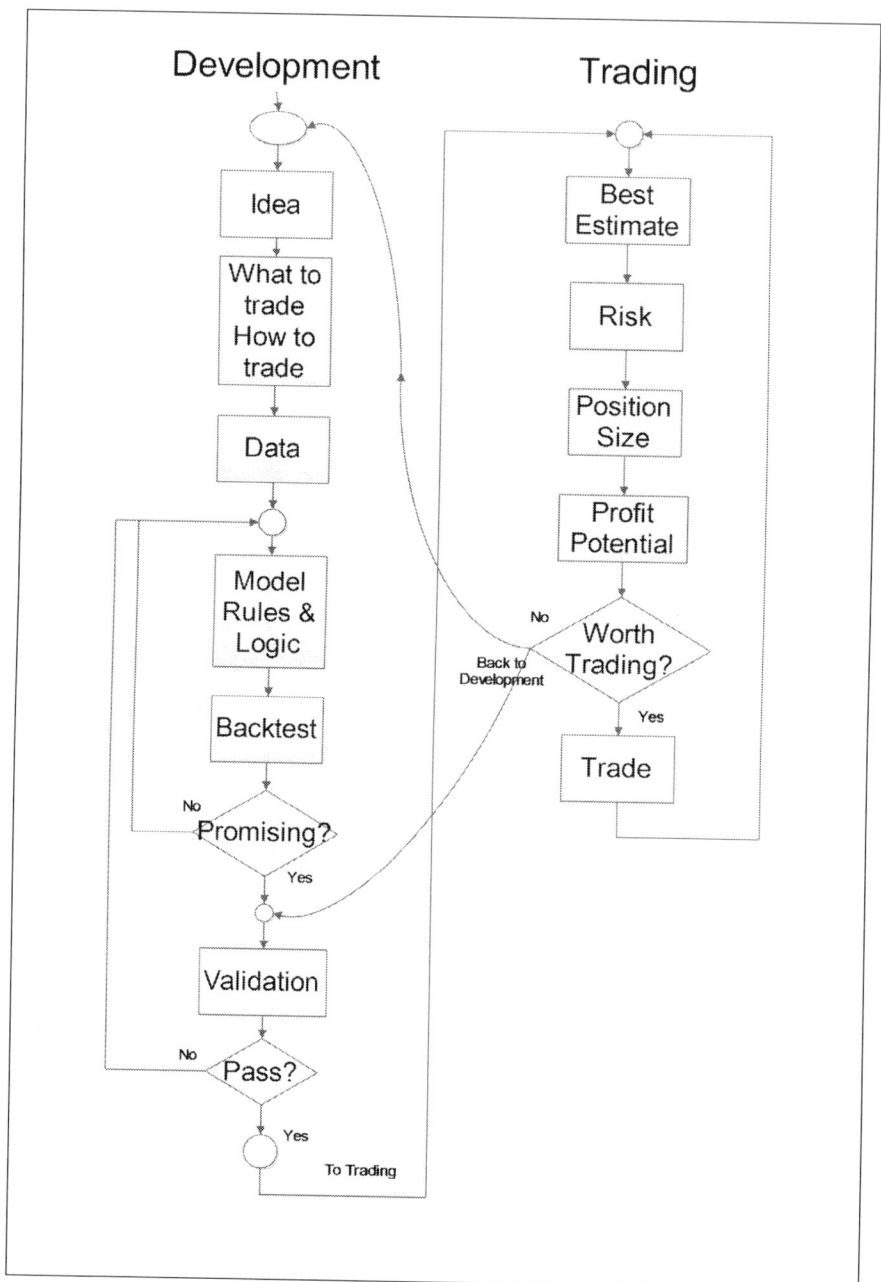

Figure 1.1 Flowchart of trading system development and trading management

Development handles issue and data selection; and the design, testing, and validation of the trading model. That includes calculation of indicators, establishment of rules for trade entry and trade exit, searching to detect patterns, metrics for measuring success, testing to validate the pattern recognition, and establishing a baseline with which to compare future performance.

Trading management focuses on monitoring the health of the system being traded, estimating risk, determining position size, estimating profit potential, and making the trades. When performance begins to decline, it may be necessary to return it to development.

The two components share a common element—the set of trades that, during development, is the *best estimate* of future performance, and, during trading, is that best estimate set of trades augmented by trades actually taken.

Each side of the flowchart has its own model.

Trading system development has long been thought of as a relatively simple process of applying some chart pattern or indicator to a lengthy series of historical price data, often including a search for the best rules and parameter values, and often including calculation of the position size to be used for each trade.

As both the thinking about that process and the tools available for use with that process have evolved, we can develop better trading systems and better trading management systems by separating the single system into two distinct components.

The first is the trading system. It models the left column—the one labeled as *development*. Its input is one or more series of prices and its output is a series of buy and sell signals and the resulting trades. It is discussed in the next few pages of this chapter, and in detail in Chapters 6, 7, and 8.

The second is the trading management system. It models the right column—the one labeled *trading*. Its input is a set of trades and its output is the position size for the next trade. It is discussed a little later in this chapter, and in detail in Chapter 9.

Position sizing

First a few words about position sizing—determining the number of shares or contracts for the next trade.

Position sizing is vitally important. Risk of account-destroying drawdown and opportunity for account-growing profit are closely linked, with position size the critical and coordinating variable.

Including position size while evaluating the data series prior to trading model development (as explained in Chapter 5, Issue Selection), and again in trading management (as explained in Chapter 9, Trading Management), is correct and important. Those two chapters discuss techniques in detail.

But position size should not be a component of the trading model itself (any of those models described in Chapters 6, 7, and 8). Including it there causes two problems:
1. During development of the trading system, using position size other than a fixed number of contracts or dollars introduces a bias that favors specific models (rules and parameter values) that benefit from specific order of trades that happen to occur in the historical data used for development but are unlikely to be repeated in the future, as compared with models whose trades are evaluated independent of order.
2. The trading system has a large number of rules and parameters that can be varied in the search for the best system. The management system has only one—position size. Including position size in the trading system removes it from the management system, leaving no variable that can be used for objective trading management.

Part of the problem of where to put position size calculation was, in the past, due to limitations of available trading system development platforms.

Position size calculations depend on estimation of distributions of results.

Trading system development platforms are very good at processing price data, producing a trade sequence, and computing single-valued metrics. But relatively poor at the complex mathematics and Monte Carlo simulations required to estimate and analyze distributions related to the trades. Until recently, there was little choice—include position size in the trading system or deal with it using a separate process and a separate analysis program—perhaps a spreadsheet.

Recent advances in software have provided new opportunities. General purpose languages, such as Python, have been augmented with libraries such as Pandas to ease the handling of time series data, and with libraries such as NumPy and SciPy to ease complex mathematics and Monte Carlo simulations, and with libraries such as Scikit-learn to assist in pattern recognition and classification. As we will see in Chapter 8, Python can be used as a trading system development platform.

The technological barriers to more accurately modeling trading systems and trading management are being removed. Dynamic position sizing, which is discussed in Chapter 9, can now be implemented in the same program that processes the price data and generates trading signals. The appearance is that position sizing is being added back into the trading system. In reality, it is that the two separate phases—development and management—can be together in a single program. The trading system recognizes the patterns in the data and issues the buy and sell signals, and the management system determines system health and correct position size. They do this through sharing the best estimate set of trades. This is something that was not available to ordinary trading system developers and traders just a few years ago.

Development

System = Model + Data

As illustrated in Figure 1.2 **a trading system is a combination of a model and some data.**

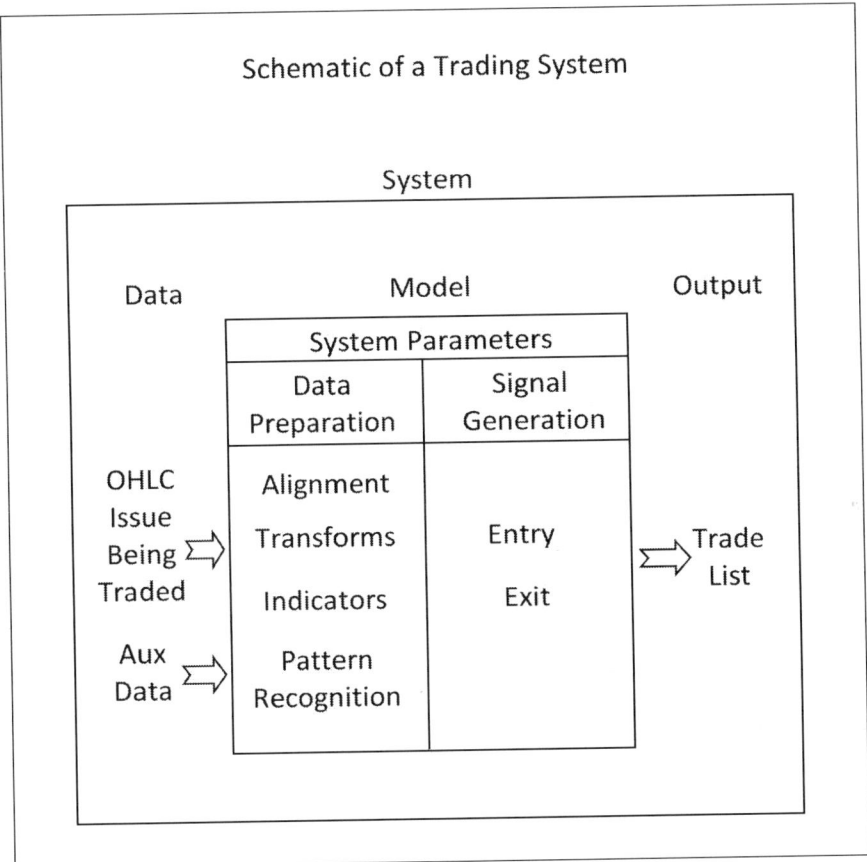

Figure 1.2 Organization of a trading system

The Model

The model accepts the data series that are being used. **The data always includes a primary series—the issue being traded.** It may also include auxiliary data, such as that used for inter-market analysis.

The model performs whatever data alignment and transformations are necessary. Parameters are chosen and indicators computed. The logic, rules, and parameters define patterns. When those patterns are found in the data, entry and exit signals are issued.

The purpose of the model is to recognize patterns that precede profitable trading opportunities.

The output from the model is a list of trades for the time period being tested, together with a summary of performance.

The model does not include any position sizing—that is handled in trading management.

Chapter 6 discusses general issues related to development of the model. Chapters 7 and 8 discuss issues related to model development using indicator-based techniques and machine learning based techniques, respectively.

The Data

Primary data

The primary data series is a time-ordered sequence of quotations. Each quotation represents the price of the issue being traded. The prices can be:
- Individual transaction prices—ticks.
- Individual quotations—bid and ask.
- A set of values that provide the range of prices for some period of time—a bar.

The data format assumed throughout this book is bars. Each bar represents a fixed length of time and is a set of numbers that specify the prices associated with that bar. When the issue is a stock, ETF, or commodity, the prices typically include the first, highest, lowest, and last for that period, referred to as open, high, low, and close. Note that, in general, we cannot assume that the first price occurred at the time the bar opened, nor that the last price occurred at the time the bar closed. We never know, nor should we assume, anything about the order of prices within the bar. Specifically, without examining bars of shorter time duration within a longer bar, we cannot determine whether the high came before the low or after it.

In some cases, such as with stocks and ETFs, the volume of shares is also included and reported.

The most common bar length is one trading day, in which case the data is described as being *daily bars* or *end-of-day* data. Bars can be as short as one second, or a few seconds, one minute, or some number of minutes. Any of these is described as *intra-day* data or intra-day bars.

When buy and sell signals are issued and trades created, the transaction prices come from this primary data series.

Chapter 5 discusses selection of the primary data series.

Auxiliary data

In addition to the prices of the issue being traded, the model might use auxiliary data. That could be the price of other tradable issues—for example, including the price of bonds in a model that trades stocks. Or it could be a non-price series—for example, the number of advancing or declining issues from a broader set, such as a market sector.

Before being analyzed, all data series must be aligned by the date and time associated with each bar, and any missing data filled in. The obvious choice to provide the master list of dates and times is the primary data series.

Assume nothing about distribution

Numerous studies have documented that financial data does not reliably follow any of the standard statistical distributions. In general, we do not know—or even need to know—the distribution of the data. It is important to accept the data as it is without making additional assumptions as to being normal, log-normal, or any other distribution.

Distributions

Emanuel Derman writes: "Models are simplifications, and simplifications can be dangerous."[1] The point I hope to make in this section is that systems developers should avoid simplification of data representation. In short—whenever possible use distributions rather than a limited number of scalar values.

The information content that describes a trading system over a given period of time can be described in many ways. The following list is in decreasing order of information.

- Reality. Trades, in sequence, that actually result from applying the system.
- List of trades, in time sequence.
- Set of trades.
- Distribution of trades.
- Four moments describing the distribution.
- Mean and standard deviation.
- Mean.
- Direction.

---

1 Derman, Emanuel, *Models.Behaving.Badly.: Why Confusing Illusion with Reality Can Lead to Disaster on Wall Street and in Life*, Free Press, 2011.

Probability and statistics distinguish between population and sample. The population is all items of the type being analyzed. The sample is a subset of the population that has been observed. The purpose of developing trading systems is to learn as much as possible about the population of trades that will occur in the future and make estimates of future performance. The results of testing trading systems form the sample that is used to make those estimates.

Reality

Reality cannot be known in advance. Estimating reality, the population, is the purpose of system validation. Reality is the logic of the system processing the future data series.

List of trades, in time sequence

The list of trades, in time sequence, that results from processing a data series that is similar to the future data, is the best estimate we can obtain of reality. There is one of these sequences for each unique series of test data and each set of logic and parameter values. Using these results to estimate future profitability and risk depends on the degree of similarity between the test data and the future data.

Set of trades

The set of trades, ignoring time sequence, relaxes the assumption of the trades occurring in a particular sequence. It provides a set of trade data with, hopefully, the same characteristics as the future data, such as amount won or lost per trade, holding period, intra-trade drawdown, and frequency of trading. Selecting trades from this set in random order gives an opportunity to evaluate the effects of similar conditions, but in different time sequence.

Distribution of trades

A distribution can be formed using any of the metrics of the individual trades. The distribution is a further simplification since there are fewer (or at most the same number of) categories for the distribution than for the data used to form it. For example, a distribution of percentage gain per trade is formed by sorting the individual trades according to gain per trade, establishing ranges and bins, assigning each trade to a bin, and counting the number of trades in each bin. A plot of the count per bin versus gain per bin gives a plot of the probability mass function (often called the probability density function, pdf).

Four moments

Distributions can be described by their moments. The four moments most commonly used are named mean, variance, skewness, and kur-

tosis. Depending on the distribution, some or all of the moments may be undefined.
- Mean. The first moment. The arithmetic average of the data points.
- Variance. Second moment. A measure of the deviation of data points from the mean. Standard deviation is the positive square root of variance.
- Skewness. Third moment. A measure of the lopsidedness of the distribution.
- Kurtosis. Fourth moment. A measure of the peakedness and tail weight of the distribution.

Mean and standard deviation

Mean and standard deviation are commonly computed and used to describe trade results. They can be used in the definition of metrics such Bollinger bands, z-score, Sharpe ratio, mean-variance portfolio, etc.

Mean

The mean gives the average of the values. Mean can be computed in several ways, such as arithmetic mean and geometric mean. Median is an alternative measure of central tendency of a sample that is often useful.

Direction

Direction of a trade describes whether it was a winning trade or a losing trade. Direction is meant to represent any way of describing the trades in a binary fashion. Other ways might be whether the result was large or small in absolute value, or whether the maximum favorable excursion met some criterion, etc.

Stay High on the List

With each step down this list, a larger number of data points are consolidated into a smaller number of categories, and information is irretrievably lost. Knowing only the information available at one level makes it impossible to know anything definite about the population that could be determined at a higher level. Working with only the mean tells us nothing about variability. Working with only mean and standard deviation tells us nothing about the heaviness of the tails. Using the four values of the first four moments enables us to calculate some information about the shape of the population, but nothing about the lumpiness or gaps that may exist.

For more discussion and examples, read Sam Savage[2] or Patrick Leach.[3]

Patterns

We will be examining data looking for patterns, for profitable trades, and the relationship between the patterns and the trades. The patterns will be described as a set of rules and coded into the model.

Non-stationary

Stationarity is a feature of data that refers to how a particular metric of the data remains relatively constant or changes as different subsets of the data are analyzed.

A process, or set of data, is described as *strictly* or *strongly* stationary when the distribution and its parameters—such as mean, variance, skew, and kurtosis—do not change over time, including showing no trends. Stationarity is a required assumption for some analysis techniques.

The techniques discussed in this book extend the concept of stationarity to whatever metric is being analyzed. In particular, we will be careful to avoid disturbing the relationship between critical patterns and the trades that follow. We want that relationship to remain stationary.

Traditional statistical analysis, including much of both probability and machine learning, assumes the data being analyzed is strongly stationary. The theorems upon which the techniques are based, in particular those that give limits to accuracy and / or error, often require strong stationarity. That assumption is reasonable for applications such as political polling, medical diagnosis, and character recognition.

But time series data is seldom stationary, and financial time series data is never stationary. **Be cautious when applying any technique that assumes the data is stationary to financial time series—there will probably be an undesirable bias.**

Synchronization

The model specifies the logic, rules, and parameters. The rules, for example, might be to enter and exit as two moving averages cross. The parameters include the lengths of the two moving averages.

The data is the price history of the issue being traded, perhaps augmented by other data series.

---

2 Savage, Sam, *The Flaw of Averages: Why We Underestimate Risk in the Face of Uncertainty*, Wiley, 2009.
3 Leach, Patrick, *Why Can't You Just Give Me the Number?*, Probabilistic Publishing, 2006.

A trading system is profitable as long as the logic identifies patterns in the data that precede profitable trading opportunities. That is, as long as the logic and data remain synchronized.

The logic of a typical trading system is relatively fixed. It is designed to detect a particular set of patterns. The data change, following changes in areas that affect the issue—economics, politics, weather, etc.

As the data changes, the patterns in the data move in and out of synchronization with the logic. When synchronized, the system is healthy, it is profitable, gains are steady, drawdowns are low; when unsynchronized, the system is broken, it is unprofitable, gains are sporadic, drawdowns are high. The profit potential and drawdown risk of a system are determined by the accuracy with which the system identifies the patterns.

During periods of close synchronization, the system is healthy and large positions may safely be taken. As synchronization weakens, position size must be reduced.

Signal and Noise

The data consists of two components—signal and noise. The signal consists of the patterns we hope to identify. What constitutes signal is determined by the model. Everything that a particular model does not explicitly consider to be signal is noise and interferes with identification of the signal patterns.

For a book-length discussion of the relationship between signal and noise in a wide variety of applications, I highly recommend Nate Silver.[4]

Data Series are Not Interchangeable

It is the combination of a model and some data that comprise a trading system.

Just as we cannot expect different models to be equally effective for a given data series, we cannot expect a given model to be equally effective applied to different data series. If one model does work for a wide range of data, that is a plus. But it is not a requirement.

Learning

Learning is the process of examining data, recognizing some patterns, observing related patterns, and hoping there is a generalization. As it applies to trading systems, we will be looking for patterns that provide either:

---

4   Silver, Nate, *The Signal and the Noise: Why So Many Predictions Fail—But Some Don't*, Penguin Press, 2012.

- Classification. Buy or Sell. Either to open a new position or to close an existing position. The issue of how much to buy or sell—position sizing—is addressed separately from pattern recognition.
- Estimation. Direction and magnitude of change anticipated. If an estimation technique is used, we may apply a threshold filter to convert the estimation into a classification category.

Learning is not possible unless there is data to be examined and patterns to find. Preferably a lot of data and a lot of patterns. This is definitely a data mining activity. The data mined is called the *in-sample* data. We are searching for patterns within the historical price data that precede profitable trades.

We cannot learn a feature that has not been seen. The in-sample data must include examples of the patterns to be learned.

Identifying patterns in the in-sample data is necessary for learning, but not sufficient. There must be generalization. The test for generalization is validation. That is, testing previously unused data to estimate the success of detecting the patterns and defining the rules. The data tested for validation is called the *out-of-sample* data.

Validation is the step designed to provide the confidence requested in the goal.

Subjectivity and Objective Functions

There are many subjective decisions to be made.

Every day, traders must make decisions:
- Whether the system is healthy.
- When to enter.
- How large a position to take.
- When to exit.

Discretionary traders acknowledge the subjectivity associated with those decisions and draw on experience.

Systematic traders use *objective functions* designed to identify important decision criteria and quantify them. An objective function is alternatively called a loss function, cost function, utility function, fitness function, or optimization metric. An objective function is a formula that includes terms for each of the criteria or variables important to the decision.

Weights proportional to the importance of the criteria are given to each of the terms, and the terms added together resulting in a single numeric quantity—an objective function score. The score is computed for each alternative being evaluated. The alternatives are sorted according to their score. Providing the objective function has been well designed, the order of subjective preference is the same as the order of objective function score.

Objective functions are important in both phases of trading:
- In development—to rank alternative systems.
- In trading management—to decide the size of the next position.

Rank Alternative Systems

A trading system is a set of computations, logic statements, and parameter values that comprise a set a rules that identify profitable trading patterns and give buy and sell signals.

There are an infinite number of possible systems.

In order to make the process manageable, relatively simple systems are designed to focus on specific trading ideas, such as trend following, mean reverting, seasonality, etc.

For any one of these ideas, there are many alternatives. A trend following system might have logic that looks at breakouts, or the crossing of two moving averages, or the projection of a regression. For each of these there are numeric parameters such as the lengths of the moving averages, or magnitude of breakout. There might be multiple rules to exit a position, such as logic, trailing exit, profit target, and / or maximum loss stop.

Designing a trading system is an iterative process of:
- Modify the logic and parameters.
- Test the performance.

Each set of logic and parameters, together with the data series, creates a new trading system—one of the alternatives to be evaluated.

The developer needs to decide which is best, and best is subjective. The purpose of the objective function is to provide an objective metric that represents the subjectivity of the developer's definition of best. The objective function she uses includes terms for important features such as gain-per-trade, holding period, and maximum loss.

Estimate Distributions of Performance

The trading system that results from the design, testing, and validation provides a single set of trades with single mean, single standard deviation, single terminal wealth, single maximum drawdown.

These results will be repeated as the system is traded only if future prices are exactly the same as the historical series used during development. In order to estimate profit potential and risk it is important to consider the distribution of potential results.

Modeling future performance, including evaluating system health, estimating risk, and estimating profit potential, is based on:

- Using the set of trade results that, in the judgment of the developer, best represents the trades that are likely to occur in the future.
- Using Monte Carlo simulation techniques to create many equally likely trade sequences.
- Analyzing the distributions of drawdown and profit resulting from the trade sequences.
- Comparing both the magnitude and probability of both the drawdown and profit potential with the trader's personal tolerance for risk and desire for profit to determine system health and position size.

Beginning with determining the maximum safe position size that normalizes the risk associated with a set of trades to keep it within your personal risk tolerance, an objective function based on the Compound Annual Rate of Return (CAR) at some confidence level, say the 25th percentile, is a nearly universal objective function. It is very useful in deciding whether a system is worth trading, and in comparing performance among alternative systems.

The process is outlined in Chapter 2 of this book. For an in-depth explanation of the Monte Carlo method used, including the free software necessary to run the Monte Carlo simulations, see my Modeling book.[5]

Trader Psychology

We often hear of the importance of psychology in successful trading. The need for the trader to understand himself, to trust the system, to take all signals, to enter the market when the buy signal appears, to set stops at a comfortable level, to exit the trade when the money management stop is hit, to exit the trade at a profit when the profit target is hit, to keep trading through drawdowns. And if the trader considers second-guessing the system, he should consult a trading coach to help him realign his beliefs and accept the system.

In my opinion, that is exactly backwards. We all have personal beliefs about the way the markets work, comfort levels with risk, and preferences related to trading. We know what trading frequency fits in with our other activities. We know what level of drawdown causes us to lose sleep. We can incorporate our own preferences into the objective function we design for our own use when developing and trading our own systems.

A system that scores high marks using our own custom objective function is already one we can expect to be comfortable using. A well designed custom objective function goes a long way toward

---

[5] Bandy, Howard, *Modeling Trading System Performance*, Blue Owl Press, 2011.

avoiding the cognitive dissonance that requires professional consultation to cure.

Trading management

The trading management sections of this book discuss a new and unique technique, *dynamic position sizing*, and introduce a new metric of system health, *safe-f*.

Position sizing is widely recognized as an important component of trading. The position sizing methods most widely discussed to date make oversimplifying assumptions. They either assume that position size is a stationary variable and a single position size can be applied to a trading system without need for periodic recalculation; or they assume that position size can be determined from within the system's model, then include the position sizing calculation with the logic and rules. Neither is true. Use of either increases the likelihood of serious equity drawdown. Position size is not stationary—position size varies as the health of the system varies. Position size cannot be determined from within the model without outside reference.

Dynamic position sizing monitors system performance trade by trade. Using Monte Carlo simulation and Bayesian analysis, it determines risk of drawdown, assesses the personal risk tolerance of the trader, computes safe-f—the maximum safe position size for the next trade—and estimates profit potential. All on a trade-by-trade basis. Safe-f gives you a clear indication of system health, including when the system should be taken offline.

The correct position size for system that is broken is zero.

Chapter 9 discusses trading management.

Risk Tolerance

Everyone has a personal tolerance for risk. Every data series has some inherent risk, independent of the model. Every trading system has some risk. In Chapter 2, we give some techniques for assessing and quantifying personal risk tolerance, for assessing the risk associated with a data series, and for a trading system.

Why Traders Stop Trading

Assume a trader has a method—mechanical, discretionary, or a combination of both—that she has been using successfully. Also assume that she understands both herself and the business of trading, and wants to continue trading. Why would she stop trading that particular system?

Here are a few possibilities:
1. The results are too good.

2. The results are not worth the effort.
3. The results are not worth the stress.
4. She has enough money.
5. There is a serious drawdown

1. Results are too good

She is afraid that this cannot possibly continue.

Her system—any system—works when the logic and the data are synchronized. There are many reasons why systems fail and should be taken offline, but a sequence of winning trades should be seen as a success.

She should continue trading it until one of the other reasons to stop happens.

2. Results are not worth the effort

There is not much gain, but not much loss either. Other things in life are more important. On balance, the time, energy, and resources would be more productively applied doing something else.

3. Results are not worth the stress

Performance is satisfactory, but at a high cost—worry and loss of sleep. Regardless of the position size indicated by the distribution of risk, the positions being taken are too large.

She should either reduce position size or have someone else execute the trades.

4. She has enough money

Not matter how good a system is, there is always a risk of serious loss.

When she has reached her goal, she should retire.

5. There is a serious drawdown

The magnitude of the drawdown needed for it to be classified as serious is subjective. Among my colleagues and clients, those who manage other people's money typically want drawdown limited to single digits. Those trading their own money may be willing to suffer drawdowns of 15 or 20 percent.

But there is a level at which everyone stops trading the system—preferably while the account still has a positive balance.

My view is that experiencing a large drawdown is the primary reason people stop trading a system.

What causes a large drawdown and how should the trader react to it?

- The system is broken.
- There was an unexpected sequence of losing trades.
- The system is out of sync.
- The position size is too high.

As the account balance drops from an equity high into a drawdown, it is not possible to determine which is The reason.

All of the reasons are true to some extent. A system that is broken breaks because the logic and the data become unsynchronized, causing an unexpected sequence of losing trades and at a time when position size was too high for conditions.

The solution is two-fold.
1. Continually monitor system performance and system health.
2. Modify position size to reflect recent performance.

During the trading system development process, a baseline of system performance is established. Using the out-of-sample trades from the walk forward phase is a good source of this data. Personal risk tolerance and system risk, taken together, determine position size for that system performance. As system performance changes, position size must also change.

Position size varies in response to system health.

Do not continue to trade a system that has entered a serious drawdown expecting that it will recover. It may recover on its own; it may require readjustment; or it may be permanently broken and never work again.

Take it offline and either observe it until recent paper-trade results demonstrate that it is healthy again, or send it back to development.

The correct position size for a system that is broken is zero.

Confidence

In the end, you must have confidence. If not confidence, then faith.

The forums that discuss trading systems and their development often ask about the value of walk forward testing. The question is usually accompanied by comments about how hard it is to get good results from the out-of-sample tests from the walk forward runs, whereas it is relatively easy to get good results from optimization and backtesting.

My first reaction is the obvious one—it is hard to get good out-of-sample results because the markets are nearly efficient and it is hard to write a set of rules that detect an inefficiency in advance.

But the first question leads to a deeper consideration about trading systems and trading. Having confidence in a system.

It is my view that the universe of trading system application divides into two—having confidence and having faith.

If you want quantifiable confidence—the kind that tells you whether to hit soft 17 at blackjack, or to hit the blot in your inner table in backgammon, or to buy a recent low, or to buy a new high breakout—my techniques are designed to provide quantifiable confidence in both development and trading.

The problem is harder than it looks at first blush. The characteristics of a trading system determine to a large extent whether it is even possible to have confidence. In order to be useful, there must be enough data points—closed trades or daily account equity values—to compute useful statistical metrics. Examples of useful statements about confidence are:
- To put a low p-value on a set of system results, such as: "we can reject the hypothesis that the expectancy is less than 0.0 with a p-value of 0.05."
- To put limits on estimates, such as: "with 95% confidence, the worst maximum drawdown for the next year for an account with an initial balance of $100,000 trading at a fraction of 0.80 is 20%."

Statistical metrics such as these can be computed for any data set—real or hypothetical. If future trades will be made based on these statistics, the data set used to compute the test statistics must be as unbiased as possible.

Using the walk forward technique with trading systems that trade frequently and have short holding periods gives the trading system developer a reasonable chance of producing a set of trades that is both large enough and unbiased enough. Even at that, it is all too easy to introduce bias—bias that will cause reward to be overestimated and risk underestimated—into even the walk forward out-of-sample results.

Compare with backtesting with little or no out-of-sample testing, (which is the all-too-common method in both the popular trading journals and many professional publications), or with systems that have such long holding periods or infrequent trading that an unbiased data set cannot, for practical purposes, be produced.

When in doubt, test it! Do not accept traditional wisdom blindly. Is the 200 day moving average is a good trend indicator? Is trend following the best system to grow a trading account with low drawdown? Those rules may be good ones, and they may lead to trading systems that are appropriate for your use. Or they may not.

Test everything yourself. Your logic, your data, your execution, your estimation of system health. If those tests give you confidence, act accordingly.

Beware of following the advice of the White Queen: "Why, sometimes I've believed as many as six impossible things before breakfast."[6]

If you must act on faith, ask yourself how the casino can build such a fine facility. Stand next to the roulette wheel and listen to the young man tell his partner: "There have been six reds in a row. Black is due."

Decisions and Uncertainty

Most of the decisions we make in life are choices that involve weighing opportunity against risk. Most of the calculations are extremely complex and involve estimating costs and values of things not easily quantified—whom to choose as a partner, where to live, what employment to pursue. All are specific applications of making decisions under uncertain conditions. It seems that the more important the decision, the less opportunity we have to practice and the more important it is to be correct early in the process.

How we handle our finances is certainly an important area, and one where we don't get many practice runs. For traders, the goal is maximizing trading profits while minimizing the risk of bankruptcy. In the spectrum of life's activities, this is a problem that is relatively easy to quantify and analyze. The major aspects already have easily measured units of value—dollars. And, given a little understanding of probability and statistics, along with some computer data analysis, we can outline a plan.

Why This is So Hard

Developing profitable trading systems is a difficult problem for many reasons.

Low Signal to Noise Ratio

The data is very noisy. The markets are nearly efficient. Thinking of the patterns we are searching for as the signal, the signal is weak and is hidden among a lot of noise.

Nonstationary

The data is not stationary. Nothing stays the same for long. The characteristics of the data change over time. A solution found for one period of time may no longer apply in a later time period. Determining the appropriate lengths of time to use for the in-sample and out-of-sample periods is difficult.

---

6   Carroll, Lewis, *Through the Looking-Glass*, 1871.

Time Series is Different

Time series data, and particularly financial time series data, is different than the data typically fed to models. The vast majority of modeling, simulation, statistics, and machine learning books and articles assume the data is stationary.

When it is, models that learn and predict accurately are relatively easy to build. The theory provides guidelines, and in some cases rigorous estimates, of out-of-sample performance.

When it is not, techniques that rely on stationarity still give results. But the theoretical justification fails to hold. Results overestimate profit and underestimate risk. Real-time trading results are much poorer than anticipated.

Feedback

The purpose of a trading system is to recognize an inefficiency in price, then make trades that capture that inefficiency. An example is the process described as "arbitraging an inefficiency out of the system." In the process, price becomes more efficient and more difficult to detect in the future.

Trend Following

Every trade is a trend following trade. No matter how the entry is made, the price must change in the direction predicted in order for the system to be profitable. The trend must complete its expected or predicted run before there is a drawdown or early exit from the trade. As more traders recognize that particular trending pattern, the trend becomes shorter in both time and price change.

Limited Profit Potential

The markets are very nearly efficient. Every successful trade removes some inefficiency and makes future profitability less likely. Given a desirable trend, the first positions taken get the best price. Later fills are at worse prices. The latest trades do not obtain enough profit to cover commission and slippage.

Different Systems, Same Trades

Trades can be categorized according to the amount of change from entry to exit, or the amount of time they are held. Over a period of time, there are only a few profitable trades for any given trade profile. Everyone developing systems that will hold trades for one to five days or one to two percent will locate the same profitable trades no matter what pattern or entry technique they are using.

Very Large Search Space

There are many potential solutions. Patterns can be described in terms of indicators, seasonality, candles, etc. Finding a pattern that works is a search among a large number of possibilities. It is very easy to overfit the model to the data.

The in-sample results are always good. With so many variables available to fit so few data points, it is easy to obtain good in-sample results.

Out-of-sample Results Matter

Out-of-sample results are the important ones. They may not be good for two reasons.
- One. The system was never good. The rules fit the in-sample noise rather than meaningful and predictive patterns.
- Two. The system is no longer good. The characteristics of the data have changed since the patterns were identified.

Financial Rewards

Rewards for success are high.

Barriers to entry are low.

Trading is competitive. Trading is nearly zero sum. My profit is some other trader's loss. Knowledge shared by one trader reduces his future profit.

Competition

There are no handicaps. Novice and journeyman golfers, bowlers, tennis players, chess players, bicycle racers, and go players can all enter tournaments knowing that they will either be competing with people whose skill level is roughly the same as their own, or they will be given a handicap that compensates for their lack of skill and experience. Not so for traders. When any of us takes a long position in a stock, ETF, or futures contract, the person taking the opposite position is very likely to be trading for a major financial institution. They are well educated, well equipped, well funded, well supported, and are using the best methods and systems.

Figure 1.1 After I win a few races, I am going to buy a really good bicycle and enter the Tour de France.

Summary

Our goal is to develop profitable trading systems that use rules that have been derived by learning patterns in price data that precede price changes.

The systems we develop will be quantitative. At every point in their development and use, there will be metrics to help make decisions.

Many trading decisions are subjective. We will use objective functions to quantify subjective preferences.

The system's characteristics are determined in part by the desires of the trader and in part by what is achievable within the specified risk tolerance. They are also determined by, and to some extent restricted by, the practicalities and realities of combining sound practices of mathematical modeling, simulation, and statistical analysis with uniqueness of financial time series and the business of trading.

George Box famously wrote: "Essentially all models are wrong, but some are useful."[7] The more complete quotation adds some qualifications, including: "all models are approximations." Understanding that trading systems are not perfect, my hope is to help you develop systems that are useful.

---

[7] Box, G. E. P., and Draper, N. R., *Empirical Model Building and Response Surfaces*, John Wiley & Sons, New York, NY, 1987.

Chapter 2
Risk and Risk Tolerance

I believe most people view risk in the context of their trading account. Risk is the risk of drawdown in the balance of the account.

The motivation for this chapter is that the primary reason traders stop trading a system is that they experience a drawdown larger than they anticipated, larger than they can afford, larger than their risk tolerance.

Measurement and Management

Measurement of risk and management of risk are related.

Management of risk has two components—system design and position sizing.

System design affects risk in issue selection, trade selection, entry, and exit. A high quality system trades an issue that has good profit potential and few large adverse price surprises. We address these issues in Chapter 5. The issue must also be easily modeled—patterns preceding trades identified, and timely entries and exits made. We address these in Chapter 6.

Position sizing is vitally important. Adjusting trade size as the model and data move in and out of synchronization enables us to take advantage of periods of good performance and reduce exposure during periods of poor performance. Using dynamic position sizing, we can maximize account growth while holding risk of serious drawdown to levels within our personal risk tolerance. We define risk tolerance in this chapter, and address dynamic position sizing in Chapter 9.

Measurement of risk helps us understand the risk inherent with the combination of :
- the issue being traded,
- accuracy of the trading system,
- holding period,
- intra-trade visibility.

We begin with a discussion of drawdown as a measure of risk, analysis of the visibility of intra-trade prices, and willingness to hold a position through a drawdown. Then continue with the definition and formulation of a statement of risk tolerance.

Drawdown Defined

Drawdown is defined as the drop in account equity, measured as a percentage relative to the highest equity achieved prior to the drawdown. Figure 2.1 shows two major drawdowns—one of 10% and one of 20%.

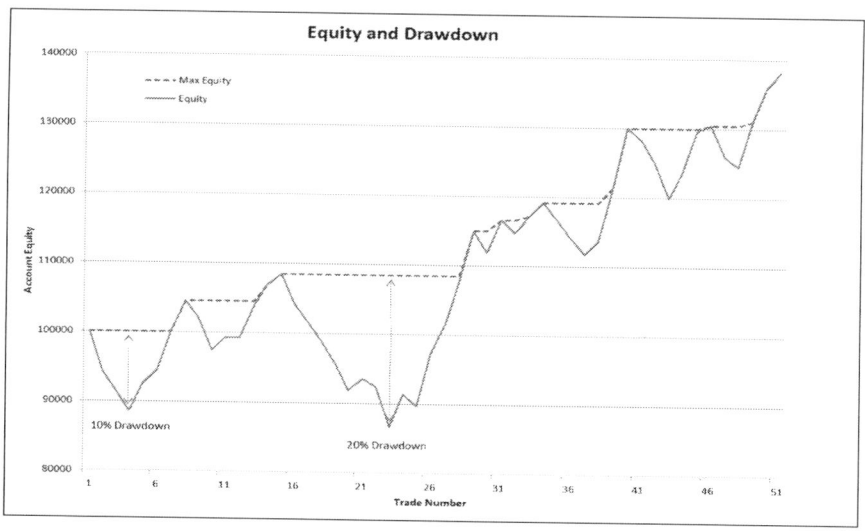

Figure 2.1 Account drawdown

As Figure 2.2 illustrates, loss of equity into a drawdown is not symmetric with the gain required to recover from it. The gain needed to recover from a drawdown is greater than the loss that caused the drawdown.

Figure 2.2 also illustrates another view of drawdown—the time required to recover. Assuming a system has an expected annual growth of 15%, recovery from a 20% drawdown will take about 20 months.

It is one thing to look at a chart showing an historical record. Perhaps of a trading system, perhaps of a broad market index, perhaps of a country's economy. The chart shows several steep drawdowns, each followed by recovery. The person imagines the final outcome and believes any current drawdown in a system, market, or economy will be followed by an equally full and pleasant recovery. It is both easy and patriotic to have faith in a recovery, but painful to personally experience the discomfort throughout the entire period. Every forecast should include consideration of how it might be different this time—or not different, as the case may be.

Drawdown percent	Recovery percent	Recovery months at 15%
1%	1.01%	0.8
2%	2.04%	1.6
3%	3.09%	2.5
4%	4.17%	3.3
5%	5.26%	4.2
6%	6.38%	5.1
7%	7.53%	6.0
8%	8.70%	7.0
9%	9.89%	7.9
10%	11.11%	8.9
15%	17.65%	14.1
20%	25.00%	20.0
30%	42.86%	34.3
40%	66.67%	53.3
50%	100.00%	80.0
60%	150.00%	120.0

Figure 2.2 Drawdown and recovery

Frequency of Action

A system's equity is either at a new high, or it is in a drawdown. Most systems are in drawdowns most of the time—70 to 90% of the time is not unusual.

Continuing to trade a system that is in a drawdown requires that you have confidence that:
1. The drawdown is within your risk tolerance.

2. Compared with the trading history and expected performance, the current drawdown is not unusually deep or long.
3. The system will recover to make a new equity high in a reasonable period of time.
4. The system is still the same. The trading opportunities still exist. The signal patterns programmed into the model still exist in the data and precede the trades. The system is healthy and in good synchronization.

Minimum Holding Period

Assume you are trading a system, it has an open long position, and the price of your issue is falling.

Is there some level of drawdown in your account equity that would cause you to not take the next trade? Or, more seriously, that would cause you to exit the open trade without waiting for the system exit?

What is the minimum period of time you are willing to hold through without taking a subjective action? Five minutes, one hour, one day, one week? Or is it independent of a specific period of time? Can you always wait until the system issues the exit?

Trade Exits

The answers depend in part on how your system exits trades.

However a new position has been opened, there are five general ways to exit. (These are discussed more fully in Chapter 6.)
- Logic—trading system rules that issue a Sell signal.
- Maximum holding period, including inactivity.
- Profit target.
- Trailing exit.
- Maximum loss exit.

The system must have at least one of these, and it may have as many as all five. The exit prices may be set at entry and left unchanged for the entire trade, or they may be adjusted intra-trade.

One of the definitive aspects of using a quantitative system is that all of the rules are in the system. There are no external rules, either objective or subjective. When the system issues a Buy, a long position is taken, and it is held until the system issues a Sell.

In order to apply the pattern recognition, risk control, and position sizing techniques described in later chapters, the answer to "what is the minimum period of time you are willing to hold through?" must be "until the system issues the exit." What does that imply?

Since drawdown can increase rapidly over a multi-day market decline, that period must be short enough that price changes, including drawdown, within it can be ignored. The system will always hold through a period at least this long. I recommend the minimum period between potential changes to position be no longer than one trading day. (Any shorter period, such as hourly, will work equally well providing intra-day data with appropriate bar lengths are used. To avoid awkward sentence construction, please interpret "daily" to mean "daily or more frequently" unless otherwise stated.)

Establishing the basic period as daily does not restrict entry and/or exit from occurring intra-day. End-of-day traders are able to use limit and stop orders to enter or exit at an intra-day price. However, with bars of any length, the inability to resolve intra-bar price action limits the number of potential trades in a single bar to the open, the close, and at most one intra-bar trade.

Maximum Adverse Excursion (MAE)

Maximum adverse excursion is a measure of the most unfavorable point in a trade, or in a period of time. MAE can be expressed as a positive number or negative; in points, dollars, or percentage. By convention we will express MAE as a positive number, and in whatever unit is appropriate. We want MAE to be small.

MAE is a measure of the risk we acknowledge.

For clarity, I refer to a bar as a day. The analysis and discussion applies equally well to bars of any length, and also to trades treated as bars.

In the first few examples that follow, intra-day prices are *visible*. That is, the intra-day high and low prices are known and used in calculations.

In later examples, intra-day prices are *invisible*. That is, the only prices known are the open and close, or perhaps only the close.

MAE for a single day

The MAE for a single period of time in isolation, such as a daily bar, is the most adverse position relative to the beginning of the that period and with respect to the direction. The MAE for a long position entered Market-on-Open (MOO) is the low relative to the open.

$$MAE = (Open - Low) / Open$$

If entry is made at some other intra-day price than the open, we cannot determine (without access to shorter, intra-day bars) whether the low came before or after the entry. The conservative analysis is to assume the worst case and compute MAE as the low relative to the entry.

$$MAE = (Entry - Low) / Entry$$

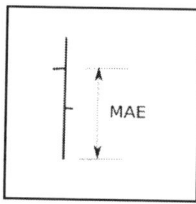

Figure 2.3 MAE for a single day Long, relative to the Open

The MAE for a short position entered MOO is the high relative to the open. For an intra-day entry, it is the high relative to the entry. (This is the only reference to short trades in this section.)

MAE = (High - Open) / Open

MAE = (High - Entry) / Entry

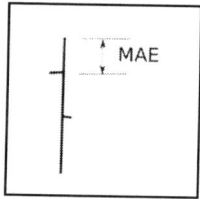

Figure 2.4 MAE for a single day Short, relative to the Open

MAE for a two-day trade

Consider a system that enters a long position market-on-close (MOC), holds one day, and exits MOC the next day, with intra-day low visible. The intra-trade MAE is the low on the second day relative to the entry.

MAE = (Close - Ref(Low,1)) / Close

MAE = (Entry - Ref(Low,1)) / Entry

where Ref(Low,1) is the low one day into the future.

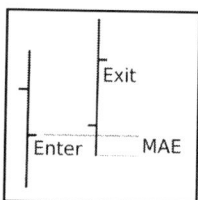

Figure 2.5 MAE for a two-day Long trade, Close to Close, intra-day visible

If intra-day prices are invisible, then only the two closing prices matter. If the trade is a winner, MAE is zero; if it is a loser, MAE is the loss of the trade.

$$MAE = Max(C - Ref(C,1)) / C, 0)$$

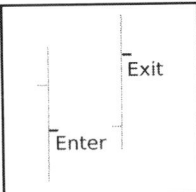

Figure 2.6 MAE for a two-day Long trade, Close to Close, intra-day invisible

MAE for a multi-day trade

For a multi-day trade, the MAE of the trade depends on how much of the intra-trade price we want to acknowledge.

Intra-day prices are visible

The adverse excursion for a long trade is the difference between the highest intra-trade equity, marked-to-market each day at some price, and that day's low. In this example, and most that follow, the mark-to-market price is the day's close. Each of the vertical arrows shows the adverse excursion for that day. The MAE for the trade is the largest of the adverse excursions.

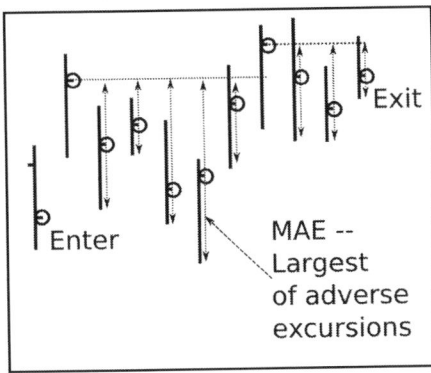

Figure 2.7 MAE for a multi-day trade, intra-day visible

Intra-day prices are invisible

Each day's price is a single value

The data in Figure 2.8 is the same as in Figure 2.7, except that there is now only a single data point for each day—the close.

The adverse excursion is the difference between the highest close, marked-to-market daily, and the day's close. Each of the arrows shows the adverse excursion for that day. The MAE for the trade is the largest of the adverse excursions. Note that in this example it occurs on a different day than when intra-day prices are visible.

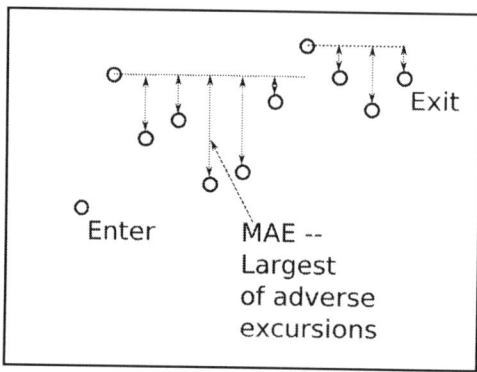

Figure 2.8 MAE for a multi-day trade, intra-day invisible

MAE for a series of trades

There is a similarity between a price bar, say a daily bar, and a trade. Each has an open, high, low, and close. Revisit Figures 2.3 through 2.8. Imagine that the opening price of the bar is the entry price of a trade and the closing price is the exit price. In this interpretation, the trade's high is its MFE and the trade's low is its MAE.

Each trade is a series of days, each of which has its own high and low. Drawdown for a series of trades could be measured relative to:
- intra-day high price
- intra-trade high equity
- closed-trade high equity

Figures 2.9 through 2.12 show four views of a multi-trade sequence of the same four trades. In each, horizontal lines show the progression of MFE and MAE, measured in the manner described for that figure. The thick dashed line indicates account equity.

Figure 2.9 shows the trades arranged so that the open of the first day of each trade is at the same equity as the close of the final day of the previous trade.

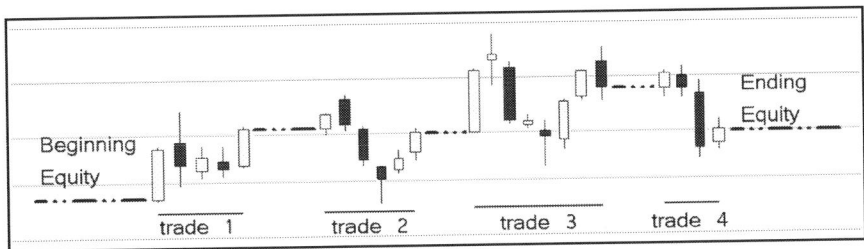

Figure 2.9 A four trade sequence

In Figure 2.10, intra-day high and low prices are visible. Although we never know the actual high for a bar until that bar is complete, the horizontal lines show what the MFE and MAE would be if measured from intra-day high and low. While not tradable, this does show the degree of anxiety-raising intra-day drawdown.

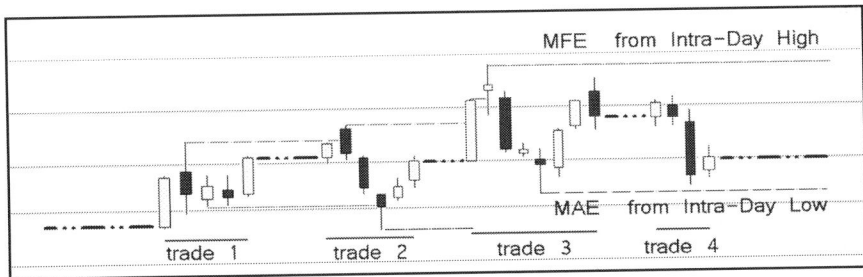

Figure 2.10 Intra-day high and low are visible

In Figure 2.11, marked-to-market closing prices define the highest bankable equity and maximum adverse excursion from that price. Point A is the highest close. You could have liquidated the position, banked the profit, and withdrawn the funds at the closing price that day. That is your money, and drawdown is calculated relative to it.

Point B is the maximum adverse excursion. It is the deepest intra-trade drawdown at a marked-to-market closing price. The difference between B and A is the amount you had lost at the close of day B. The two lines leading out of the right side represent the highest bankable equity and the account balance after the trade was closed.

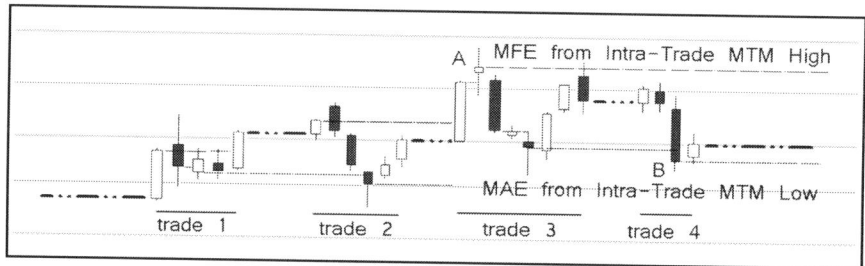

Figure 2.11 Intra-trade high and low marked-to-market are visible

Figure 2.12 ignores all intra-trade equity changes. There is still an MAE, but it only compares current closed equity with maximum closed equity.

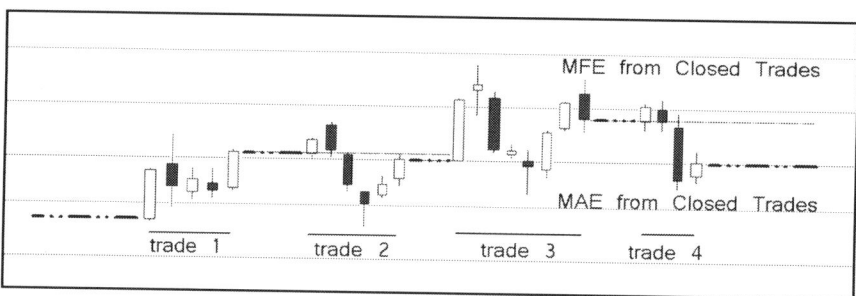

Figure 2.12 Only closed trades are visible

Maximum Favorable Excursion

Similar to MAE, maximum favorable excursion (MFE) records the most favorable price. In a long trade, it is the highest high. When using mark-to-market, whenever there is a new MFE and it establishes a new high for the account equity, adjust the equity to reflect that gain.

If you subscribe to the idea that there are *two* absorbing boundaries—success and failure—a new maximum equity may cause you to stop trading because you have *gained enough*.

Accumulated MAE (AMAE)

Every trade has its own MAE, computed and reported daily. The accumulated drawdown spans trades and measures the highest marked-to-market bankable equity to lowest marked-to-market equity.

AMAE is the drawdown we use to measure risk.

Your goal in trading the system is to determine the proper maximum safe position size, on a trade-by-trade basis, so that the AMAE rarely—hopefully never—exceeds your risk tolerance.

Bad Stuff Can Happen

In spite of your best system development efforts, there might be—probably will be—situations where a larger loss than the system—or you—anticipated occurred, but there are still open trades.

Management and measurement should coincide.

If it is necessary to do so, your action to declare the system broken, override the rules, exit open positions, and take the system offline should coincide with a point in time or in the trade where drawdown is measured. That is the point at which trades are marked-to-market.

If the intra-day drawdown is too severe, use shorter bars and mark-to-market after each bar.

Your measurement period must agree with your management period.

Does intra-trade drawdown matter?

Yes. Consider the Will Rogers system.

> *Don't gamble; take all your savings and buy some good stock and hold it till it goes up, then sell it. If it don't go up, don't buy it.*

Written as a trading system, that might be:
```
Buy when the price rises above its 100 day moving average
Sell when there is a 5% profit
```

Figure 2.13 shows the equity curve, based on closed trades, for trading SPY using that system beginning in 1999.

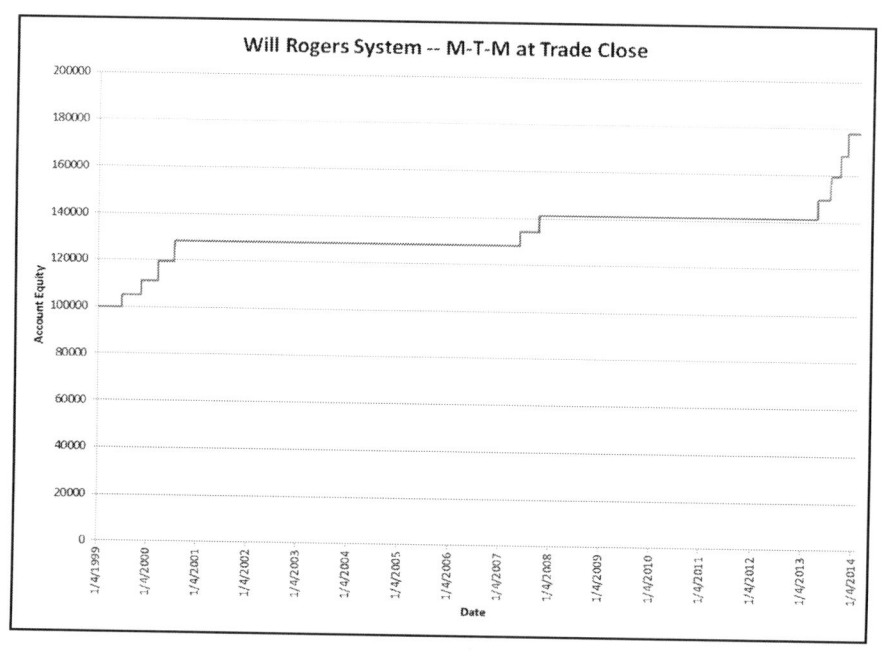

Figure 2.13 Closed trade equity for Will Rogers system

Figure 2.14 shows the equity curve with daily account balance changes.

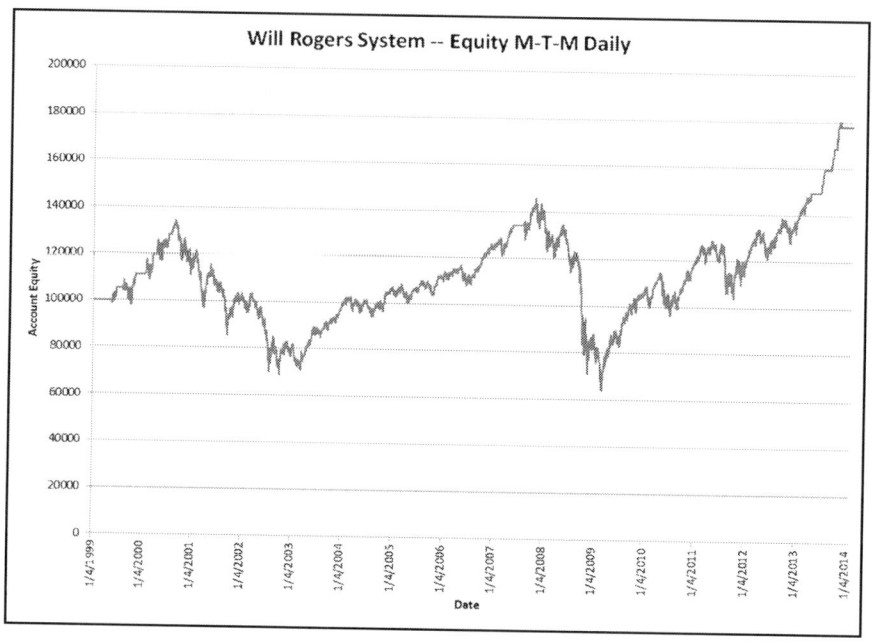

Figure 2.14 Daily equity for Will Rogers system

Imagine if the system had been trading Enron rather than SPY.

Mark-to-Market Equivalence

Figure 2.15 shows a table representing three multi-day trades. Entry to a long position is made at the close of the first day, at the closing price. Exit is at the close of the final day, at the closing price. The column headed "Trade" gives the gain of that trade—exit price divided by entry price. "Trade Sequence" gives the cumulative gain for the trade sequence. "Daily Change" is the day-by-day percentage change from the previous day. "Daily Cumulative" is the cumulative gain for the sequence of days within each trade. Note agreement between "Trade" and "Daily Cumulative" at the end of each trade. "Daily Sequence" is the cumulative gain for the sequence of days for the entire three trade sequence. Note the agreement between "Trade Sequence" and "Daily Sequence" at the end of the trade sequence.

	Daily price SPY Close		Trade	Trade Sequence	Daily Change	Daily Cumulative	Daily Sequence
4/11/2002	110.59	buy		1		1	1
4/12/2002	111.42				1.0075	1.0075	1.0075
4/15/2002	110.57				0.9924	0.9998	0.9998
4/16/2002	113.20				1.0238	1.0236	1.0236
4/17/2002	112.96				0.9979	1.0214	1.0214
4/18/2002	112.47				0.9957	1.0170	1.0170
4/19/2002	112.88	sell	1.0207	1.0207	1.0036	1.0207	1.0207
4/26/2002	107.39	buy				1	
4/29/2002	106.86				0.9951	0.9951	1.0157
4/30/2002	107.86				1.0094	1.0044	1.0252
5/1/2002	109.18				1.0122	1.0167	1.0377
5/2/2002	108.76	sell	1.0128	1.0337	0.9962	1.0128	1.0337
5/8/2002	109.01	buy				1	
5/9/2002	107.75				0.9884	0.9884	1.0218
5/10/2002	105.72	sell	0.9698	1.0025	0.9812	0.9698	1.0025

Figure 2.15 Equity change by trade and by day

From a mathematical perspective, the net equity change from a sequence of trades is identical whether the trades are considered as complete trades or as sequences of marked-to-market days.

From a trading management perspective, marking-to-market daily gives finer resolution to the performance of the system and the opportunity to make subjective trading decisions, should they become necessary.

From a trading system design perspective, marking-to-market daily transforms every system, no matter how often it buys and sells, into a system that has 252 daily results every year. This reduces distortion that occurs at the start and end of every evaluation period. It also increases the number of data points available for trade selection, and entry and exit signals.

The technique for converting between impulse signals (traditional signals that identify the boundaries of multi-day trades) and state signals (used with mark-to-market evaluation to indicate the position to hold for the next day) is described in Chapter 6.

Although the trades extend over multiple days, the system design and system management focus is on the mark-to-market period—daily.

This does not imply changing positions every day. It does imply evaluating every day, and willingness to change positions daily. It allows us to ask the questions "What is the distribution of next day return?" and "Should the position for the next day be long, flat, or short?"

In terms of changes to account equity and drawdown, an n-day trade is equivalent to n one-day trades.

Risk Tolerance

Every trader or trading company has a level of risk tolerance. It is the level of drawdown that, when reached or exceeded, causes the trader to accept that the system is broken and must be taken offline. Risk tolerance can be quantified.

Statement of Risk Tolerance

An example of a statement of risk tolerance is:

> I am trading a $100,000 account and looking forward two years. I am willing to accept a 5% risk of a 20% drawdown, measured from highest equity to date.

It has four parameters:
- Account size.
- Forecast horizon.
- Maximum drawdown.
- Degree of certainty.

Account Size

The initial balance of the trading account at the beginning of the period. With the understanding that the utility of money is an important issue, it is ignored here. But, needing specific numbers for examples, the initial balance is set at $100,000 for most examples.

Since we are measuring in percentage changes, it is not a critical issue at this point.

Forecast Horizon

The depth of a drawdown sometime in the future depends on how far into the future we look. Pick a length of time that fits your business plan and trading activity. We call this the *forecast horizon*. It will be set to two years for these examples. Both estimates of future drawdowns and realized drawdowns increase as the length of the forecast horizon is increased. Think of the oft-quoted warning that "your greatest drawdown lies in the future."

Maximum Drawdown

The trader's risk tolerance is the drawdown at which the system is taken offline in recognition that it is not working as expected. As we will see, account growth, position size, and drawdown are linked. Being too conservative on maximum drawdown limits account growth. Being too liberal increases the probability of a steep drawdown, and the difficulty of recovering from it. Individual traders might be willing to accept 20%.

Money managers who prefer to hold drawdowns to single digits and have no losing years might use 10% instead of 20%.

Use whatever level you are comfortable with. In Chapter 9 we see some examples of position sizing in action, and of the relationship between the maximum drawdown level specified in the statement of risk tolerance and the drawdown experienced trade-by-trade as a system fails.

As we will see in the next chapter, risk increases as holding period increases. **Traders preferring longer holding periods must be prepared to either accept higher risk or trade at a smaller position size.**

Degree of Certainty

We seldom get opportunities to recover from serious mistakes, so we should reduce the chances of having even one drawdown as severe as the limit we have chosen. If one chance in twenty sounds about right, that is a 5% chance. 5% corresponds well with our understanding of statistical significance. We say that an event is *significant* at the 5% level.

A Chart Illustrating Risk Tolerance

Good! We have a well defined statement of risk tolerance. We know enough to draw a picture illustrating the risk tolerance. Figure 2.16 shows the cumulative distribution function (CDF) of drawdown for a simple trading system (the code is shown at the end of this chapter). The circle at the right edge of the page identifies the risk tolerance of the example statement on the previous page—a 5% chance of a 20% maximum drawdown. The next few sections describe how to create this chart from a set of trades.

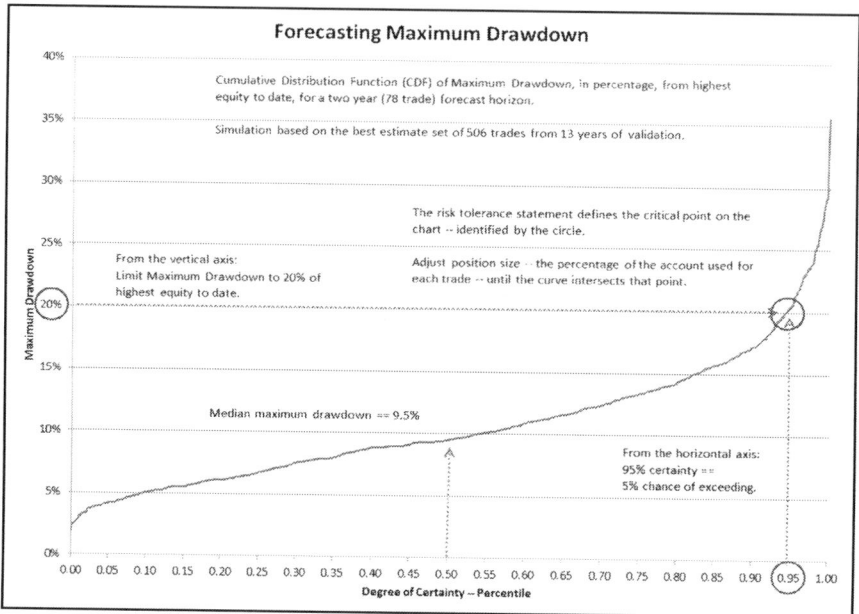

Figure 2.16 Chart illustrating a statement of risk tolerance

This chart (and the others that are similar to it later in the book) came from a Monte Carlo simulation. A trading system was designed, coded, and tested using daily end-of-day data for the period 1/1/1999 through 1/1/2012. Validation produced a set of 506 trades for the 13 year period. That set of trades was used as the *best estimate* of future performance. Assuming that future performance is similar to that of the best estimate, a two-year forecast horizon will have about 78 trades. A Monte Carlo simulation was coded in Excel using the techniques described in my Modeling book.[1]

The fixed fraction technique was used for position sizing. The fraction of the account used for each trade that produced this curve is 63%. This means that whenever a Buy signal is generated by the system, buy as many shares as possible using 63% of the current balance of the trading account. That value, 63%, was determined by an iterative search. The fraction was adjusted in order to find the value where there was a 5% chance that the maximum drawdown would exceed 20%. That is, to find the fraction where the CDF curve passed through the point defining the statement of risk tolerance.

The resulting cumulative distribution function of percentage maximum drawdown is plotted in Figure 2.16. The 5% certainty comes from the horizontal axis, where the 95th percentile corresponds to a 5% chance

---

1 Bandy, Howard, *Modeling Trading System Performance*, Blue Owl Press, 2011.

of a greater drawdown. The 20% maximum drawdown comes from the vertical axis.

Tail Risk and Black Swans

We can estimate the *tail risk*—the depth of the worst drawdown—by observing the extreme right side of the distribution—the area above the 95th percentile. The extreme tail risk for Figure 2.16 is 36%. **Black swans live and hide in the tail of the distribution.**

Producing the CDF for Estimate of Risk

The histogram in Figure 2.17 represents a probability mass function (pmf). A pmf is for discrete data what a probability density function (pdf) is for continuous data. The maximum drawdown from each of the 1000 simulation runs described above was recorded, then sorted into bins 0.5% wide. The heights of the histogram bars show the proportion of drawdowns in each of the respective bins. For an interpretation, consider the tallest histogram bar—the bin at 9%, is 6.3% high. That means that of the 1000 simulation runs, 6.3%, or 63, of them had a maximum drawdown between 8.75% and 9.25%. (Since the bins are each 0.5% wide, the 9% bin includes 8.75% to 9.25%.)

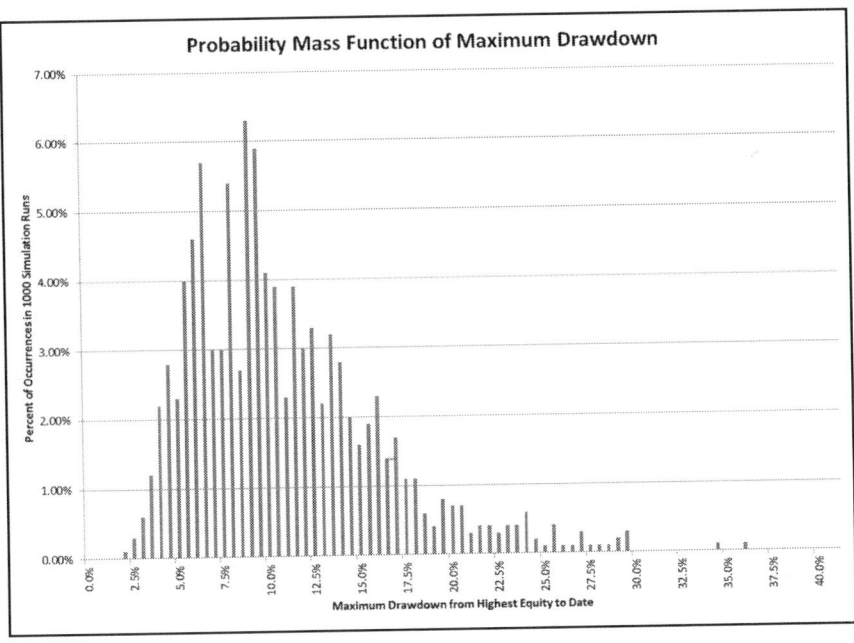

Figure 2.17 Probability mass function of maximum drawdown

The CDF is more useful for our purposes. To form the CDF, beginning at the leftmost bin of the histogram of the pmf, compute the running sum of percentages. CDFs always have a range of 0.0 to 1.0. The resulting CDF is shown in Figure 2.18.

Figures 2.16 and 2.18 show the same data, but with the axes exchanged. In Figure 2.16, the percentile scale is on the horizontal axis, and the function is more properly called the *inverse CDF*. Most of the CDFs we will work with are displayed like Figure 2.16 and are inverse CDFs. Since there will likely be no confusion, either format of the function will be referred to as a CDF.

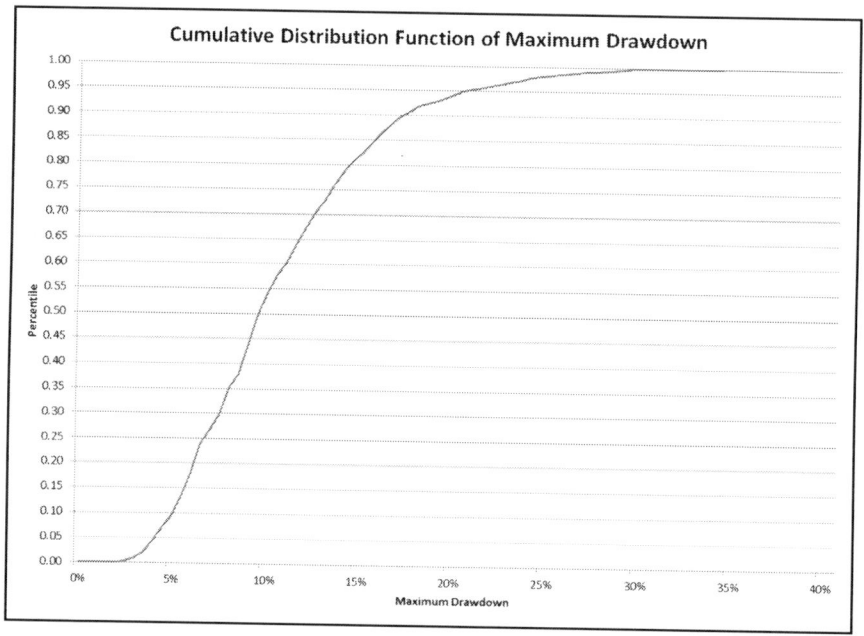

Figure 2.18 Cumulative distribution function

Backtest Equity Curve

For interest, Figure 2.19 shows the equity curve for the validation trades for the system. There is no compounding or other position sizing—each trade is the number of shares that can be purchased by the same dollar amount. This is about as benign, smooth, and safe looking an equity curve as ever results from an out-of-sample test.

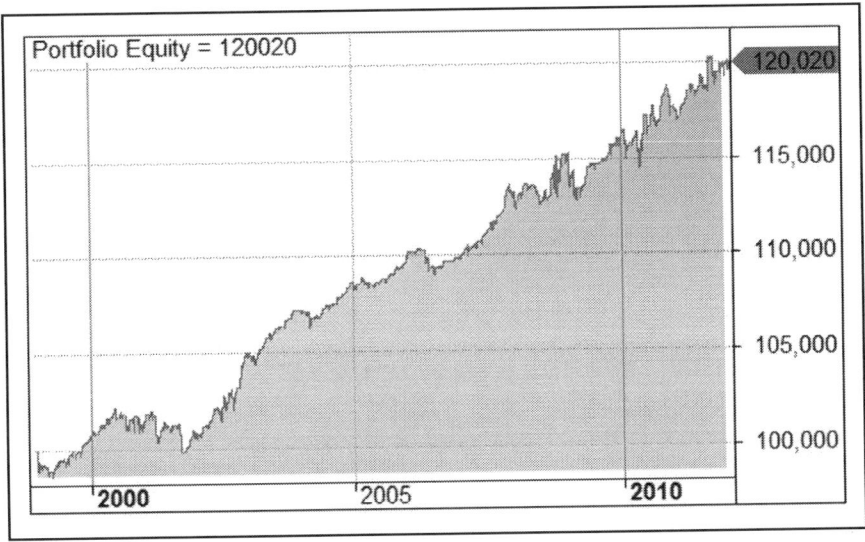

Figure 2.19 Equity curve for example system

Trade at Full Fraction

Yet, this system can only be traded at a fraction of 0.63 without risk exceeding the desired limits. If all funds were used for each trade—trading the system at a fraction of 1.00, or *full fraction*— the risk rises considerably, as the CDF in Figure 2.20 shows. Figures 2.16 and 2.20 use the same scales. If the certainty remains at 5%, maximum drawdown increases from 20% to 30%—the tail of large drawdowns increases. Alternatively, if the maximum drawdown remains at 20%, the certainty drops from 5% to 25%—from a 1 in 20 chance to a 1 in 4 chance of a 20% drawdown. Not shown because it is truncated by the scale limitation, extreme tail risk when traded at full fraction rises to more than 48%.

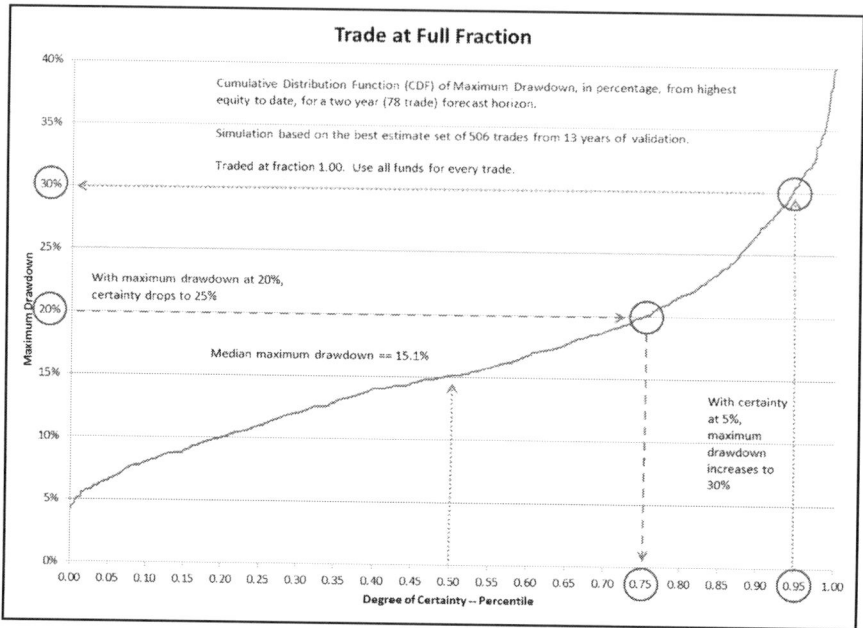

Figure 2.20 CDF of maximum drawdown traded at full fraction

Position Size — safe-f

There are many alternative methods of determining position size. See Chapter 10 of my Modeling book[2] for a description and discussion of several of the most popular, including Kelly, single contract, constant dollar, volatility weighted, margin requirement, fixed fraction, fixed ratio, and generalized ratio. In that discussion, I conclude that fixed fraction is a reasonable, usually optimal, and easily implemented technique. **I recommend using fixed fraction as the position sizing technique.**

For a given set of trades, maximum drawdown is highly dependent on position size. As the fraction of the account used for each trade is increased, maximum drawdown also increases. As shown in Figure 2.21, the relationship is nearly linear in the range any of us will be using.

---

2 Bandy, Howard, *Modeling Trading System Performance*, Blue Owl Press, 2011.

Risk and Risk Tolerance

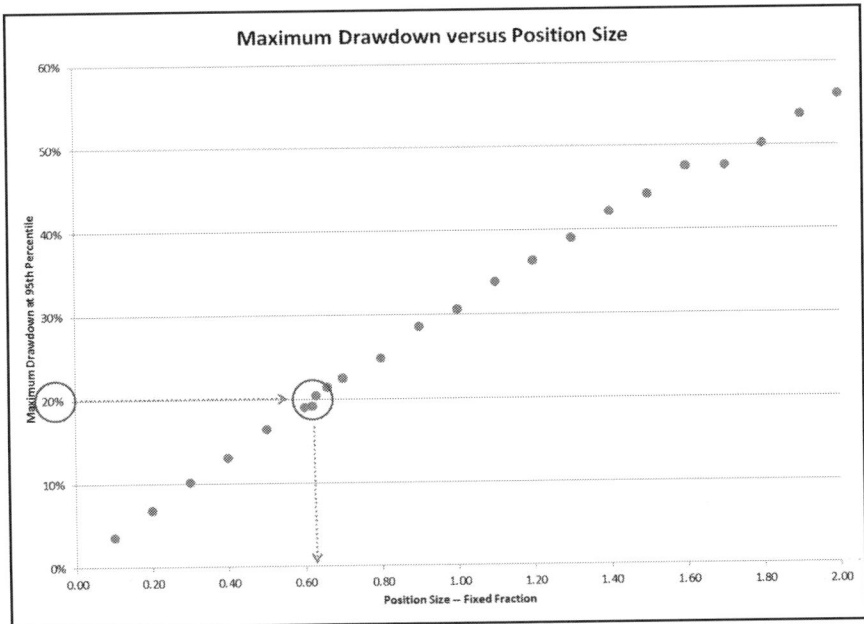

Figure 2.21 Maximum drawdown versus position size

Position size, the fraction used for each trade, was varied from 0.1 to 2.0. The simulation was run for each value, estimating maximum drawdown at the 95th percentile. To hold maximum drawdown to a limit of 20%, use a fixed fraction position size of 0.63.

0.63 is the value of safe-f that is associated with this set of trades and this risk tolerance.

If the set of trades changes—and it definitely will change as future trades are included in the set—the risk of drawdown changes, and safe-f changes. If the newly added trades are losing trades, risk increases, and the fraction of the account exposed to risk must decrease in order to hold overall risk within the trader's tolerance.

Safe-f is position size. It is recalculated after every trade and used to determine the size of the next trade.

When using mark-to-market evaluation, safe-f is computed at that same frequency—daily. Daily intra-trade changes are added to the set of trades. If an intra-trade drawdown develops, safe-f will drop, indicating to the trader to lighten position.

This is the dynamic position sizing technique.

Equity of the trading account also depends on position size. As shown in Figure 2.22, as the fraction is increased through the range of 0.2 to 1.0, median final equity at the end of the two year horizon is progressively higher. The solid line—the center of the five lines—shows the CDF of final equity when the fraction is 0.60.

Final equity is relative to initial equity. Using the terminology of Ralph Vince, final equity is Terminal Wealth Relative, TWR.[3] Note that all five lines are above 1.0 for percentile levels of about 0.10. Interpret this to indicate that there is about a 90% probability that the account will show some profit after two years. Also note that as the probability of a large TWR increases with increased position size, the magnitude of the potential loss of account equity also increases.

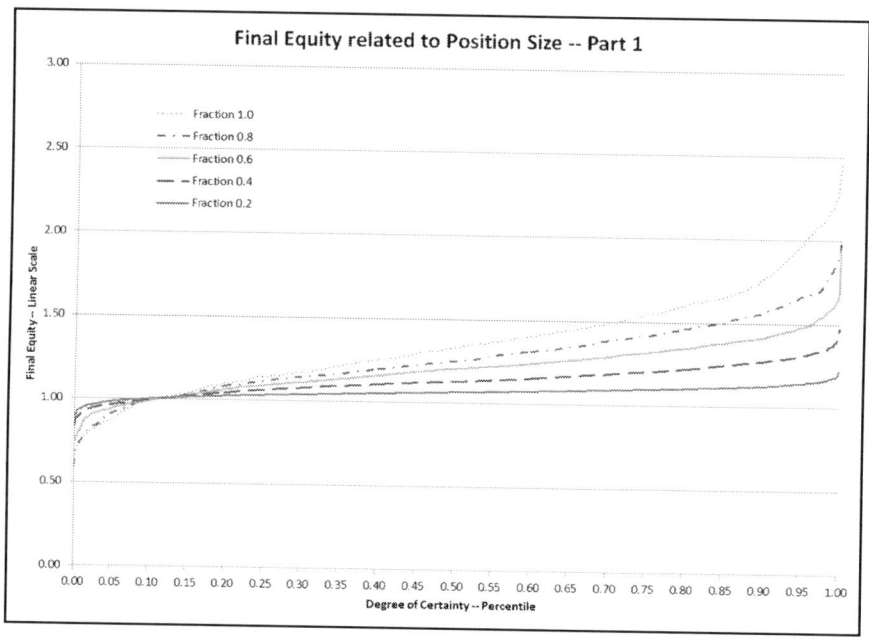

Figure 2.22 Final equity related to position size -- part 1

Continuing to increase position size for fractions 1.0, 2.0, 3.0, and 4.0, results in increased TWR, as shown in Figure 2.23. The gains, provided the trader is lucky, are very great, requiring a switch to log scale to show the potential profit. Also note the increase in potential loss. And the increase in probability that there will be a loss.

---

3   Vince, Ralph, *Portfolio Management Formulas*, Wiley, 1990.

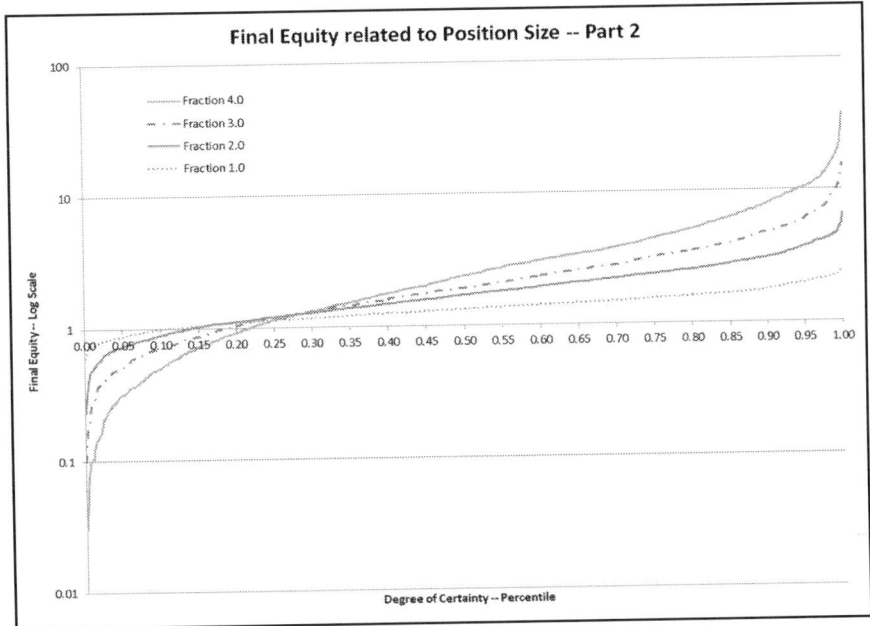

Figure 2.23 Final equity related to position size -- part 2

As Figure 2.24 shows, the risk increases dramatically. The lowest line is fraction 1.0. As mentioned earlier, and as can be read from the chart, the probability of a 20% drawdown is about 25% and the tail risk is nearly 50%. ETFs with leverages up to 3.0 are available for some indexes. Using all funds—a fraction of 1.0—to take a position in a fund with 3X leverage is equivalent to trading with a fraction of 3.0. The CDF for fraction 3.0 is the dashed line second from the top. The median (50th percentile) maximum drawdown is 44%, and there is only a 5% chance that maximum drawdown will be below 20%.

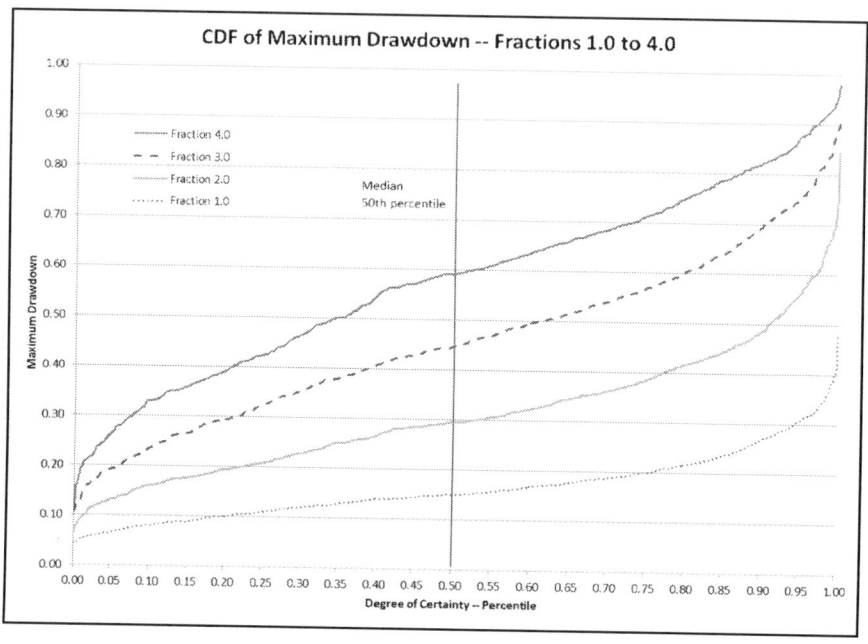

Figure 2.24 Maximum drawdown related to position size -- part 2

Using Final Equity as a Metric

As the previous analysis demonstrates, final equity increases with position size. It is tempting to use final equity, terminal wealth, or compound annual rate of return (CAR)—all equivalent metrics—to evaluate system performance. The difficulty is that the distribution of final equity expands quite rapidly as position size increases. Figure 2.25 shows the probability mass function of final equity for three values of the position size fraction—0.2, 0.6, and 1.0. The median (50th percentile) final equity values are 1.06, 1.20, and 1.33, respectively. These correspond to CAR values of 2.9%, 9.5%, and 15.3%. Based on the risk tolerance analysis described earlier, the maximum safe position size is 0.63, with a corresponding CAR of about 9.6%. Moving from position size of 0.6 to 0.2 reduces CAR, but tightens the distribution; while moving to 1.0 increases CAR, but expands the distribution.

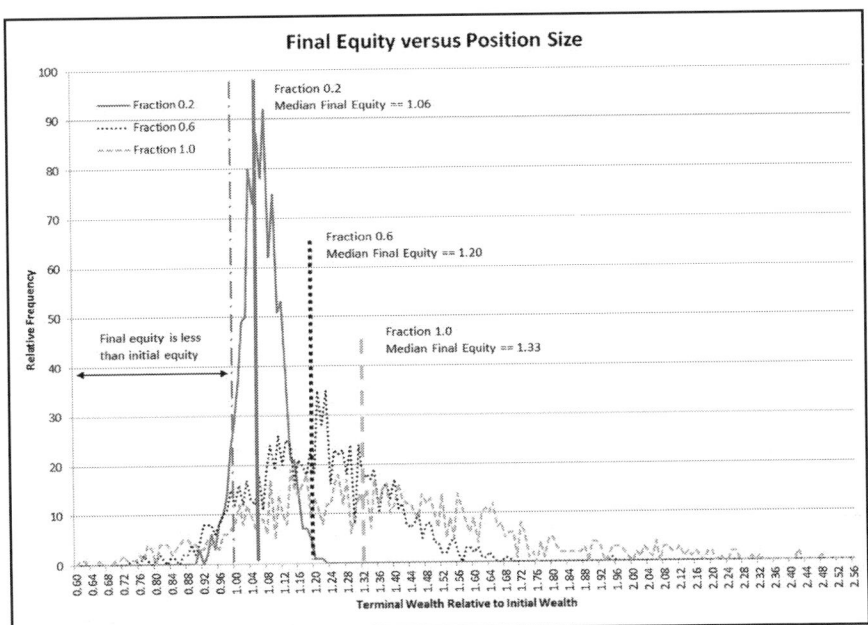

Figure 2.25 Final equity versus position size

Figure 2.26 expands the area where final equity is less than initial equity—below final equity of 1.0. It is the increased possibility that the next two years could produce a net loss of capital that recommends against using a fraction greater than 0.63.

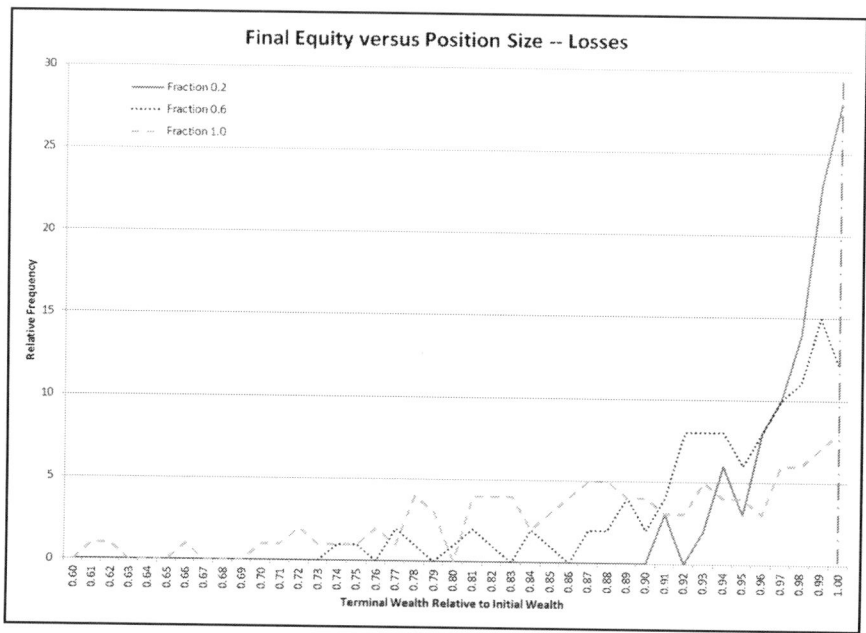

Figure 2.26 Final equity versus position size -- losses

Evaluating Mark-to-Market Equivalence

The system whose risk was analyzed in Figures 2.19 through 2.26 used end-of-day data with entry and exit at the close of the day the signal was generated. We saw the mark-to-market equivalence between a sequence of multi-day trades and a sequence of single-days, each marked-to-market, in Figure 2.15. We can, and should, test whether mark-to-market equivalence holds for risk, calculation of safe-f, and profit potential.

Recall that the original, trade-by-trade, system produced 506 trades over the 13 year period, 78 trades were used to forecast a two year horizon, and safe-f was found to be 0.63.

The trading system code was modified so its output included a series of daily price changes along with the trade listing. The 506 trades covered 1151 days. The simulation to forecast a two year period used 177 days. Nothing else was changed.

Safe-f using daily marked-to-market data is 0.57. Figure 2.27 compares the CDFs of maximum drawdown for trade-by-trade with day-by-day. Safe-f was determined such that the two curves would agree at the 95th percentile.

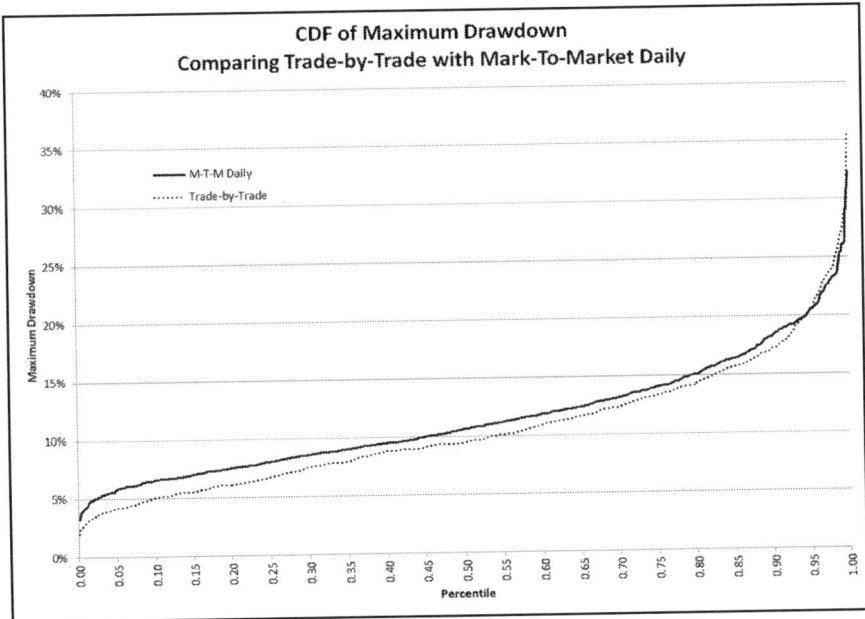

Figure 2.27 CDF of maximum drawdown comparing trade-by-trade with daily marked-to-market

Figure 2.28 compares the CDFs of final equity using safe-f of 63% for trade-by-trade and 57% for day-by-day.

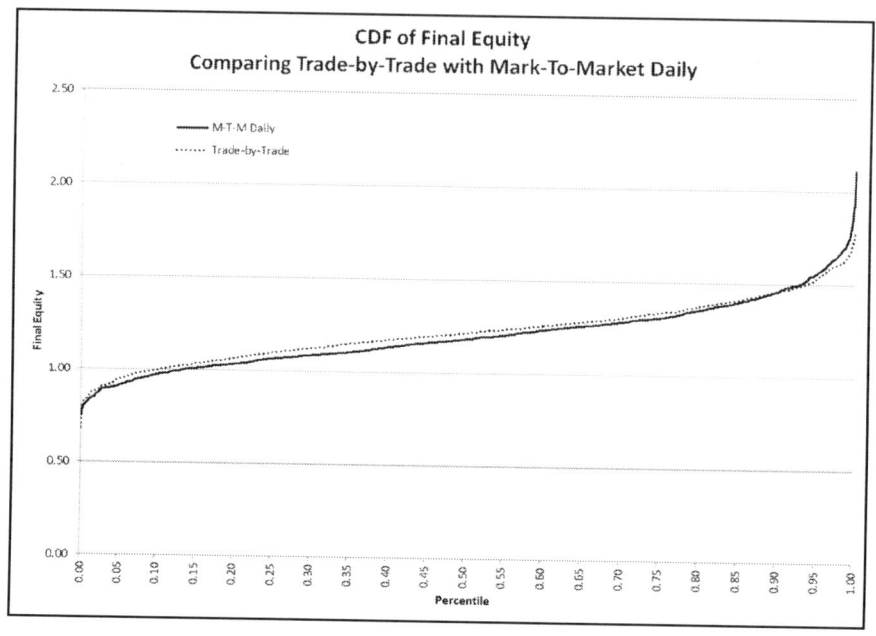

Figure 2.28 CDF of final equity comparing trade-by-trade with daily marked-to-market

We should hope for results that are close, as they are; but we should not expect perfect agreement. For one thing, replacing 78 trades by 177 days destroyed whatever serial correlation existed between the days in trades. For another, simulations usually produce results that differ slightly from run to run.

Our use of this information is comparisons of alternatives. The advantages of marking to market daily—increased control over changes in position, increased number of data points per year, less distortion at the boundaries of evaluation periods—easily compensate for slight differences in forecasts of safe-f, drawdown, and final equity.

No Guarantee

You have used the best modeling and simulation techniques during development, and profitably traded live for a period of time. You have confidence in the system. Never-the-less, the system cannot deal with all contingencies. Extreme situations—perhaps such as Enron or October 1987—will cause even the best systems to fail. There is still a possibility that drawdown exceeds your tolerance. That should be unlikely.

Technique for Risk Management

The statement of risk tolerance is a personal statement. If the drawdown reaches the maximum level, that is an indication that the system is broken, and the system is taken offline.

The *dynamic position sizing* method described in detail in Chapter 9 uses recent trading results, together with the best estimate set of trades and a Monte Carlo simulation, to estimate the distribution of the drawdown that can be expected in the future. That estimate is compared with the statement of risk tolerance to calculate safe-f—the maximum safe position size. Properly implemented, dynamic position sizing will reduce the position size when trading results are poor. In practice, the dynamic position sizing technique will usually have reduced the maximum safe position size to zero before the drawdown reaches the maximum tolerable level.

Trade Quality

We periodically read articles that recommend holding long positions for long periods of time. The argument revolves around an analysis of equity gain related to missing a very few of the best days in a period, suggesting it is essential to remain invested in order to benefit from those few special days. Since this is a book about trading system development, and we are looking for alternatives to buy and hold that provide for account growth while avoiding large drawdowns, we can answer the best day versus worst day question using the techniques just described—compare profit potential on a risk-normalized basis.

Example System

We begin with a trading system described at the beginning of this chapter. Recall that the primary indicator is the two period RSI of closing price. Call it RSI2. The system enters a long position when RSI2 falls through a level of 36, and exits when RSI2 rises through a level of 36. The program is listed at the end of this chapter. The system was tested on major equity index ETFs for the 13 year period of 1999 through 2011. Figure 2.29 shows the equity curve for one of the issues.

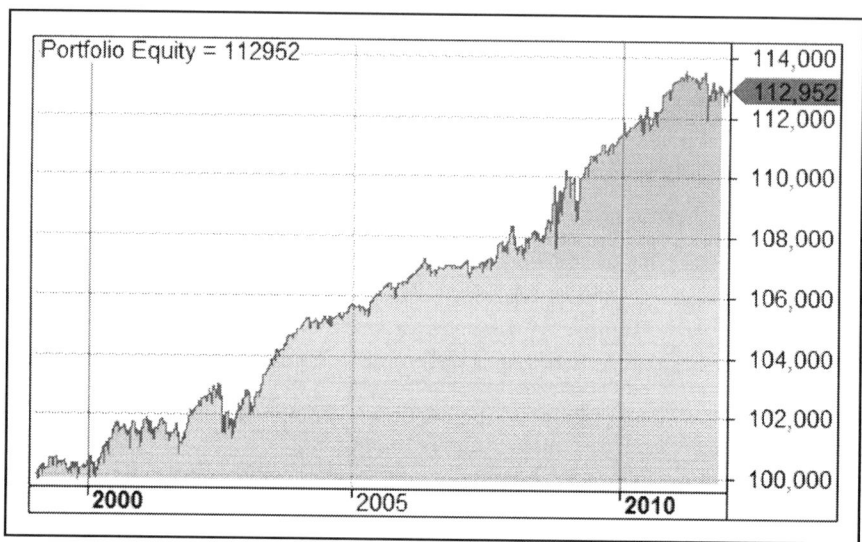

Figure 2.29 Equity curve for constant size trades

Figure 2.30 shows the statistics. There are 517 trades, each of which gains about 0.25%, on average. The summary report in Figure 2.30 shows average bars held to be 3.22. AmiBroker counts the entry day. For this system, there is no equity change on entry day, so we will not count it as one of the holding period days, making the average holding period 2.22 days. Trade accuracy is about 71%. On average, losing trades are held longer than winning trades, and the magnitude of the average loss is greater than of the average win.

Statistics

	All trades	Long trades	Short trades
Initial capital	100000.00	100000.00	100000.00
Ending capital	112952.12	112952.12	100000.00
Net Profit	12952.12	12952.12	0.00
Net Profit %	12.95 %	12.95 %	0.00 %
Exposure %	3.31 %	3.31 %	0.00 %
Net Risk Adjusted Return %	391.58 %	391.58 %	N/A
Annual Return %	0.94 %	0.94 %	0.00 %
Risk Adjusted Return %	28.47 %	28.47 %	N/A
Total transaction costs	0.00	0.00	0.00
All trades	517	517 (100.00 %)	0 (0.00 %)
Avg. Profit/Loss	25.05	25.05	N/A
Avg. Profit/Loss %	0.25 %	0.25 %	N/A
Avg. Bars Held	3.22	3.22	N/A
Winners	367 (70.99 %)	367 (70.99 %)	0 (0.00 %)
Total Profit	39180.54	39180.54	0.00
Avg. Profit	106.76	106.76	N/A
Avg. Profit %	1.07 %	1.07 %	N/A
Avg. Bars Held	2.49	2.49	N/A
Max. Consecutive	14	14	0
Largest win	718.29	718.29	0.00
# bars in largest win	2	2	0
Losers	150 (29.01 %)	150 (29.01 %)	0 (0.00 %)
Total Loss	-26228.42	-26228.42	0.00
Avg. Loss	-174.86	-174.86	N/A
Avg. Loss %	-1.75 %	-1.75 %	N/A
Avg. Bars Held	5.00	5.00	N/A
Max. Consecutive	4	4	0
Largest loss	-1188.78	-1188.78	0.00
# bars in largest loss	11	11	0

Figure 2.30 Statistics for trades

Figure 2.31 shows the 517 trades, sorted by gain.

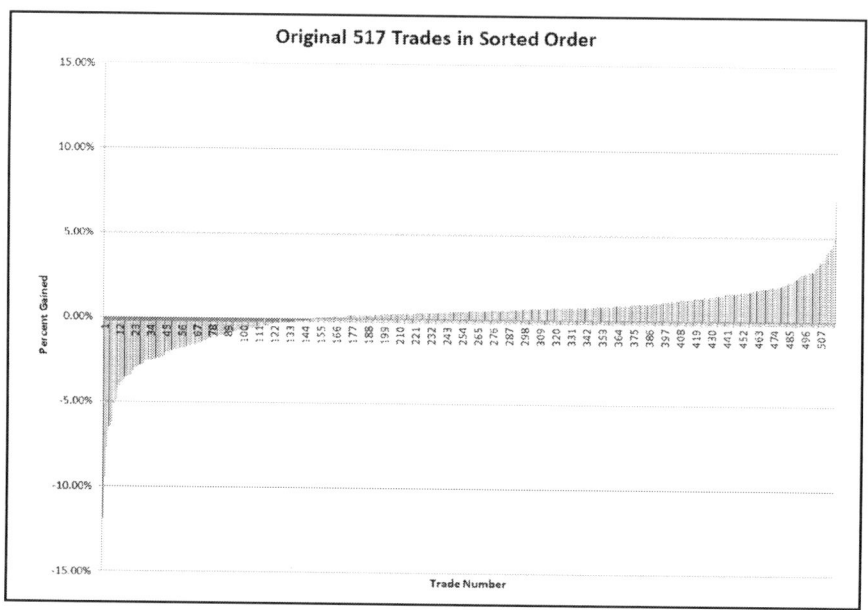

Figure 2.31 Trades in sorted order

The by-now-familiar simulation is used to compute safe-f for a risk tolerance of 5% / 20% / 2 years. It turns out to be 0.883, and the interquartile CAR values are CAR25 = 3.4% and CAR75 = 14.3%.

To study how the best trades and the worst trades affect performance, we will analyze four more sets of trades. Each simulation run begins with the same 517 trades, then modified by adding or removing five percent (26) winning trades or losing trades. The five simulations are:

A. The original 517 trades.
B. Add winners. Copy the best 26 trades and add them to the trade list, resulting in 543 trades.
C. Add losers. Copy the worst 26 trades and add them to the trade list.
D. Remove winners. Remove the 26 best trades from the list, resulting in 491 trades.
E. Remove losers. Remove the 26 worst trades from the list.

Five simulation runs were made, each trading full fraction. The five CDFs of maximum drawdown are shown in Figure 2.32.

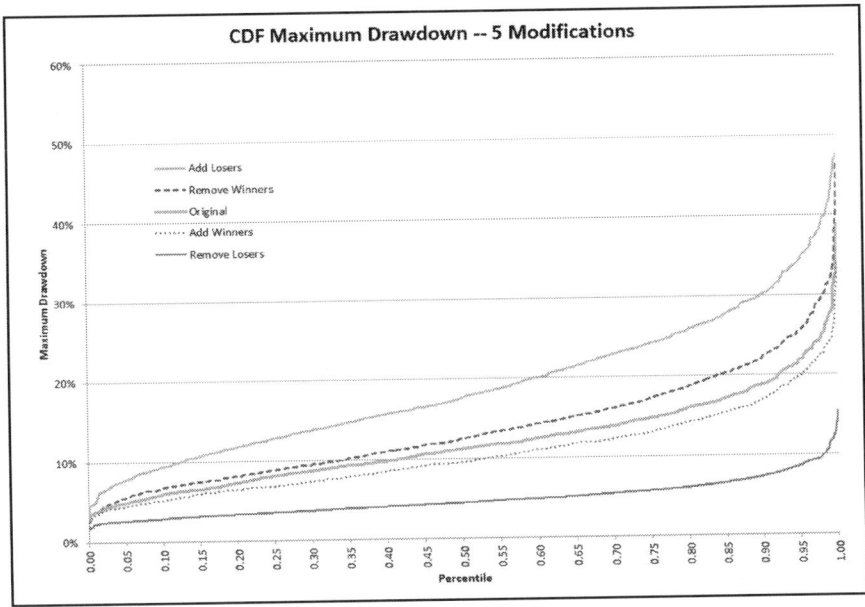

Figure 2.32 CDFs of maximum drawdown for modified trade list

We prefer systems with lower drawdown—those lower on the chart. The uppermost curve is the one where losing trades were added. Increasing losing trades increases drawdown. The lowermost curve is the one where losing trades were removed. Decreasing losing trades decreases drawdown. The curves where winners were either added or removed—just above and below the middle curve—did not change the result much.

Losing trades are clearly more important than winning trades in determining risk.

Limitation to any trading system is the number and magnitude of losing trades. When these occur close together in sequence, they cause large drawdowns.

Recall that safe-f is computed so that the risk of a 20% drawdown is 5%. We can describe this as *normalizing for risk*. When normalized for risk, the profit potential of alternative trading systems can be compared directly.

Safe-f was determined for each of the five sets of trades, normalizing the drawdown at the 95th percentile, and the profit potential of each was computed. The safe-f values, in A, B, C, D, E order, were 0.88, 1.01, 0.55, 0.72, and 2.53. Figure 2.33 shows the five CDFs of final equity when each is traded at its safe-f position size. Higher is better. Note the significantly higher profit for the trade list that had the worst five percent of trades removed.

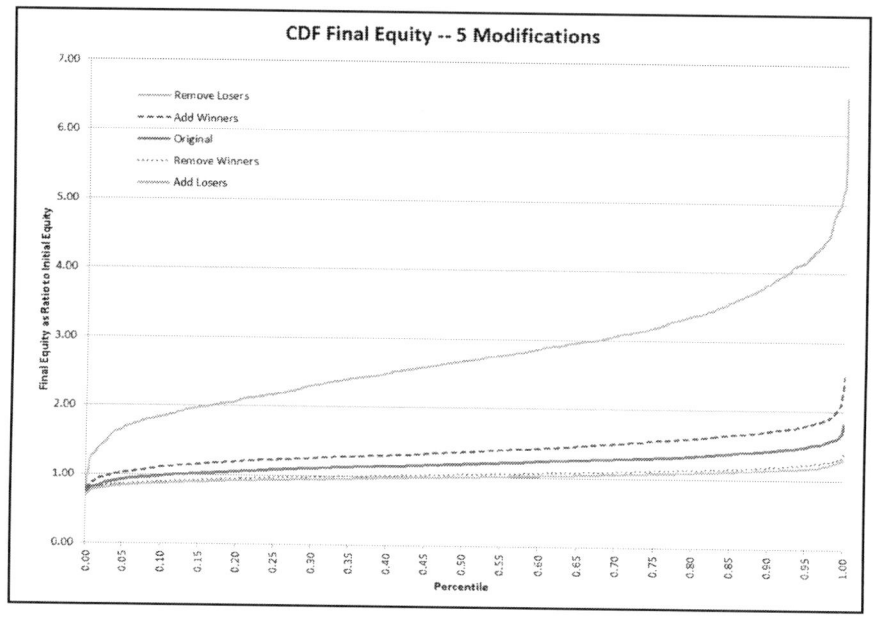

Figure 2.33 CDFs of profit potential

While it would be ideal to remove only the worst trades, that will be difficult. Figure 2.34 shows an interesting comparison where both the five percent best trades and the five percent worst trades have been removed. Normalized for risk, performance is significantly better for the set of trades that do not include the losing trades. There is less risk of having a loss at the end of the two year period, and CAR is higher across the distribution.

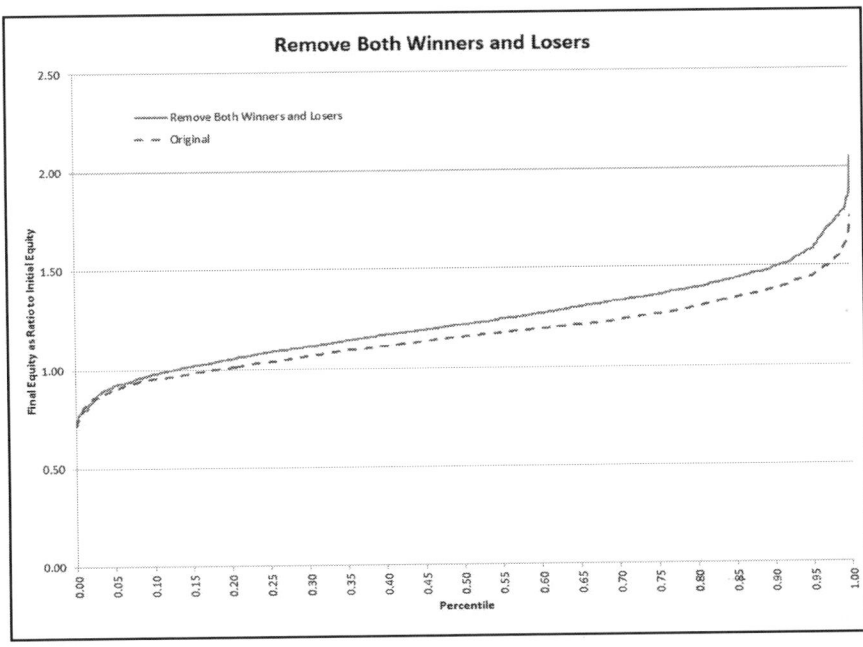

Figure 2.34 Remove both best and worst trades

Even at the expense of missing good trades, it is important to avoid bad trades.

Summary

Other factors in life, or utility of money, may cause people to stop trading systems. Dealing with drawdown is the only reason being considered in this book.

It is psychologically easier to hold through a drawdown to the end of a shorter trade than a longer trade.

Daily, or intra-day, bars are used within the system.

Daily bars are used for reporting and for trading management.

Following the thought that the main reason people stop trading a system is because they had a large drawdown, this chapter:
- Shows how to define a personal statement of risk tolerance in terms of drawdown.
- Shows how to measure the risk of any trading system.

There are natural choices of when to mark-to-market.
- Prices of issues are marked-to-market at the closing price.
- Account equity is marked-to-market daily.
- Drawdown is computed daily.
- Trade results are computed and recorded at the close of every trade.
- The best estimate set of trades is used to establish a performance baseline, monitor system health, and compute position size.
- Monte Carlo simulations produce distributions of trade metrics and estimates.
- Maximum safe position size for the next trade is computed between trades.

When accumulating gains and losses for risk analysis, the periodicity of marking-to-market makes accounting of finer detail invisible. Marking prices to market daily makes the high and low invisible. Marking trade gain to market upon completion makes the intra-trade MFE and MAE invisible.

While account growth increases with increase in position size (at the level of position size appropriate for systems trading shares), evaluating system performance on the basis of final equity or compound annual rate of return ignores drawdown and leads to excessively risky trading.

Program Listing

The AmiBroker code for program that produced the equity curve displayed in Figure 2.19 and the trades analyzed beginning in Figure 2.16 is shown below. The program was tested using many price series, including major indexes such as SPY, QQQ, IWM, and EEM, and country funds such as EWA, EWC, and EWP.

```
//  Program_2_1.afl
//
//  Generate a lot of trades
//          for book example
//

SetOption( "InitialEquity", 100000 );
SetPositionSize( 10000, spsValue );
MaxPos = 1;
SetOption( "MaxOpenPositions", MaxPos );
SetOption( "ExtraColumnsLocation", 1 );
SetTradeDelays( 0, 0, 0, 0 );
BuyPrice = SellPrice = Close;

BuyLevel = 36;
SellLevel = 36;
MaxHold = 9;
RSI2 = RSI( 2 );

Buy = Cross( BuyLevel, RSI2 );
Sell = Cross( RSI2, SellLevel )
       OR BarsSince( Buy ) >= MaxHold;

Buy = ExRem( Buy, Sell );
Sell = ExRem( Sell, Buy );

//////// Plots //////////////

Plot( C, "C", colorBlack, styleCandle );
shapes = IIf( Buy, shapeUpArrow,
              IIf( Sell, shapeDownArrow, shapeNone ) );
shapecolors = IIf( Buy, colorGreen,
                   IIf( Sell, colorRed, colorWhite ) );
PlotShapes( shapes, shapecolors );

//////// end ///////////////
```

Program 2.1 Trading system to produce the trades and equity curve analyzed in Chapter 2

Chapter 3
Programming Environments

Technical analysts who plot price and volume, inspect the chart, and use their experience and expert judgement to trade, can use one of the many excellent charting packages to prepare their data.

Quantitative technical analysts use precisely defined logical and mathematical expressions to identify signals and trades. Whether simple, such as moving averages, or complex, such as support vector machines using non-linear kernels, the mathematics is invariably implemented as a computer program.

Your success as a quantitative technical analyst depends very much on your ability to understand the mathematics and logic that represent these techniques, and to accurately translate and implement them as computer programs.

There is no alternative. You must understand the techniques and the associated math. You must be able to read, write, and execute computer programs.

As we approach quantitative analysis from two different perspectives, we need two different programming environments. One for traditional trading system development, computation of indicators, and generation of buy and sell signals. The other for data science and machine learning. This chapter outlines the installation of some recommended choices.

Figure 3.1 shows the development process and illustrates that the two approaches occupy the same position in the development process. You may decide to do all your development using one environment, or you may decide to use both.

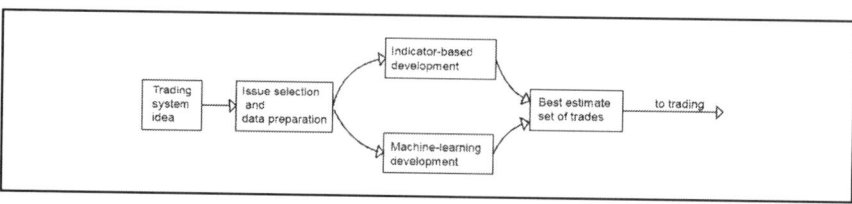

Figure 3.1 Two development paths

Trading System Development Platform

For traditional technical analysis, chart-based, and indicator-based systems our choice has long been, and continues to be, AmiBroker. I recommend AmiBroker as being the best available to individuals and small trading companies based on a combination of superior capabilities and reasonable cost.

AmiBroker is distributed from its website.[1] A free and fully functional trial is available. There is extensive support and reference material on the AmiBroker site. Complete instructions for installing AmiBroker and setting up several sources of data, as well as a set of ten graduated exercises that guide new users through the capabilities of the program, can be found in my book, *Introduction to AmiBroker*,[2] available free in downloadable pdf format.[3]

My earlier books, *Quantitative Trading Systems*[4] and *Mean Reversion Trading Systems*,[5] address the design, testing, and validation of trading systems from the indicator-based perspective. They both use AmiBroker to illustrate and implement the ideas and techniques.

The next few sections of this book outline the procedure for installation of AmiBroker and establishment of a database of stocks using free data downloaded from Yahoo Finance.

AmiBroker runs under Windows. Both 32 bit and 64 bit operating systems are supported, and AmiBroker itself comes in both 32 bit and 64 bit versions.

---

1   https://www.amibroker.com/
2   Bandy, Howard, *Introduction to AmiBroker, Second Edition*, Blue Owl Press, 2012.
3   http://www.introductiontoamibroker.com/
4   Bandy, Howard, *Quantitative Trading Systems, Second Edition*, Blue Owl Press, 2011.
5   Bandy, Howard, *Mean Reversion Trading Systems*, Blue Owl Press, 2013.

All versions of AmiBroker—trial and registered, standard and professional, end-of-day and real-time—begin with a visit to the AmiBroker web site and downloading the installation file. As of this writing, the latest version is 5.80. Click the Download AmiBroker link, choose the 32 bit or 64 bit version, and download the installation file. The current file for the 64 bit version is named AmiBroker5803x64.exe, and is about 9 MB. Save it to your hard disc. Double click the file to begin installation. Accept all defaults.

When the installation is complete, launch AmiBroker. The installation will have created an AmiBroker icon on your desktop. Just double-click that. When AmiBroker starts, it displays a message that it is Standard Edition and Unregistered. This is the trial version, but will be instantly converted to Registered (and Professional Edition, if you requested that) when your AmiBroker Registration file is processed. In the mean time, AmiBroker is ready for your use in Trial mode.

The User's Guide is included in the download, is indexed and searchable, and is accessible by pressing the F1 key when in AmiBroker.

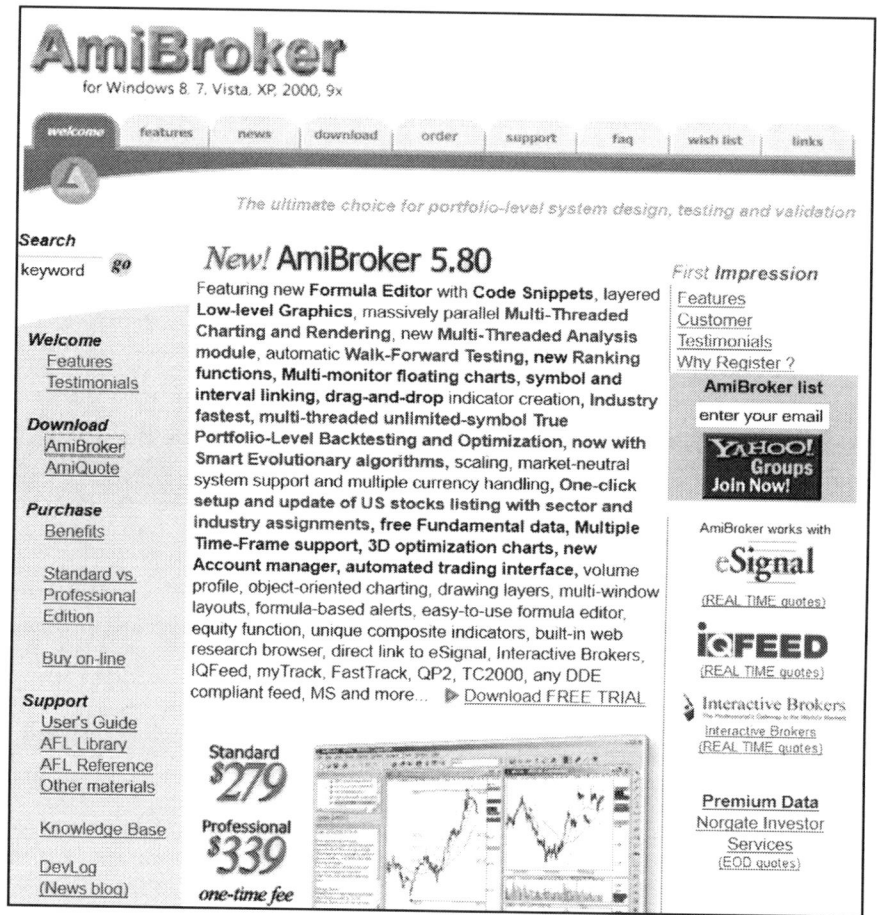

Figure 3.2 AmiBroker web site

The trial version is fully functional with a few exceptions:
- The trial version is limited to 30 days.
- When processing multiple symbols, the maximum allowed for the trial version is five.
- Changes, particularly to the database or to chart panes, are not saved.

Default Database

When you install AmiBroker, a small database is also installed. Its name is Data and it contains end-of-day price history for the stocks in the Dow Jones Industrial Average, and for the DJIA itself. The date range is short, and the data is not up-to-date. But it is useful for verifying that the installation was successful and for investigating AmiBroker.

You will definitely want a longer history and more issues. You can have as many databases as you wish. Data is one. You can expand it or add other databases. As Figure 3.3 shows, AmiBroker has two levels of database files—native and external.

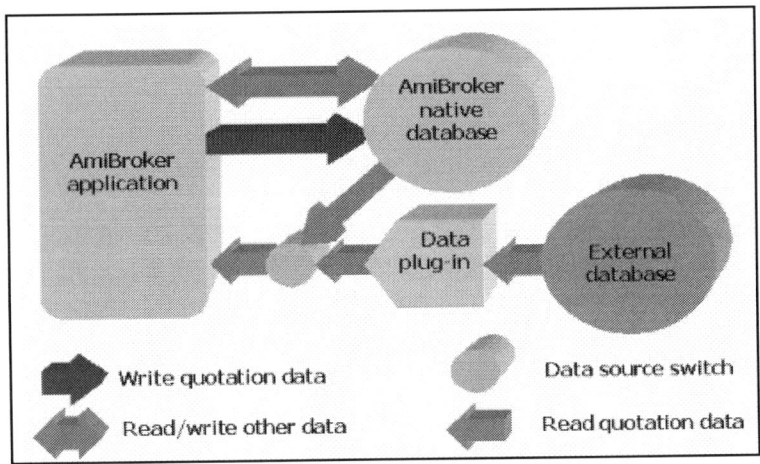

Figure 3.3 Block diagram of AmiBroker databases

The native database is maintained by AmiBroker and AmiQuote, and can be modified by you using the Quote Editor within AmiBroker. The Data database is an AmiBroker native database.

When you subscribe to a data provider, that provider will set up an external database that they exclusively maintain. As AmiBroker needs quotes to place on a chart or process in a backtest, the Data Plug-in reads the external database and passes the data to AmiBroker.

Database Setup—End-of-Day

Setting up a database is a two step operation. Step one is establishing the database within AmiBroker and specifying which tickers will be stored in it. Step two is filling the database with historical price quotations. Depending on the processes being used, you may be aware of the two separate steps, or they may be combined and appear to you as a single step.

If you will be subscribing to a data service, such as Norgate Premium Data[6], the installation procedure for that service will set up a database specifically for quotes from that service and will be maintained by that service. Norgate is in the process of changing their database format and installation procedures. Check their website for the latest information.

---

6 http://www.premiumdata.net/

If you want to use one of the free data providers, such as Yahoo, you can either expand Data or create a new database.

Free data may have no monetary cost, but consider the time and effort you will spend maintaining the free data. Subscription data services not only provide the price and volume data, but also manage tasks such as splits and correcting data errors. I recommend subscribing to a high quality data provider. To my mind, the approximately $40 per month they charge is well worth while. Visit the AmiBroker website[7] for a list of supported data vendors, their products, and their fees. Choose one (or more) that provides the data you need—stocks, mutual funds, ETFs, futures, Forex, end-of-day, real-time.

Free Database using AmiQuote

AmiQuote is a companion program to AmiBroker that manages downloading of price quotes, from Yahoo[8], Google[9], msn[10], or Quandl[11], and storing those quotes in the AmiBroker database.

Return to the AmiBroker download page, download the setup file for AmiQuote, and install AmiQuote.

The procedure described here uses only the ticker symbol. If you are serious enough to want the full name and industry category stored with the symbol, I assume you will be using a subscription data service where all of that is provided for you automatically for the majority of your data. The procedures explained here will let you create data files for those few issues that your primary vendor does not supply.

Begin by deciding which issues you want in your database. Find or create a list of their tickers. This does not need to be the final list—you will be able to add additional tickers and historical data at any time in the future. For example, you might want all the stocks in the Russell 1000 index—the 1000 largest capitalization stocks listed on US exchanges. (According to the Russell Investments website,[12] the Russell 1000 represents approximately 92% of the US equities market. That website also has a list of the current components of all the Russell indices.) Other lists you might want are the stocks in the S&P 100, S&P 500, and NASDAQ 100. Many stocks are constituents of several indexes or lists. You only need one copy of the historic price data for each issue. AmiBroker manages the lists and associations.

---

7 http://www.amibroker.com/guide/h_quotes.html
8 http://finance.yahoo.com/
9 https://www.google.com/finance
10 http://www.msn.com/en-us/money/personalfinance
11 https://www.quandl.com/
12 http://www.russell.com/indexes/americas/indexes/fact-sheet.page?ic=US1000

This example updates the database named Data with data for the tickers in the NASDAQ 100 list.
1. Get the current list of constituents of the NASDAQ 100 from the London Stock Exchange web page.[13]
2. Using a simple text editor, such as NotePad, or a spreadsheet, create a file with one ticker per line. The tickers should be in all capital letters. Each ticker must be spelled the same as your data provider spells it. Save that file in the AmiQuote directory with a meaningful file name, such as Nasdaq100.tls. If you accepted all the defaults during installation, that directory is C:\Program Files\AmiBroker\AmiQuote. tls files are ordinary text files that are recognized by AmiBroker and AmiQuote as containing lists of ticker symbols.

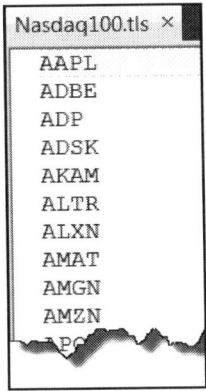

3. Open AmiBroker.
4. Using the AmiBroker File menu, click Open Database, select the Data database, click OK.
5. Leave AmiBroker open as the next steps are performed.
6. Decide the date you want the historical data to begin. If you plan to do extensive trading system development, I suggest having at least ten years of data available. The characteristics of the markets changed after the October 1987 crash, so data before that date has limited value in developing systems for current conditions. A starting date (From Date) of 1/1/1995 or 1/1/2000 might be reasonable. Use today's date for the end date (the To Date).
7. Using the Windows Start menu, select the AmiQuote program and run it. You will find it under All Programs > AmiBroker > AmiQuote > AmiQuote.

---

13 http://www.londonstockexchange.com/exchange/prices-and-markets/international-markets/indices/home/nasdaq-100.html

8. Using AmiQuote's File menu, select Open. Then select the file with the tickers you want to get historical data for, Nasdaq100.tls, and click Open.

   Be sure that AmiBroker is running and that the database you want updated is the current database. The name of the database in current use is displayed in the status bar in the bottom right-hand corner of the AmiBroker window. If necessary, use the AmiBroker File menu and open the desired database.

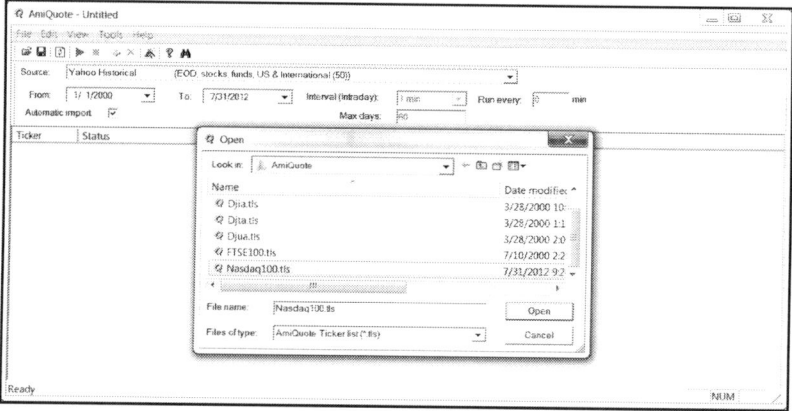

9. Be sure that the From and To dates are set as you want them, and that AmiQuote's Automatic Import box is Checked.
10. Click the Green Triangle to begin the download. You have asked for over 1,200 years of data, each with 252 sets of Open, High, Low, Close, and Volume. Depending on the speed of your Internet connection, it will take a few minutes to a few hours for the download to complete.
11. AmiQuote will inform you of the progress of the download. If the amount of data stretches the capacity of your communications or your patience, divide the Nasdaq100.tls file into several smaller files and work with each part in turn. As soon as the data for any individual stock has been downloaded, it is immediately available for use within AmiBroker. You may continue to work with AmiBroker while downloading proceeds.

    When the download is complete, scroll through the Ticker List in AmiQuote. If there were problems with any of the tickers, there will be messages displayed. A common problem is that the spelling of the ticker in the tls file is not the same as the spelling the data provider uses. For example, the list supplied by the exchange used a period when specifying the Class A stock, while Yahoo uses a dash character. Make a list of all the

tickers that did not download properly, spelling them as the data provider spells them, and create a file named NewTickers. tls Add the tickers of any other stocks you want. Using the same procedure, have AmiQuote download the new tickers. A good source for researching companies and verifying tickers that will be downloaded from Yahoo is the Yahoo financial site.[14]
12. Close AmiQuote.
13. In AmiBroker, using the File menu, click Save Database.

Data Updates

Once the database has been established and the historical data loaded, maintaining the data by adding the latest quotes is very easy. In AmiBroker, using the Tools menu, select AutoUpdateQuotes. AmiBroker will examine the database that is open, determine the date range needed to bring the quotes for all the issues in this database up to current date, and call AmiQuote to do the download. Since only a few days data is needed for each ticker, the process takes only a short time.

Sources of Free Data

The examples above illustrate using Yahoo as the source of historical data. There are other sources.
- For US markets, msn and Google also provide free end-of-day historical data.
- Google recently began offering free intra-day data.
- Quandl offers free end-of-day historical price data, along with a wide variety of other economic data series.

If you wish to use any of those sources, use the pull down menu in AmiQuote to select one of them instead of Yahoo. Keep in mind that consistency is important. Different data suppliers will have different ways of preparing and presenting the data. For example, the volume multiplier may be different, or the ticker spelling may be different. After you load your database with quotes from one supplier, keep the database up-to-date using that same supplier.

ASCII Import

There are two methods of importing ASCII data: the ASCII Import Wizard (file menu, Import Wizard), and the full ASCII Importer (file menu, Import ASCII). The wizard is good for one-off imports. Its features are a subset of the full importer. If you will be importing the same files regularly, set up the full importer. (Note: the ASCII Import Wizard can create a format definition file for later use with the ASCII Importer.)

---

14 http://finance.yahoo.com/

Before you start, decide which database you want the imported data to go into. If you are just practicing, create a test database and open it. Do not import into your high quality database until you are confident the import procedure is working correctly.

Download the data files and, if necessary, unzip or expand them. Open the files using a text editor such as Notepad. There should be one quote per line, fields separated by space, semicolon, or comma.

There may be a header line describing the fields. If not, identify the fields yourself. If necessary, go to the site from which the data was obtained and read their documentation.

The date field is the trickiest. The wizard understands many formats. If your data is in one of them, all you need to do is identify the order of month, day, and year. The codes are DMY, MDY, YMD. If your data does not follow one of the recognized date formats, you will need to reformat the date (for example, by using a spreadsheet) and rewrite the data file before proceeding.

The year can be either four digits or two (the final two of the year). The month can be either two digits or three characters (such as Dec or Jan). The day is two digits. The separator can be / (slash), \ (backslash), - (minus), or not separated at all.

Assume the date for one quote is December 31, 2000. YMD formats that are recognized include:

20001231

2000-12-31

2000/12/31

2000-Dec-31

001231

00-12-31

00/12/31

00\12\31

If your data has a ticker symbol as a field in each line, the data will be stored under that symbol. If there is not an explicit ticker, the file name will be used. If your data file is downloaded as, for example, IBM.csv, the data will be stored as IBM. If your data file is downloaded with a generic name, such as Table.csv (Yahoo uses this file name for all its individual downloads), rename it before proceeding.

Yahoo Historical Data Download

The Yahoo site[15] is a good place to get stock and index historical data. Using the investing tab, select stocks. Under research tools, click historical quotes to get to the page with historical data.

Follow these steps to download the historical data for a stock or index:
1. Enter the ticker (say it is XOM)
2. Click GO
3. The screen will display the most recent data
4. Click Download to Spreadsheet.
   On your desktop, or wherever your default directory to receive downloads is, you will find a file named Table.csv.
5. Rename Table.csv to XOM.csv. Use capital letters if you want your symbol to be in capitals.
6. Proceed to import XOM.csv into AmiBroker using either the ASCII Import Wizard (see next section) or Import ASCII.

ASCII Import Wizard

The following steps illustrate how to use the ASCII Import Wizard. Before beginning, a database named Test has been created and opened. It already has a few symbols and data for them. Data has been down loaded from Yahoo for two stocks, GE and XOM, but not yet imported. Since Yahoo downloads all data using the file name Table.csv, the downloaded file was renamed between downloads, so the files are GE.csv and XOM.csv.

1. Using the File menu, select Import Wizard.
2. When the dialog box opens, click Pick Files.
3. Navigate to the directory holding the files you have downloaded.
4. Since the files have identical formats, you can process multiple files in one pass, so select both GE.csv and XOM.csv. (Click one file, press the Control key and click the other.)
5. Click Open.

The Define Fields dialog box will open.
1. Note the format of the data in the .csv files.
2. Using the pull-down menus, define the fields for each element of data. Each element in the entire row of data must be defined. Select SKIP to ignore data in the csv file that you do not want in your AmiBroker database
3. Select comma as the separator.
4. Skip 1 line—the header.
5. Check Automatically add new symbols.

---

15 http://finance.yahoo.com/

6. Click Next.
   The Additional Settings screen will come up. It is on this screen that you can save the format settings that you just used. They will not help for future uses of the ASCII Import Wizard, but they will be available in the full ASCII importer. To do this, Check Add current settings to ASCII importer definitions, and give meaningful Description and File Name—such as From Yahoo. You will see your format as we look at the full ASCII Importer in the next section.
7. Click Finish.
   The data will be converted from ASCII, imported into the open database, and be immediately ready for use in AmiBroker.

ASCII Importer

The full ASCII Importer is much more efficient, has more capabilities, and is more complex. Rather than having to fill in a form each time you want to import an ASCII file, you can set up a format definition file, or use one of the pre-defined files. The file that was created for the import done manually using the wizard in the previous section is:

```
# Format definition file generated automatically
# by AmiBroker's ASCII Import Wizard
$FORMAT Date_YMD, Open, High, Low, Close, Volume, Skip
$SKIPLINES 1
$SEPARATOR ,
$CONT 1
$GROUP 255
$AUTOADD 1
$DEBUG 1
```

The definition files are stored in the C:\Program Files\AmiBroker\Formats directory. By copying the format file that you will be using regularly to be Default.Format, all that is necessary to import ASCII files is:
1. Using the File Menu, select Import ASCII.
2. On the Open screen, select the file you want to import.
3. Enter the file type, such as From Yahoo.
4. Click Open.
   The file will be converted, imported, and made available within AmiBroker for immediate use.

The options available for controlling the processing of ASCII data are extensive. Read about them all in the AmiBroker User's Guide.

Subscription Data Providers

Free data has a cost to you—the cost of checking the data for missing quotes, bad values, unadjusted splits, and so forth, and correcting those problems. Subscription data services, such as Norgate Premium Data, Quandl, and others, provide that maintenance for you and deliver cleaner, more consistent data with less effort on your part. End-of-day stock data costs about $40 per month—more for some services, less for others. Some end-of-day vendors include mutual funds at no charge; others charge extra. Commodities and futures data is an additional cost, depending in part on the fees the exchanges that clear those trades and report that data charge. Some subscription vendors provide custom indexes, custom indicators, and have a wider selection of issues—and often charge an extra amount for those. Some services charge a one-time fee for loading the historical data, others do not.

If you plan to use a subscription service, be aware that each service has its own database format. Once you begin with one subscription service, they will be the only service that can keep your data in that database up-to-date.

The installation procedure for each service will be unique to that service, but it is generally simple and well documented. Typically, the installation does three things for you:
1. Establishes the external database and the communications between the database and AmiBroker.
2. Loads the definitions of the tickers, including the ticker symbol, the full name, and the industry assignment.
3. Loads the historical price data.

After the close of trading each day, you initiate communication with the data vendor. The database is brought up-to-date, and errors and inconsistencies are corrected and re-downloaded, all automatically. Some vendors provide intra-day updating—treating the latest price as though it is the closing price. At subsequent updatings, the earlier prices are replaced by the more recent ones. Some vendors provide a Windows system process that automatically communicates with the data vendor's server.

Data Science and Machine Learning

For the data science approach, there are literally hundreds of computer languages that could be used. Ideally, the one we use will have these characteristics and capabilities:
- readily available
- inexpensive
- widely supported
- easily learned
- flexible input and output
- flexible display of graphical output
- efficient at handling financial time series
- efficient numeric computation
- efficient matrix computation
- library of machine learning applications
- library of statistical analysis applications

As recently as 2010, the choice was not clear, and the solution involved multiple languages and applications packages inefficiently cobbled together. Components typically included, among many others:
- General programming: C++, Java, Visual Basic, Python.
- Financial time series: AmiBroker, TradeStation.
- Statistical analysis: R, SPSS, Stata.
- Scientific library: C, C++, FORTRAN, MATLAB, Excel.

Python was just one of the contenders to be a single-application platform for quantitative analysis.

Python

In 2011, with the publication of *pandas*[16] by Wes McKinney, it became crystal clear that Python had risen to be the top choice. McKinney developed pandas for his own use while a quantitative analyst at AQR Capital Management. Pandas provides several capabilities—most importantly the DataFrame data structure and the set of functions that handle financial time series. His book[17] is essential reading. Set this book down for a minute while you order a copy.

The Python language was developed, beginning in 1989, by Guido van Rossum in the Netherlands. It is open source. It is free. It runs under Windows, Mac OS, UNIX / Linux, and even Raspberry Pi, among others.

It was released to the public in February 1991; Version 2.0 was released in October 2000, and Version 3.0 in December 2008. By design, Python

---

16 http://pandas.pydata.org/
17 McKinney, Wes, *Python for Data Analysis*, O'Reilly, 2012.

is highly readable and easily programmed. It uses English keywords and indentation to define program structure. It is highly extensible. As of January 2014 it is supported by over 38,000 libraries and packages.

Python, with the scientific stack of NumPy, SciPy, pandas, and matplotlib, is exceptionally easy to work with, well supported, powerful, and inexpensive. Many packages, such as scikit-learn, are available to provide classification, regression, dimension reduction, and other modeling and machine learning capabilities. If the analysis requires faster execution, critical routines can be written in compiled languages such as FORTRAN or C++ and linked in transparently. If the analysis requires functions specific to R, MATLAB, or Excel, data can be prepared in Python, processed in those programs, with results returned to Python for further analysis. It meets all of the requirements to be a single-language, data science-based, quantitative technical analysis platform.

The components you will need are:
- Python—base language
- NumPy—support for multidimensional arrays
- SciPy—modules for scientific computing
- pandas—time series library
- matplotlib—plotting library
- scikit-learn—machine learning

Environments

Your Python environment can be on your machine, or you can use one of the many web-based or cloud-based service providers. Some of the on-line choices are free services whose main application is on-line tutorials, such as:
- Learn Python
  www.learnpython.org
- Code Academy
  www.codeacademy.com
- Online Python Tutor
  www.pythontutor.com

Others are powerful cloud-based sites, intended to support always-on computation, such as Python Anywhere
   www.pythonanywhere.com

and joint-effort program development, such as cloud9
   https://c9.io

On-line services are easy to use, accessible from any computer, and do not require installation of software on your computer.

Trading system development is computationally intensive, and you will soon reach the limits of the free services provided. Assuming you might want to install a Python development environment on your own computer, there are some excellent alternatives.

In order to make easy use of Wes McKinney's book, I recommend using the operating environment he uses. That is Python version 2.7, iPython, NumPy, SciPy, pandas, and matplotlib.

One reference that stands out is Dr. Allen Downey's book, *Think Python*.[18] It is an introduction to both Python and to computer science. The book is available in print, and also as a free e-book.[19] Downey's website provides downloadable code for programs in his book.[20]

The terminology and notation used in this book closely follows that of McKinney and Downey.

The next sections outline installation of Python in three alternative environments. They are Enthought's Canopy, the Continuum Analytics Anaconda version of Spyder, and Google's command line based Python. Canopy and Spyder have graphical user interfaces (GUIs) and iPython. Take your pick.

But evaluate carefully before installing your choice on your development computer. Although each Python environment states that it is independent, my experience is that installing multiple Python environments on a single computer does cause conflicts. On Windows computers, the confusion is in the path and the registry.

---

18 Downey, Allen, *Think Python*, O'Reilly, 2012.
19 http://www.greenteapress.com/thinkpython/
20 http://www.greenteapress.com/thinkpython/code/

Enthought Canopy

The (free) Enthought Canopy Express environment includes all of the components listed above. Visit their website[21] for details. The next few sections give instructions for installation of Python from Enthought onto a Windows system.

Installation

Canopy is the successor to the EDP Free described in McKinney's book. Jonathan March of Enthought posted this comment in the Enthought Knowledge Base:[22]

> The excellent book *Python for Data Analysis*, by Wes McKinney (O'Reilly, 2012) describes how to install and set up Enthought Python Distribution (EPD) Free.
>
> EPD Free has been superseded by Enthought Canopy Express, which provides all the same packages as EPD Free (including everything that is used in the book), plus a GUI application with a text editor, IPython shell, IPython notebook, file browser, package manager, and documentation browser. This Canopy GUI provides a convenient environment for writing and running Python code. (Python for Data Analysis, pg 11: "When asked about my standard development environment, I almost always say 'IPython plus a text editor'" ... voila Canopy!)
>
> You can download Canopy Express from https://enthought.com/downloads/.
>
> While you are on the Enthought web site, we recommend that you register ("Sign up") for a free Enthought account. This login will enable you to use the Package Manager to easily update all the packages in Canopy Express, or, with a Basic subscription or Academic license, all 100+ packages in the Enthought package repository.

---

21 https://www.enthought.com/canopy-express/
22 https://support.enthought.com/entries/21842400-Canopy-for-readers-of-Python-for-Data-Analysis-by-McKinney

After download, please see the step-by-step installation and startup instructions at http://docs.enthought.com/canopy/quick-start.html.

After you have completed Canopy's installation and startup, please go to the Canopy Help menu and check for updates.

Canopy Express directly installs Numpy, SciPy, IPython, Matplotlib, Pandas, SymPy, Chaco, and other core scientific Python packages.

Enjoy Python!

Python is undergoing a transition from version 2 to version 3. While the future of Python is clearly version 3, the highest Enthought Canopy version that is stable and includes all the features we need is 2.7.

Begin with a visit to the Enthought website and create an account.
https://www.enthought.com/products/canopy/

Click the "Create Account" link in the upper right corner. Even though Canopy is free and can be run without being logged in to a user account, an account is required in order to receive updates for some of the packages. Enthought offers free use of Canopy and EPD (Enthought Python Distribution) to students and staff at degree-granting institutions. Inquire at the website.

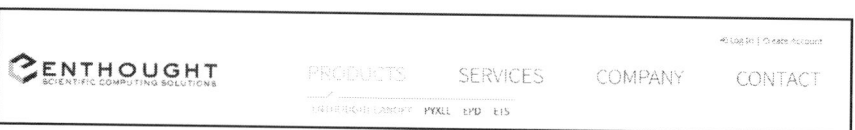

Watch the introductory video. Then click the Get Canopy button.

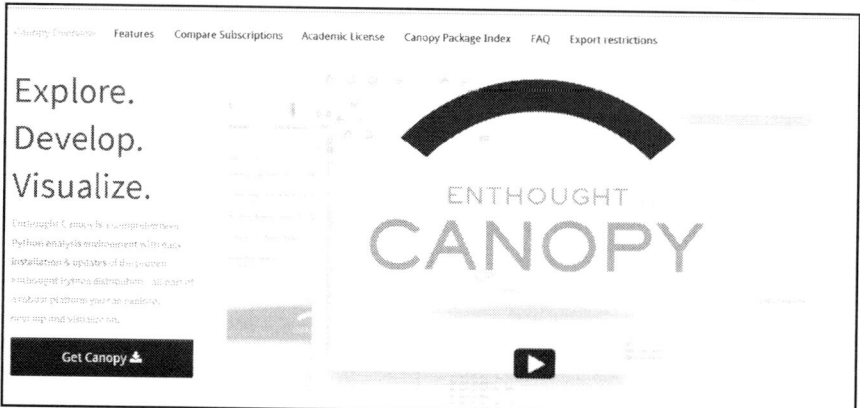

Programming Environments

Click the button to Download Canopy Express.

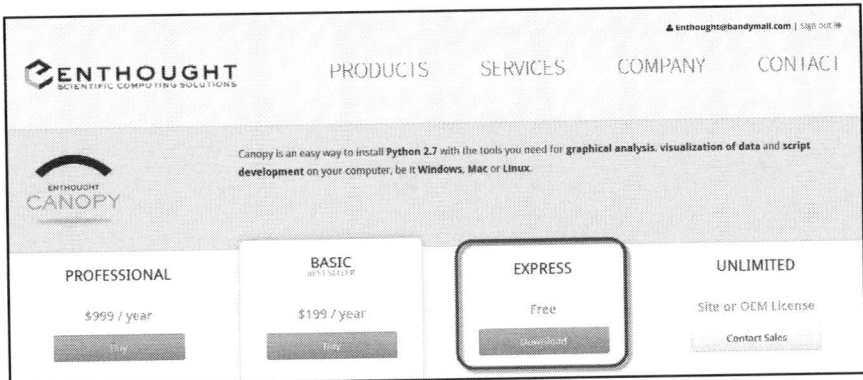

Choose 64 bit or 32 bit version. There are several links (not shown here) on that page to additional information, including Installation Help, User Guide, and Knowledge Base.

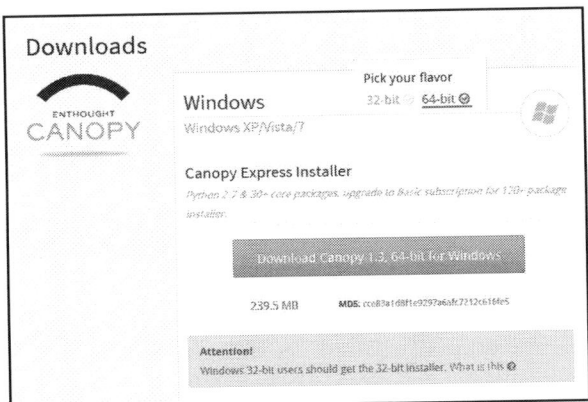

You will be downloading Canopy-1-3-0-win.64.msi (or whatever is current), a Windows installer file, of about 240 MB. Copy the file to a subdirectory of its own, then double click it to begin installation.

Agree to everything and accept all the defaults. At the final dialog, check the box to Launch Canopy when setup exits. Click Finish.

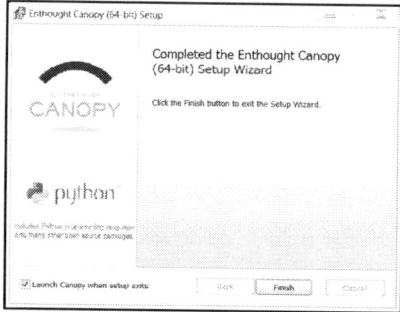

The Canopy Windows GUI will open. Login to your account.

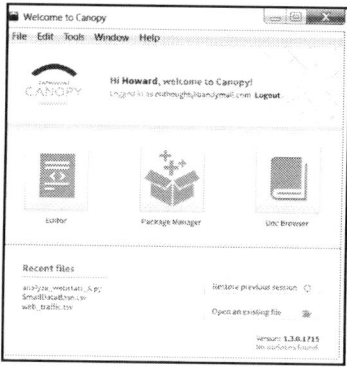

Pull down the Tools menu, Select Package Manager, then Installed Packages. Scroll up and down to view the packages that have been installed. You should see iPython, matplotlib, NumPy, pandas, scikit-learn, and SciPy—all with green check marks indicating that they have been installed. If you click Available Packages, you will see a list of the some 14,000 additional libraries that are available through Enthought, should you need them.

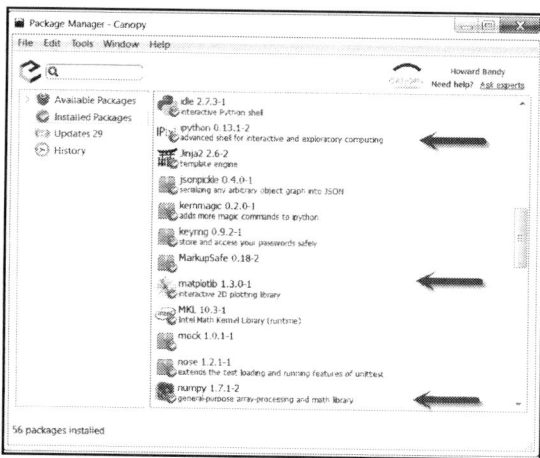

Running Canopy

Installation of Enthought Canopy put two icons on your desktop. They both initiate a Python session, but in different environments.

iPython Shell

If you want to run Python / iPython from the Command Shell, click the PyLab icon.

The PyLab shell will open. (The background on your computer will be black. The colors in this figure have been inverted for clarity when printed.)

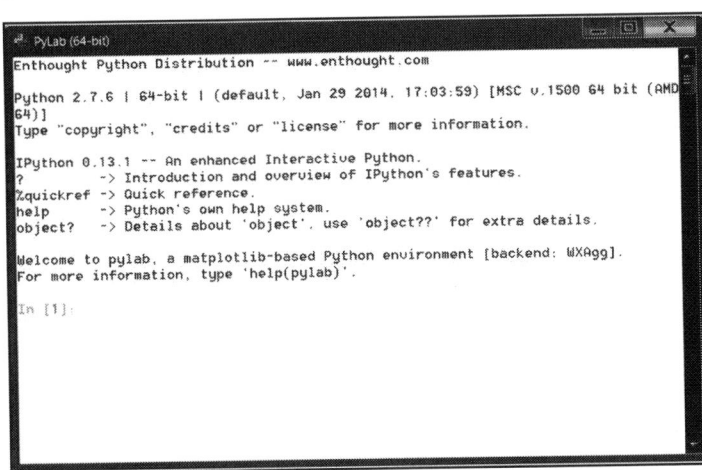

You can enter Python commands for immediate execution.

```
PyLab (64-bit)
Enthought Python Distribution -- www.enthought.com

Python 2.7.6 | 64-bit | (default, Jan 29 2014, 17:03:59) [MSC v.1500 64 bit (AMD
64)]
Type "copyright", "credits" or "license" for more information.

IPython 0.13.1 -- An enhanced Interactive Python.
?         -> Introduction and overview of IPython's features.
%quickref -> Quick reference.
help      -> Python's own help system.
object?   -> Details about 'object', use 'object??' for extra details.

Welcome to pylab, a matplotlib-based Python environment [backend: WXAgg].
For more information, type 'help(pylab)'.

In [1]: a = 6

In [2]: b = 7

In [3]: a*b
Out[3]: 42

In [4]: print "hello world"
hello world

In [5]:
```

Canopy Environment

More likely, you will want to run Python / iPython from the Canopy GUI. Click the Canopy GUI icon.

The GUI Welcome Dialog will open.

Click the Editor Icon. The Canopy Editor will open.

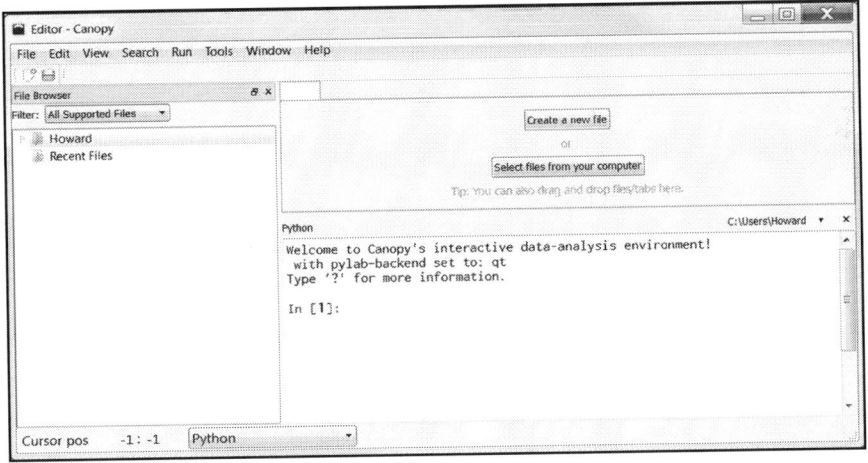

Use the File pull-down menu, select New, Click iPython notebook.

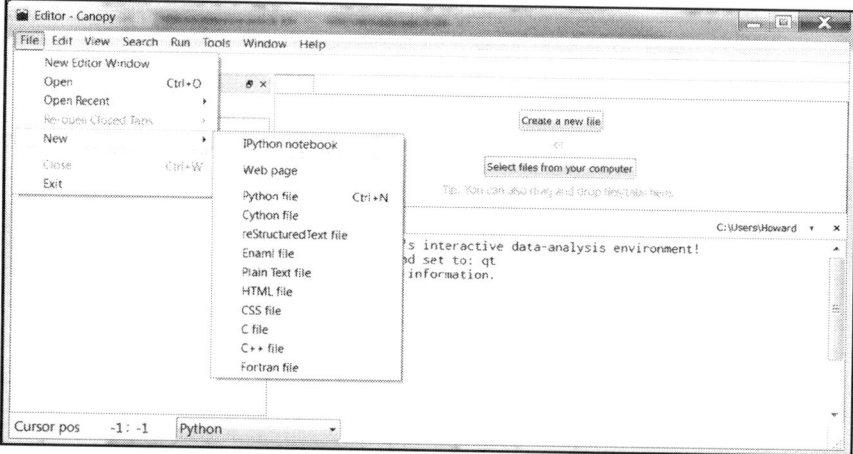

A new iPython Notebook will open. Type in a short program or some calculator commands and run it.

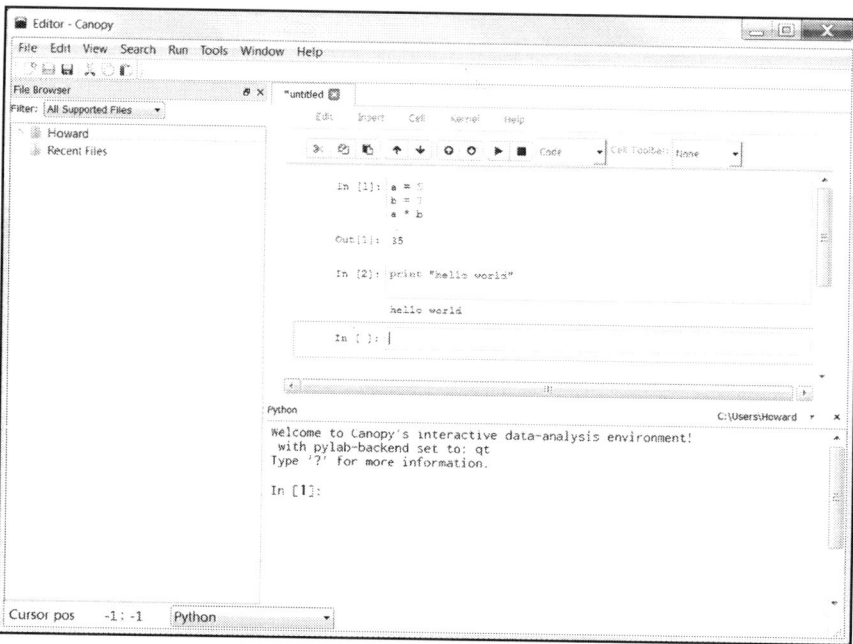

Spyder

Spyder is an open source cross-platform interactive development environment for scientific programming in Python. Spyder integrates the same set of libraries as Canopy—NumPy, SciPy, pandas, matplotlib, scikit-learn, and iPython. The Spyder website[23] has documentation, including links to several installation options.

Installation

I used the (free) Anaconda version of Spyder distributed by Continuum Analytics. Begin with a visit to their website.

```
https://store.continuum.io/cshop/anaconda/
```

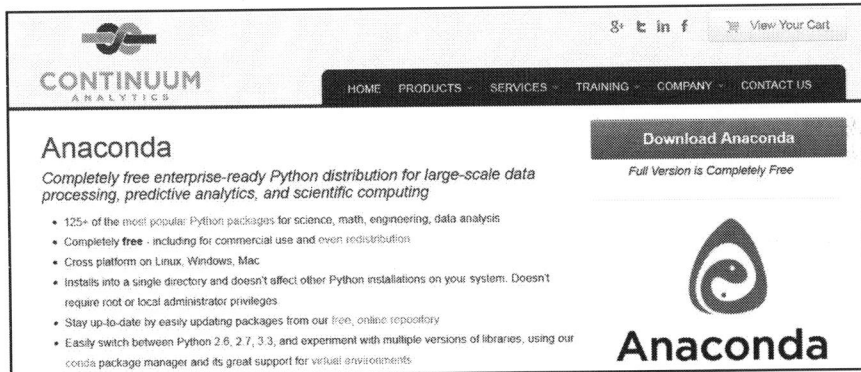

Scroll down a little and click Download Anaconda. Enter your e-mail address and create an account.

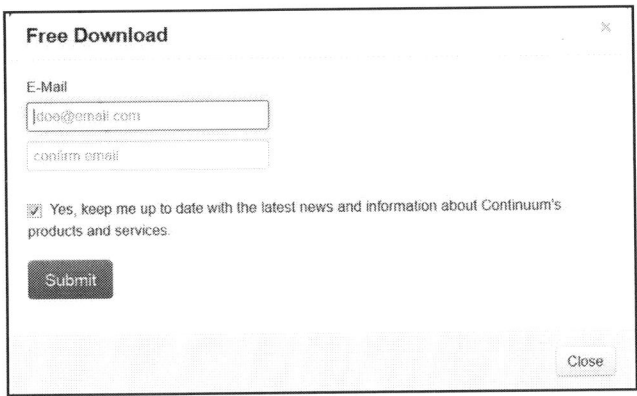

---

23 https://pythonhosted.org/spyder/

By default, Anaconda comes with Python 2.7. Click the download link to your choice of the 32 bit or 64 bit version. Also note the link to the "Get Started ... Guide."

> **Windows**
> After downloading the installer double click the .exe file and follow the instructions on the screen.
> **Please note**: the Anaconda default install comes with Python 2.7. Python 2.6 and 3.3 are available through the conda command.
>
> Get Started with the Anaconda Quick Start Guide [pdf]
>
> Downloads
>
> Anaconda
>
> Free for all to use: (including commercial)
>
> **Linux installers**
> Linux 32-bit / 411M / md5: f1505963a1c7d2bfe7a73c079b22762d
> Linux 64-bit / 483M / md5: 9d973e9ac715ce3241c3785704505971
>
> **Mac OS X installers**
> Mac OS X (10.7 or higher - GUI installer) 64-bit / 280M / md5: 772b8e5dc385bf5ea3f78cdd21a8ec71
> Mac OS X (10.5 or higher - bash installer) 64-bit / 245M / md5: 6ef81bc54a6ab506f352b5589ea80f61
>
> **Windows installers**
> Windows 32-bit / 311M / md5: 5404da4f89dca1a4f5c9efd5ae6fbc5a
> Windows 64-bit / 367M / md5: b8a404c9f5bfd2452316db3710d2b8ef

You are downloading 300 MB or so. Save the file. Double-click it when the download is complete. Agree to everything and accept all the defaults.

If the installer did not put an icon on your desktop, put one there yourself. Click it to start Spyder.

Programming Environments

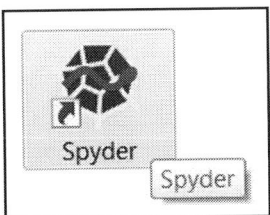

Enter a small program. Click the Green Run icon. Spyder is operational.

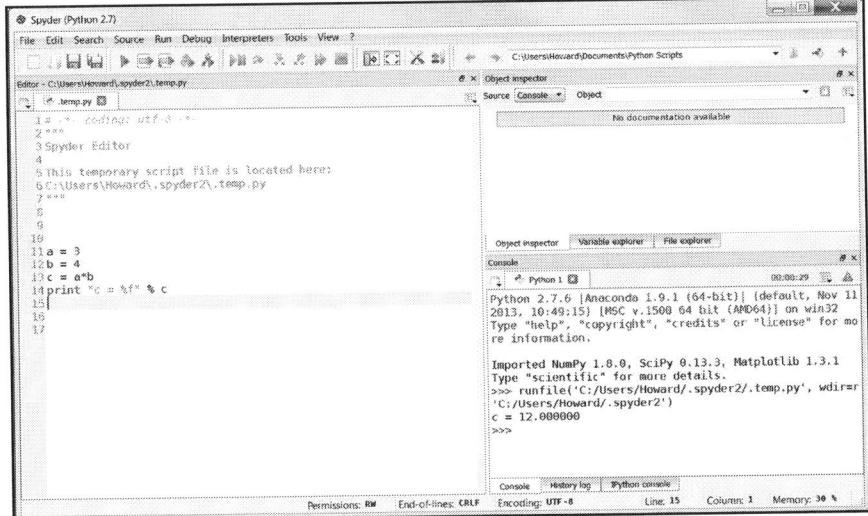

Google

Google has an outstanding set of Python tutorials. You can use any of the Python environments, including either Canopy or Spyder, to do the Google exercises. If you want to follow Google exactly, set up Python as they recommend. Begin with a visit to their website.

    https://developers.google.com/edu/python/

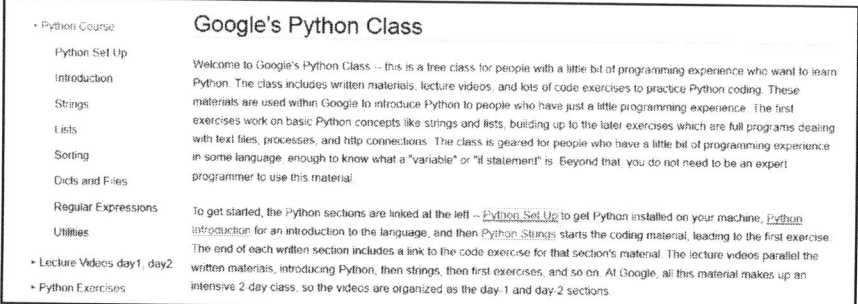

Click the link to Python Setup. The link to the set of exercises is near the top of the page.

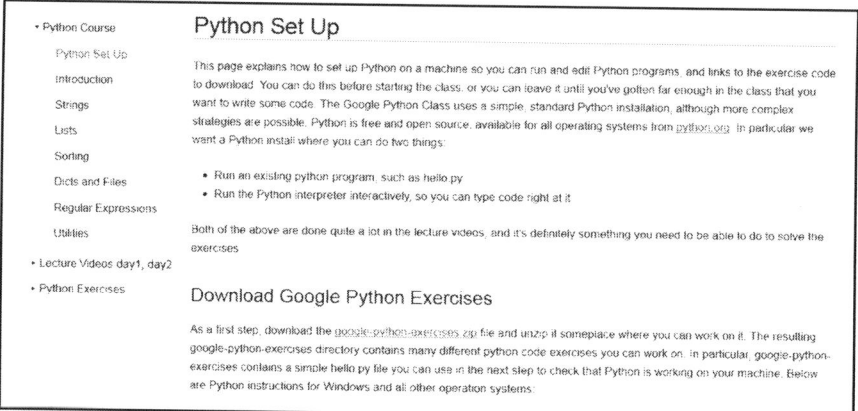

Further down that page are instructions for installing Python. That page also contains instructions for installation on a Mac or Linux system. As of this writing, the current production version is 2.7.6. The installer file for the 64 bit version is about 15 MB.

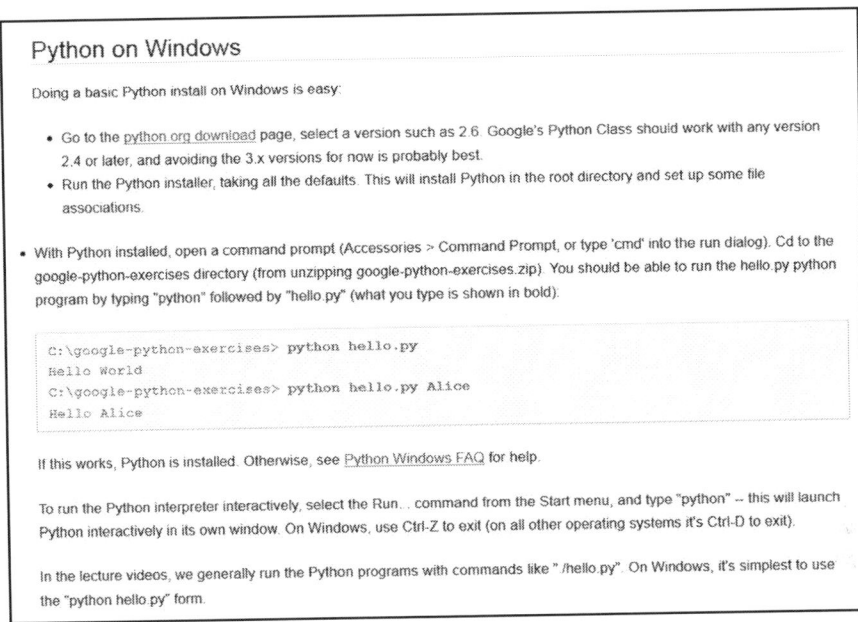

Locate the installer file on your computer, double click it, agree to everything and accept all defaults. As Google suggests, open a command prompt, navigate to the directory with the exercises, and run the hello.py program. It should look like this.

If you are using the command line version of Python, you will need a program editor. Follow Google's recommendation. Download and use Notepad++.[24] Note their warning to avoid Notepad, Wordpad, or any program designed for word processing and output formatting, such as MS Word.

> **Editing Python (all operating systems)**
>
> A Python program is just a text file that you edit directly. As above, you should have a command line open, where you can type "python hello.py Alice" to run whatever exercise you are working on. At the command line prompt, just hit the up-arrow key to recall previously typed commands, so it's easy to run previous commands without retyping them.
>
> You want a text editor with a little understanding of code and indentation. There are many good free ones.
>
> - Windows -- **do not use Notepad or Wordpad**. Try the free and open source Notepad++ or the free and open source JEdit.
> - Mac -- The built-in TextEdit works, but not very well. Try the free TextWrangler or the free and open source JEdit.
> - Linux -- any unix text editor is fine, or try the above JEdit.
>
> **Editor Settings**
>
> To edit Python, we advocate the strategy that when you hit the tab key, your editor inserts spaces rather than a real tab character. All our files use 2-spaces as the indent, and 4-spaces is another popular choice. It's also handy if the editor will "auto indent" so when you hit return, the new line starts with the same indentation as the previous line. We also recommend saving your files with the unix line-ending convention, since that's how the various starter files are set up. If running hello.py gives the error "Unknown option...", the file may have the wrong line-ending. Here are the preferences to set for common editors to treat tabs and line-endings correctly for Python:
>
> - Windows Notepad++ -- Tabs: Settings > Preferences > Edit Components > Tab settings, and Settings > Preferences > MISC for auto-indent. Line endings: Format > Convert set to Unix.
> - JEdit (any OS) -- Line endings: Little 'U' 'W' 'M' on status bar, set it to 'U' (i.e. Unix line-endings).
> - Windows Notepad or Wordpad -- do not use

Tutorials

If there were problems during installation, refer to the guides provided by the publisher of the version of Python you are using. While there will be differences in the interfaces among Python distributions, the Python code itself will be the same.

Please read some of the books and visit some of the sites that specialize in Python tutorials. While you do eventually need to become a competent programmer, you can continue reading this book while you practice Python.

---

[24] http://notepad-plus-plus.org/

Chapter 4
Data

The final step in development and use of a trading system is trading. Thinking ahead to trading clarifies the mandatory and desirable characteristics of the data used for development.

Every trade is because the rules have identified a pattern in the data. First in the data used to develop the system; then in the current, as yet unseen, data used to trade. Development data must have sequences of patterns followed by price changes similar to those being sought in the trading data.

At a minimum:
- All series and fields referenced by the model must be present in the data.
- All data series used must be aligned to the same periodicity and the same time zone.
- All missing data must be filled in—copied forward as necessary.

Sound business practice suggests that the data also:
- Be current.
- Be reported by an independent clearing agency.
- Be the public record of trades freely made between willing parties.
- Be reported to the public no later than to any other private parties.
- Have the same level of revision history in both development and trading.

These requirements imply consequences for several categories of data.

Simulated Data

Artificial data, random data, simulated data, or data generated from a standard distribution is of very limited value. Real trades result only when a pattern is detected in the real data being processed. In order to be useful in training, the training data must contain instances of the pattern. If we knew the pattern accurately enough to be able to create useful training data, we would already have the information we needed to define the rules, and we would not need any development.

Fundamental Data

In order to be valuable, any data series or indicator, company data or economic series, must be:
- Timely
- Accurate
- Predictive

There are several issues that complicate use of fundamental economic or company data for trading.
- *Timeliness related to reporting granularity.* Fundamental data is reported annually, quarterly, monthly, or weekly. Trading decisions are made monthly, weekly, daily, or intra-day. If the stock price is reported and acted upon more frequently than the economic indicator is reported, there will be many time periods (data bars) where there is no new data for the economic indicator. In order to have a value to use in calculations, the latest value that does exist will be copied forward until a new value is received. Useful patterns are based on changes in data series. The only time that value can change is on those days when a new report is received.
- *Timeliness related to revision.* Economic indicators, and other fundamental data, are reported, then revised at later dates. When the historical data is retrieved from the data provider, it will usually be a series that consists of only the final revision data. In order to maintain consistency, the data value associated with a given time period cannot be used in the trading system until after the date and time its final revision is published. See Figure 4.1, a chart showing the dates associated with the US government GDP report. The GDP report covers the months January, February, and March. The *advance* report is issued at the end of April, the month following the quarter, followed by the *preliminary* report one month later, and the *final* report two months later. In July, the series is *rebased*, adjusting

and changing all previously reported values.

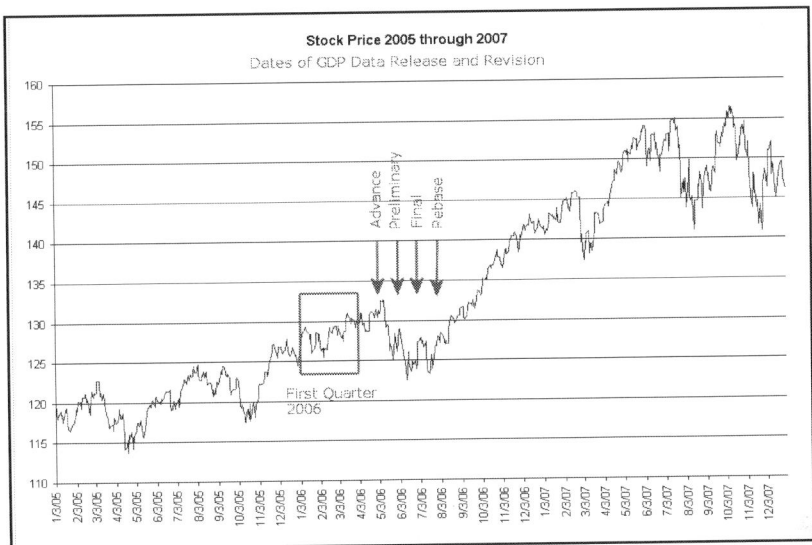

Figure 4.1 Revision history of fundamental data

An alternative is to use a series that consists solely of data initially released, with no revisions or adjustments applied. The trading system would then be based on initial release data rather than final release data. For some series, this is workable. For others, not even the signs of the values published in the preliminary and final reports agree.

- *Accuracy related to revision.* Government statistical series are regularly given annual adjustments, are re-based, and re-benchmarked. Re-basing sets a new date for the base of the index (the date it has a value of, say, 100) and adjusts all data in the series accordingly. Re-benchmarking recalculates the relationship between indicator series, adjusting those that depend on others. Any of these operations result in a revised historical data series, potentially changing patterns and signals.
- *Accuracy related to bias.* There is a bias to any reported data. That bias is unknown, and unknowable, to users of the data. Whether the report is unintentionally biased due to an innocent data preparation error or omission, or intentionally misleading, outsiders probably cannot detect the bias, its amount, or its reason. They have little alternative but to accept and use the data as reported. Bias introduces a systematic error into the reported statistic that lasts as long as that particular bias persists.
- *Accuracy related to measurement.* The fundamental statistic reported is the result of subjective interpretation of reports,

questionnaires, and interviews. Preparers of these reports must be careful to avoid confusing precision with accuracy. Measurement introduces a random error into the reported statistic.
- *Degrees of freedom.* There are hundreds of series of economic data that could be chosen. Each series has a limited number of data points. Choosing a series risks selection bias. Fitting rules to the few data points risks overfitting.
- *Predictive.* Whether the fundamental data is predictive depends on the strength of the relationship, the efficiency with which the market assimilates the information, and the insight and skill of the developer of the trading system. Remember to follow good modeling and validation practices. Keep enough data reserved for out-of-sample testing. In-sample results are always good and have no value in predicting the profitability of a system when traded on unseen data.

For all of these reasons, it is difficult to incorporate the fundamental data series with the daily, or even weekly, price series representing the trading prices. An alternative is to find surrogate data series such as indexes, ETFs, stocks, or mutual funds that:
- Reflect changes in the fundamental data.
- Represent transactions made in public and reported through a clearing agency.
- Are reported on the same time schedule as the price series being traded.
- Are never revised.

Inclusion of intermarket data, such as interest rates, can be used for broad market timing, or to create filters to permit or block equity trades.

Surrogate data, primarily in the form of sector indexes defined and maintained by financial services companies, can be useful in active trading systems.

Over-the-counter Data

These include:
- Transactions between private parties.
- Bids and offers not open to the public.
- Transactions not recorded by an independent clearing agency.
- Transactions reported to a limited audience before being reported publicly.
- Records changed after initial reporting.

All of these characteristics are faults and skew the advantage toward a potentially biased counterparty.

Data Sources

The best situation would be to use the same data for development as for trading. Unfortunately, that is unlikely.

The bid, ask, and execution prices available on your broker's screen are provided by your broker for your convenience. The broker's business is brokerage, not data distribution. Under normal circumstances you can expect a reputable broker to display the best bid and ask and a stream of transaction records in near real time. When there is a resource limitation—such as saturated communications—the brokerage data stream will be reduced to fit the available capacity. The trade history recorded from a single broker is nearly certain to be incomplete and will not agree with the historical trade data downloaded some time after those trades were made.

Be aware of the possible problems associated with broker-supplied data for use in trading system development.

Data supplied by a data service that is not a broker is more likely to be complete, but it cannot be directly traded.

My suggestion is a compromise:
- For development, use high quality data obtained from a source whose stated purpose is to distribute complete and accurate data.
- For trading:
    * Feed your trading system program from the same source used for development.
    * Generate the buy and sell signals from the trading system running in the development platform.
    * Verify on your broker's screen that the broker's quotations are accurate.
    * Place your trades using your broker's utilities.

The sections that follow identify and briefly discuss several sources of price data. Some provide only historical data—end-of-day data some time after the markets close, or intra-day data reported after a delay of some time. Others distribute real-time data, reported as soon after the data was created as possible. Most have a range of products and services at a range of prices, allowing you to select what you need. The completeness of the data provided varies with vendor—do enough research to satisfy yourself that the data provided meets your needs. All are data vendors, and all are currently in business. You should expect changes as new vendors enter the business and others drop out. Join the user groups and discussion forums for the platform you use and the data vendors you are using or considering using.

You have some choices to make related to the data you will use for development.

- The source—where the data will come from.
  * Free.
  * Subscription.
- Database location.
  * Locally, on your own computer.
  * On the data server's computer, downloading what you need when you need it.
- Database maintenance.
  * The data vendor corrects errors and adjusts for splits and distributions. (In most cases, you are unable to make modifications to the vendor-maintained database.)
  * You maintain the database.

csi
http://www.csidata.com/

End-of-day historical data for US and Canadian stocks, world futures, Forex, indexes, government rates, ETFs, mutual funds. Subscription. Data is stored on your computer in a proprietary format. Data is maintained by the vendor.

dtn.iq
http://www.interquote.com/

Real-time, tick-by-tick streaming data for stocks, futures, options. Subscription. Your software requires a "client process" to receive the quotes, functions to interpret the data, and functions to store it to your local database (if you want to record the data for future use).

eoddata
http://www.eoddata.com/

End-of-day and one minute-based intra-day data for stocks, ETFs, mutual funds, commodities on markets around the world. A limited amount is available free, most require a subscription. Data is downloaded to your computer and stored in one of a number of formats, including ASCII, MetaStock, and several specific to trading system development platforms.

eSignal
http://www.esignal.com/

Real-time, tick-by-tick, streaming data for stocks, futures, options. Subscription. Uses eSignal and third-party software.

Google
https://www.google.com/finance

End-of-day historical data for stocks, indexes, mutual funds for US and many world markets. Real-time data for stocks using beta-test data feed. Free. API procedures for direct feed to your application are available for many development platforms. Or download in csv format and store in your local database.

Interactive Brokers
    https://www.interactivebrokers.com/ind/en/main.php

End-of-day and intra-day historical, and real-time streaming, data through the TWS (Trader Work Station). Some free, some subscription. Download in csv format and store in your local database. Direct access to AmiBroker through the TWS API.

msn money
    http://money.msn.com/

End-of-day historical data for stocks, indexes, mutual funds for US and many world markets. Free. Download in csv format and store in your local database.

nasdaq
    http://www.nasdaq.com/quotes/historical-quotes.aspx

End-of-day data for stocks and ETFs listed on the all US exchanges. Free. Download historical data in csv format. Intra-day prices, including pre-market and after-hours, are available for view—some real-time, some with 20 minute delay. Historical commodity prices viewable but not downloadable.

Norgate Premium Data
    http://www.premiumdata.net/

End-of-day historical data for stocks, futures, Forex for US and many world markets. Subscription. Vendor maintains a database (in several formats including MetaStock, ASCII, and the preferred proprietary) on your computer, updating content with each download. Extensive historical data, including survivorship adjusted data, is available.

Quandl
    http://www.quandl.com/

A large number of end-of-day datasets for global markets, including indexes, commodities, stocks, interest rates. Free. Extensive historical data download in csv, Excel, json, R, or xml format. Free API for direct access of Quandl by AmiBroker, Python, C/C++/C#, Excel, Java, Maple, Matlab, R, Stata, and more. Quandl is a data aggregator and redistributor. Their premium data is available shortly after market close.

US Treasury
    www.treasury.gov/

Daily T-Bill, T-Note, T-Bond, and yield-curve spread rates. Free. Copy and paste to your spreadsheet. Store in your local database.

Yahoo! Finance
http://finance.yahoo.com/

End-of-day historical data for stocks, indexes, mutual funds for US and many world markets. Free. API procedures for direct feed to your application are available for many development platforms. Or download in csv format and store in your local database.

Read and Write Data Files

Essentially every run of every trading system—live or development—begins by reading one or more data series into that program's data structures. Files on your computer's storage devices are sometimes used for temporary storage or for data exchange. This section describes several basic procedures, in both AmiBroker and Python, for reading and writing data series.

AmiBroker

Read data series from disk

Reading price data from an ASCII file and importing it into an AmiBroker database was described in Chapter 3. While AmiBroker supports any number of databases, at present, only one can be open at a time. Any data already in the currently open database can be read into the program using the AmiBroker Foreign statement. Reading from a csv file on disk could be used to bring a data series not already in the open database into a running AmiBroker program, but that is complex and error prone. A better solution is to add the desired data to one of the AmiBroker databases, then use the Foreign statement to load it into the running program.

Write data series to disk

Figure 4.2 shows the AmiBroker code that writes an ASCII file to a disk in csv format. While the example writes price quotations, the technique applies to any series available in the first phase of analysis. With a little modification, it could be writing indicator values.

```
//  WriteDataToFile.afl
//
//  This program exports the data for
//  the current stock in comma separated
//  separated file format.
//
//  Usage:
//         Open this file using Formula Editor.
//         Click the Verify Syntax icon.
//
//  The data will be written to a file in the AmiBroker directory.
```

Data

```
//  If you want it in some other directory, modify the path
        variable.
//
//  Whatever periodicity is displayed will be used for the output.
//  If it is set to Daily, then Hour and Minute will each be 0
//
//  The first few lines of the file are:
//  Ticker,Date,Hr:Min,Open,High,Low,Close,Volume
//  IWM,2008-01-02,07:05,76.5000, 76.5000, 76.5000, 76.5000,   100
//  IWM,2008-01-02,07:10,76.4500, 76.4500, 76.3700, 76.3700,  3400
//  IWM,2008-01-02,07:15,76.3900, 76.3900, 76.3900, 76.3900,   200
//  IWM,2008-01-02,07:20,76.4200, 76.4200, 76.4200, 76.4200,   200
//  IWM,2008-01-02,07:55,76.2900, 76.2900, 76.2900, 76.2900, 25000
//
//  Excel will open it without further modification.
//  AmiBroker will re-import it using the Import ASCII Wizard.
//
//  As you copy and paste, be aware that line wrap and quote marks
//  may cause unexpected errors and need attention.
//

path = "quotes.csv";
fh = fopen( path, "w" );

if ( fh )
{
    fputs( "Ticker,Date,Hr:Min,Open,High,Low,Close,Volume\n",
        fh );

    nm = Name();

    y = Year();
    m = Month();
    d = Day();

    Hr = Hour();
    Mn = Minute();

    for ( i = 0; i < BarCount; i++ )
    {
        ns = nm + ",";
        fputs( ns, fh );
        ds = StrFormat( "%02.0f-%02.0f-%02.0f,",
                        y[ i ], m[ i ], d[ i ] );
        fputs( ds, fh );

        ts = StrFormat( "%02.0f:%02.0f,",
                        hr[ i ], mn[ i ] );
        fputs( ts, fh );

        qs = StrFormat( "%.4f, %.4f, %.4f, %.4f, %.0f\n",
                        O[ i ], H[ i ], L[ i ], C[ i ], V[ i ] );
        fputs( qs, fh );
    }

    fclose( fh );
}
//////////////  end  //////////////
```

Figure 4.2 Write data series to a disk file—AmiBroker

Write trades to disk

Figure 4.3 shows the AmiBroker code that writes an ASCII file to a disk in csv format. In this example, the data are trades. This example applies to any series available in the second phase of analysis.

```
//  WriteTradesToFile.afl
//
//  Writes a list of trades to a disk file
//    in the Custom Backtester phase of analysis.
//

// System settings have been omitted for clarity

// Custom Backtester begins here
SetCustomBacktestProc( "" );
if ( Status( "action" ) == actionPortfolio )
{
    bo = GetBacktesterObject();
    bo.Backtest( 1 );
    path = "writeShadowTrades.csv";
    fh = fopen( path, "w" );
    if ( fh )
    {
        trnum = 0;
        for ( trade = bo.GetFirstTrade(); trade;
                    trade = bo.GetNextTrade() )
        {
            trnum = trnum + 1;
            trp = trade.GetPercentProfit();
            outstr =
                StrFormat( "Trade Number %5.0f PctGain %3.6f\n",
                            trnum, trp );
            fputs( outstr, fh );
        }
        outstr = StrFormat( "Number of trades  %5.0f \n",
                            trnum );
        fputs( outstr, fh );
        fclose( fh );
    }
    else
    {
        Error( "Error -- file cannot be opened" );
    }

//bo.ListTrades();
}

//  Trading system begins here

Buy = DayOfWeek() == 4;
Sell = DayOfWeek() == 5;

//  end //
```

Figure 4.3 Write trade list to a disk file—AmiBroker

Python

The first illustration, reading end-of-day historical data from Yahoo Finance, is shown as code, then in the context of the Canopy IDE and the Spyder IDE. Following that, the examples are shown without the IDE. The same Python / pandas / NumPy / SciPy / scikit-learn code works identically in all environments.

The format of each program will usually follow this template:
- An introductory comment block that includes the name of the program and its purpose.
- Import statements defining libraries used.
- Definitions and assignments of major data structures and variables.
- Program code.

Read end-of-day history from Yahoo Finance

```
"""
ReadYahoo.py
Read price history of a single issue from Yahoo
"""

from pandas.io.data import DataReader

ticker = 'SPY'
source = 'yahoo'
start = '01/01/2012'
end = '03/22/2014'

qt_spy = DataReader(ticker, source, start, end)
print qt_spy.head()
print qt_spy.tail()
```

Figure 4.4 Read price history from Yahoo—Python code

Canopy IDE

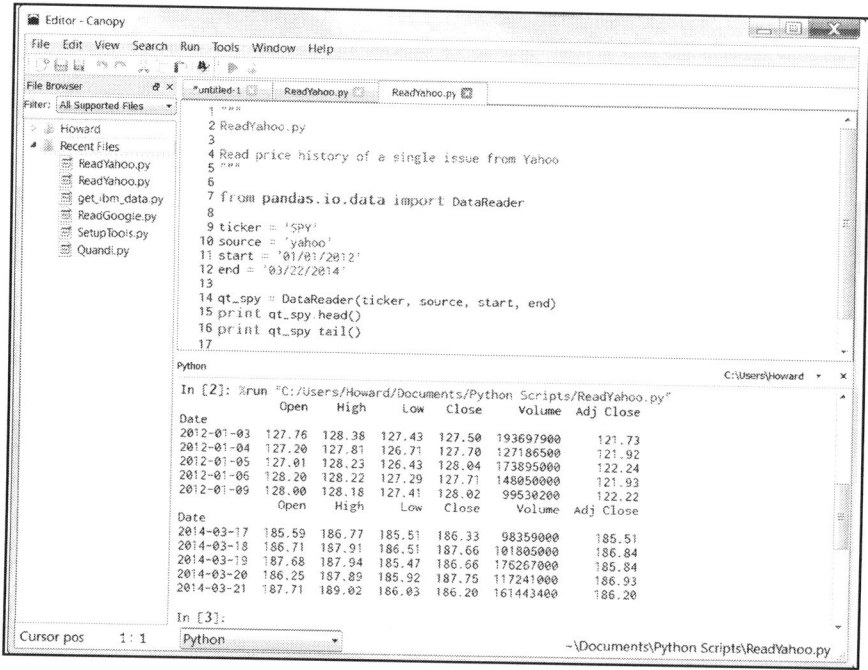

Figure 4.5 Read price history from Yahoo—using the Canopy IDE

Spyder IDE

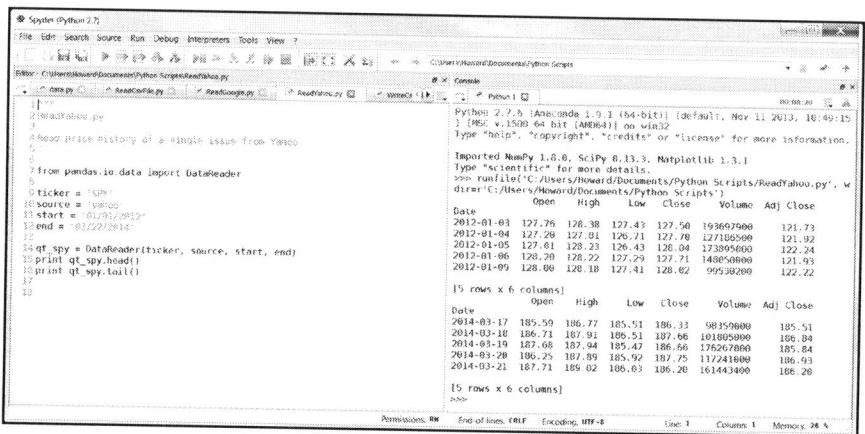

Figure 4.6 Read price history from Yahoo—using the Spyder IDE

Read end-of-day data from Google Finance

```
"""
ReadGoogle.py
Read price history of a single issue from Google
"""

from pandas.io.data import DataReader

ticker = 'SPY'
source = 'google'
start = '01/01/2012'
end = '03/22/2014'

qt = DataReader(ticker, source, start, end)
print qt.head()
print qt.tail()
```

Figure 4.7 Read end-of-day data from Google Finance

Read intra-day data from Google Finance

Intra-day historical data is available from Google Finance. It is free, not well documented, and not guaranteed to be an ongoing resource. It can be accessed directly using a url. Enter the following line in the address bar of your browser as a single line:

```
http://www.google.com/finance/
       getprices?q=AAPL&i=300&p=20d&f=d,o,h,l,c,v
```

You are asking for historical intra-day data for Apple Corporation, 5 minute (300 second) bars or intervals, for the past 20 trading days. Your browser window will look something like Figure 4.8.

```
EXCHANGE%3DNASDAQ
MARKET_OPEN_MINUTE=570
MARKET_CLOSE_MINUTE=960
INTERVAL=300
COLUMNS=DATE,CLOSE,HIGH,LOW,OPEN,VOLUME
DATA=
TIMEZONE_OFFSET=-300
a1417703400,115.8,115.83,115.71,115.77,345616
1,115.9,116.18,115.65,115.81,1012745
2,115.99,116.09,115.61,115.9,662454
3,115.964,116.12,115.8501,115.99,599331
4,116.29,116.31,115.95,115.97,709628
5,116.2,116.3,116.07,116.29,503950
6,116.68,116.76,116.18,116.209,1264154
7,116.65,116.82,116.6,116.69,944825
8,116.82,116.925,116.62,116.65,1032169
9,116.78,116.861,116.62,116.82,410099
10,116.97,116.99,116.68,116.78,649447
11,117.1597,117.2,116.935,116.98,1119213
```

Figure 4.8 Intra-day data from Google using browser

There are seven header lines. 570 seconds is 9 hours, 30 minutes—the opening time of floor trading. 960 seconds is 16 hours (1600 hours in 24 hour time)—the closing time of floor trading. The first data line begins with "a" and is followed by the full date and time—call it the *base* time. Following data lines begin with an integer specifying the number of intervals beyond the base time. Be aware that parameters provided to the Google app may result in unusual results. Visually inspect all data before using it. The steps performed in the code that is shown in Figure 4.9 are:

- Defines a Python function, then works within it.
- Configures a line of text that can and will be used as a url.
- Uses the Python *requests* library and *requests.get* function to retrieve the data from that url.
- Parses the data that was retrieved, converting the first field into a series of fully formed and independent dates and times.
- Assigns the parsed data to a pandas dataframe, which it returns.

```
"""
GoogleIntraday.py

Disclaimer continues to apply

Copyright  2014 Blue Owl Press, Inc
Dr. Howard Bandy
"""

import datetime
import pandas as pd
import requests

def getGoogleIntradayData(ticker,numSeconds,numDays):

    #  Define some variables
    parsedData = []
    syncChar = 'a'
    numSkipLines = 7

    # Form the url
    urlStr = 'http://www.google.com/finance/getprices?q='
    urlStr += ticker
    urlStr += '&i=' + str(numSeconds)
    urlStr += '&p=' + str(numDays) + 'd'
    urlStr += '&f=d,o,h,l,c,v'

    # Open the url
    resp = requests.get(urlStr)

    rawData = resp.text
    lines = rawData.split('\n')
    nrows = len(lines)

    for i in range(numSkipLines,nrows):
        #  check for empty line at end of data
        if (lines[i]==""): continue
        dtField, o, h, l, c, v = lines[i].split(',')
```

```
            if dtField[0]==syncChar:
                #  Full datetime
                dtBase = dtField[1:]
                dtIncr = 0
            else:
                #  Datetime increment
                dtIncr = int(dtField)
            dtValue = datetime.datetime.fromtimestamp\
                    (float(dtBase) + (dtIncr*numSeconds))
            o, h, l, c = [float(x) for x in [o, h, l, c]]
            parsedData.append((dtValue, o, h, l, c, v))

    qt = pd.DataFrame(parsedData)
    qt.columns = ['datetime', 'open', 'high', 'low', 'close',
            'volume']
    qt.index = qt.datetime
    del qt['datetime']
    return qt

# Call the function to retrieve historical intra-day data
qtIntra = getGoogleIntradayData('AAPL',300,5)

print type(qtIntra)
print qtIntra.head()
print qtIntra.tail()

##########   end   ###########
```

Figure 4.9 Read intra-day data from Google Finance

Figure 4.10 shows the result of calling the function and asking for 5 days of 5 minute (300 second) bars for Apple stock.

```
>>> runfile('C:/Users/Howard/Documents/Python Scripts/GoogleIntraday.py', wd:
cuments/Python Scripts')
<class 'pandas.core.frame.DataFrame'>
                      open      high      low      close    volume
datetime
2014-12-26 06:30:00   112.0800  112.1000  112.050  112.100  300458
2014-12-26 06:35:00   112.0999  112.2901  112.010  112.060  408239
2014-12-26 06:40:00   112.3000  112.4600  112.100  112.100  408048
2014-12-26 06:45:00   112.3700  112.5900  112.308  112.308  446215
2014-12-26 06:50:00   112.7900  112.7900  112.340  112.370  484740

[5 rows x 5 columns]
                      open      high      low      close    volume
datetime
2015-01-02 12:40:00   109.100   109.140   109.0399 109.112  402650
2015-01-02 12:45:00   109.245   109.524   109.1050 109.110  882742
2015-01-02 12:50:00   109.450   109.510   109.2260 109.240  740948
2015-01-02 12:55:00   109.400   109.480   109.3600 109.450  841872
2015-01-02 13:00:00   109.330   109.430   109.2500 109.390  3588633

[5 rows x 5 columns]
>>>
```

Figure 4.10 Results from Google intra-day data

Figure 4.11 lists a Python program that reads some end-of-day data from Yahoo Finance, then writes that data to a disk file in csv format.

Write csv file to disk

```
"""
WriteCsvFile.py

Read price history of a single issue from Yahoo
Write the data (from DataFrame) to disk file in .csv format
"""

from pandas.io.data import DataReader

ticker = 'SPY'
source = 'yahoo'
start = '01/01/2012'
end = '03/22/2014'

qt = DataReader(ticker, source, start, end)
print qt.head()
print qt.tail()

qt.to_csv('F:\\StockData\\SPY.csv')
```

Figure 4.11 Write csv file—Python code

The program in Figure 4.12 reads data from a disk file.

Read csv file from disk

```
"""
ReadCsvFile.py

Read price history of a single issue from a csv file
"""

import pandas as pd

fromDisk = pd.read_csv('F:\\StockData\\SPY.csv')

print(fromDisk)
```

Figure 4.12 Read csv file—Python code

Chapter 5
Issue Selection

Figure 5.1 shows a chart of SPY, the ETF that tracks the S&P 500 Index. Is it tradable? Or is any other stock, ETF, mutual fund, or future tradable? The answer is in three parts.
- How much risk is there?
- How much profit is available?
- Can we develop a system to extract the profit?

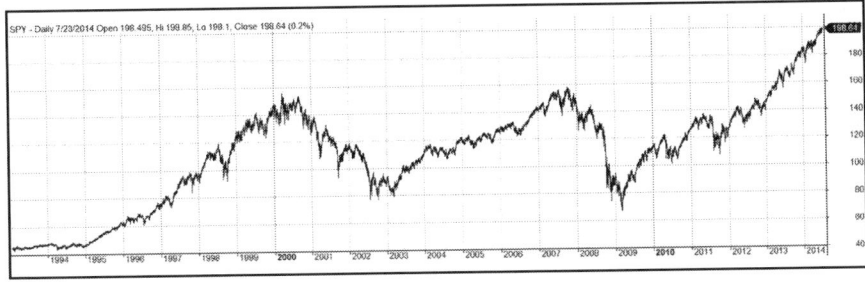

Figure 5.1 SPY

Market Research

Market research is a natural part of a business plan. If you were considering starting a company to sell running shoes, you would do some market research. You would find out how many potential customers there were and how much profit there was in each pair sold. There is no guarantee your product would be successful. Developing a good product line and selling are yet to come. But you would be unwise to start if you knew there was no market or the profit margin was too low.

Or perhaps you have a case of gold fever. Is there gold in those hills over there? How much? How hard to extract? Before buying the property and bringing in the heavy equipment, let's send in a prospector.

Blue Owl Prospecting, Inc.

Let us dig around in your data.

We will identify the risks and estimate the profit potential. We will tell you how accurate your system must be. Then you can decide which issues have the best prospects and begin developing those systems.

There is an analogy with trading systems. The best issues to trade combine three characteristics:
- Adequate profit potential—some price variation.
- Absence of extreme adverse price changes—not too much price variation.
- Existence of detectable signal patterns—not too efficient.

Goldilocks, to be sure.

Additionally, the issue must be sufficiently liquid. I recommend enough liquidity so you can exit your entire position any minute of any day without substantially affecting the bid-ask spread.

The complete trading system consists of the model and the data series. Even before we begin model development, we can determine how much profit is potentially available by analyzing the data series itself.

Risk and Profit Potential

There is quantifiable risk inherent in any data series. Whatever system is eventually developed to trade it, some trades will be winners and some will be losers. All trades, winners as well as losers, have adverse excursions that contribute to the drawdown.

Given a data series and two variables—holding period and system accuracy—we can estimate the risk inherent in the series. Given the risk inherent in the series and your personal statement of risk tolerance, we can determine safe-f. Given safe-f, we can estimate profit potential.

The analysis described here assumes:
- You have a trading system that trades a single issue and is either long or flat.
- All the rules have been included in the model.
- There will be no subjective position changes or early exits.
- Equity is marked-to-market at the close of every trading day.

Simulation Outline

The analysis is done using a Monte Carlo simulator implemented in a Python program. The code is listed at the end of this chapter.

We are choosing trades that total two years of long exposure, however many trades that requires and however much time that covers. Imagine you are alternately long and flat, then squeeze out the flat periods, resulting in two years of long trades.

The major control variables are:
- Your risk tolerance. Say a maximum 5% chance of a drawdown greater than 20% over a 2 year horizon.
- The issue being tested. Say SPY. The simulator is set up for daily data. Closing prices are required. If daily high and low are present, they can be used.
- Any time period longer than the forecast period can be used. The ideal is what is representative of the future. Within reason, longer is better. Say 1999 through 2014.
- The holding period of each trade in days. Any value up to the length of the forecast is valid. Say 5 days.
- Accuracy of the trading system. Any value from 0.00 (every trade is a loser) to 1.00 (every trade is a winner) can be used. Say 65%, represented as 0.65.
- The number of simulation runs. Say 1000.

The simulation works as follows.

Preliminaries.
1. Set the control variables.
2. Select a daily price series.
3. Given the holding period, examine every day as an entry day. Positions will be taken market on close, at the closing price. Look ahead the number of days of the holding period. That will be the exit day. If the closing price on the exit day is higher, mark this entry day as a "gainer" entry day; otherwise it is a "loser" entry day.
4. Divide the number of days in the forecast period by the holding period, giving the number of trades.
5. Set the fraction used for each trade to 1.00.

For each of the required number of simulation runs, repeat the following sequence for as many trades as are needed to complete the forecast horizon:
1. Pick a random number (uniform, 0.00 to 1.00) to determine whether the next trade will be a winner or a loser. Over the course of many runs, the proportion of winning trades matches the trade accuracy you want to study.
2. From whichever list—"gainer" or "loser"—was chosen, select a trade entry day at random. Note the entry price. Buy as many shares as you can with the fraction of equity allowed.
3. In the sequence they occur in the historical price series, process the trade day-by-day. Keep daily track of:
    * Intra-day drawdown, measured using daily high and low.
    * Intra-trade drawdown, measured using mark-to-market daily closing price.
    * Trade drawdown, measured from the trade open to trade close.
    * Account equity—value of shares held plus cash.

At the completion of those trades, the simulator reports the three drawdown metrics and the final equity.

Figure 5.2 shows ten equally likely equity curves resulting from trading SPY with a holding period of 5 days, an accuracy of 65%, and a fraction of 1.00. The Python program that creates and displays equity curves is listed at the end of the chapter.

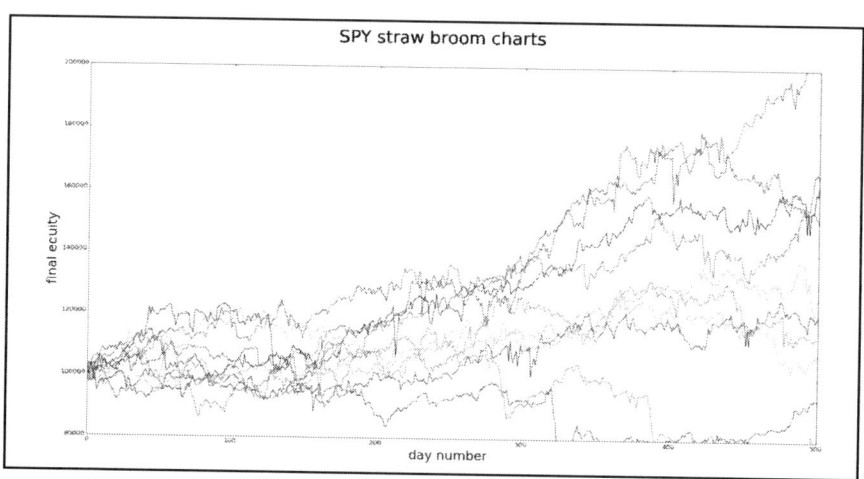

Figure 5.2 Equity, two years of SPY, fraction 1.00

Figure 5.3 shows a table with the metrics for those ten runs. The first few lines of output document the values of the control variables. Not shown, initial equity is $100,000.

There is one row for each run. Interpretation of the columns, using the first row as an example, is:
- Max IDDD is the maximum intra-day drawdown over the two year period. The value in the first run is 0.3620, meaning there was a 36.2% drawdown in equity measured from highest daily high price to date to a subsequent daily low price.
- Max ITDD is the maximum intra-trade drawdown. The first run had a drawdown of 34.09% using mark-to-market closing prices. This is the metric we wish to hold to 20%.
- Max TRDD is the maximum trade-by-trade drawdown—33.3%. This is the drawdown using only the sequence of 100 5-day trades, ignoring all intra-trade price variation.
- EqAtClose is the final equity—$93,285.
- CAR is the compound annual rate of return—a loss of 3.42% per year.

```
Issue: spy
Dates: 01 Jan 1999 to: 01 Jan 2015
Hold Days: 5
System Accuracy:  0.650000
DD 95 limit: 0.200000
Fraction: 1.000000
Forecast Horizon: 504
Number Forecasts: 10
Max IDDD: 0.3620    Max ITDD: 0.3409    Max TRDD: 0.3330    EqAtClose: 93285     CAR: -3.42
Max IDDD: 0.1689    Max ITDD: 0.1573    Max TRDD: 0.1434    EqAtClose: 113211    CAR:  6.40
Max IDDD: 0.1399    Max ITDD: 0.1206    Max TRDD: 0.0855    EqAtClose: 208173    CAR: 44.28
Max IDDD: 0.1410    Max ITDD: 0.1345    Max TRDD: 0.0928    EqAtClose: 125937    CAR: 12.22
Max IDDD: 0.1635    Max ITDD: 0.1379    Max TRDD: 0.1184    EqAtClose: 151131    CAR: 22.94
Max IDDD: 0.2075    Max ITDD: 0.2032    Max TRDD: 0.1713    EqAtClose: 107548    CAR:  3.71
Max IDDD: 0.1477    Max ITDD: 0.1336    Max TRDD: 0.0743    EqAtClose: 162239    CAR: 27.37
Max IDDD: 0.2600    Max ITDD: 0.2499    Max TRDD: 0.2263    EqAtClose: 120118    CAR:  9.60
Max IDDD: 0.3941    Max ITDD: 0.3852    Max TRDD: 0.3696    EqAtClose: 75432     CAR: -13.15
Max IDDD: 0.1607    Max ITDD: 0.1484    Max TRDD: 0.1345    EqAtClose: 164959    CAR: 28.44
```

Figure 5.3 Metrics for the ten equity curves

Sidebar—Calculating CAR

Terminal wealth relative, TWR, is the term coined by Ralph Vince to represent the ratio of final equity to initial equity. In terms of the simulation, TWR is EqAtClose / initial equity. Final equity (TWR), compound annual rate of return (CAR), and number of years (N), are related by these formulas:

$$TWR = (1+CAR)^N$$

$$CAR = \exp(\ln(TWR)/N) - 1$$

For a two year forecast period, a close approximation of CAR, expressed as a percent, is given by:

$$CAR = 100.0 * (\sqrt{TWR} - 1)$$

For example, if an account grows from $100,000 to $115,000 in two years, TWR is 1.15. The corresponding compound annual rate of growth is 7.2%

The simulation continues.

The risk tolerance requires intra-trade marked-to-market daily drawdown at the 95th percentile to be no greater than 20 percent. Intra-trade marked-to-market-daily drawdown is the second column—Max ITDD. If results for all 1000 runs were listed and sorted by that column, we want the first 950 to have values less than 0.2000, the final 50 to be greater. There is no advantage in having the final 50 be less than 0.2000, a situation that would occur only if the fraction of available equity used for each trade was lower than the maximum safe-f. Intentionally using a lower fraction does lower risk, but it lowers profit even more. You do want to coordinate your risk tolerance with the fraction used and take the largest positions that are safe.

Note that four of the ten runs shown in Figure 5.3 have values greater than 0.2000. This combination—5 day holding with 65% accuracy—is too risky when traded at full fraction.

This does not mean that a system that is 65% accurate and holds trades five days cannot be profitably traded. It does mean that, in order to avoid unacceptable drawdowns, only a fraction of the available funds can be safely used. The remainder must remain in a risk free account to act as a ballast.

What is the largest that fraction should be? The metrics shown in Figures 5.2 and 5.3 result from taking every trade with all available funds—fraction of 1.00. The 95th percentile maximum intra-trade drawdown for all 1000 runs was 30.1 percent.

The simulation searches for the highest fraction for which the metric Max ITDD is 0.20 or less in 95% of the runs. That is safe-f for this issue, holding period, and accuracy. Safe-f is found to be 0.646.

> We know that position size is not stationary. Safe-f varies over time as the characteristics of the data change. In a later chapter we will adjust position size periodically. For now, using an assumption of stationarity considerably simplifies the analysis and explanation.

Figure 5.4 shows ten equally likely equity curves for the same holding period and accuracy as those shown in Figure 5.2, but with a fraction of 0.646 rather than 1.00.

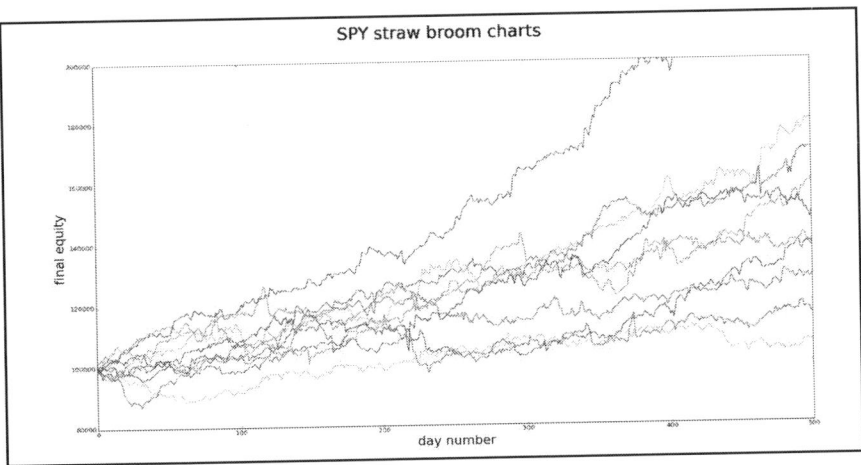

Figure 5.4 Equity, two years of SPY, fraction 0.646

Figure 5.5 shows the associated table.

```
Issue: spy
Dates: 01 Jan 1999 to: 01 Jan 2015
Hold Days: 5
System Accuracy:  0.650000
DD 95 limit: 0.200000
Fraction: 0.646000
Forecast Horizon: 504
Number Forecasts: 10
Max IDDD: 0.1223    Max ITDD: 0.1010    Max TRDD: 0.0728    EqAtClose: 138520    CAR: 17.69
Max IDDD: 0.1271    Max ITDD: 0.1157    Max TRDD: 0.0917    EqAtClose: 137760    CAR: 17.37
Max IDDD: 0.1998    Max ITDD: 0.1667    Max TRDD: 0.1286    EqAtClose: 115721    CAR: 7.57
Max IDDD: 0.0962    Max ITDD: 0.0837    Max TRDD: 0.0773    EqAtClose: 179749    CAR: 34.07
Max IDDD: 0.1025    Max ITDD: 0.0941    Max TRDD: 0.0882    EqAtClose: 128546    CAR: 13.38
Max IDDD: 0.1225    Max ITDD: 0.1155    Max TRDD: 0.1086    EqAtClose: 107178    CAR: 3.53
Max IDDD: 0.1589    Max ITDD: 0.1275    Max TRDD: 0.0811    EqAtClose: 149333    CAR: 22.20
Max IDDD: 0.0818    Max ITDD: 0.0759    Max TRDD: 0.0672    EqAtClose: 228167    CAR: 51.05
Max IDDD: 0.1549    Max ITDD: 0.1492    Max TRDD: 0.0958    EqAtClose: 159437    CAR: 26.27
Max IDDD: 0.1355    Max ITDD: 0.1310    Max TRDD: 0.1230    EqAtClose: 170265    CAR: 30.49
```

Figure 5.5 Metrics for the ten equity curves

Drawdown as a Function of Holding Period

Continuing to use SPY as the issue, set fraction to 1.00, and use the 5% / 20% / 2 year statement of risk tolerance. Run a series of simulations. Begin with trade accuracy at 50%, then 55, 60, 65, 70, 80, and 90. For each of the seven levels of trade accuracy, vary the holding period from 1 day to 252 days. Record the value of ITDD95—the 95th percentile intra-trade drawdown. This is the number you want to hold to 20% or less.

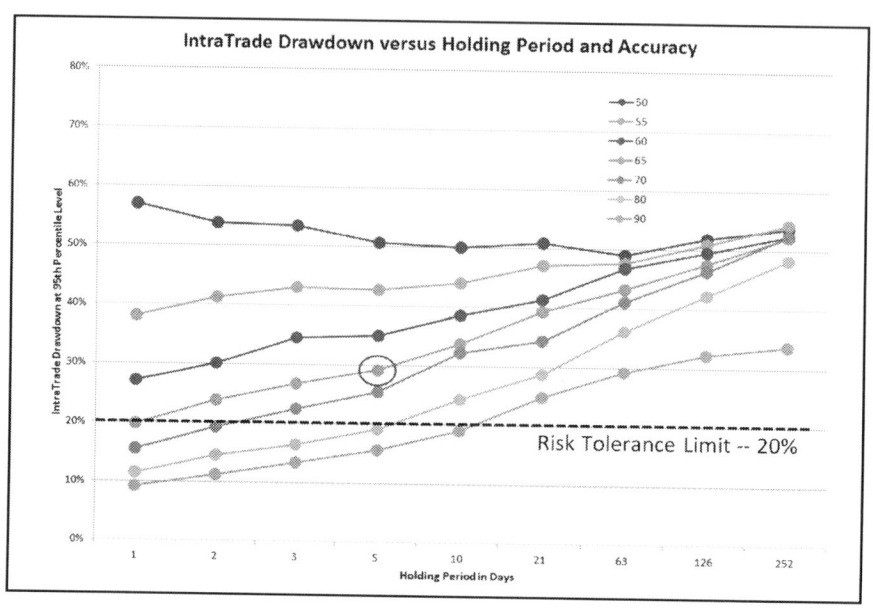

Figure 5.6 Drawdown related to holding period and accuracy

Figure 5.6 shows the relationship between drawdown and holding period and accuracy. The horizontal axis is holding period in days; the vertical axis is maximum drawdown in percent; the dashed horizontal line at 20% is your risk tolerance. Each of the lines with dots represents one of the levels of trade accuracy. The 50% level is closest to the top of the chart, progressing downward with 90% accuracy the lowest line. On this chart, lower is better. The circled dot is 65% accurate, 5 day hold—the values analyzed in detail in the preceding sections. Sharp-eyed readers will note the circled value is slightly less than 30%, while the figure given for safe-f earlier was 30.1%. Variations of this sort are to be expected when working with Monte Carlo simulations.

Figure 5.6 shows that the maximum safe position size decreases as holding period increases, and it decreases as accuracy decreases.

Drawdown increases as holding period increases.

Drawdown increases as trade accuracy decreases.

This does not mean systems that hold longer than 5 days or have accuracy less than 70% cannot be profitable. It does mean they cannot be traded at full fraction.

Only those combinations of trade accuracy and holding period plotted below the 20% drawdown limit can be traded at full fraction. To get a very rough estimate of the fraction that is safe for any combination of holding period and trade accuracy, locate that point on the graph, note the corresponding value of maximum drawdown from the vertical axis, and divide 0.20 by that value. For example, if your system is 60% accurate in selecting trades that hold one month (21 trading days), go up from 21 days to the 60% curve, then left to the axis, and read off the value of about 42%. 0.20 divided by 0.42 gives 0.48. The interpretation is that the maximum safe fraction for this system is to use 48% of available funds to buy shares, keeping the remaining 52% in cash. (Really in cash and really allocated solely to this system. These funds are not available to be used "twice" by also using them as the cash reserve for another system.) The relationship is not quite as linear as the simple division would suggest—the further above 0.20 the system is, the lower the safe fraction.

Profit Potential

When 65% accurate holding 5 days, maximum intra-trade drawdown is about 30%, and maximum safe fraction is about 64%. Given these parameters, we can estimate the potential profit. That is, trading SPY for two years of exposure, using a yet-to-be-defined model that results in trades that are held five days, of which 65 percent are winners, we can compute the distribution of final equity and associated compound annual rate of return (CAR). Figure 5.7 is that cumulative distribution function (CDF).

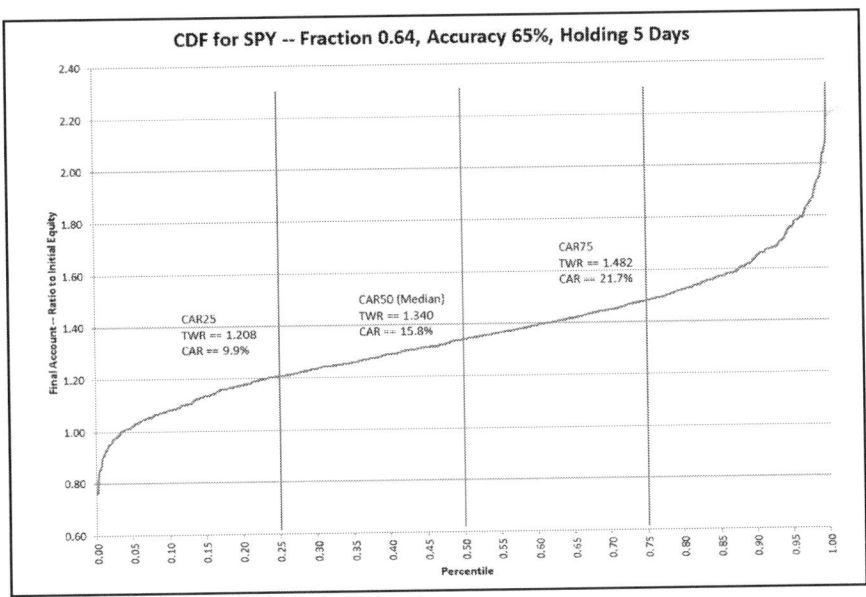

Figure 5.7 CDF for SPY

The CAR actually experienced will depend on the specific trades, but if the future resembles the past — where the past is 1999 to 2014 data — estimates can be read from the graph.

The 50th percentile is the median. The interquartile range is another useful metric. It is the difference between the values at the 25th percentile and those at the 75th percentile. Results are equally likely to be within this range as to be outside it to one extreme or the other.

For conciseness, these three will be called CAR25, CAR50, and CAR75. The results for SPY traded at a fraction of 64% are 9.9, 15.8, and 21.7.

It is typical for CAR75 to be about one and one-half to two times CAR25, with CAR50 about at their midpoint. Any large differences should be checked for unadjusted splits or data errors. In a few cases, CAR75 is much greater than typical. These are probably because of a few rapid prices rises.

Thus defined, profit potential is related to accuracy and holding period. As shown in Figure 5.8, profit potential increases as holding period is reduced and as trade accuracy is increased. The area outlined in the upper right corner contains those combinations where CAR25 is 10% or greater.

Compound Annual Rate of Return -- SPY -- Long Positions

Holding	Accuracy							
	40	50	55	60	65	70	80	90
1	-7.4	-2.6	5.9	28.0	74.0	161.0	725.0	3546.0
2	-6.4	-2.1	4.3	17.0	40.0	75.0	228.0	725.0
3	-6.4	-2.0	1.6	10.0	25.0	46.0	129.0	294.0
5	-5.4	-1.7	1.8	7.7	15.3	29.0	70.0	145.0
10	-4.6	-1.8	0.4	3.5	8.1	14.3	31.0	62.0
21	-3.7	-1.5	0.2	2.0	4.3	7.3	15.1	28.0
63	-2.0	-0.5	0.3	1.4	2.7	4.6	7.8	15.0
126	-1.6	-0.3	0.3	0.8	1.9	3.0	5.2	9.1
252	-1.7	-0.8	-0.5	-0.2	1.3	1.9	3.8	5.7

Figure 5.8 Median CAR versus Accuracy and Holding Period — Long

Note that the CAR figures reported in Figure 5.8 represent two years of holding a position. A system that is either long or flat would be long only a portion of that time, say, one-third. If so, it would take about six total years to accumulate two years of long exposure. Consequently, the reported CAR figures should be divided by three to estimate the maximum effective rate of return before the model is developed.

Risk in being Short

We hear that being short is dangerous. That it is riskier than being long. We are told that the potential loss from a long stock position is "only" the amount lost when the price goes to zero, but the potential loss from a short position is unlimited because price has no upper limit.

The maximum drawdown for a long position is the entry price minus the lowest close of the holding period. The risk to a long position is a sharp price drop. The maximum drawdown for a short position is the highest close of the holding period minus the entry price. The risk to a short position is a sharp price rise.

Continuing with the same technique of estimating the risk inherent in a data series for a given holding period and trade accuracy, the maximum drawdown, safe-f, and median CAR is computed for short positions in SPY. If being short is indeed riskier, safe-f will be smaller, CAR will be lower, and the outlined area will be smaller.

The risk-normalized CAR25 for short positions is shown in Figure 5.9. These values are directly comparable with those for long positions in Figure 5.8. There is a program listing at the end of this chapter you can use to study your own choice of data series, holding period, accuracy, and resulting risk and profit potential.

Compound Annual Rate of Return -- SPY -- Short Positions

Holding	Accuracy							
	40	50	55	60	65	70	80	90
1	-6.1	2.2	22.2	59.0	142.0	252.0	825.0	12180.0
2	-5.4	2.2	13.4	32.2	72.0	128.0	256.0	797.0
3	-4.3	3.0	12.0	27.2	51.0	80.0	202.0	507.0
5	-4.1	1.1	6.3	15.6	27.3	44.0	102.0	203.0
10	-2.8	1.9	5.3	10.6	16.4	25.6	51.0	91.0
21	-2.6	1.6	4.0	8.8	11.9	16.3	32.9	51.0
63	-1.9	0.5	1.2	2.8	5.2	5.7	12.1	17.3
126	-2.0	0.9	-0.4	2.1	4.4	6.4	7.9	12.3
252	0.2	0.8	1.1	2.3	4.0	5.3	6.9	9.9

Figure 5.9 Median CAR versus Accuracy and Holding Period—Short

In both figures, the outlined area encloses those combinations that result in CAR25 greater than 10 percent. In every cell in the outlined area, CAR for a short position is higher than CAR for a long position.

There may be other reasons for not taking short positions, but riskiness is not one of them. Being short is inherently safer than being long.

This should come as no surprise. Research suggests and experience confirms that sharp drops in price are more common than sharp rises.

The outlined areas in Figures 5.8 and 5.9 contain those accuracy and holding period combinations that have a CAR25 of 10 percent or higher for a period of exposure of two years. This is the maximum potential inherent in the data for the given risk tolerance. We will not know what portion of this potential is achievable until a model is developed to detect patterns and trade this data series. Outside the outlined area, even with a trading system that captures all of the available profit, the return is equivalent to bank interest or less. There is an implication that will make many people very uncomfortable.

Not only is the sweet spot highly accurate trade selection with a holding period of only a few days. The further the system performance is away from the sweet spot area, the lower the possibility of a return greater than risk-free bank interest without experiencing drawdowns that will exceed your risk tolerance.

What the Prospector Found

The analysis described so far in this chapter has been for SPY. Expanding our analysis, we asked the Blue Owl Prospector to evaluate a variety of stocks and ETFs. We want to know what accuracy and holding period we might use with what data series.

Before spending the effort trying to develop a model to use with a data series, we want some assurance the resulting system has the possibility of satisfactory performance. Recall that we want a combination of:
- Enough variability to give opportunity for profitable trades.
- Enough stability that sharp price changes are infrequent.
- Enough history to assess performance in rising and falling markets.
- Enough liquidity to be able to exit a position easily.

We will pick issues to develop models from those that pass these screens.

Everything is in the context of a statement of personal risk tolerance. We are using 5% / 20% / 2 years. If you are using the program at the end of this chapter, adjust it as necessary to reflect your tolerance.

The metrics we will examine and compare are:
- History. The most recent five years have been a strongly rising market. About eight years, 2000 days, of data will ensure both enough data points to give consistent simulation results and experience in a weak market. Plot every data series you are considering. Look for anomalies and correct any you find before beginning model development.
- CAR25 high enough to beat bank interest. CAR25 was chosen because it describes a lower limit for 75 percent of the distribution. For this analysis, we want a minimum CAR25 of 30. The long/flat or short/flat analysis is for two years of exposure. Assuming roughly equal periods of long, flat, and short, it will take six years of trading to get two years of exposure, a factor of three. So, divide 30 by three. We do

not have a model yet. Some of the profit potential reported is random and cannot be predicted by any model. We do not know what portion that is, so let's assume a yet-to-be-developed model might capture half, a factor of two. So, divide again—this time by two. Ideal CAR25 of 30 becomes potential CAR25 of 5—just high enough to compete with bank interest, or your risk-free alternative.

- Safe-f is the maximum fraction of the account that can be used to take positions. The remainder must be held in reserve to act as a ballast. We want the maximum drawdown of the account to be 20 percent. The account is a combination of the portion exposed to risk in trades that produce drawdown and the amount held risk-free with no drawdown. The higher safe-f, the lower the drawdowns in trades. Setting a lower limit of 0.66 on safe-f restricts to those series with drawdowns in the trade portion of the equity curve less than 30 percent (20% / 0.66 == 30%).
- Liquidity and bid-ask spread. For the examples here, the limit was set at $5,000,000 per day, on average for the most recent three months. Choose limits appropriate for your trading.

Setting control variables for accuracy to 65% and holding period to 5 days, none of the roughly 5000 issues we tested passed the screens.

Resetting accuracy to 75% and holding period to 5 days, several hundred passed. Those that were long / flat that passed are listed in Figure 5.10. The columns are: ticker, safe-f, and CAR25. DD95 is 0.20 in all cases, so is omitted. Accuracy of 65% and holding 3 days also produced good results (not shown).

Ticker	safe-f	CAR25	Ticker	safe-f	CAR25	Ticker	safe-f	CAR25	Ticker	safe-f	CAR25
ACC	0.66	46	BOH	0.68	49	DD	0.69	53	ENH	0.71	48
ACN	0.67	48	BPL	0.66	36	DEO	0.93	56	EQY	0.67	45
ADM	0.77	69	BR	0.78	64	DIA	0.94	32	ESS	0.75	48
ADP	0.82	53	BTI	0.80	57	DJP	1.01	46	ETR	0.77	38
AEE	0.85	41	BXP	0.65	42	DLN	0.87	28	EWA	0.67	39
APD	0.68	49	CAG	0.76	42	DOG	1.16	60	EWG	0.66	41
APU	0.69	33	CASY	0.72	71	DOV	0.70	56	EWH	0.83	59
ATO	0.89	47	CBSH	0.66	32	DTE	0.77	39	EWI	0.65	36
AVY	0.70	56	CEF	0.79	66	DTV	0.74	50	EWJ	0.95	58
AZN	0.83	62	CINF	0.67	38	DVY	0.82	28	EWL	1.00	47
AZO	0.81	67	CM	0.65	48	DXJ	0.89	44	EWM	0.88	67
BAP	0.69	65	COL	0.65	48	ED	1.00	42	EWP	0.69	43
BDX	0.80	48	COV	0.74	43	EE	0.90	70	EWQ	0.77	47
BKH	0.67	45	CPB	0.80	42	EFG	0.75	32	EWS	0.79	56
BLV	1.84	47	DBA	0.91	46	EFV	0.73	38	EWU	0.82	40
BOBE	0.68	61	DBC	0.87	37	EGP	0.66	42	FBT	0.74	55

Figure 5.10A Stocks and ETFs that held long / flat that pass the screen

Ticker	safe-f	CAR25	Ticker	safe-f	CAR25	Ticker	safe-f	CAR25	Ticker	safe-f	CAR25
FCNCA	0.75	55	GAS	1.00	49	IDA	0.76	40	IWR	0.74	30
FDN	0.77	48	GHC	0.74	44	IDU	0.97	41	IWV	0.88	35
FE	0.72	34	GLD	1.00	53	IEF	2.80	52	IXJ	1.00	35
FEX	0.87	39	GPC	0.93	63	IEI	4.92	55	IYH	1.15	44
FEZ	0.67	40	GSG	0.78	40	IFF	0.74	46	IYJ	0.80	40
FMER	0.70	52	GSK	0.84	47	IGV	0.72	47	IYT	0.78	44
FRT	0.67	43	GVI	4.24	40	IHI	0.77	35	IYW	0.73	42
FTA	0.75	38	GWW	0.73	61	IHS	0.66	57	IYZ	0.81	43
FXA	1.11	37	GXP	0.72	35	ITA	0.77	37	K	0.93	42
FXD	0.76	47	HCN	0.80	46	IVE	0.81	35	KMB	1.07	52
FXE	2.13	62	HQH	0.68	44	IVV	1.05	40	LANC	0.75	48
FXG	1.00	42	HSBC	0.66	42	IVW	0.91	32	LDOS	0.76	46
FXH	0.90	41	HSH	0.71	48	IWB	1.01	39	LG	0.90	51
FXL	0.77	49	HTH	0.84	63	IWC	0.75	37	LLY	0.66	45
FXR	0.68	38	HUB-B	0.77	60	IWD	0.91	36	LMT	0.73	46
FXU	0.95	35	IBB	0.67	39	IWF	0.86	31	LNCE	0.70	56
FXY	2.16	70	IBKC	0.74	62	IWO	0.74	46	MAA	0.66	34

Figure 5.10B Stocks and ETFs that held long / flat that pass the screen

Ticker	safe-f	CAR25	Ticker	safe-f	CAR25	Ticker	safe-f	CAR25	Ticker	safe-f	CAR25
MCY	0.75	45	OEF	0.99	34	PSB	0.71	41	SJM	0.82	52
MDP	0.66	51	PCL	0.72	49	PSO	0.67	63	SNA	0.67	54
MDY	0.86	44	PDP	0.74	37	PSQ	1.00	64	SNY	0.75	47
MGLN	0.84	64	PEG	0.66	40	PTP	1.00	74	SON	0.73	46
MKL	0.74	40	PEP	0.92	43	RBC	0.66	63	SPH	0.78	38
MLM	0.65	61	PJP	1.08	49	RDS-A	0.71	46	SPY	0.89	35
MTD	0.67	59	PKG	0.69	62	RE	0.79	69	SRE	0.79	46
NGG	0.78	37	PKW	0.92	35	RPG	0.78	39	SWX	0.86	47
NI	0.75	41	PLL	0.69	59	RWM	0.65	49	SXT	0.82	60
NNN	0.69	43	PNW	0.74	40	RWX	0.67	36	SYT	0.73	57
NS	0.76	43	POM	0.70	40	RYT	0.71	36	T	0.74	53
NSC	0.67	60	POR	0.88	45	SCG	1.00	48	TCP	0.73	44
NSH	0.69	68	PPG	0.76	49	SDY	0.84	32	TDG	0.69	65
NTT	0.75	61	PRE	0.66	42	SE	0.69	38	TEG	0.84	43
NU	0.87	46	PRF	0.82	36	SH	0.95	50	TFX	0.78	52
NWN	1.00	58	PSA	0.70	47	SHW	0.69	49	THI	0.95	61

Figure 5.10C Stocks and ETFs that held long / flat that pass the screen

Ticker	safe-f	CAR25	Ticker	safe-f	CAR25	Ticker	safe-f	CAR25	Ticker	safe-f	CAR25
THS	0.66	53	VBK	0.76	40	VTV	0.94	36	XBI	0.73	53
TLT	1.61	57	VBR	0.78	37	VUG	1.00	37	XLB	0.74	47
TM	0.72	59	VCR	0.85	42	VV	0.96	35	XLE	0.74	50
TMO	0.69	55	VDC	1.27	35	VVC	0.81	43	XLF	0.58	32
TRI	0.78	50	VDE	0.67	42	VYM	0.79	24	XLI	0.84	44
TRMK	0.66	45	VEU	0.72	36	VZ	0.80	48	XLK	0.73	39
TRP	0.77	44	VGK	0.76	36	WABC	0.80	65	XLP	1.25	44
TRV	0.71	59	VGT	0.94	42	WDFC	0.76	59	XLU	1.03	43
TSCDY	0.74	56	VHT	1.08	38	WGL	0.92	45	XLV	1.11	47
TW	0.69	51	VIG	1.00	33	WIN	0.73	47	XLY	0.81	45
UDN	2.26	50	VIS	0.81	42	WPC	0.77	51	XPH	0.78	42
UNF	0.68	73	VO	0.75	31	WR	0.82	40	XRT	0.70	41
UNS	0.83	51	VOE	0.75	32	WRE	0.70	45	XSD	0.67	50
UPS	0.89	46	VPL	0.77	37	WSH	0.67	52	Y	0.72	34
UUP	2.27	58	VPU	1.00	37	WTM	0.70	47	ZMH	0.66	45
VB	0.74	39									

Figure 5.10D *Stocks and ETFs that held long / flat that pass the screen*

There are two reasons issues failed to pass the screen.

One is inadequate profit potential. The CAR25 is below the level that can provide a return that exceeds a risk-free alternative without exceeding the stated risk tolerance. These issues can be ignored—they will not be profitable using any model.

The second is history shorter than eight years. There are issues that pass the CAR25 screen but fail the 2000 day screen. Some of these are good candidates for trading, and you might want to use them. If you do, be rigorous in validating the system. Since most of their history is in a period when the broad market moved strongly in one direction, there is a greater chance a system trading them will fail in other market conditions.

Figure 5.10E lists a 50 issue subset that have the highest safe-f, highest CAR25, and seem to be relatively easy to model.

ADP	EWJ	K	RE	VPU
ATO	EWM	KMB	SJM	VTV
AZN	EWS	LG	SWX	VUG
AZO	GAS	MDY	SXT	VZ
BDX	GPC	MGLN	THI	WABC
BTI	HCN	NU	UPS	WGL
CEF	IVV	OEF	VDC	XLI
DEO	IWB	PEP	VGT	XLP
EE	IXJ	PJP	VHT	XLU
EWH	IYH	PTP	VIG	XLV

Figure 5.10E *List of issues that are good candidates for development*

Which Issues are "Best?"

We do not know yet, but we are narrowing the field. What we do know is that the issues that passed the screens and are listed in Figure 5.10 are best in terms of the first two goldilocks characteristics. They have high profit potential without excessive volatility.

To be profitable as components of a trading system, there must be identifiable patterns that precede the price changes. It is the model that has the logic and rules that identify patterns and generate buy and sell signals. We will not know how much of the potential can be captured until the data series is combined with a model to form a trading system.

Universal Objective Function

CAR25 is the compound annual rate of return at the 25th percentile of the cumulative distribution of profit.

CAR25 of the risk-normalized distribution of profit is as close to a universal objective function as I have found.

True, CAR25 is a single value. I warn about using single values as metrics of evaluation, and prefer to use as much of the data or distribution of the data as possible. But when ranking alternatives, particularly in automated search-and-selection procedures such as we will encounter in both indicator-based and machine-learning model development, a single-valued objective function is a near-requirement.

Given that the primary limitation on trading is risk of drawdown that exceeds our personal tolerance, normalizing trading results by using the position size that limits risk to the desired tolerance puts alternative results on equal basis. At that point, whether during development or in live trading, they can be can be compared by examination of the distribution of potential profit. CAR25 is the point on the CDF that is likely to be exceeded about 75 percent of the time. It is a conservative, but realistic, estimate of future performance.

That said, continue to examine the distribution of drawdown. Black swans live and hide in its tail above the 95th percentile.

Holding Longer

There are many reasons for holding positions longer than a few days. There may be restrictions that forbid or penalties that discourage selling a position earlier than some limit. You may have read or heard an anecdote where a large profit was made as a result of holding a position for a long time.

Large profits improve any trading system. But limiting losses is more critical than achieving gains. As holding periods increase, adverse price movements increase in proportion to the square root of the holding period, just from the random changes in prices. If a series of trades that hold 5 days has intra-trade drawdowns of, say, 4 percent, we can expect that a series of trades over the same data where the trades are held 20 days will have intra-trade drawdowns of 8 percent. If an error is made predicting whether a trade will be a winner or a loser, losers that are held 20 days will have losses double those of losers held 5 days.

The math is pretty clear—the sweet spot in terms of maximum profit for a specified level of risk is a holding period of few days. And until the holding period is very short, where transactional costs erode profits, shorter is better.

Nevertheless, you may ask, what are the implications of insisting on a longer holding period? Say one calendar month—21 trading days.

The CAR is limited by position size, which is limited by risk, which is limited by the inherent characteristics of a price series for a given trade accuracy and holding period. So far, we have been estimating CAR for a fixed risk tolerance. We can use the same simulation to test other settings. If the holding period must be 21 trading days, we can fix that variable and examine CAR versus risk.

Given a set of trades, or well defined potential trades, and a risk tolerance, safe-f is completely determined. Safe-f is the highest fractional position size that places the CDF of drawdown no higher than the 5% / 20% point defined by the risk tolerance statement.

Given a set of trades, or well defined potential trades, and a value of safe-f, the CDF of profit is completely determined. CAR25 is completely determined.

For SPY, using a risk tolerance of 5% / 20% / 2 years, 70% accuracy, 21 day holding period, based on 1/1/1999 through 1/1/2012, the safe-f fraction is 0.563 and CAR25 is 5.4%. The CDF of drawdown is shown in Figure 5.11.

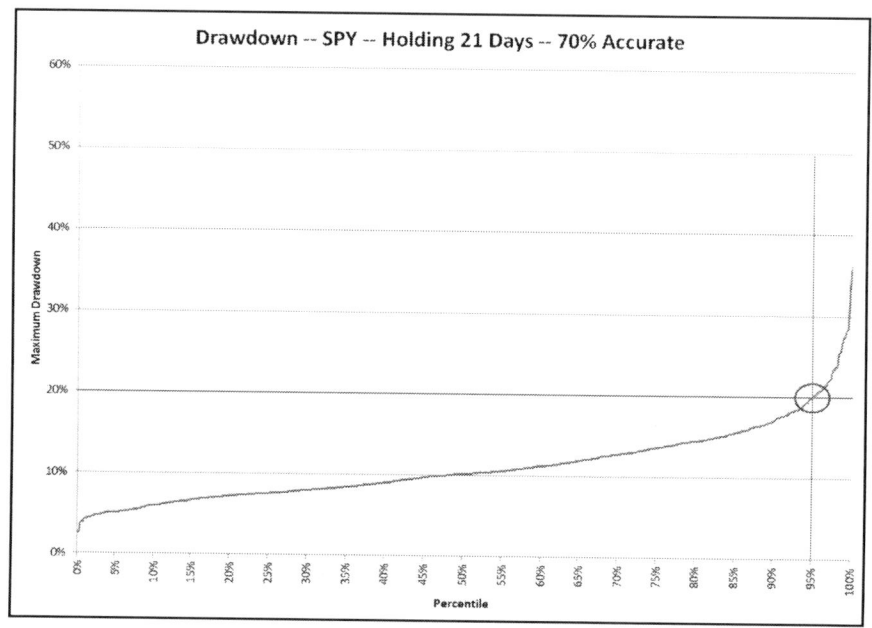

Figure 5.11 CDF of drawdown for SPY, 70% accuracy, holding 21 days

No other assumptions are necessary to produce the CDF of profit. It is shown in Figure 5.12. We can read CAR25 from the curve. It is 5.4%

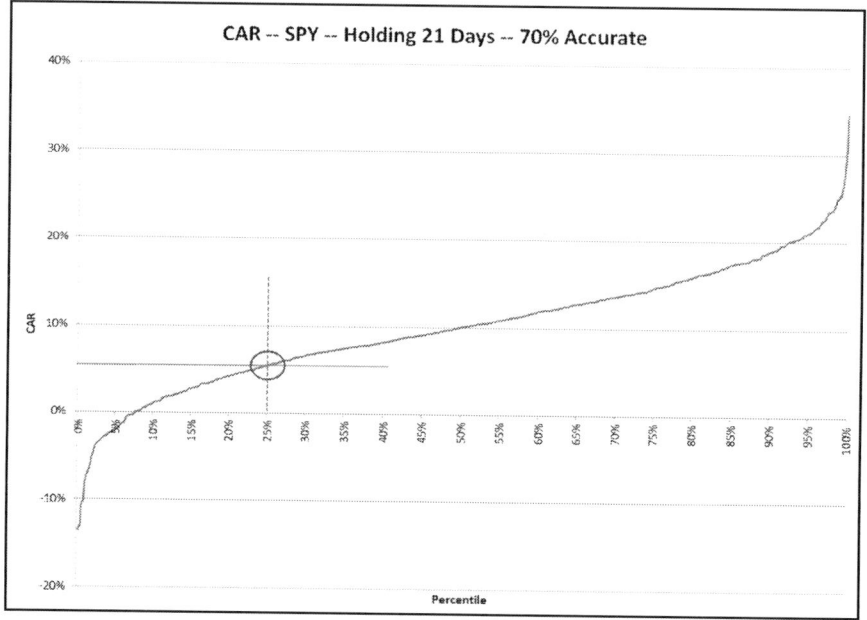

Figure 5.12 CDF of Compound Annual Rate of Return, 70%, 21 days

If we want to change the value of CAR25 without changing the trades, we must change the position size fraction. There is no other knob to turn. For a given set of trades, position size completely determines the position of the CDF. To increase CAR25 is to drag the entire CDF of profit upward, as illustrated in Figure 5.13. Fraction is increased from 0.563 to 1.000—take all trades with all available funds.

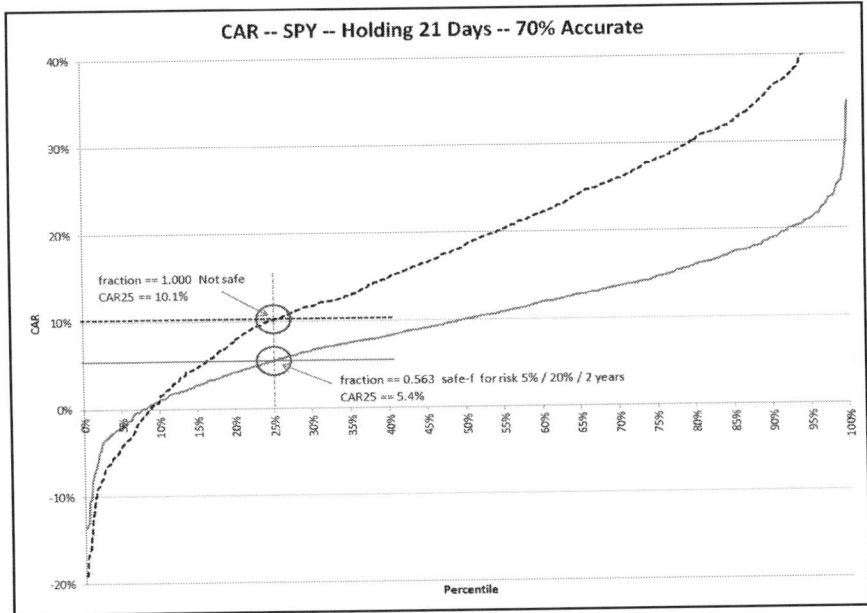

Figure 5.13 CDF of CAR, fraction increased to 1.000

Changing the fraction changes the position of the CDF of risk. Those two curves are linked together. Intended or not, changing one changes the other, as shown in Figure 5.14.

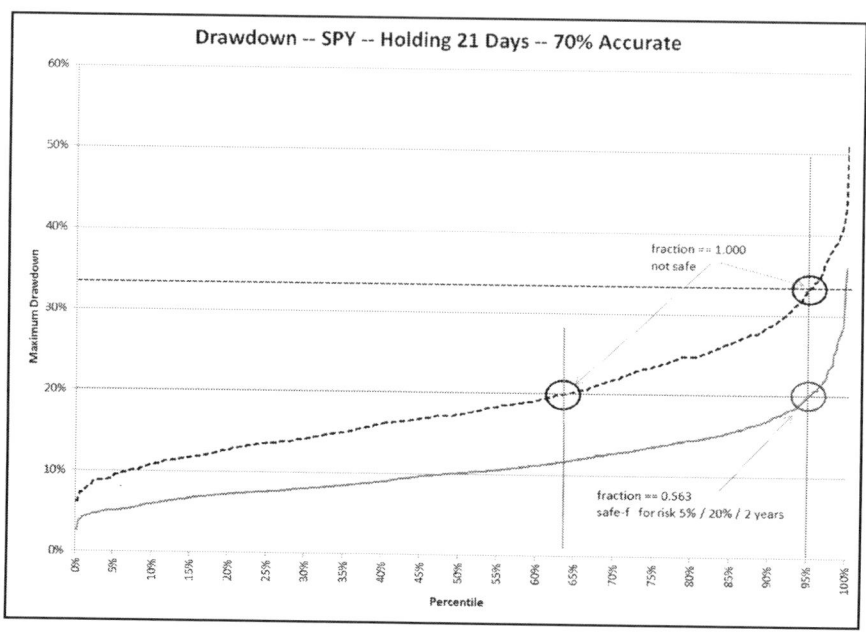

Figure 5.14 CDF of drawdown fraction = 1.000

Traded at full fraction, position size is no longer safe. Risk of drawdown at the 5% level (95th percentile) has increased from 20% to 34%. Seen another way, risk of 20% drawdown has increased from 5% to 37% (95th to 63rd percentile). These are represented by the two circles on the dotted line.

Potential CAR at full fraction is 10.1%, before application of a yet-to-be-developed model. Increasing CAR further requires either increasing position size above 1.00—by using margin, trading an ETF with a beta greater than 1, or using options—or increasing accuracy of trades selected beyond 70%.

Accuracy at 90% increases CAR25 to 21.8 at safe-f with a fraction of 0.779. Accuracy at 95% increases CAR25 to 35.5 at safe-f of 1.000.

The task of predicting whether the price of SPY will be higher or lower one month ahead with 70 percent accuracy, or higher, is daunting. It has left the realm of technical analysis. I know of no indicators that accurate that far in the future.

We might have expected that all we needed to do was increase our tolerance limit and we would see profit potential rise. At ordinary levels of accuracy, that is not what we found. Accuracy of 60% holding 21 days did not show profit potential at any level of risk. Profit potential at 70% accuracy is marginal. Profit potential begins to rise in step with willingness to accept additional risk at 80% accuracy, and even those values are not worth the risk. **Increasing risk tolerance for a poor system does not increase profit—it only increases risk and drawdown.**

My conclusion is that holding through 21 days is too difficult, or too risky, or insufficiently profitable. 21 days is too long a holding period.

In my opinion, and supported by the math, it appears that holding positions in SPY for 21 days with reasonable risk and CAR greater than risk-free bank interest is not achievable. No matter how much we wish it would be.

Long and Short

SPY and SH both passed screens, as did DIA and DOG, UUP and UDN. These pairs are ETF derivatives of the same underlying, SP 500, DJIA, and US dollar, respectively. One of the pair has a positive beta, the other negative. They make good candidates for pairs of systems that will never both have positions. They can share an account, using the same ballast funds. Together the pair has a position two-thirds of the time, covering periods of both rising and falling prices in the underlying.

When it comes time to develop models, there are two approaches. One uses a single model of the underlying, taking positions in the positive or negative derivative according to the signals. The second uses two models—one for each of the ETFs themselves. Try both ways.

Note that while neither QQQ nor IWM passed the screens, both because of excessive volatility, their inverses PSQ and RWM did pass. These may give additional opportunities to develop systems that profit from falling prices through holding long positions.

Portfolios

The ideas on which portfolios are based are:
- diversification.
- mean-variance optimization.
- rotate to whatever is rising in price.

According to modern portfolio theory (MPT), a carefully weighted combination of a small number of issues selected from a larger pool gives an opportunity to tune reward relative to risk. MPT uses the recent performance of each issue, calculating gain per unit of time, variance in price per unit of time, and correlation of price movement with other issues in the pool as indicators. There is no buy and sell logic—MPT is the model. In my opinion, it suffers some drawbacks:
- It does not distinguish the unique characteristics of each issue. All issues in the pool are evaluated using the same criteria and the same periodicity. While I consider this a flaw in design, I

would also criticize an MPT-like model that applied individual rules because of the increase in the number of variables and likelihood of overfitting.
- It assumes correlations among issues are stationary. Not only are they not stationary, the diversity breaks down in precisely the conditions when it is most needed—a crisis.[1] Unless the issues are explicit inverses and can never be positively correlated, correlations tend to rise during crises. Prices of all issues fall together. As traders reduce exposure, issues to be sold are chosen for their liquidity rather than based on patterns in the data.
- Issues included in the pool are selected for subjective and quasi-statistical reasons, not including the risk-normalized profit potential inherent in the data as we have been discussing it.
- MPT assumes the distribution of prices is Normal. It is not.
- MPT uses standard deviation of price movement as a metric of both risk and reward, and that is not appropriate. Risk comes from adverse price movements, while profits come from favorable price movements. Standard deviation treats all price movements as identical without distinguishing between those that are favorable versus unfavorable.
- Diversity is not universally desirable. In a phrase, diversity is for people who are not sure. A diverse holding produces a return that represents the average. Studies regularly report how few holdings are necessary for the total return to track a broad index.

My preference is shifting from portfolios to more focused systems. Each system taking a single direction (long/flat or short/flat, not both long and short in the same model) in a single issue. Select a few issues that have attractive risk and profit potential based on your criteria, develop a system for each, then manage trading of each separately. Allocate most of your trading account to the system that is performing best.

The sweet spot is a few days and being accurate in entry and exit. This is much easier to achieve with a system designed for one issue than for many issues simultaneously.

If you must have a rotational portfolio, consider creating the pool not as a group of issues, rather as a group of systems. The dynamic position sizing techniques described in Chapter 9 can be modified to select the current best among several systems. All nine of the S&P Sector ETFs (XLx) passed the screens—they are a good place to begin. (Well, eight of the nine passed. I included XLF for completeness.) And eleven country ETFs (EWx) passed.

---

[1] http://www.businessinsider.com/troublesome-commonality-during-recent-market-volatility-2014-12

Summary

Every person has a quantifiable risk tolerance.

All data series are not equally tradable. Good series have enough variability to provide profit, but not so much variability that risk is too high.

Data series can be screened in advance of their use for system development.

No matter what model will eventually be developed, high system performance requires limiting risk, high accuracy in trade selection, and short holding periods.

Given a set of trades, or a well defined procedure for selecting trades from a data series, future performance can be estimated.

The combination of trading performance and risk tolerance determines an upper limit to the position size that can be safely used.

Trading results or forecasts can be directly compared after being normalized for risk using the maximum safe fraction position size.

CAR25 is a near-universal objective function.

The sweet spot for trading any series that can provide profit in excess of risk-free bank interest is being accurate in trade selection and holding only a few days.

Until we have a model that generates specific buy and sell signals and produces a set of specific trades, the accuracy and holding period are sufficient to create a well defined set of potential trades. Whenever there is a specific set of trades, we will use those, and the same analysis will hold.

This analysis is not related to the model. It is inherent in the data.

We can use this information and techniques described in this chapter to select issues, but we still need to find a model—logic, rules, and parameters—that achieve that accuracy, for that holding period, for that data series. The model could equally have the entry signal come from a mean reversion indicator, a trend indicator, seasonality, or a pattern.

We address that in the three model development chapters that follow.

Estimating Profit Potential — A Monte Carlo Simulation Program

For a given set of trades, risk, as measured by drawdown, depends on the sequence of trades.

The position size—the fraction of the dollar amount allocated to a system that is used to take a position for each of that system's trades—affects both equity growth and drawdown. Assuming the system has a positive expectation, increasing position size results in faster equity growth, a higher final equity balance, and higher drawdown. If the position size is too high, drawdown will cause bankruptcy and end trading. We want to estimate the highest position size—the largest fraction—that can be used while keeping drawdown within tolerable limits.

A Monte Carlo simulation will give that estimate.

The technique described in Chapter 2—monitoring and accumulating adverse price excursions—is used to compute the drawdown of a sequence of trades.

Drawdown can be recognized at three levels:
- intra-day
- intra-trade
- trade

Using daily price bars and marking to market at the close of every day, intra-trade drawdown is the level this program uses to determine safe-f.

The simulation is straight-forward:
1. State risk tolerance.
2. Choose a data series and date range.
3. State holding period and trading accuracy.
4. Create or import a "best estimate" set of trades.
5. Search for safe-f:
    A. Pick an initial estimate of the fraction.
    B. Generate many trade sequences.
    C. Compare estimated risk from the trades with risk tolerance from the statement.
    D. Adjust the fraction and repeat until the estimated risk matches the risk tolerance.

The program listed here generates the set of trades based on trading accuracy and holding period. Alternatively, a set of real or hypothetical trades could be imported.

Begin with a statement of risk tolerance. Say it is a limit of a 5% chance of a drawdown of equity greater than 20%, measured from highest equity to date, marked-to-market using daily closing prices, over the period of a 2 year forecast.

Choose the holding period, say 5 days. Specify a desired trading accuracy, say 65 percent.

The trade generation and trade-by-trade performance process is as follows:

For every possible entry day, note the entry price. Look into the future and note the exit price at the end of the holding period. Assign a label of either "gainer" or "loser" to the entry day.

If you are working with 10 years of daily data, there are 2520 possible entry days. Adjust for the boundary at the end of the test period. Either use 2515 entry days to ensure that every trade entered will be completed within the test data; or use all 2520 entry days, and allow the final 5 days to look into the subsequent period.

Divide the length of the forecast period by the length of the holding period, returning an integer. That result is the number of trades needed to cover the forecast period. You will need 100 5-day trades to cover the 504 days in two years.

Each trade sequence / equity curve will be a sequence of 100 trades, each trade drawn at random using "sampling with replacement" from the best estimate set.

For a system that is long or flat, a winning trade is one where the exit price is higher than the entry price—a "gainer."

Whenever you need a trade to add to the sequence, begin with a random choice of "gainer" or "loser" with "gainer" chosen 65% of the time. Given the resulting category, select any entry day at random. Determine the size of the trade by the fraction being used.

Generate many, say 1000, such trade sequences, each covering two years of long exposure. For each sequence, compute and remember the metrics—final equity, maximum drawdown, and whatever else is of interest. Sort by maximum drawdown and note the value at the 95th percentile. If it is about 20%, the fraction is safe-f. If it is not, adjust the fraction and repeat generating a new set of 1000 sequences.

When the fraction is correct so that the 95th percentile maximum drawdown matches the stated risk tolerance, use the final equity value from each sequence to construct the distribution of final equity. Report the values for the 25th, 50th, and 75th percentile.

Program Listing

Listing 5.1. Python code for the simulator that computes risk, determines maximum safe position size, and estimates profit potential.

```
"""
ComputeRiskLong.py

A Python program that implements the
Monte Carlo simulation analysis described
in Chapter 5 of the book
"Quantitative Technical Analysis"
written by Dr. Howard Bandy
and published by Blue Owl Press, Inc.

Copyright © 2014 Howard Bandy

Author: Howard Bandy
Blue Owl Press, Inc.
www.BlueOwlPress.com

Trimmed down version that only looks
at marked to market closing price.

This program is intended to be an educational tool.
It has not been reviewed.
It is not guaranteed to be error free.
Use of any kind by any person or organization
is with the understanding that the program is as is,
including any and all of its faults.
It is provided without warranty of any kind.
No support for this program will be provided.
It is not trading advice.

The programming is intended to be clear,
but not necessarily efficient.
It was developed using Python version 2.7.

Be careful of line wrap and quotation marks.

There are several options within the program
that allow various information to be saved to
disc for further analysis, formatting, or display.
Using them requires understanding of the program,
modifications to the program's control parameters,
and removal of comment marks.

Permission to use, copy, and share is granted.

Please include author credits with any distribution.
"""

from datetime import datetime
import math
import matplotlib.pyplot as plt
import numpy as np
import pandas as pd
from pandas.io.data import DataReader
import random
from scipy import stats
```

Issue Selection

```python
import time

accuracy_tolerance = 0.005

# ------------------------
#   User sets parameter values here
#   Scalars, unless otherwise noted

issue = 'spy'
data_source = 'yahoo'
start_date = datetime(1999,1,1)
end_date = datetime(2012,1,1)

hold_days = 5
system_accuracy = .75
DD95_limit = 0.20
initial_equity = 100000.0
fraction = 1.00
forecast_horizon = 504  #  trading days
number_forecasts = 10   # Number of simulated forecasts

print '\n\nNew simulation run '
print '  Testing profit potential for Long positions\n '
print 'Issue:              ' + issue
print 'Dates:              ' + start_date.strftime('%d %b %Y')
print ' to:                ' + end_date.strftime('%d %b %Y')
print 'Hold Days:              %i ' % hold_days
print 'System Accuracy:        %.2f ' % system_accuracy
print 'DD 95 limit:            %.2f ' % DD95_limit
print 'Forecast Horizon:       %i ' % forecast_horizon
print 'Number Forecasts:       %i ' % number_forecasts
print 'Initial Equity:         %i ' % initial_equity

# ------------------------
#  Variables used for simulation

qt = DataReader(issue, data_source, start_date, end_date)
#print qt.shape
#print qt.head()

nrows = qt.shape[0]
print 'Number Rows:            %d ' % nrows

qtC = qt.Close

number_trades = forecast_horizon / hold_days
number_days = number_trades*hold_days
print 'Number Days:            %i ' % number_days
print 'Number Trades:          %d ' % number_trades

al = number_days+1
#   These arrays are the number of days in the forecast
account_balance = np.zeros(al)      # account balance

pltx = np.zeros(al)
plty = np.zeros(al)

max_IT_DD = np.zeros(al)      # Maximum Intra-Trade drawdown
max_IT_Eq = np.zeros(al)      # Maximum Intra-Trade equity

#   These arrays are the number of simulation runs
# Max intra-trade drawdown
```

```python
FC_max_IT_DD = np.zeros(number_forecasts)
# Trade equity (TWR)
FC_tr_eq = np.zeros(number_forecasts)

# ------------------------
#   Set up gainer and loser lists
gainer = np.zeros(nrows)
loser = np.zeros(nrows)
i_gainer = 0
i_loser = 0

for i in range(0,nrows-hold_days):
    if (qtC[i+hold_days]>qtC[i]):
        gainer[i_gainer] = i
        i_gainer = i_gainer + 1
    else:
        loser[i_loser] = i
        i_loser = i_loser + 1
number_gainers = i_gainer
number_losers = i_loser

print 'Number Gainers:       %d ' % number_gainers
print 'Number Losers:        %d ' % number_losers

########################################################
#   Solve for fraction
fraction = 1.00
done = False

while not done:
    done = True
    print 'Using fraction: %.3f ' % fraction,
    # ----------------------------
    #    Beginning a new forecast run
    for i_forecast in range(number_forecasts):
    #    Initialize for trade sequence
        i_day = 0       # i_day counts to end of forecast
        # Daily arrays, so running history can be plotted
        # Starting account balance
        account_balance[0] = initial_equity
        # Maximum intra-trade equity
        max_IT_Eq[0] = account_balance[0]
        max_IT_DD[0] = 0

        #   for each trade
        for i_trade in range(0,number_trades):
            #   Select the trade and retrieve its index
            #   into the price array
            #   gainer or loser?
            #   Uniform for win/loss
            gainer_loser_random = np.random.random()
            #   pick a trade accordingly
            #   for long positions, test is "<"
            #   for short positions, test is ">"
            if gainer_loser_random < system_accuracy:
                #  choose a gaining trade
                gainer_index = np.random.
                        random_integers(0,number_gainers)
                entry_index = gainer[gainer_index]
            else:
                #  choose a losing trade
```

Issue Selection

```
            loser_index = np.random.
                    random_integers(0,number_losers)
            entry_index = loser[loser_index]

        #  Process the trade, day by day
        for i_day_in_trade in range(0,hold_days+1):
            if i_day_in_trade==0:
                #  Things that happen immediately
                #  after the close of the signal day
                #  Initialize for the trade
                buy_price = qtC[entry_index]
                number_shares = account_balance[i_day] * \
                            fraction / buy_price
                share_dollars = number_shares * buy_price
                cash = account_balance[i_day] - \
                        share_dollars
            else:
                #  Things that change during a
                #  day the trade is held
                i_day = i_day + 1
                j = entry_index + i_day_in_trade
                #  Drawdown for the trade
                profit = number_shares * (qtC[j]
                                    - buy_price)
                MTM_equity = cash + share_dollars + profit
                IT_DD = (max_IT_Eq[i_day-1] - MTM_equity) \
                        / max_IT_Eq[i_day-1]
                max_IT_DD[i_day] = max(max_IT_DD[i_day-1], \
                        IT_DD)
                max_IT_Eq[i_day] = max(max_IT_Eq[i_day-1], \
                        MTM_equity)
                account_balance[i_day] = MTM_equity
            if i_day_in_trade==hold_days:
                #   Exit at the close
                sell_price = qtC[j]
                #  Check for end of forecast
                if i_day >= number_days:
                    FC_max_IT_DD[i_forecast] =
                                max_IT_DD[i_day]
                    FC_tr_eq[i_forecast] = MTM_equity

    #  All the forecasts have been run
    #  Find the drawdown at the 95th percentile
    DD_95 = stats.scoreatpercentile(FC_max_IT_DD,95)
    print '   DD95: %.3f ' % DD_95
    if (abs(DD95_limit - DD_95) < accuracy_tolerance):
        #  Close enough
        done = True
    else:
        #  Adjust fraction and make a new set of forecasts
        fraction = fraction * DD95_limit / DD_95
        done = False

#  Report
#IT_DD_25 = stats.scoreatpercentile(FC_max_IT_DD,25)
#IT_DD_50 = stats.scoreatpercentile(FC_max_IT_DD,50)
IT_DD_95 = stats.scoreatpercentile(FC_max_IT_DD,95)
print 'DD95: %.3f ' % IT_DD_95,

years_in_forecast = forecast_horizon / 252.0

TWR_25 = stats.scoreatpercentile(FC_tr_eq,25)
```

```
        CAR_25 = 100*(((TWR_25/initial_equity) ** (1.0/
                years_in_forecast))-1.0)
        TWR_50 = stats.scoreatpercentile(FC_tr_eq,50)
        CAR_50 = 100*(((TWR_50/initial_equity) ** (1.0/
                years_in_forecast))-1.0)
        TWR_75 = stats.scoreatpercentile(FC_tr_eq,75)
        CAR_75 = 100*(((TWR_75/initial_equity) ** (1.0/
                years_in_forecast))-1.0)

        print 'CAR25: %.2f ' % CAR_25,
        print 'CAR50: %.2f ' % CAR_50,
        print 'CAR75: %.2f ' % CAR_75

        #  Save equity curve to disc
        #np.savetxt('account_balance.csv', account_balance,
                delimiter=',')

        #  Save CDF data to disc
        #np.savetxt('FC_maxIT_DD.csv', FC_max_IT_DD, delimiter=',')
        #np.savetxt('FCTr.csv', FC_tr_eq, delimiter=',')

        #  Plot maximum drawdown
        #for i in range(al):
        #    pltx[i] = i
        #    plty[i] = max_IT_DD[i]
        #
        #plt.plot(pltx,plty)

        #  /////  end  /////
```

Listing 5.1. Python code for the simulator that computes risk, determines maximum safe position size, and estimates profit potential.

Chapter 6
Model Development Preliminaries

Introduction

There are two approaches to trading system development. In a brief phrase, they can be described as:
- Compute an indicator, then observe price changes that follow.
- Observe a notable price change, then identify patterns that precede.

As a shorthand, they will be referred to as *indicator-based* and *machine learning*, respectively.

This is the first of three chapters devoted to the development and selection of the model. We begin with an overview, outlining general considerations for the model development process—those things that must always be taken into account. It is followed by a chapter describing indicator-based model development using a trading system development platform, using AmiBroker. Then by a chapter that discusses machine learning model development using Python and associated libraries.

The purpose of the model is to accept time series data that represent trades, process that data searching for patterns that precede profitable trading opportunities, learn those patterns, and issue orders to buy, sell, short, and cover in response to live real-time or end-of-day data.

The quality of the model is judged by its usefulness in live trading. Everything done in model development is in preparation for live trading.

The diagram in Figure 6.1 shows the common data preparation tasks, the two paths of model development, and the common transition to trading.

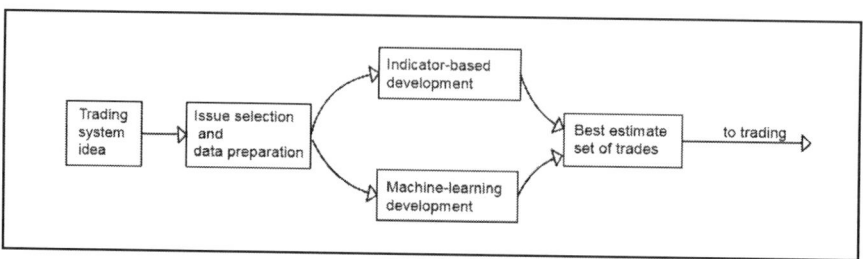

Figure 6.1 Alternative development paths

The two approaches share a considerable amount.
- They both fit naturally into the development flowchart shown in Chapter 1, Figure 1.1.
- The trading system idea and issue selection come first.
- Both rely on the general principles of learning—observe past data, generalize, test using unseen data.
- Both use technical analysis indicators as major components of their model.
- Both produce a model that accepts data and, using the rules, generates signals.
- Both require an iterative process of testing and modification, followed by validation, before the system is deemed finished.
- Both produce a *best estimate* set of trades that is the basis for determination of risk of drawdown, maximum safe position size, profit potential, and on-going monitoring of system health.

As seen from the perspective of trading management, there is no difference.

A Mining Analogy

We love to hear the tales of success—the lottery winner, trading champion, or lucky prospector. But we are all experts at deceiving ourselves—we seldom see the piles of losing tickets. (Daniel Kahneman[1] should be required reading for all aspiring traders.)

I think mining analogies fit fairly well. In the early days ordinary people picked up precious stones and gold nuggets. Individual prospectors using simple tools moved small amounts of dirt and found more treasure. Large companies funded multiple mining operations

---

1 Kahneman, Daniel, *Thinking, Fast and Slow*, Farrar, Straus, and Giroux, 2011.

(anticipating that not all would be profitable) moved large amounts of dirt and found still more.

These days, an individual prospector occasionally finds a gem or two. But most of us are either combing through tailings looking for small gains previously overlooked, or exploring at random hoping to get lucky.

Developing or discovering high quality models is difficult.

Setting aside insider information—or funding twenty entries into a trading competition knowing that at least nineteen will blow up—we have a very general, but very difficult, modeling problem to solve before becoming rich.

The rewards for success are high—financial independence and perhaps fame.

The barriers to entry are low—inexpensive computers, inexpensive (or even free) software, inexpensive or free data, multiple markets, plentiful brokers, low commissions.

The competition is well educated, has the best equipment, uses the best software, knows proprietary methods, and is trading other people's money.

The Past and the Future

In the pre-personal computer era, the models were primarily subjective application of expert knowledge—reading the tape and interpreting hand drawn charts. These were followed by computer models that compute technical indicators and issue buy and sell signals based on rules—AmiBroker programs, for example.

The modeling techniques are changing. In part because tools have improved and the techniques can change. In part because the problem has become more difficult, yesterday's tried-and-true systems are losing their edge, and the techniques must change.

The markets are nearly efficient. Everyone is looking for the same profitable trades. Every profitable trade removes some of the inefficiency the system was designed to find.

It appears to me that future models will increasingly be based on machine learning—mining of data in search of patterns using sophisticated mathematical techniques.

Two Processes to be Modeled

As we will see in later chapters, there are two modeling processes involved in trading system development.

The first is developing the trading system, as we are preparing for in this chapter and will explore in more detail in the two chapters that follow. It is developing the rules, identifying the patterns, analyzing the trades found in historical data, validating the system through walk forward testing or some similar confidence-building technique. During trading system development, the data is historical OHLCV, and the model is rules that identify patterns and generate buy and sell signals.

The second is managing trading. That is deciding whether the system is working or broken, and what size position is best for the next trade. The data for that phase is no longer OHLCV. It is trades. The model for that is rules determining the position size for the next trade. When the system is broken, position size will be zero.

It is important to recognize this early, so that development of the model used to signal trades does not interfere with the later model used to determine position size. If the position sizing technique is treated as stationary, or as fixed, or is included in the trading system code, there is no data left for the second model to use to control the trading management function.

For the discussion of the general aspects of trading system development in this chapter, and for the specifics in Chapters 7 and 8, all trades are a fixed size. Chapter 9 deals with calculation of position size.

Aspects of Model Development

There are several aspects of model development that must be addressed regardless of whether the models are indicator-based or machine learning. They exist in all models, and they are so inter-related that it is difficult to discuss any one independent of the others. Or to present them in a sequence that explains all individual techniques before using them in discussions of others. If a term does not seem to be completely clear when you first encounter it, keep reading. Everything comes together by the end of the chapter.

They include:
- Goal
- Pattern recognition
- Data
- Trend following
- Indicators
- Entries and exits
- Trading signals
- Model constraints
- Fitting and overfitting
- Objective function
- Backtesting
- Optimization

- Stationarity and synchronization
- Validation

Goal

The goal of the model—its sole purpose—is to identify profitable trades. Nothing else.

In the general sense, we are attempting to first design, then fit, a model to a set of data. The problem is complicated because there are a truly uncountable number of possible models, and a nearly uncountable number of data series. The signal is weak and in a noisy background, and the data is not stationary.

We definitely need to simplify. We began this book with discussion of quantifying our own risk tolerance, and for quantifying the risk inherent in a data series. These simplifications allow us to work with a limited pool of data series that we know to have reasonable risk and profit potential.

While the number of data series is reduced to a reasonable size, the number of possible models remains nearly uncountable.

There are a myriad of one-line rules, words of wisdom, and analogies that are intended to ease, simplify, and guide development of trading systems. Some relate to trading frequency or holding period, but are contradictory—"the early bird gets the worm" and "the second mouse gets the cheese." Some suggest careful thought, others to rely on instinct—"think it through" and "trust your instinct." Some deny progress, wanting to practice medicine without antibiotics or astronomy with Galileo's telescope. Others hide opportunity behind effort, suggesting simple solutions to avoid learning computer programming and complex mathematics.

Simplifying approaches, justifying and rationalizing as necessary, include:
- Restricting the model. Be long-only, trend-following, hold a long time, trade infrequently.
- Restricting the data. Trade only large cap stocks traded on US exchanges, or traditional mutual funds.
- Choosing techniques for their ease of application rather than appropriateness. Use only elementary functional relationships. Treat the data as being stationary.
- Choosing techniques because of their historical success. Buy breakouts to new highs.
- Accepting limitations that favor other participants. Be long-only, trade infrequently, or work within the universe of a single fund manager or broker.
- Restricting the modeling process. Evaluate a limited number of alternative models.

These simplifications may help limit the scope of the development problem, but they do not address the central questions:
- Are we finding the best models?
- Are the signals predictive?
- What performance can be reasonably expected in the future?
- Are metrics of system health available?

Throughout the remainder of this book, we will attempt to develop the best systems, setting aside arbitrary constraints.

Pattern Recognition

Signals to Patterns

Every series of trade prices is a combination of:
- Signals that are useful and potentially profitable.
- Noise that obscures the signal, is at best useless, and often contributes to losing trades.

Signal, in this sense, is the information component of the data. It will eventually be translated to buy and sell trading signals by the model. The signal portion of the data contains the patterns our model is designed to recognize. The model performs a pattern recognition operation as it searches for patterns that will become profitable trading signals.

Sea of Noise

As seen by our model, everything that is not signal is noise—even if it contains profitable signals that could be identified by some other model.

If it is easy to pick the signals out of the surrounding noise, we say there is a high signal-to-noise ratio. As either the distinctiveness of the signal decreases or the amount of noise increases, the signal-to-noise ratio drops, the model identifies fewer signal patterns or identifies them less accurately, risk increases, and profitability drops.

Selection of rules and adjustment of parameters is done by a trial and error process fitting the model to a period of data. The stronger the signal-to-noise ratio, the easier it is to identify the patterns, and the more profitable the trades.

Our development goal is to create a model that identifies patterns that precede profitable trading opportunities. We are looking for non-stationary, weak signals in a noisy background. Nate Silver describes it well.[2]

---

2   Silver, Nate, *The Signal and the Noise*, Penguin Press, 2012.

Data

Bar Types

Data bars represent the prices at which the issue traded during some period of time (timed bars) or for some number of trades (tick bars). Timed bars are the kind we are most familiar with. They always have one or more times associated with them. Tick bars do not necessarily. Timed bars fall into two categories—daily (or longer) and intra-day.

Daily Bars

When daily data, often described as end-of-day data, is being used, one bar represents the trades made for an entire day. The definition of the day might be the period an exchange is open or it might be a 24 hour day.

A daily data bar typically has four prices—open, high, low, and close. The open price—the price listed in the historical data as Open—is a price in some way representing the first trade of the day. That might mean it is the actual first trade, or it might be the price established by an organization such as an exchange or clearing house to be treated as the opening price. If the issue is heavily traded, the open price is representative of the price at the time associated with the open. If the issue is lightly traded, the open price is still the price of the first trade of the day, but not necessarily at the time listed to be the open.

Similarly, the close is a price that in some way represents the last trade of the day. It might be the price of the actual last trade, or some agreed-upon closing or settlement price.

High and low are the highest and lowest prices of the day. Without additional information, it is not possible to associate either high or low with a specific time, or even to determine which occurred first.

Daily bars sometimes have fields for additional information such as volume, open interest, and/or distributions such as dividends.

Multi-day bars, including weekly and monthly bars, are similar to daily bars, but cover a longer period of time.

As suggested by being called end-of-day data, daily bars are usually prepared some time after the close of the period. In the evening for daily bars, on weekends for weekly bars.

The trading system development platform recognizes daily bars as distinct data records with date and time fields. When historical daily data is downloaded for use in system development, it is already in the format the platform expects.

When the platform is collecting data from a live data feed during the trading day, each trade or tick is assumed to be the final or closing trade for that bar. Additional data belonging to the same bar updates the close, and perhaps the high or low. It is the responsibility of the platform to read the time stamp of each data value, compare that with the computer's real-time clock, and start a new bar at the correct time.

If the daily bar represents only a portion of the 24 hour day, there might be changes in price during the period that is not immediately reported. Those changes are reflected in the opening price of the next bar and might create a price gap.

Some daily data has fewer fields. It might be because the vendor does not distribute some fields, such as omitting the open. Or it might be because the issue has a limited number of price points per day, such as traditional mutual funds. Some fields might be updated after a delay, such as the volume and open interest fields for commodities that do not have continuous clearing.

Intra-day Bars

Intra-day bars, bars that represent a time period or trading volume less than a full trading day, have some of the same fields as daily bars. Typically date, time, open, high, low, close, and volume. Some data vendors supply data preformatted into fixed length intra-day bars, such as one-minute or five-minute bars. If you are considering using intra-day bars, be certain the data vendor supplies historical data in such a way that you can prepare bars with the lengths you want. One-minute bars are a typical common denominator, allowing the platform to consolidate them into bars of any number of minutes.

If the system being developed uses intra-day bars, we can assume that system will be traded by people who are monitoring the market throughout the trading day. Intra-day bars seldom have large price gaps from the close of one bar to the open of the next bar.

Tick bars are typically created on-the-fly by the platform as it receives prices from individual trades. Tick bars are usually very short duration intra-day bars, minutes or seconds long. They are outside the scope of this text.

Trend Following

No matter which entry technique is used, no matter which patterns are found to be predictive, the trades sought are always trend following. To be profitable, the price at which the position is sold must be higher than the price at which it is bought. Every long position must trend up from entry to exit. Every short position must trend down from entry to exit.

Indicators

Indicators can be based on anything—price, volume, patterns, calendar, multiple time frames, auxiliary data, diffusion indexes. Indicators are most useful when they have significant events, such as crossings or bottoms, at about the same frequency as the trades we hope to identify.

Filters are similar to indicators in most aspects, but change state less frequently.

Ideal Indicator

Assume we want to predict extreme oversold, enter at a near-bottom in anticipation of a one percent price rise, and exit within two days. We will take a 1% profit at our first opportunity, exiting market-on-close of the second day if the profit target has not been met.

Entry is based on an indicator that oscillates with about the same frequency as the trades we are looking for. At this level of activity, all indicators (z-score, RSI, stochastic, %B, detrended oscillator, etc.) are interchangeable. OK, that is a slight over-generalization. But not by much, and it is pretty accurate for fast cycle indicators based on price. Techniques that relax the requirement that lookback periods for indicators be integers, such as the CustomRSI described in my Mean Reversion book, allow greater flexibility in tuning indicators to data. For this example, we will use the 2-period RSI.

In AmiBroker, the code is:

```
// OnePercentProfit.afl

RSI2 = RSI( 2 );
Buy = RSI2 < 36;

Sell = 0;
ProfitTarget = 1.0;
HoldDays = 2;
ApplyStop( stopTypeProfit, stopModePercent, ProfitTarget );
ApplyStop( stopTypeNBar, stopModeBars, HoldDays );
/////////////// end ////////////
```

Ideally, there would be a clear relationship between the value of an indicator, such as the RSI2, and the price change the day ahead. Figure 6.2 shows how it would look, where:

GainAhead = 100 * (Ref(C,1)-C) / C

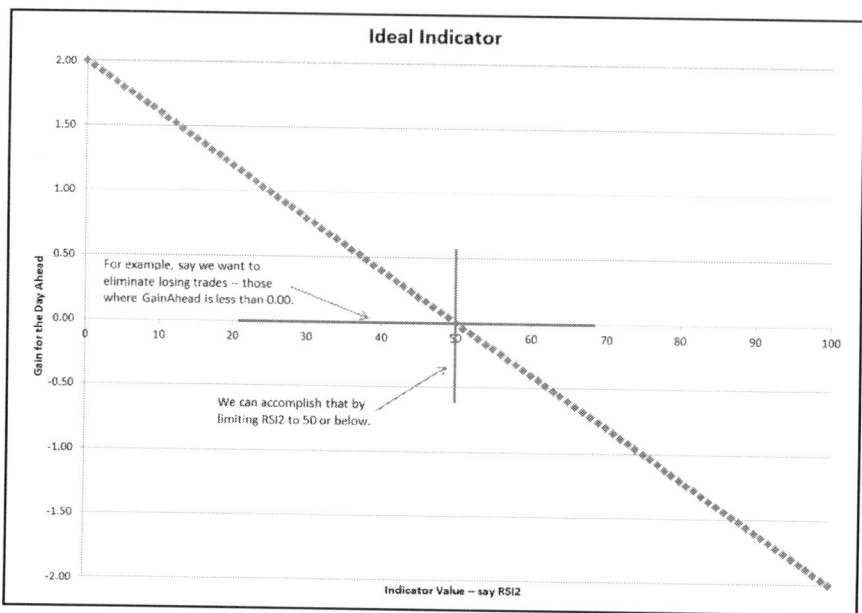

Figure 6.2 Ideal indicator

There is a perfect relationship between the indicator and the gain for the day ahead. If we want to eliminate all losing trades, those trades below the horizontal line, we can accomplish that by taking long positions only when RSI2 is below 50, those trades to the left of the vertical line.

Fuzzy Indicator

With just a little fuzziness in the data, as shown in Figure 6.3, the indicator is less accurate, and consequently less useful.

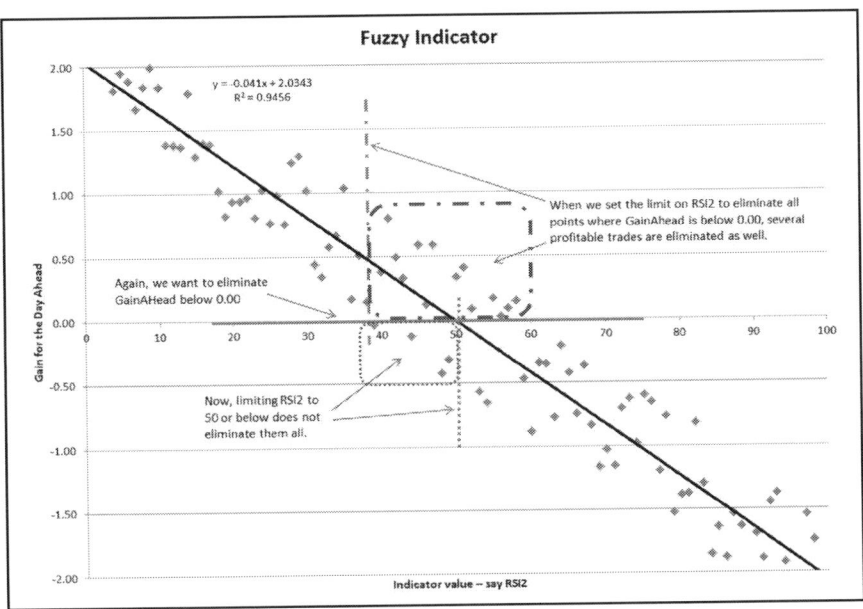

Figure 6.3 Slightly fuzzy indicator

The diagonal line shows the linear regression fit to the data points. R-squared is 0.94—a very good fit by most standards. Again, we want to eliminate losing trades using the same indicator. When we set RSI2 to 50, the dotted vertical line, the result is not perfect. Not all of the losing trades are eliminated, and some winning trades are eliminated. When the limit on RSI2 is changed so that it does eliminate all of the losing trades, the dashed vertical line at about 39, a side effect is that it also eliminates a large number of winning trades—those in the large dashed area.

Realistic Indicator

Figure 6.4 shows the relationship between GainAhead and the RSI2 indicator for the actual data for SPY for several years. When a trading system rule states we should hold a long position whenever RSI2 is less than 36, this is the data it is using.

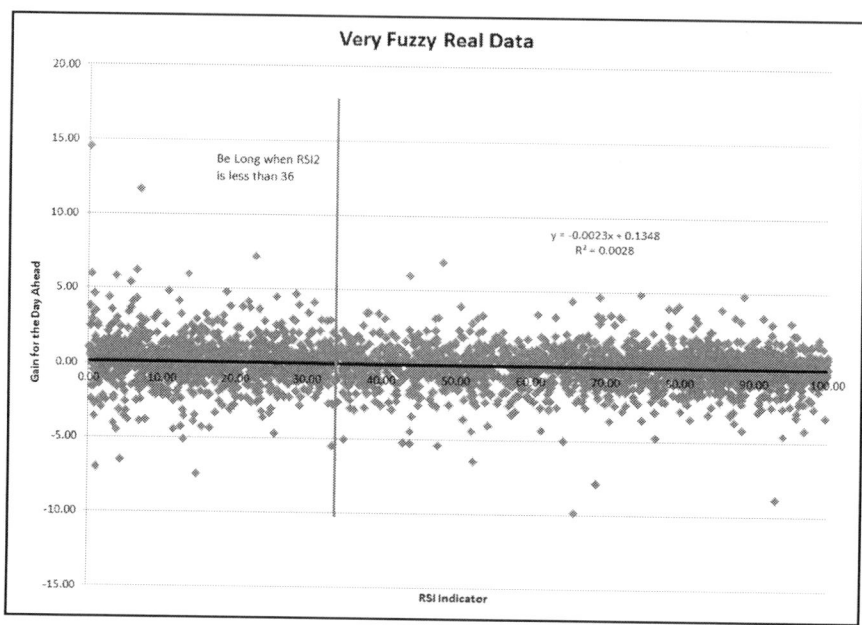

Figure 6.4 Very fuzzy real data

The trendline shows an r-squared of 0.0028. This is essentially zero and was in the round-off error for Figure 6.3. The vertical line is set at 36, the value determined during system development.

Looking at this chart, there is no apparent best place to set the vertical line that limits RSI2. The relationship is a little clearer when the 1146 pairs of RSI2 and GainAhead are sorted by RSI2 and combined into bins of 5 RSI units. As Figure 6.5 shows, there is a net positive gain of about 136 "gain ahead points" from being long when RSI2 is less than 36.

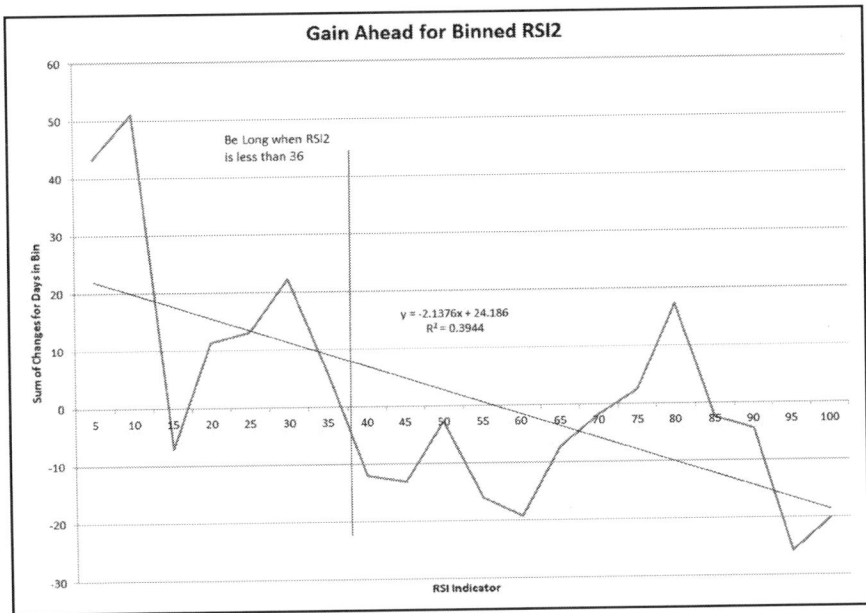

Figure 6.5 Gain ahead for binned RSI2

This illustrates several points:
- Based on traditional frequentist statistical analysis, waiting until the end of the data period, and treating the relationship as stationary, the correlation between RSI2 and GainAhead is indistinguishable from random.
- Even for a relationship between indicator and profit that is known to be tradable, there is remarkably little "edge."
- Anything we can do to improve the relationship will be immensely profitable.

Entries and Exits

Perfect Bottoms and Tops

My preference is for trades that occur frequently and hold one to three days. Yours may be for something different, such as the best five days in every month. Whatever it is, a useful development practice is to intentionally look into the future to:
1. Identify the best entry point.
2. Identify the best exit point.
3. Evaluate the risk.
4. Evaluate the profit.
5. Explore patterns that precede entry and exit.
6. Analyze results when either the entry or exit is not perfect.

The classical lookahead indicator is ZigZag. It identifies tops and bottoms perfectly. The pseudocode syntax is:

z = zigzag(p,n)

where:

p is the price series, such as the Close,

n is the minimum percentage between successive tops and bottoms,

z is the new series where the interpolated zigzag prices are stored.

Figure 6.6 shows a 2% zigzag of closing prices of SPY for a recent period.

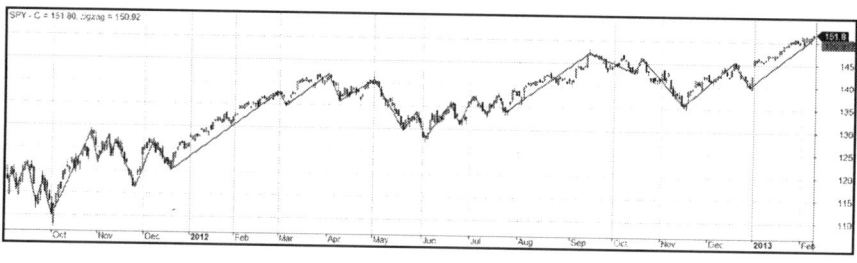

Figure 6.6 2% zigzag of SPY

The zigzag function has done the hard work. Determining the ideal day to buy is now easy. Look for a day where the value of z is lower than both the preceding and following day. If day-by-day bars are indexed by a variable, i, the ideal bottoms are found using logic in a loop that processes all bars.

Bottom[0] = 0

Bottom[BarCount-1] = 0

For (i=1; i<BarCount-1;i++)

Bottom[i] = z[i]<z[i-1] and z[i]<z[i+1]

For those platforms that have array functions, such as AmiBroker, an alternative formula in a single statement that replaces the entire loop is:

Bottom = z<Ref(z,-1) and z<Ref(z,1)

(The numeric value in the Ref statement specifies the number of days or bars in the future.)

In either case, Bottom is an array that has a value of True (1, for most platforms) for those bars that are lows and a value of False (0) for all others. Figure 6.7 shows the bottoms, marked with impulse signals.

Model Development—Preliminaries

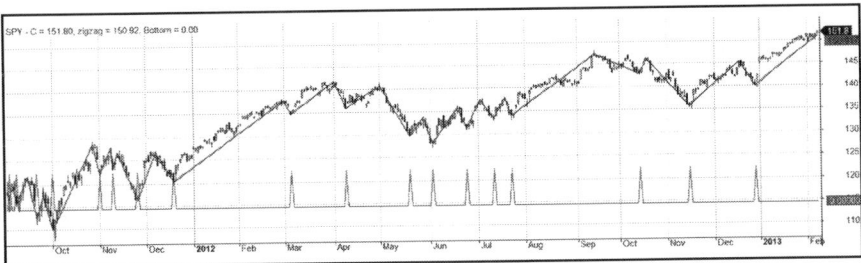

Figure 6.7 Bottoms identified

If you want to analyze perfect entries, buy at the close of bars where Bottom is True.

   Buy = Bottom

Tops can similarly be identified:

   Top = z>Ref(z,-1) and z>Ref(z,1)

Exiting at the top creates perfect trades:

   Sell = Top

Every trade, both long and short (if shorts are taken), will have a gain of at least 2%, and will have intra-trade drawdown (based on closing prices) no greater than 2%. These trades can be exported from the trading system development platform, imported into Excel, and analyzed using the techniques described in my Modeling book.[3] If you are working in Python, the entire process can be done in a single program. The outline of the analysis is:
1. Identify trades. Using daily prices:
   A. compute zigzag or some other indicator of your choice
   B. identify entry
   C. identify exit
   D. identify trade and store it in an array
2. Analyze performance. Using the array of trades, perform Monte Carlo analysis to:
   A. assess risk
   B. normalize for risk
   C. determine safe-f
   D. estimate profit, including CAR25

This procedure defines an upper limit to profitability. It is also valuable in studying the price series and alternative rules. For example, if you want to analyze the effect of entering a day late, use the following rule. It specifies that the bottom occurred one day in the past:

   Buy = Ref(Bottom,-1)

---

[3] Bandy, Howard, *Modeling Trading System Performance*, Blue Owl Press, 2011.

You can use perfect entries together with other exits—profit targets or trailing exits. You can study stability and consistency of prices, indicators, and trades. Etc.

Trading Signals

Impulse Signals

Impulse signals mark transitions, such as the beginning or end of a trade. They arise from an event that occurs on a single bar—such as when an RSI indicator falls through a critical level. That event produces a signal on that bar, but none on the following bars until the RSI recovers above, then again falls through that level. The trade which that signal initiates begins with the one-bar impulse interpreted as a buy signal. The long position is held until the one-bar impulse interpreted as a sell signal occurs.

Using impulse signals, one *trade* is one data point—however many days that trade lasts.

State Signals

While impulse signals mark boundaries, state signals identify conditions—such as whether the position being held is long, flat, or short.

Figure 6.8 illustrates a multi-day trade with corresponding state and impulse signals.

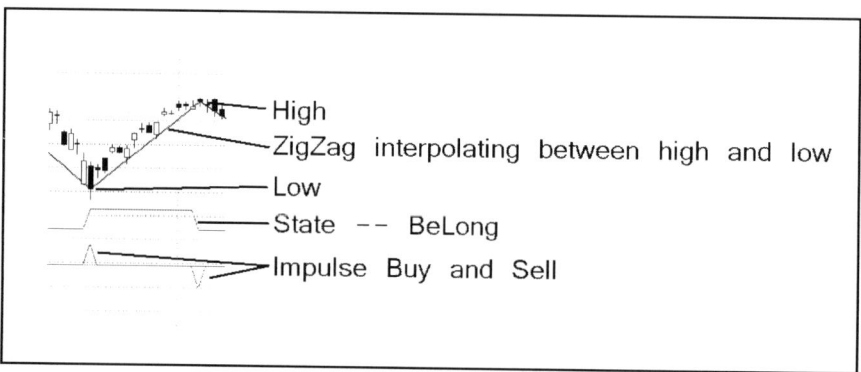

Figure 6.8 Multi-day trade with impulse and state signals

Changing from impulse signals to state signals changes the way we view trades—from some number of bars between the buy and sell impulses where no action or opportunity for trade management exists, to a series of single-day marked-to-market trades.

Model Development—Preliminaries

Using state signals, every day is evaluated on its own. With exception of trades that are open across the boundaries of the test period, performance results are identical.

Using state signals, marking to market daily, each *day* is one data point.

When a sequence of days that has the same state, the position is held over and appears as a single multi-day trade. With state signals, there will be as many trade-related data points as days the system holds an open position, perhaps minus one day at each end of the test period.

Your trading system development platform has functions that allow you to create state or impulse signals, as you wish, and to convert between them. Examples using AmiBroker follow.

```
//   Impulse entry and exit signals
buy  = Cross(36, RSI(2));
sell = Cross(RSI(2),36);

//   State entry and exit signals converted from impulse
entry = Cross(36, RSI(2));
exit  = Cross(RSI(2),36);
//   State equivalent
buy  = Flip(entry,exit);
sell = Flip(exit,entry);

//   Direct computation of state signals
buy  = RSI(2) < 36;
sell = RSI(2) >= 36;

///////////   end   ////////
```

Finer control

One advantage to state signals is providing opportunity for finer control of trade management throughout the trade. The health of the system is reevaluated every day at the same time it is marked-to-market. This is also the frequency that position size is readjusted using the dynamic position sizing technique used to calculate safe-f for the next trade. We will see this in more detail in Chapter 9.

Reduced distortion

Another advantage is greatly reducing distortion caused by trades that are open either at the beginning of a test period or at the end.

This can be important when there are relatively few trades in a test period. Assume, for example, a one year test period has, say, three trades, each about 20 days long:
1. One was entered 10 days before the one year period began and is still open as the period begins.
2. One entered and exited within the one year period.

3. One entered within the period, say 5 days before the end of the year, and still in a position as the period ended.

With impulse signals, only one of the trades can be completely evaluated—the one that is entered and exited within the period. For the other two, it is complex—perhaps impossible in the context of a practical trading system simulator—to determine whether there is a trade open upon entry or exit, and, if there is, how to account for the trade. There is one "complete" trade data point (for the 20-day trade) in the one year period. There are perhaps two "incomplete" data points which may or may not even show up.

With state signals, the 10 days of the partial trade at the beginning of the year, 20 days of the complete trade, and 5 days of the partial trade at the end of the year, are all "visible." There are 35 1-day trades.

Filters

Filters are similar to trade signals, but usually hold their state for longer periods of time. They are used to identify favorable and unfavorable periods, allowing or blocking trades accordingly. Filters are typically represented using state variables.

For example, advice is sometimes heard to "trade with the trend," where the trend is defined as upward and favorable to long positions when the current close is above its 200 day moving average, and downward when below. To use such a rule as a filter:
1. Compute the 200 day moving average.
2. Compare the current close with the average.
3. Set a variable according to the filter condition.
4. Combine the filter with the indicator.

If the signal to be in a long position is based on RSI being below 36, creating and using the filter takes the following form:

```
FilterPermit = C>MA(C,200);
Buy = RSI(2)<36 And FilterPermit;
```

Exit from a trade can be based on the indicator alone, such as:

```
Sell = RSI(2)>36:
```

Or either the indicator or the filter, such as:

```
Sell = RSI(2)>36 Or Not FilterPermit;
```

200 Day Moving Average Filter

Two short programs illustrate how filters are used, and compare use of the 200 day moving average as a trend filter with allowing all trades.

A simple program enters long positions when the short lookback period RSI drops through a critical level, and exits the position when the RSI rises through a slightly higher level.

Model Development—Preliminaries

The first version of the program requires that the current price be above the 200 day moving average. That is, no matter what the RSI value is, no long position will be entered unless the close is above the long term moving average. The AmiBroker code for it follows, along with a chart of the equity curve and a table of trade statistics.

```
// 200Day_MA_Filter.afl
//
// Testing whether the performance of a short term system
// is improved by using a 200 day moving average filter.

FilterMALength = 200;
RSILB = Optimize( "RSILB", 4, 2, 10, 1 );
RSIBuyLevel = Optimize( "RSBuyLevel", 23, 1, 90, 1 );
RSISellIncr = Optimize( "RSISellIncr", 1, 1, 90, 1 );
RSISellLevel = Min( RSIBuyLevel + RSISellIncr, 99 );

FilterPass = C >= MA( C, FilterMALength );

RSI2 = RSI( RSILB );

// Require permission from a moving average filter
Buy = Cross( RSIBuyLevel, RSI2 ) AND FilterPass;
Sell = Cross ( RSI2, RSISellLevel ) OR NOT FilterPass;

//////////////  end  /////////////////
```

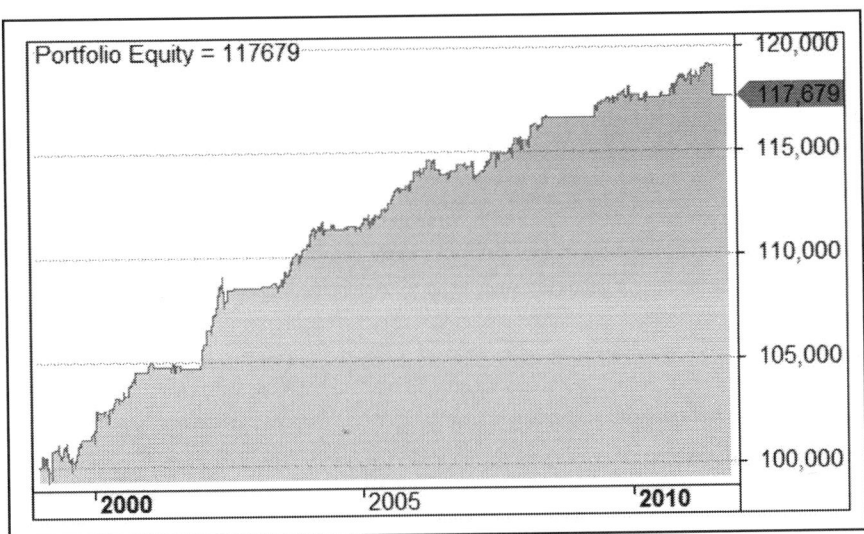

Figure 6.13 Equity curve when 200 day moving average filter is used

| Statistics | Charts | Trades | Formula | Settings | Symbols |

Statistics

	All trades	Long trades	Short trades
Initial capital	100000.00	100000.00	100000.00
Ending capital	117679.49	117679.49	100000.00
Net Profit	17679.49	17679.49	0.00
Net Profit %	17.68 %	17.68 %	0.00 %
Exposure %	1.82 %	1.82 %	0.00 %
Net Risk Adjusted Return %	973.78 %	973.78 %	N/A
Annual Return %	1.26 %	1.26 %	0.00 %
Risk Adjusted Return %	69.44 %	69.44 %	N/A
Total transaction costs	0.00	0.00	0.00
All trades	366	366 (100.00 %)	0 (0.00 %)
Avg. Profit/Loss	48.30	48.30	N/A
Avg. Profit/Loss %	0.48 %	0.48 %	N/A
Avg. Bars Held	2.80	2.80	N/A
Winners	261 (71.31 %)	261 (71.31 %)	0 (0.00 %)
Total Profit	36714.76	36714.76	0.00
Avg. Profit	140.67	140.67	N/A
Avg. Profit %	1.41 %	1.41 %	N/A
Avg. Bars Held	2.33	2.33	N/A
Max. Consecutive	23	23	0
Largest win	1020.38	1020.38	0.00
# bars in largest win	8	8	0
Losers	105 (28.69 %)	105 (28.69 %)	0 (0.00 %)
Total Loss	-19035.27	-19035.27	0.00
Avg. Loss	-181.29	-181.29	N/A
Avg. Loss %	-1.82 %	-1.82 %	N/A
Avg. Bars Held	3.97	3.97	N/A
Max. Consecutive	3	3	0
Largest loss	-797.16	-797.16	0.00
# bars in largest loss	3	3	0

Figure 6.14 Statistics when 200 day moving average filter is used

The second version of the program is identical to the first, but has the length of the moving average used for the filter set to 1 day. The filter requirement is that the current close is greater than or equal to the filtering moving average. Since the current close is always equal to its own 1 period moving average, the filter always allows the RSI value to govern entry. The AmiBroker code, equity curve, and statistics follow.

Model Development—Preliminaries

```
// 1Day_MA_Filter.afl
//
// Testing whether the performance of a short term system
// is improved by using a 200 day moving average filter.

FilterMALength = 1;
RSILB = Optimize( "RSILB", 4, 2, 10, 1 );
RSIBuyLevel = Optimize( "RSBuyLevel", 23, 1, 90, 1 );
RSISellIncr = Optimize( "RSISellIncr", 1, 1, 90, 1 );
RSISellLevel = Min( RSIBuyLevel + RSISellIncr, 99 );

FilterPass = C >= MA( C, FilterMALength );

RSI2 = RSI( RSILB );

//  Require permission from a moving average filter
Buy = Cross( RSIBuyLevel, RSI2 ) AND FilterPass;
Sell = Cross ( RSI2, RSISellLevel ) OR NOT FilterPass;

/////////////// end //////////////////
```

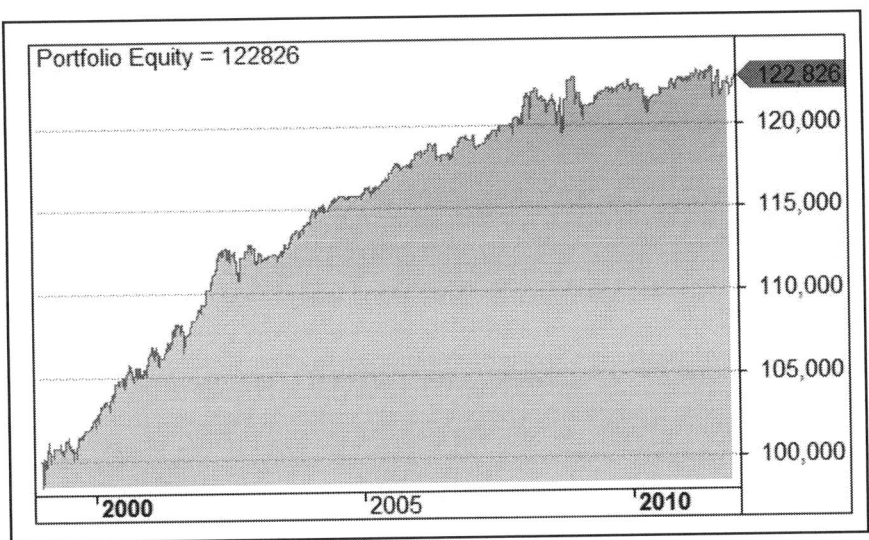

Figure 6.15 Equity curve when 200 day moving average filter is not used

| Statistics | Charts | Trades | Formula | Settings | Symbols |

Statistics	All trades	Long trades	Short trades
Initial capital	100000.00	100000.00	100000.00
Ending capital	122825.81	122825.81	100000.00
Net Profit	22825.81	22825.81	0.00
Net Profit %	22.83 %	22.83 %	0.00 %
Exposure %	3.27 %	3.27 %	0.00 %
Net Risk Adjusted Return %	697.29 %	697.29 %	N/A
Annual Return %	1.59 %	1.59 %	0.00 %
Risk Adjusted Return %	48.72 %	48.72 %	N/A
Total transaction costs	0.00	0.00	0.00
All trades	573	573 (100.00 %)	0 (0.00 %)
Avg. Profit/Loss	39.84	39.84	N/A
Avg. Profit/Loss %	0.40 %	0.40 %	N/A
Avg. Bars Held	3.13	3.13	N/A
Winners	404 (70.51 %)	404 (70.51 %)	0 (0.00 %)
Total Profit	59465.45	59465.45	0.00
Avg. Profit	147.19	147.19	N/A
Avg. Profit %	1.47 %	1.47 %	N/A
Avg. Bars Held	2.43	2.43	N/A
Max. Consecutive	20	20	0
Largest win	1083.91	1083.91	0.00
# bars in largest win	2	2	0
Losers	169 (29.49 %)	169 (29.49 %)	0 (0.00 %)
Total Loss	-36639.64	-36639.64	0.00
Avg. Loss	-216.80	-216.80	N/A
Avg. Loss %	-2.17 %	-2.17 %	N/A
Avg. Bars Held	4.82	4.82	N/A
Max. Consecutive	4	4	0
Largest loss	-1376.00	-1376.00	0.00
# bars in largest loss	7	7	0

Figure 6.16 Statistics when 200 day moving average filter is not used

Repainting

Beware of *repainting*. Repainting refers to the value of an indicator, impulse signal, or state changing as additional data is received. This commonly occurs in intra-day bars as real-time data is received tick-by-tick. Traders using intra-day bars during trading hours are aware that each newly received tick is interpreted by the platform as the final tick of whatever bar is currently being built. Consequently, each tick is processed as if it is the Close of the bar, and it may also be the High or the Low.

Whatever indicator, signal, and state calculations are made by the model are based on the then-current bar. This might cause a trading signal to be generated mid-bar. If the period the bar represents expires without further changes, that signal remains and should never change or be repainted. If subsequent data within the same bar causes a new calculation and a revised signal, it is the responsibility of either the model or the trader to recognize that and act accordingly.

Some techniques, such as Elliott wave, Fibonacci, and ZigZag, revise their critical points or levels or counts as additional data is received. That is, an indicator value or signal calculated after the close on Tuesday, using Tuesday's data, might be revised after the close on Wednesday, even though no data prior to Wednesday changed.

In my opinion, repainting of anything associated with any closed bar should never occur. The model should be designed so that it is immune to conditions that might cause repainting.

Order Placement

When you will process data, generate signals, and place orders depends on what length data bars are being used and what else is going on in your life.

Clearly, if you are using real-time intra-day data and monitoring the market throughout the trading day, you can trade at any time.

If you cannot follow the market during the trading day, are using daily data, download data and run the trading system in the evening, the soonest opportunity to trade will be the open of the next day. You can enter orders for execution at the open (described as next day's open, NDO), at the next day's close (as you might for mutual funds), or at a pre-computed intra-day price to be filled using limit or stop orders placed with your broker.

Anticipate Signals

My research and experience shows that if your system is accurate using end-of-day data to predict the direction of tomorrow's close relative to today's close, it is worthwhile entering the position at today's close. For issues listed on US exchanges, a large part—typically about one-third—of the close-to-close price change occurs in the overnight market. Do your own research to verify this is true for your system. If it is, there are several ways you can anticipate the signal in time to place your order at today's close using today's closing price.

If your job is trading, or your activities allow you to monitor the market near the close of trading, you have several options, even when using end-of-day data. You can:
- Use a real-time data feed. Have your system receive live data and interpret each tick as if it is the close. Check your system for signals a few minutes before the close, planning ahead by whatever amount of time you need to place your order to have it executed as one of the Market-on-Close orders.
- Wait for the official close, then trade in the extended trading period. That is, where applicable.

Even if you cannot monitor the market near the close, you can:
- Precompute the price at which your system will generate a signal. If your model uses simple mathematical calculations, such as simple moving averages, you can reverse the calculation and compute the price at which some condition will become true. If your model uses complex calculations, use one of the root finding methods to search for the price at which some condition will become true. See Chapter 7 for an example in AmiBroker code, and Chapter 8 for an example in Python code.

These same precomputation techniques can be used to calculate the price at which some intra-day signal would be generated, allowing you to place limit or stop orders with your broker for unattended intra-day execution.

Model Constraints

Much of the discussion among traders focuses on the definition of the pattern that signals the trades. People describe themselves, or their technique through themselves, as being trend following, mean reverting, seasonal, or pattern traders. What they are describing is the pattern they are using to enter trades. To my thinking, we can develop better systems if we relax our insistence that entries conform to particular categories or traditions.

Comparison of Two Moving Average Systems

Two developers are discussing the design of a trading system based on the cross of two moving averages. They agree to test using SPY as the data series, 1/1/1999 through 1/1/2012. The initial balance is $100,000. All trades are fixed size of $10,000. There is no position sizing and no compounding.

One insists that long positions should be taken when the faster moving average (that is, the one with the shorter length) rises up through the slower moving average, stating that is the "proper" trend following technique.

His program is MA_Cross_Restricted.afl. The model has two parameters—the lengths of the two moving averages. As the AmiBroker Cross function works, an impulse value of True (1) is generated when the first series (MA1) crosses up through the second series (MA2). To ensure that the shorter - longer length relationship is maintained, the longer length is computed by adding an increment to the shorter length. The range of lengths tested was:
- For MA1, the shorter: 1 day (just the latest Close) to 30 days.
- For MA2, the longer: 1 day longer than the shorter to 20 days longer.

The AmiBroker code, equity curve, and performance statistics follow. The best values for lengths, chosen for highest final equity, are 19 days for the shorter and 21 days for the longer. Long positions are entered when the 19 day moving average crosses up through the 21 day moving average.

Restricted Model

```
//  MA_Cross_Restricted.afl
//
//  Trading system based on crossing of two moving averages.
//  Restricted to buying only when the fast crosses up
//  through the slow.

MALen1 = Optimize( "MALen1", 19, 1, 30, 1 );
MAIncrement = Optimize( "MAIncrement", 2, 1, 20, 1 );

MALen2 = MALen1 + MAIncrement;

MA1 = MA( C, MALen1 );
MA2 = MA( C, MALen2 );

Buy = Cross( MA1, MA2 );
Sell = Cross ( MA2, MA1 );

Plot( C, "C", colorBlack, styleCandle );
Plot( MA1, "MA1", colorGreen, styleLine );
Plot( MA2, "MA2", colorGreen, styleLine );

///////////////////// end /////////////////////
```

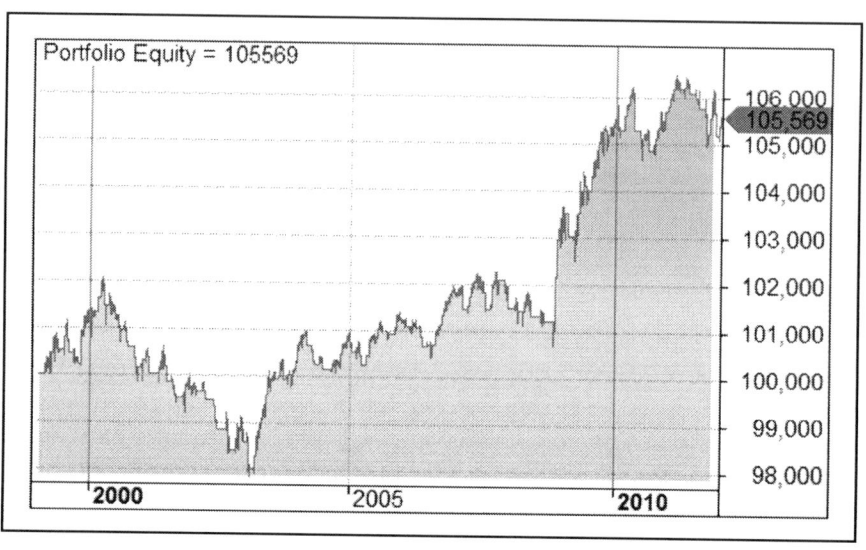

Figure 6.9 Equity curve for restricted crossover system

| **Statistics** | Charts | Trades | Formula | Settings | Symbols |

	Statistics		
	All trades	**Long trades**	**Short trades**
Initial capital	100000.00	100000.00	100000.00
Ending capital	105568.95	105568.95	100000.00
Net Profit	5568.95	5568.95	0.00
Net Profit %	5.57 %	5.57 %	0.00 %
Exposure %	5.50 %	5.50 %	0.00 %
Net Risk Adjusted Return %	101.31 %	101.31 %	N/A
Annual Return %	0.42 %	0.42 %	0.00 %
Risk Adjusted Return %	7.60 %	7.60 %	N/A
Total transaction costs	0.00	0.00	0.00
All trades	146	146 (100.00 %)	0 (0.00 %)
Avg. Profit/Loss	38.14	38.14	N/A
Avg. Profit/Loss %	0.38 %	0.38 %	N/A
Avg. Bars Held	13.37	13.37	N/A
Winners	71 (48.63 %)	71 (48.63 %)	0 (0.00 %)
Total Profit	20531.30	20531.30	0.00
Avg. Profit	289.17	289.17	N/A
Avg. Profit %	2.91 %	2.91 %	N/A
Avg. Bars Held	15.82	15.82	N/A
Max. Consecutive	5	5	0
Largest win	1347.72	1347.72	0.00
# bars in largest win	4	4	0
Losers	75 (51.37 %)	75 (51.37 %)	0 (0.00 %)
Total Loss	-14962.34	-14962.34	0.00
Avg. Loss	-199.50	-199.50	N/A
Avg. Loss %	-2.01 %	-2.01 %	N/A
Avg. Bars Held	11.05	11.05	N/A
Max. Consecutive	5	5	0
Largest loss	-641.78	-641.78	0.00
# bars in largest loss	11	11	0
Max. trade drawdown	-1029.70	-1029.70	0.00
Max. trade % drawdown	-9.89 %	-9.89 %	0.00 %

Figure 6.10 Statistics for restricted crossover system

Unrestricted Model

The other is willing to consider crossing in either direction.

His program is MA_Cross_Unrestricted.afl. Since the restriction on which moving average length is greater has been removed, the range of lengths tested was 1 day to 30 days for both MA1 and MA2.

The AmiBroker code, equity curve, and performance statistics follow. The best values for lengths, chosen using the same criteria, are 11 days for the first and 5 days for the second. Long positions are entered when the 11 day moving average crosses up through the 5 day moving average. Or, equivalently, when the 5 day crosses down through the 11 day.

```
//  MA_Cross_Unrestricted.afl
//
//  Trading system based on crossing of two moving averages.
//  Unrestricted
//  Buy when either crosses up
//  through the other.

MALen1 = Optimize( "MALen1", 11, 1, 30, 1 );
MALen2 = Optimize( "MALen2", 5, 1, 30, 1 );

MA1 = MA( C, MALen1 );
MA2 = MA( C, MALen2 );

Buy = Cross( MA1, MA2 );
Sell = Cross ( MA2, MA1 );

Plot( C, "C", colorBlack, styleCandle );
Plot( MA1, "MA1", colorGreen, styleLine );
Plot( MA2, "MA2", colorGreen, styleLine );

////////////////////  end  ////////////////////
```

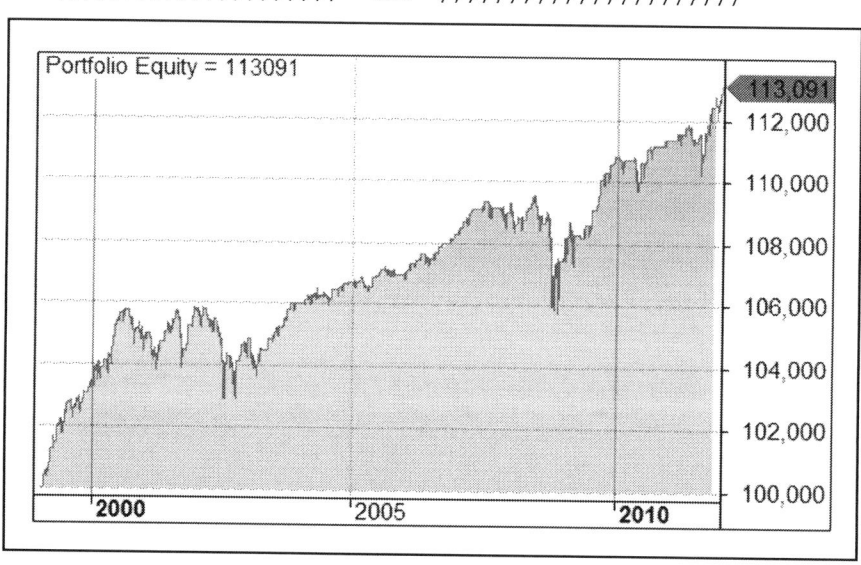

Figure 6.11 Equity curve for unrestricted crossover system

Statistics | Charts | Trades | Formula | Settings | Symbols

	Statistics		
	All trades	**Long trades**	**Short trades**
Initial capital	100000.00	100000.00	100000.00
Ending capital	113090.91	113090.91	100000.00
Net Profit	13090.91	13090.91	0.00
Net Profit %	13.09 %	13.09 %	0.00 %
Exposure %	4.14 %	4.14 %	0.00 %
Net Risk Adjusted Return %	316.39 %	316.39 %	N/A
Annual Return %	0.95 %	0.95 %	0.00 %
Risk Adjusted Return %	22.99 %	22.99 %	N/A
Total transaction costs	0.00	0.00	0.00
All trades	170	170 (100.00 %)	0 (0.00 %)
Avg. Profit/Loss	77.01	77.01	N/A
Avg. Profit/Loss %	0.77 %	0.77 %	N/A
Avg. Bars Held	9.69	9.69	N/A
Winners	122 (71.76 %)	122 (71.76 %)	0 (0.00 %)
Total Profit	28344.84	28344.84	0.00
Avg. Profit	232.33	232.33	N/A
Avg. Profit %	2.34 %	2.34 %	N/A
Avg. Bars Held	7.24	7.24	N/A
Max. Consecutive	15	15	0
Largest win	1147.98	1147.98	0.00
# bars in largest win	7	7	0
Losers	48 (28.24 %)	48 (28.24 %)	0 (0.00 %)
Total Loss	-15253.93	-15253.93	0.00
Avg. Loss	-317.79	-317.79	N/A
Avg. Loss %	-3.20 %	-3.20 %	N/A
Avg. Bars Held	15.92	15.92	N/A
Max. Consecutive	3	3	0
Largest loss	-2587.20	-2587.20	0.00
# bars in largest loss	36	36	0
Max. trade drawdown	-3079.20	-3079.20	0.00
Max. trade % drawdown	-30.31 %	-30.31 %	0.00 %

Figure 6.12 Statistics for unrestricted crossover system

The two models are simplistic. Neither is tradable. There is a losing trade in the unrestricted version that none of us would find acceptable. Some logic would be needed to address that.

The point of the comparison is that if we want the determining factor of system acceptability to be results, rather than the constraints, we must be willing to relax tradition-bound requirements. Traditions such as that signals must be derived from specific patterns or that trades must have certain characteristics.

Fitting and Overfitting

Recall the premises of technical analysis as described in Chapter 2.
- The markets are not completely efficient.
- There are patterns in the historical price series that can be used to identify profitable trading opportunities.
- Trading systems can be designed to recognize the patterns and give buy and sell signals.
- Patterns similar to those found in the historical data will continue to be found in future data.

For each tradable issue, there is a large population of data—all of the historical price and volume data. Working with samples of the data, our task is to develop a model that describes the population well enough to make predictions about its future.

The fit of a model to a process or data series has two metrics—accuracy and precision.

Imagine shooting. We aim at the center of a target, then we shoot. The shots land on the target, but not all at the exact point of aim. There is error, and it comes from two sources—poor accuracy and poor precision.

Accuracy refers to errors in missing the center of the target. It is how far the typical shot is from the center.

Precision refers to the distance between shots.

In statistical experiments, accuracy measures the between-sample error, while precision measures the within-sample error.

Precision can be calculated from the experiment—from the in-sample results. Accuracy requires knowledge of the reference class. We never have complete knowledge of that. The best estimate we have of it comes from out-of-sample testing, and that will be affected by non-stationarity in the data. Chapter 7 has an example comparing precision and accuracy.

Overfitting can be defined as an overly precise solution to a general problem based on a limited sample. Overfitting is emphasizing precision over accuracy.

Fitting a Trading Model

We are trying to discover a functional relationship between pattern, signal, and trade. We have some data. We can describe the trades we want, and determine whether the ones selected were correctly identified. Our model is a combination of rules and parameters that represent the function.

The only purpose of a trading system's model is to identify patterns in the data.

We begin with a data series and a very general model. General in the sense that the rules are incomplete and the parameters incorrect.

The fitting process is a series of modifications to the rules and parameters. Each iteration of modification results in a new model—different than the one previously tested.

We are looking for a sequence of:
1. **Some frequent patterns based on rules and indicators.**
2. **That are consistently followed by trades with the characteristics we desire.**

The first model created was probably completely unfit. The trades following the patterns it identified were not profitable. As successive models were created, through changes to rules and parameters, the fit improved, and trades became more profitable.

The model is becoming more and more precise. It is attempting to memorize the data. In some modeling processes, the purpose of the model *is* memorization for later recall. For the purpose of trading, we want accuracy and generalization, *not* memorization. We will be using the model for prediction.

As the model development process continues, the model becomes increasingly fit to the specific data—including the noise as well as the signal. During the fitting process, the model adjusts to all the data. It cannot distinguish between "real" instances of the patterns that are followed by profitable trades and "fakes" that are artifacts of random data values.

The danger is confusing accuracy with precision. Seeing precision in the in-sample testing, we assume there will be accuracy in the out-of-sample period and in live trading.

The test of whether the model is properly fit or is overfit—whether it has learned or memorized—is testing with previously unseen data. That new data will contain some real, profitable patterns that are important to trading. We want the model to recognize those and generate buy and sell signals. The new data will also contain some new and different noise. Some of the noise will be recognized as *the* pattern and signals will be generated, but the following trades will not be profitable. Needless to say, we hope there will be few of those.

Objective Function

In order to manage the fitting process, there must be an appropriate metric of goodness of fit that can be measured.

If we were fitting a polynomial equation to a set of data points, the metric of fitness would be an error term—perhaps residuals after a regression.

If the model was assigning classification, the metric of fitness might be a confusion matrix and the associated receiver operating characteristic.

For quantitative technical analysis, it is an objective function.

What is "Best?"

Given two or more alternatives or choices, the one we prefer is "best."

This is true whether we are deciding between toast or an English muffin for breakfast, or between which of two trading systems to put into live trading. Whether we are conscious of it or not, we choose by evaluating and weighing features, and computing a sum of benefits and costs.

If you are looking for a new pair of shoes, stores and catalogs have a wide choice, already manufactured. Which pair is best depends on how well the shoes fit your needs. You evaluate them by a number of criteria you deem to be important, such as their size, comfort, material, appearance, practicality, and price. As an aspiring technical analyst who is shopping for shoes, you could write out a check list, assign a weight to each criterion, and total up the score for each pair you consider. The sheet would look different if you were looking for running shoes than if you were looking for dress shoes or work boots. The formula combining the weights is your objective function. If you have included all the important criteria and assigned weights reasonably, those shoes that score highest are most likely to be the ones you prefer.

Some choices are trivial and errors are inexpensive. We can try out 40 different breakfast cereals for a few hundred dollars (that we were already prepared to spend for food), and have it done in two or three months.

Life's more important choices are more expensive, more difficult to get right, and more difficult to correct. Choosing a profession, and a school for the necessary education, for example.

There are always benefits that carry rewards, and undesirable features with associated costs. A lot of work has been done studying what people prefer and how they decide. Important decisions involve many factors, sometimes not easily ranked or compared. The frame of reference and utility matters. A gift of $1000 is more important and more valuable to a person living on a limited and fixed income than to a debt-free person with a good job. Nonetheless, most choices can be quantified by creating a list of important features, assigning weights in proportion to relative importance, assigning relative costs or rewards to each, computing a single-valued score. The computation, or function, that computes the score is the objective function. The alternative with the highest score is "best."

If, after scoring alternative breakfast cereals or potential professions, the scores do not align with our subjective choice, then either:
- The list of features, weights, and costs needs adjustment.
- The process has identified important criteria not previously considered.

The purpose of the objective function is to provide a single-valued score for each alternative, where the ranking of the alternatives is in the same order as our subjective preferences.

We are using the objective function to quantify subjectivity.

Just doing the analysis, weighting, scoring, and ranking does not assure success. A perfect score may be unattainable—too rare or too expensive.

Or we might find we do not need the very best—any of the alternatives with scores above some threshold are satisfactory.

Objective Function for Trading

Objective functions are extremely important both in trading system development and later in trading management. There are many millions of combinations of data series, rules, and parameters, each one of which defines a trading system. Which is best?

The trading system development process consists of generating many alternatives—combinations of data series, indicators, rules, and parameters—and choosing the best from among them.

Best, seen from trading results, is subjective. It includes positive growth of the trading account, limited drawdowns to the trading account, and conformity of results to real or artificially imposed constraints such as trading frequency and holding period.

Best, seen from within the development process, is the score computed using an objective function and associated with each of the alternatives being compared.

Compared with many decisions we must make in life, trading system development is relatively easy. The common unit of measurement is dollars, or your currency equivalent. Winning trades gain dollars, losing trades cost dollars. Personal risk tolerance sets a lower threshold. Provided that threshold is not violated in the time period, higher gains are better, the highest gain is the best.

There are some limitations. Trading system development platforms limit what objective functions can be defined, calculated, and referenced during development test runs.

In early chapters, I described:
- How to determine and quantify your personal risk tolerance.
- Given a set of trades—the "best estimate"—how to determine safe-f, the maximum position size given your risk tolerance.
- Given a value for safe-f, how to estimate the profit potential if future trades are similar to those in the best estimate.
- How to read a single value—CAR25—from the distribution of potential profit.

CAR25 is the credible value of expected equity growth associated with the risk-normalized forecast of a trading system. It is the most universal objective function for trading system development and trading management I have found.

As you saw as early as the program used in Chapter 2, it is possible to perform the entire stack of operations—from creation of the best estimate to computation of CAR25—in a single program run, given a programming environment that supports the data structures and computation functions needed. Python is such an environment. When we discuss trading system development using machine learning in Chapter 8, we will use CAR25 as the objective function, compute it on-the-fly as a system is being tested, and use it to guide model selection. When we discuss trading management in Chapter 9, we will use CAR25 as the objective function to measure system health.

Metrics for Trading

If we are working with a traditional trading system development platform (at least those available today), direct calculation of CAR25 is not possible. The objective function that is used must be defined from the metrics available during backtesting and optimization runs.

Some platforms, such as AmiBroker, provide easy access to a rich selection of metrics, allow custom objective functions that include those metrics, and use that objective function to guide optimization. This is one of the very important capabilities a trading system development platform should have. It is one of the reasons I prefer and recommend AmiBroker.

Assuming you are working with a trading system development platform that provides a rich variety of metrics, what makes a good objective function?

Model Development—Preliminaries

The model identifies patterns, issues buy and sell signals, resulting in a sequence of trades. Eventually another analysis of trades gives a value for CAR25. What characteristics of the series of trades give high CAR25?

- We know that relying on the single specific sequence is misleading, so we will not use metrics that are sequence dependent. That excludes maximum series drawdown. But it does not exclude trade-by-trade loss or maximum adverse excursion.
- We should reward gain and penalize loss. Exclude Sharpe ratio, but not necessarily Sortino ratio.
- TWR = G ^ N. G should be high, after transactional costs. Insist on a positive expectation. N should be high, so trade frequently.
- Drawdown increases in proportion to the square root of holding period. Reward short holding periods.
- It is psychologically easier to trade a system with a high percentage of winning trades. Reward a high ratio of winning trades.
- Determination of system health is easier when accuracy is high. Reward a high ratio of winning trades.
- The sweet spot for risk inherent in a data series is high accuracy and short holding period.
- Avoiding toxic trades is important. Penalize large losses.

The list of features to be rewarded includes:
- Trade frequently.
- Trade accurately.
- Hold a short period.
- Have a high gain per trade.

The list of features to be penalized includes:
- Maximum trade drawdown or maximum adverse excursion.

Look for metrics provided by your platform that allow you to identify and weight these features.

Backtesting

A backtest is an evaluation of a system using data previously collected—historical data.

For development done using a trading system development platform, the platform has the control settings. For development done using a machine learning environment, the same structure is required, much of it supplied by you.

As the operator, you decide which trading system module to load. Data is selected, either through the user interface of the platform, or as specified by the code in the system module. There is always a primary data series—the one being traded. There may be additional data series that will be used as well. A date range or bar count may be entered to specify which data or how much data to use.

The system module contains the computer code for the model, plus settings and instructions that govern the test run. Depending on the platform, values for control variables may be set using a user interface, or by the system module. These include:
- primary data series
- auxiliary data series
- dates of data to load
- bar length to use
- dates of period to test
- objective function
- positions that are allowed—long, short, or both
- delay between signal and execution
- initial account balance
- margin availability and use
- position sizing
- contract specification—shares or contracts, and details
- commission schedule
- slippage

After the control variables have been set, the test begins. One-time tasks are performed:
- Data for the range specified is loaded into memory in data structures designed for financial time series.
- Data is scanned for errors, such as close greater than high.
- Data is aligned to a known series of reference dates and times.
- If there are multiple data series, they are adjusted to a common time zone—preferably the trader's time zone.
- Missing data is filled with copies of last known values.
- Indicators, such as moving averages, may be either pre-computed for the entire date range and stored in memory, or computed bar by bar. Provision must be made for an initialization period. For example, a 50 day simple moving average does not have stable values for the first 49 days.
- The structures and variables needed to keep track of important information such as funds, positions, and transaction prices are created and initialized.

The test proceeds chronologically, bar by bar. Each bar is processed in stages:
1. at the open
2. intra-bar
3. at the close

For each bar, at each stage, the rules of the model together with the data values and indicator values for that stage of that bar are used to determine whether any of the patterns the model was designed to recognize are present. When a pattern is detected, a trading signal is issued.

Perhaps immediately, or perhaps in a second phase of the test, trade signals are interpreted, funds allocated, trade by trade results produced, and performance metrics computed.

At the end of the test period, trade lists, charts, and statistics are available.

The advantage of using a trading system development platform is that it was designed to do the behind-the-scenes processing transparently. You specify some data and a model, click "test," and view the resulting charts.

If you are using machine learning, you have fewer choices for the support of the trading simulator, but more choices for the model.

Optimization

While the term is optimization, the process is:
1. Generate a large number of alternatives—typically alternative models.
2. Choose the best.

Generating alternatives is easy.

The intelligence is in the objective function used to assign each of the alternatives a score so they can be sorted into the order you prefer them.

The alternatives are typically distinguished by having different rules, indicators, and / or parameter values.

For example, if a model is based on the crossing of two moving averages, we want to know the best lengths. We create a list with pairs of numbers, one number for the length of each moving average.

A series of backtests is made, one test for each pair on the list, using the lengths set to the values listed. As each test is completed, the objective function score for that pair is recorded. After all the tests have been run, the list is sorted by objective function score. The best test is at the top of the list, and we note the best lengths for the two moving averages.

Dimensions in a Search Space

The optimization is a search through a search space. Each indicator (or other feature being searched) defines a dimension in a search space. In this example, there are two indicators, each with one parameter—length. They define a two-dimensional search space. One dimension is associated with the length of the first moving average. The second dimension is associated with the second moving average.

The values of the lengths being tested can be visualized as being on the x and y axes of a two-dimensional graph. Vertical and horizontal lines define a grid. Each intersection represents one specific alternative model with those two specific lengths.

As the backtests are run, a value for each on the objective functions is computed and associated with one of the grid intersections. A contour-like plot connecting points of equal objective function values can be created. It looks like a typographical map, and is called a response surface. Figure 6.13 shows an example. The objective function value is represented on the z-axis. We are searching for the highest stable area of that surface.

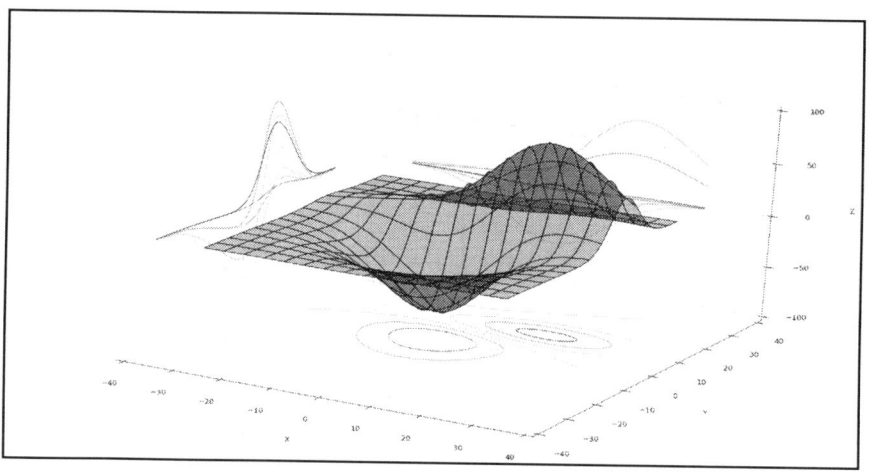

Figure 6.13 Response surface for two-dimensional search space

Each of the dimensions has a list of values to be tested. It is common, but not necessary, for the values to be equally spaced over some range. A moving average might be tested for all integer lengths from 1 to 20. There are 20 values to search in this dimension.

The designer of the model might want the second moving average to be a multiple of ten, between 10 and 100. (Perhaps in an attempt to avoid overfitting, or perhaps to shorten run times while doing preliminary explorations.) There are 10 values to search in this dimension.

The number of points in the search space is the product of the number of points in each of the dimensions. This search space has 200 points. Each represents one of the alternative models being considered.

The search can be expanded to include other indicators, such as the lookback length used to compute an oscillator, and the level at which the oscillator gives a signal.

Each indicator adds a dimension to the search space. Searching for the best combination of two moving averages, an oscillator lookback, and an oscillator critical level is a four-dimensional space. If there are 10 values for the lookback length and 20 values for the critical level, the search space expands from 200 points to 40,000 points.

Global Optimum

Some response surfaces, such as the one shown in Figure 6.13, have a single "mountain" that rises above the "plain." The alternative associated with the grid location of the top of that mountain is the undisputed best. Sometimes there is a single tall hill and several smaller hills. An undisputed tallest hill has the highest objective function score and is the global optimum. The other hills are local optima. Figure 6.14 shows an example.

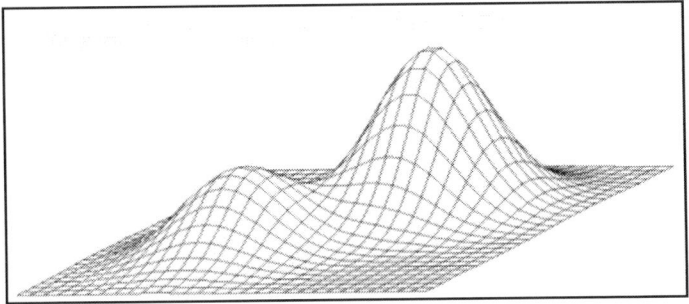

Figure 6.14 A global optimum and one local optimum

Exhaustive Search

An exhaustive search runs a backtest for each and every point in the search space. Since every grid location is tested and scored, an exhaustive search is guaranteed to find the global optimum. When the number of tests is small, execution time is short, and exhaustive searches are preferred.

Non-exhaustive Search

A non-exhaustive search runs fewer backtests than the number of points in the search space. It will still compute an objective function score for each test run, sort them, and choose the highest one as the optimum. The risk is that a poor search algorithm, combined with a poor starting point, may result in the global optimum being missed, with the best found being a local optimum.

Fortunately, there are several algorithms that perform intelligent, non-exhaustive searches that will shorten the computation time considerably while being reasonably certain of finding the global optimum. One that receives good reviews from professional mathematicians, works well in practice, and is available in some trading system development platforms, including AmiBroker, is covariance matrix adaptation evolution strategy (CMA-ES).[4][5]

One of the very big advantages of non-exhaustive searches is that increasing the search space does not increase search time in proportion to the increase in tests requested.

Things to Watch For

If run times are acceptable, use exhaustive search. But search spaces are often so large that exhaustive searches are too lengthy. In that case, use CMA-ES.

Check for spikes in the response surface. Preferred solutions are located in "plateaus" with smooth slopes. The data series will change over time, changing the performance of the system and the location of the optimum parameter values. If the optimum being traded is on an isolated spike of good performance, it will take only a small change in the characteristics of the data for performance to fall off rapidly.

Check the value returned as optimal for each of the variables being optimized. Unless you specifically want a rigid limit, be aware when an optimal value is at one of the limits of the range. If you asked for a search over 1 to 10, and the reported optimum is 10, there might be an even better result for values greater than 10.

If the objective function is well behaved, you can do exploratory searching of a large search space piecemeal. Set wide limits for each variable and use non-exhaustive search. Based on the preliminary results, focus on a narrower region. Fix some of the parameter values and optimize others, then fix some of those identified as optimal and test the ones that had been fixed. Repeat for a few iterations. This technique is called evolutionary operation. If the objective function is not well behaved, it may not converge. But it is worth a try.

Do not obsess over perfection. A good local optimum may be satisfactory. Prefer a robust system with lower performance to a fragile system with higher performance.

---

4   Hansen and Ostermeier, Adapting Arbitrary Normal Mutation Distributions in Evolution Strategies: The Covariance Matrix Adaptation. *Proceedings of the IEEE International Conference on Evolutionary Computation,* pages 312-317, 1996.
5   https://www.lri.fr/~hansen/cmaesintro.html

Stationarity and Synchronization

In-sample and Out-of-sample

To be profitable, a system must:
1. Learn the predictive patterns by analysis of the training data.
2. Identify those patterns in the validation data, and eventually in live-trading data.

Training data is in-sample data. Data that is extensively searched in order to identify patterns and define the rules.

Validation data is out-of-sample data. Data that has not been used in the development of the model. The truest out-of-sample data is tomorrow—future data that *cannot* be known during development.

Figure 6.15 shows the ideal relationship between in-sample (IS) and out-of-sample (OOS) periods and data, with the OOS period immediately following the IS period. That is, after all, how data processed during live trading relates to data used during development.

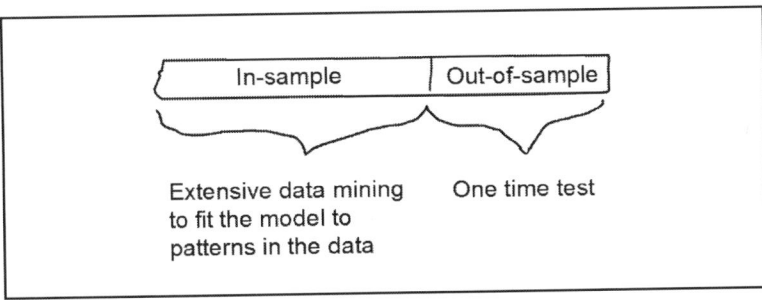

Figure 6.15 Relationship between in-sample and out-of-sample

Stationarity

As described in Chapter 1, stationarity is a feature of data that refers to how a particular metric of the data remains relatively constant or changes as different subsets of the data are analyzed.

The bugaboo of financial trading systems is lack of stationarity.

The trading system—the combination of model and data—is not stationary. Almost all other references to system development treat synchronization, and many other features of trading systems, as though they are stationary. Whether the reason is ignorance, naïvety, or simplification, the result is the same. Applying techniques that are appropriate for stationary processes to models that are not stationary produces inaccurate and unreliable results—over-estimates of profit potential, under-estimates of risk, and unprofitable trading systems.

As Figures 6.16 and 6.17 illustrate, nothing about financial time series is stationary for an extended period.

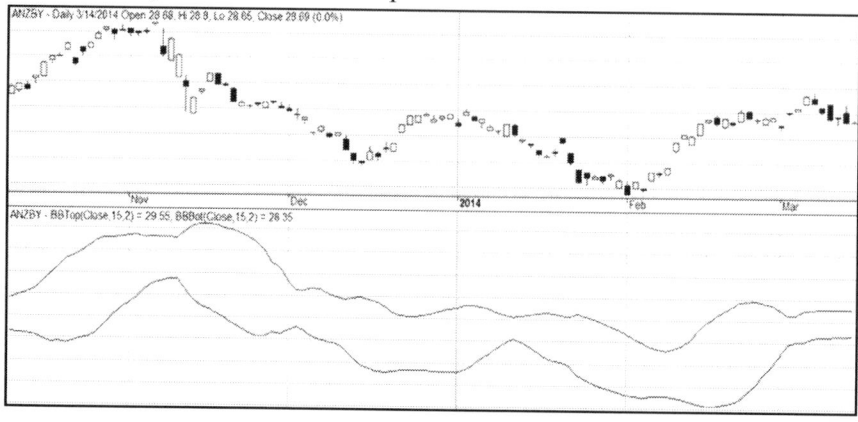

Figure 6.16 Neither price nor volatility is stationary

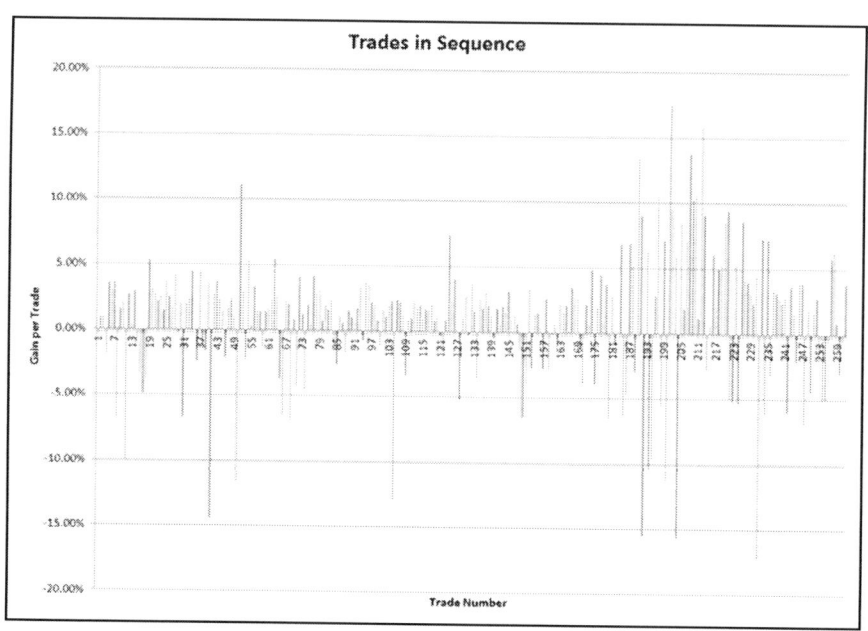

Figure 6.17 Neither patterns nor profits are stationary

No rules of thumb exist, or are even possible, estimating the length of the period of stationarity. Experiments are needed.

In-sample Data Length

The signal or pattern component of the data must be stationary throughout the in-sample training period. The in-sample period may be short-

Model Development—Preliminaries

er than the period of synchronization, but avoid longer periods. The issue is not the length of the period in days so much as it is the length of the period of stationarity.

Naive developers are sometimes heard to recommend using as much data and as long a period as possible for each test period. Their reasoning is that the model will be exposed to as many different conditions as possible and will be able to perform well in all of them. My view is quite the opposite. I recommend that the test periods—particularly the in-sample periods over which the model is fit to the data—be as short as practical. Using data that includes many different conditions decreases the fit to any of the conditions. In a phrase, stale data is worse than no data. The best models use short periods and regularly resynchronize the rules and parameters to keep the model tuned to the signal.

The in-sample fit is always good. It is guaranteed to be good. We do not stop fooling with the model and choosing data to test until it is good. There are 252 daily closing prices in a year. There are many thousands of alternative models that we can be apply to many thousands of data series. We find at least one good combination before we are finished.

Out-of-sample Data Length

Unfortunately, out-of-sample performance is usually poor. That is, of all the alternative models we apply to a series of data during in-sample data mining, most do not identify patterns that precede profitable trades out-of-sample. Either they are fit to noise—to non-recurring patterns unique to the specific data being tested—or the characteristics of the data have changed by the end of the period and the profitable patterns do not persist beyond it.

To be useful for trading, the signals must be identifiable beyond the in-sample period, and those signals must be profitable.

There are no rules, or even rules-of-thumb, for estimating the length of time a model continues to be profitable. There is no way, either within the model's logic or external to it, to estimate the length time the system will be profitable out-of-sample. Only monitoring the performance of the system over time gives us that information.

In any event, that length is non-stationary and changes as characteristics of the data change. If the system falls out of synchronization before the end of the out-of-sample period, the day-to-day monitoring of system health and associated risk, relative to the risk tolerance of the trader and attractiveness of alternative uses of the funds, will cause safe-f to drop and the system will be taken offline. This is part of the dynamic position sizing technique discussed in Chapter 9.

In my opinion, there is no minimum length for the out-of-sample period. It is, or at least can be, appropriate to treat each day as a one-day long out-of-sample period, with parameter values readjusted daily. Testing out-of-sample performance is part of the validation process, and will be discussed in a later section.

In General

In general, the lengths of the in-sample and out-of-sample periods are related only to the extent that the system must remain synchronized for the total length of those two periods.

One thing you can expect is that longer holding periods require longer periods of stationarity in order to identify and validate signal recognition. That implies both longer in-sample periods, and longer out-of-sample periods. Increasing the length of time increases the probability that conditions change, stationarity is lost, and profitability drops.

Additionally, drawdown increases as holding period increases. Longer holding periods imply greater risk, smaller safe-f, and lower CAR25.

Number of Data Points

Again, we have a familiar tradeoff. We want more data points for finer granularity, better precision, and easier statistical significance. But not so many data points that some of them represent conditions that are no longer current.

There must be data points in every test period. At least several, preferably many.

If you are using impulse signals, trading frequency and holding period affect test period length. Each data point is a trade that is both opened and closed within the test period.

The longer positions are held:
- The longer the test period must be to span several trades.
- The greater the intra-trade drawdown.

The longer the test period, the more likely the model and the data will lose synchronization.

A system that trades a single issue long / flat, trades frequently, and holds a few days, might complete 15 to 20 trades in each year. In-sample length might be one year—perhaps as short as a few months. Out-of-sample length a few months or longer.

Contrast with a system that holds several months. The in-sample length must be several years, and the out-of-sample period long enough to include several trades.

If you are using state signals, each data point is a mark-to-market period. You have much more flexibility in setting the length of both the in-sample and out-of-sample periods, even for trades that are held for a long time.

Validation

The purpose of the validation process is to give you confidence that the signals given by the system precede profitable trades. The key word is confidence.

The real test comes when real trades are made with real money, and the market performs its own validation. The best validation performed during development mirrors this. It is out-of-sample testing on the same data series used for development, with the validation data following the development data.

Be as rigorous as you can during your own development. Disappointing results in a computer validation run are less painful than losses in the market.

Midterm Exam

You have worked hard. Read, thought, studied, experimented, tested, analyzed. You have done all of the following steps, and are satisfied with the results:
- Decided how much money to allocate to trading.
- Reviewed your trading history, imagined some scenarios, decided how much risk you can tolerate, and defined your personal risk tolerance.
- Picked an issue to trade that has enough volatility so trading is potentially profitable, but not so much that its inherent risk is too great.
- Will use CAR25 as your objective function. (If your platform supports it.)
- Designed and programmed a custom objective function that reflects your trading preferences and ranks test results in the order you prefer them. (If your platform does not support CAR25.)
- Learned to evaluate the risk in a set of trades, compute the maximum safe position size, and estimate the profit potential.
- Developed a model that works with the data, producing trades that are profitable, but not too risky.
- Determined the lengths of the in-sample and out-of-sample periods.

Everything looks good on the drawing board. It is time for a midterm exam. Live trading will be the final exam.

Walk Forward Testing

The gold standard of validation is walk forward testing. Figures 6.18 through 6.21 illustrate the process.

Walk forward is a sequence of steps. Each step consists of finding the best model using the in-sample data, then using that model to test the out-of-sample data.

Earlier testing and experimentation has determined the length of the in-sample and out-of-sample periods. The search for the best model is an optimization that tests many alternative models, sorting them into order by objective function score, and choosing the one that is highest ranked. It is important to have confidence that the objective function used ranks alternatives into the same order you subjectively prefer them. Or, at least, you have confidence that the one ranked at the top is satisfactory. During the walk forward process, the choice is made automatically—you do not have an opportunity to evaluate the top choice or any other. It is automatically chosen and applied to the out-of-sample data. The results for the out-of-sample test are stored.

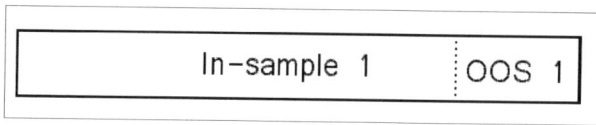

Figure 6.18 A single walk forward step

The process is repeated several times. After each step, the beginning and ending dates of both periods are stepped forward by the length of the out-of-sample period.

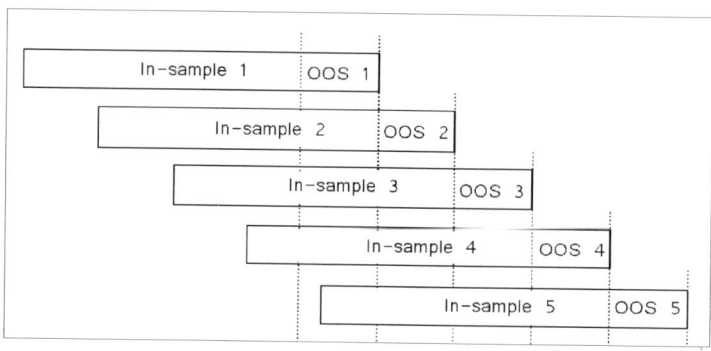

Figure 6.19 A sequence of walk forward steps

The results from all of the out-of-sample tests are accumulated and analyzed. This set of trades is the "best estimate" set of trades. The decision to pass the system forward to trading or return it to development is based on analysis of these trades. See Figure 1.1.

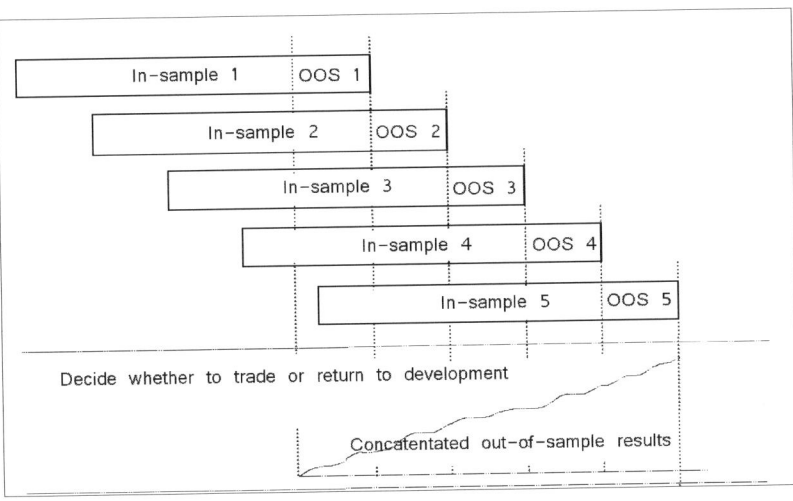

Figure 6.20 Accumulate all the out-of-sample results

If the system is passed on to trading, the process continues. Periodically, either according to the walk forward schedule, or whenever trading results are deteriorating, resynchronize the model to the data using the same process. Take live trades with the most recent model.

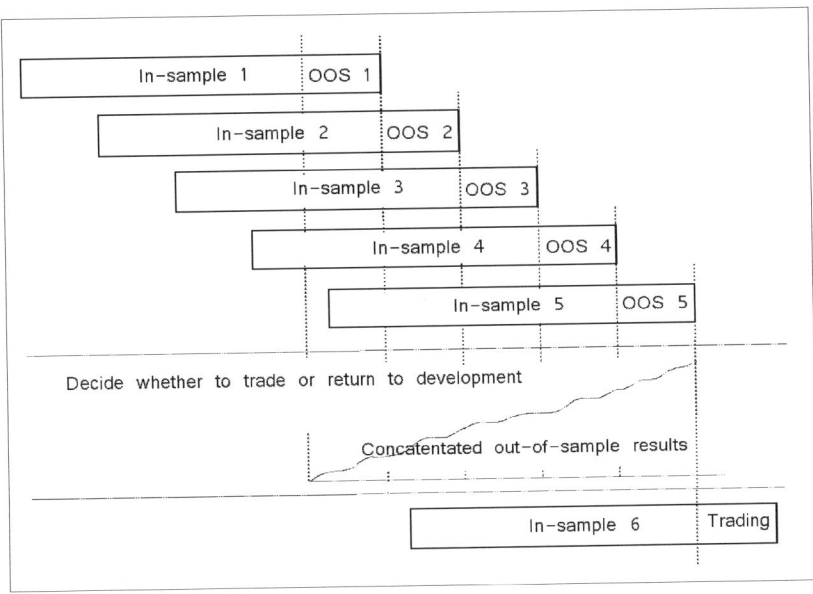

Figure 6.21 Walking forward into trading

These conditions are required for walk forward to work:
- The system is stationary for the combined length of the in-sample and out-of-sample periods.
- You have confidence that the model selected by your objective function as best based on in-sample optimization is satisfactory.
- There are several, preferably many, trades in each test period.

Try to make it work.
- It is a testing process that is very similar to the way the model will be adjusted and the system managed during live trading.
- The set of trades produced by the out-of-sample tests are the best estimate of future performance.

What if walk forward fails to work?
- One, or more, of the three conditions do not hold. Try to determine why.
- If the process failed in walk forward testing, do you have confidence that it will work any better when the out-of-sample period is live trading?

Some Other Way

Most validation techniques produce metrics that can be compared with alternative systems, or perhaps with statistical tables. In the end, however, confidence is subjective.

If satisfactory walk forward results cannot be obtained, weaker validation techniques can be used:
- Testing on other data series. If the model works for SPY, for example, test it on other major US indexes, such as QQQ, IWM, XLB, XLE, etc.
- Testing on earlier time periods. This is a very weak technique. Profitable trading removes inefficiencies from the market being traded. If the system you are developing identifies and profitably trades some pattern that other systems have also identified, current data may already have fewer inefficiencies than past data. Profitable trades will be easier to detect in the earlier data, and those results will be over-estimate profitability.

It is important that validation be based in some way on out-of-sample results. In-sample results alone have no value in estimating future performance.

Model Airplanes are Fun

System development on your computer at home, using historical data, and imaginary money is fun. You have the freedom to use any methods you can imagine—any logic, any rules, any data series. If you wish, you can ignore biases, look into the future, make unreasonable assumptions, apply outrageous money management techniques, and watch your imaginary trading account grow large enough to buy anything you ever imagined wanting.

As a teenager, I flew model airplanes. I built, and flew, and crashed, and fixed, many planes. At that time, the planes were "free flight" or "control line." It did not cost much money, just a lot of time. Hoping to have more free time in the future, my interest in model planes is returning. I enjoy both building and flying. In my town, almost all flying is now radio controlled. I am practicing flying in the comfort of my home using a flight simulator. I can choose perfect conditions and stable airplanes as I learn the basics. Then progress to aerobatic planes and random system failures as my skills increase. I can fly piper cubs, jumbo jets, and World War I biplanes.

Flying the simulator is a hobby in itself. Crashes cost nothing—no plane to fix, no bones to heal. When I take a real plane—60 inch wingspan, 12 pounds, $400 in parts, 200 hours of labor—out to the flight line, I need skills, confidence, and a measure of good luck to have a good day.

A friend regularly reminds me that takeoffs are optional. But, once in the air, landings are mandatory. Placing a real order using real money is a takeoff. It is optional. You are not required to trade. But if and when you do, the laws of the financial market equivalent to gravity, wind, and radio malfunction can no longer be ignored.

The better you do during development, the better chance you have of profitably trading. Do the hard work. Be rigorous. Learn math and programming. Anticipate black swan events.

Next Chapters

There is a logical sequence of operations that model development follows. These, including some that are optional, are:
- Specify the goal and performance metrics
- Choose the primary data series
- Choose auxiliary data series
- Date and time align the data series
- Select and compute functions and indicators
- Select the target
- Reduce dimension or change basis
- Determine lengths of in-sample and out-of-sample periods
- Learn
- Test
- Evaluate performance
- Predict and trade

We address these in the next two chapters. First, Chapter 7, for models developed using a trading system development platform. Then, Chapter 8, machine learning and pattern recognition models.

At the end of the model development process, whichever path is used, we will have a model—a computer program that contains the logic, rules, and parameters that recognize patterns and generate signals. We will have results of applying the model to a tradable data series, including a set of trades that is the best estimate of future performance of the system. We will be ready to pass the system from development to trading, where its performance and health will be monitored, and the maximum safe position size computed for each trade.

Your choice of platform has some implications for the trading systems you will be developing.

Indicator-based platforms, such as AmiBroker and TradeStation, are designed with trading system development in mind. They have built-in functions to compute indicators, graphical displays that include features for charting prices and displaying indicators, data structures that are prepared for financial price series with open, high, low, close, volume, and open interest. Their development language and backtesting engines are designed to scan data for patterns, issue orders, and track trade results. Their strengths lie in areas related to trading; their weaknesses lie in limited capabilities beyond trading.

Machine learning platforms are typically general purpose programming languages, such as Python, augmented by applications libraries. They rely on special purpose libraries to compute indicators, generate trading signals, and track trade results. Their strengths lie in the applications libraries, giving powerful capabilities in areas such as linear algebra, graphical display, and machine learning; their weaknesses are the reliance on add-on libraries.

Chapter 7
Model Development Indicator Based

Indicator-based Development

Indicator-based development begins with the selection of indicators. Often the developer has an idea of how the indicators will be used and an idea of the characteristics of the trades that will result. The development process revolves around computing a variety of alternative versions of indicators using a range of parameter values, applying rules to interpret the indicators and generate the signals, testing many tradable issues, and analyzing the resulting trades. The process is repeated until a satisfactory combination of indicators, parameters, rules, and data has been discovered.

Program Template

I find it helpful to have a standard format for the trading system program. Figure 7.1 gives an example that will be used throughout this chapter.
- A comment block where the program is documented.
- References to code being retrieved from a library directory to compute custom functions.
- Statements that define the settings such as initial account balance and trade size. The AmiBroker platform allows many of these settings to be specified on dialog screens which set default values. Values defined in the program take precedence

and override the defaults. Explicitly including them in the code documents the settings used and gives an opportunity to easily modify them.
- Definitions and initializations of global variables.
- Code for functions defined within (local to) the program.
- Definitions and initializations of local variables. The variables that will use Param and / or Optimize statements are grouped together first.
  Param gives the user the ability to change variables manually, using a slider control, and immediately observe the effect through plots in the chart window.
  Optimize gives the program the ability to change variables in the search for the best settings.
- Computation of indicators.
- Rules to define and identify patterns and conditions of interest.
- Rules to interpret conditions and issue buy and sell orders.
- Statements to compute and display plots and tables.

```
// TemplateMOC.afl
//
// This program is contained in the book
// "Quantitative Technical Analysis"
// which is copyright © 2014 Blue Owl Press, Inc
//
// The author of the book and programmer
// of the code is Dr. Howard B. Bandy.
//
// Please read and understand the disclaimer
// associated with all materials related to the book.
//
// To obtain a copy of the book,
// visit the book's website:
// www.QuantitativeTechnicalAnalysis.com
// or
// Amazon.com
//
// This code is provided for the convenience of
// readers of the book.
// Please respect the copyright.
// Do not post this listing without
// the express written consent of Dr. Bandy
//
// Template for a mean reversion trading system.
// Signals generated at the close
// for action at the close.
//

// Objective Function
#include <ObFnDemo1.afl>;

// System settings
OptimizerSetEngine( "cmae" );
SetOption( "ExtraColumnsLocation", 1 );
SetBacktestMode( backtestRegular );
SetOption( "initialEquity", 100000 );
```

Model Development—Indicator-Based

```
MaxPos = 1;
SetOption( "maxOpenPositions", MaxPos );
SetPositionSize( 10000, spsValue );
SetOption ( "CommissionMode", 3 ); // $ per share
SetOption( "CommissionAmount", 0.005 );
SetTradeDelays( 0, 0, 0, 0 );
BuyPrice = SellPrice = Close;

// Global variables and parameters

// User Functions
function ZScore(p,lookback)
{
    //     Compute the z-score of series p,
    //     using lookback as the length of
    //     the mean and standard deviation
    m = MA(p,lookback);
    s = StDev(p,lookback);
    z = (p-m)/s;
    return z;
}

// Local variables, beginning with Param and Optimize
zLookback = Optimize("zLookback",3,2,6,1);
zBuyLevel = Optimize("zBuyLevel",-1.3,-2,0,0.1);
zSellIncrem = Optimize("zSellIncrem",2.2,0,3,0.1);

zSellLevel = zBuyLevel + zSellIncrem;

// Indicators
z = ZScore(C,zLookback);

// Buy and Sell rules
Buy = Cross(zBuyLevel,z);
Sell = Cross(z,zSellLevel);

// Plots
Plot( C, "C", colorBlack, styleCandle );
Plot( z, "zscore",colorRed,styleLine|styleownscale);

// Explore

///////////////////////////// end ////////////////
```

Figure 7.1 Program template for a trading system

Objective Function

One of the first steps in indicator-based development is choice of the objective function. The objective function must satisfy several requirements:

1. It encapsulates and quantifies the subjective preferences of the trader / developer. This provides for a comfortable description of the ranking. There should be terms in the objective function that correspond to features the developer deems important.
2. It assigns a single-valued score to each set of trades evaluated. The score is computed as a combination of terms. The

individual terms reward desirable characteristics and penalize undesirable characteristics. This guides the development process.
3. If the objective function was designed properly, the order of ranking via the objective function is the same order of subjective preference of the trader. This is important during validation phase—in particular the walk forward process. When one alternative is chosen as the "best," it is based on having the highest objective function score. The developer must have confidence that choice is acceptable.
4. It prefers alternatives that are more likely to perform well in live trading. That is, it introduces as little bias into the process as possible. This is a caution. There are some characteristics of a trading system that are difficult to assess during development, drawdown being a prime example. Including an objective function component based on maximum drawdown over a test period introduces an unfavorable bias and should be avoided.

Important metrics that can, and should, be components of the objective function include:
- Percentage gained per trade.
- Number of bars held.
- Number of trades per year.
- Percentage of trades that are winners.
- Percentage of time a position is held.
- Magnitude of losing trades.

Because they are sequence dependent, these metrics should be avoided:
- Maximum drawdown for the test period.
- Maximum losers in a row.
- Time between new highs.

Ideally the objective function meets these criteria, but there may be limitations imposed by the trading system development platform. Every modern platform offers at least one default objective function—often a variation of total profit for the test period. Other built-in objective functions may be available. Evaluate those and choose one that best meets the criteria and reflects your preferences. The best platforms provide capability for the developer to define, program, and use custom objective functions.

If available, CAR25 would be the preferred objective function. Recall that CAR25 is computed from a distribution of risk normalized equally likely equity curves. AmiBroker provides the trades that are used in those computations, but it is not possible to compute CAR25 from within an AmiBroker program.

AmiBroker does support custom objective functions, and provides access to a wide range of metrics related to the system performance through its "Custom Backtester Interface." The AmiBroker User Guide has two related documents; one that gives an overview[1] and the other more details.[2] There is also a pdf file with slides from one of Tomasz Janeczko's presentations.[3]

Metrics are provided at two levels:
- Summary statistics, such as number of trades, percent of trades that are winners, and average percent gained per trade. These are available from predefined variables built in to the reports.
- Trade by trade, such as maximum adverse excursion. These are available by traversing a list of trades and computing custom metrics.

Figure 7.2 lists an example objective function that is intended to reward
- frequent trading
- accurate trading
- short holding period

and penalize
- severe losses.

It uses "decathlon" scoring. To begin, several factors are identified as important by the developer. Each has an associated metric computed. Each metric is scaled, and they are combined to give a composite score for the objective function. The combination can be by addition, as in the olympic decathlon event, or by multiplication, as in the example shown here.

This example has been written for clarity. Several passes are made over the trade list—one for each of the terms that require trade by trade metrics. In a more efficient coding, these could be consolidated. But, since the function is not computed often, it might be left in its expanded form for ease of understanding and maintenance.

It is a draft. You will want to consider other metrics and other weightings, and adjust it to meet your needs and preferences.

Note the multiple occurrences of the statement "addcustommetric" near the end of the program. Each of the metrics so assigned will have its own column on the backtest and walk forward screens, and will be summarized in the statistics report.

---

1 *How to add user-defined metrics to backtest / optimization report*, http://www.amibroker.com/guide/a_custommetrics.html
2 *Portfolio Backtester Interface Reference Guide*, http://www.amibroker.com/guide/a_custombacktest.html
3 *Advanced Users' Workshop: Custom Backtester Interface*, http://www.amibroker.com/docs/Houston2.pdf

```
//  ObFnDemo1.afl
//
//  Please read and understand the disclaimer.
//
//  This is a draft document.
//  It may or may not reflect the objective function
//  used to rank tests described in the text.
//  It may or may not reflect criteria important
//  to you.
//  It may or may not rank alternative trading
//  systems in the same order you prefer them.
//  Run tests and make adjustments so that it does.
//
//  Copyright © 2014 Blue Owl Press, Inc
//
//  Use:   #include <ObFnDemo1.afl>;
//  Refer to the metric by its name:  ObFnDemo1
//

SetCustomBacktestProc( "" );

if ( Status( "action" ) == actionPortfolio )
{
    bo = GetBacktesterObject();
    bo.backtest();

//  From trade list
//  For clarity, Several passes are made

//  Maximum loss
//  Terminal equity at full fraction
    numberTrades = 0;
    MaxLoss = 0;
    TWRCalc = 1.0;

    for ( trade = bo.GetFirstTrade();
          trade;
          trade = bo.GetNextTrade() )
    {
        numberTrades = numberTrades + 1;
        Profit = trade.GetProfit();
        EntryValue = trade.GetEntryValue();
        GeometricGain = Profit / EntryValue;
        TWRCalc = TWRCalc * ( 1 + GeometricGain );

        if ( GeometricGain < MaxLoss )
        {
            MaxLoss = GeometricGain;
        }
    }

    MaxLoss = 100.0 * abs( MaxLoss );

    NumberYears = ( BarCount / 252 );
    NumberTradesPerYear = numberTrades / NumberYears;
    CAR50 = 100.0
            * ( exp( ln( TWRCalc ) / NumberYears ) - 1 );
//  Sortino Ratio (in a single pass)
    k = 0;
    m = 0;
```

```
    mold = 0;
    s = 0;
    sold = 0;

    for ( trade = bo.GetFirstTrade();
          trade;
          trade = bo.GetNextTrade() )
    {
        k = k + 1;
        Profit = trade.GetProfit();
        EntryValue = trade.GetEntryValue();
        g = GeometricGain = Profit / EntryValue;

        if ( k == 1 )
        {
            m = GeometricGain;
            s = 0;
        }
        else
        {
            m = mold + ( g - mold ) / k;

            if ( g < 0 )
                s = sold + ( g - mold ) * ( g - m );
            else
                s = sold + ( 0 - mold ) * ( 0 - m );
        }

        sold = s;
        mold = m;
    }

    if ( k >= 2 )
        Sortino = 100.0 * m / sqrt( s / ( k - 1 ) );
    else
        Sortino = 0.0;

// From the statistics
    st = bo.getperformancestats( 0 );

    NetProfit = st.getvalue( "NetProfit" );
    expectancy = st.getvalue( "AllAvgProfitLossPercent" );
    percentwins = st.getvalue( "WinnersPercent" );
    barsheld = st.getvalue( "AllAvgBarsHeld" );

// Reward these -- set minimums

// Expectancy
    ExpectancyULimit = 0.25;
    ExpectancyLLimit = 0.10;

//    if ( Expectancy > ExpectancyULimit )
//        ExpectancyScore = 1.0;
//    else
    if ( Expectancy < ExpectancyLLimit )
        ExpectancyScore = 0.0;
    else
        ExpectancyScore
            = ( Expectancy - ExpectancyLLimit )
            / ( ExpectancyULimit - ExpectancyLLimit );

// Percent winning trades
```

```
    PercentWinsULimit = 70.0;
    PercentWinsLLimit = 55.0;
//    if ( PercentWins > PercentWinsULimit )
//        PercentWinsScore = 1.0;
//    else
    if ( PercentWins < PercentWinsLLimit )
        PercentWinsScore = 0.0;
    else
        PercentWinsScore
        = ( PercentWins - PercentWinsLLimit )
          / ( PercentWinsULimit - PercentWinsLLimit );
// Number of trades per year
    NumberTradesPerYearULimit = 20.0;
    NumberTradesPerYearLLimit = 8.0;
//    if ( NumberTradesPerYear > NumberTradesPerYearULimit )
//        NumberTradesPerYearScore = 1.0;
//    else
    if ( NumberTradesPerYear < NumberTradesPerYearLLimit )
        NumberTradesPerYearScore = 0.0;
    else
        NumberTradesPerYearScore =
            ( NumberTradesPerYear
              - NumberTradesPerYearLLimit )
            / ( NumberTradesPerYearULimit
                - NumberTradesPerYearLLimit );
// Sortino ratio
    SortinoULimit = 20.0;
    SortinoLLimit = 10.0;
//    if ( Sortino > SortinoULimit )
//        SortinoScore = 1.0;
//    else
    if ( Sortino < SortinoLLimit )
        SortinoScore = 0.0;
    else
        SortinoScore =
            ( Sortino - SortinoLLimit )
            / ( SortinoULimit - SortinoLLimit );
// CAR50 (estimated at full fraction)
    CAR50ULimit = 10.0;
    CAR50LLimit = 0.0;
//    if ( CAR50 > CAR50ULimit )
//        CAR50Score = 1.0;
//    else
    if ( CAR50 < CAR50LLimit )
        CAR50Score = 0.0;
    else
        CAR50Score =
            ( CAR50 - CAR50LLimit )
            / ( CAR50ULimit - CAR50LLimit );
// Penalize these -- set maximums

// Maximum Loss -- reward a small number
    MaxLossULimit = 20.0;
    MaxLossLLimit = 5.0;
```

Model Development—Indicator-Based

```
        if ( MaxLoss > MaxLossULimit )
            MaxLossScore = 0.0;
//      else
//          if ( MaxLoss < MaxLossLLimit )
//              MaxLossScore = 1.0;
        else
            MaxLossScore
                = Min( 1.0 - ( ( MaxLoss - MaxLossLLimit )
                       / ( MaxLossULimit - MaxLossLLimit ) ), 1.5 );

//  Bars held -- reward a small number
        BarsHeldULimit = 10.0;

        BarsHeldLLimit = 5.0;

        if ( BarsHeld > BarsHeldULimit )
            BarsHeldScore = 0.0;

//      else
//          if ( BarsHeld < BarsHeldLLimit )
//              BarsHeldScore = 1.0;
        else
            BarsHeldScore
                = Min( 1.0 - ( ( BarsHeld - BarsHeldLLimit )
                       / ( BarsHeldULimit - BarsHeldLLimit ) ), 1.5
                   );

//  Combine terms

        ObFnDemo1 = CAR50
                    * ExpectancyScore
                    * PercentWinsScore
                    * NumberTradesPerYearScore
                    * SortinoScore
//                  * MaxLossScore
                    * BarsHeldScore;

//  Expose metrics

        bo.addcustommetric( "ObFnDemo1", ObFnDemo1, 0, 0, 2, 4 );
        bo.addcustommetric( "NetProfit", NetProfit, 0, 0, 2, 4 );
        bo.AddCustomMetric( "BarCount", BarCount, 0, 0, 0, 4 );
        bo.addcustommetric( "numbertrades", numberTrades, 0, 0, 0,
                4 );
        bo.AddCustomMetric( "Trades Per Year", Numbertradesperyear,
                0, 0, 2, 4 );
        bo.addcustommetric( "percentwins", percentwins, 0, 0, 2, 4
               );
        bo.addcustommetric( "expectancy", expectancy, 0, 0, 2, 4 );
        bo.addcustommetric( "Bars Held", BarsHeld, 0, 0, 2, 4 );
        bo.addcustommetric( "MaxLoss", MaxLoss, 0, 0, 2, 4 );
        bo.addcustommetric( "TWRCalc", TWRCalc, 0, 0, 2, 4 );
        bo.addcustommetric( "CAR 50", CAR50, 0, 0, 2, 4 );
        bo.addcustommetric( "Sortino", Sortino, 0, 0, 2, 4 );
    }
///////////////   end   ///////////////
```

Figure 7.2 Custom objective function

Indicators

Trading system development platforms work well with impulse signals. We will begin with those, using daily data, and a system well known to fit the trade profile we prefer. A long position is entered when an oscillating indicator suggests the price is oversold, anticipating that price will rise toward the mean.

There are several choices to make:
- which data series
- which oscillator
- how long a lookback length
- how deeply oversold
- what condition gives the signal
- how to enter the trade
- how to exit the trade
- how to measure success

What the Data Tells Us

Chapter 2 discussed the risk inherent in a data series, independent of the model. Recall we want:
- Enough volatility to provide for profitable trades.
- Not so much volatility that the intra-trade risk is excessive.
- Detectable and persistent patterns that precede profitable trades.

We can measure the first two from the data alone. The third requires a model that identifies the patterns. We will not know whether there are identifiable and discoverable patterns until we develop the model. We are beginning to answer the third now.

Review Figure 5.10. Begin with those series that have passed the risk and profit screen, are very liquid, and easily traded. Prefer those with high safe-f scores and high CAR25 scores. Some research indicates that those listed in Figure 5.10E are somewhat easier to model.

Of course, you can use any data series you want to. Some that have not passed the screens have easily identifiable and persistent patterns. Given sufficiently high trade accuracy, both safe-f and CAR25 can be high enough that the resulting system is tradable. The advantage of beginning with one of the issues on the list is that the required accuracy of identification of profitable patterns is lower. It is easier to develop profitable, safe, tradable systems with these.

System Overview

The system will be long / flat. A steeply rising price makes it easy to be long. If the price continues to rise, that is a good thing. But we need to be aware of, and perhaps adjust for, an upward bias. There are good trading opportunities even in periods of falling prices. At very least, we need to know how the system performs during those periods. If performance is poor when price is falling, we can try adding filters to block long trades during those periods.

While there may be a short / flat system for the same data series, I recommend developing long / flat separately first because:
- It is easier to identify bottoms and entries for long trades than tops and entries for short trades.
- Long / flat has fewer rules and parameters than long / flat / short.
- There is an upward bias in price related to factors such as inflation, population growth, and productivity increase that favor being long equities.
- The characteristics of profitable long trades and profitable short trades are different for most issues. If a short / flat system does exist, it is probably not a reversal or symmetrical system.

Indicator Selection

We expect there to be about 15 to 50 ideal trades per year, each 1 to 3 days, perhaps 5 days, long. To pick a specific number for discussion, say 24 trades per year. 24 trades each year requires 24 signals each year.

Signals generated by indicators are crossings or turnings. One indicator crosses another indicator, an indicator crosses a critical level, an indicator changes direction, or something similar.

Part of the development process is fitting the indicator to the price changes and generating buy and sell signals—trade events. The frequency of these events is related to the length of the cycle of the indicator and the number of bars used to compute it. For generality, we will describe the number of bars as the "lookback." Taking a moving average of price as an example, to obtain 24 turns from rising to falling, or 24 crosses of the closing price with the moving average, there must be 24 cycles in the year of 252 trading days. If the data was perfectly aligned with the cycles, that implies a cycle length of about 10 days. The indicators we use and the data we process are never perfectly aligned. The cycles are seldom cooperatively stationary. The length that best identifies the signal event is often about half the cycle length. Useful lookbacks are typically shorter than 10 days—sometimes as short as 2 days. For the trades we hope to identify, choosing a lookback that is shorter than ideal is more forgiving than choosing one that is longer than ideal.

Figure 7.4 is a listing for a program that computes an ideal data series of sine wave and plots it in the same pane as an issue being tested. The ideal data can be adjusted manually using sliders and the Param statements to adjust the length of the cycle and the offset.

```
//  FitSineCycle.afl
//
//  Disclaimer continues to apply
//
//  Copyright © 2014 Blue Owl Press, Inc
//
//  Generate a sine wave data series
//  and manually fit it to a price series.
//

SetBarsRequired( sbrAll, sbrAll );   // Require all data

// Parameters
CycleLength = Param( "CycleLength", 10, 2, 25, 1 );
Offset = Param( "Offset", 5, 0, 25, 1 );

// Use SPY for the dates
CycleData = Foreign( "SPY", "C" );

// Variables
MiddlePrice = EMA( C, 100 );
Amplitude = ATR( 10 );

ZigPPct = 0.5;   // ZigZag percent for the primary data
ZigCPct = 0.5;   // ZigZag percent for the sine wave data

// Compute the ZigZag indicator of the primary data
zp = Zig( c, ZigPPct );
// Set a "Buy" arrow at the low
Buy = zp < Ref( zp, -1 ) AND zp < Ref( zp, 1 );

// Compute the sine wave data
// Skip the elements for the offset
for ( i = 0; i < Offset; i++ )
{
    CycleData[i] = C[i];
}
for ( i = Offset; i < BarCount; i++ )
{
    CycleData[i] = MiddlePrice[i] + Amplitude[i]
                * ( sin( ( i - Offset ) * 2
                * 3.14159 / CycleLength ) );
}
// Compute the ZigZag indicator for the sine wave data
// to make it easier to position
zc = Zig( CycleData, ZigCPct );

// Plots
Plot( c, "PrimarySeries", colorBlack, styleLine | stylethick );
shapes = IIf( Buy, shapeUpArrow, shapeNone );
shapecolors = IIf( Buy, colorGreen, colorWhite );
PlotShapes( shapes, shapecolors );

Plot( CycleData, "CycleData", colorBlue, styleLine );
Plot( zc, "Zig of Cycle", colorBlue, styleLine | stylethick );

///////////// end /////////////
```

Figure 7.4 *Fit sine cycle*

Figure 7.5 shows the application of the program to EWM—the MSCI Malaysia ETF. The cycle length for the sine wave data shown is 6 days.

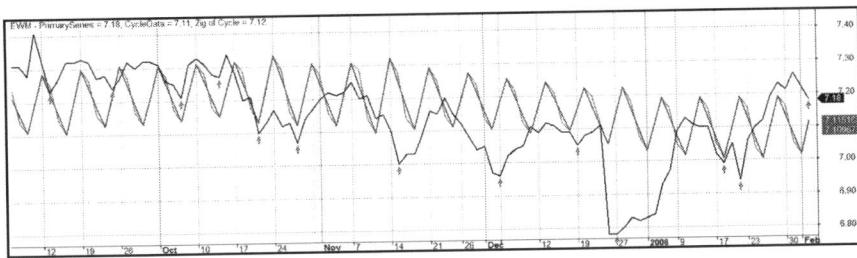

Figure 7.5 EWM with 6 days cycle overlay

Examples

The next sections show the AmiBroker code for the model, along with the results, for several technical indicators used to signal entries. These are "selected" results. They are entirely in-sample. They are not the result of walk forward runs. We are still prospecting to see if profitable patterns exist in the data, and if we can identify them. As you replicate these examples, although your specific results will probably differ, the general shape of the equity curve you obtain should be similar.

RSI -- Relative Strength Indicator

My Mean Reversion book[4] discusses the RSI indicator in much more detail, including techniques for using non-integer lookback lengths.

```
// RSIModel.afl
//
// Disclaimer continues to apply
//
// Copyright © 2014 Blue Owl Press, Inc
//
// Signals are generated at the close of daily trading
// for execution at the close of the same bar.

// Objective Function ObFnDemo1, from the Include directory
#include <ObFnDemo1.afl>;

// System settings
OptimizerSetEngine( "cmae" );
SetOption( "ExtraColumnsLocation", 1 );
SetBacktestMode( backtestRegular );
SetOption( "initialequity", 100000 );
MaxPos = 1;
SetOption( "maxopenpositions", MaxPos );
SetPositionSize( 10000, spsValue );
```

---

4 http://www.meanreversiontradingsystems.com/

```
SetOption ( "CommissionMode", 3 );  // $ per share
SetOption( "CommissionAmount", 0.005 );
SetTradeDelays( 0, 0, 0, 0 );
BuyPrice = SellPrice = Close;

// Global variables and parameters

// User Functions
function RSI_Custom( p, Lambda )
{
    //      p == series having its RSI computed
    //      lambda == weight given to latest value
    UpMove = Max( p - Ref( p, -1 ), 0 );
    DnMove = Max( Ref( p, -1 ) - p, 0 );

    //      Initialze arrays
    UpMoveSm = p;
    DnMoveSm = p;

    for ( i = 1;i < BarCount;i++ )
    {
        UpMoveSm[i] = Lambda * UpMove[i] + ( 1.0 - Lambda ) *
            UpMoveSM[i-1];
        DnMoveSm[i] = Lambda * DnMove[i] + ( 1.0 - Lambda ) *
            DnMoveSM[i-1];
    }
    Numer = UpMoveSm;
    Denom = UpMoveSm + DnMoveSm;
    return ( 100 * IIf( Denom <= 0, 0.5, Numer / Denom ) );
}

// Local variables, beginning with Param and Optimize
Lambda = Optimize( "Lambda", 0.47, 0.40, 0.80, 0.01 );
RSIBuyLevel = Optimize( "RSIBuyLevel", 16, 1, 99, 1 );
RSISellIncrem = Optimize( "RSISellIncrem", 40, 0, 40, 1 );

RSISellLevel = Min( RSIBuyLevel + RSISellIncrem, 99 );

// Indicators
RSI_C = RSI_Custom( C, Lambda );

// Buy and Sell rules
Buy = Cross( RSIBuyLevel, RSI_C );
Sell = Cross( RSI_C, RSISellLevel );

// Plots
Plot( C, "C", colorBlack, styleCandle );
Plot( RSI_C, "RSICustom", colorGreen, styleLine
            | styleOwnScale, 0, 100 );

///////////////////////////// end //////////////////
```

Figure 7.6 RSI model listing

Model Development—Indicator-Based

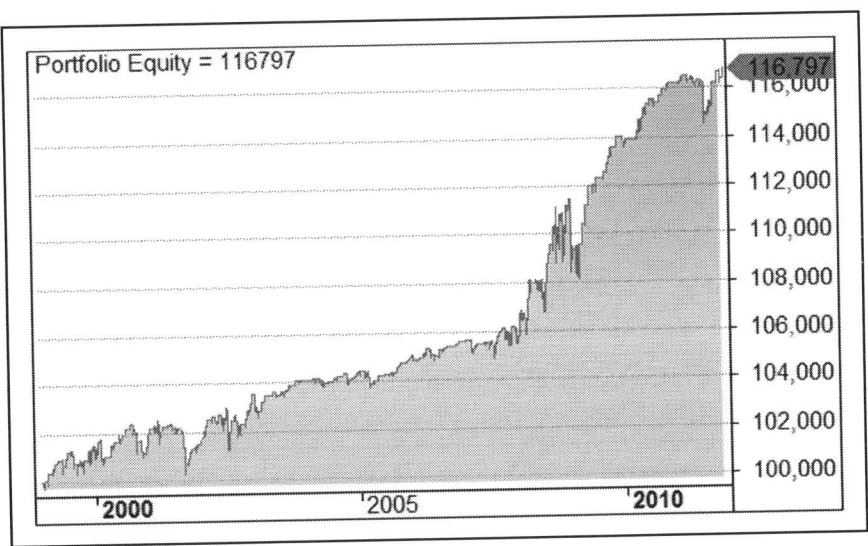

Figure 7.7 XLF with RSI Model

The summary of the RSI system:
- Compute RSI of daily closing prices using the technique I developed in my Mean Reversion book. The value of "lambda" is 0.47. This corresponds to a lookback length of about 3.125 days when using a standard (not Wilder's) exponential moving average.
- Buy at the close of the daily bar when RSI crosses downward through 16.
- Sell at the close of the daily bar when the RSI crosses upward through 56.
- There are 223 trades in 13 years.
- 72% are winners.
- Average gain per trade is 0.75%.
- Average holding period is 3.8 days.
- Total profit is $16,797.
- Is profitable for 50 of 50 of the list in Figure 7.3.
- Is profitable for 432 of the S&P 500.
- Is profitable for 500 of the S&P 600.

Z-score

The z statistic is the number of standard deviations of a single point from the data's mean over a lookback window. In this case, and in most cases, the single point is at the most recent end of the window.

```
// ZScoreModel.afl
//
// Disclaimer continues to apply
```

```
//
// Copyright © 2014 Blue Owl Press, Inc
//
// Signals are generated at the close of daily trading
// for execution at the close of the same bar.

// Objective Function ObFnDemo1, from the Include directory
#include <ObFnDemo1.afl>;

// System settings
OptimizerSetEngine( "cmae" );
SetOption( "ExtraColumnsLocation", 1 );
SetBacktestMode( backtestRegular );
SetOption( "initialequity", 100000 );
MaxPos = 1;
SetOption( "maxopenpositions", MaxPos );
SetPositionSize( 10000, spsValue );
SetOption ( "CommissionMode", 3 );  // $ per share
SetOption( "CommissionAmount", 0.005 );
SetTradeDelays( 0, 0, 0, 0 );
BuyPrice = SellPrice = Close;

// Global variables and parameters

// User Functions
function ZScore( p, Lookback )
{
    //     Compute the z-score of series p,
    //     using lookback as the length of
    //     the mean and standard deviation
    m = MA( p, lookback );
    s = StDev( p, lookback );
    z = ( p - m ) / s;
    return z;
}

// Local variables, beginning with Param and Optimize
zLookback = Optimize( "zLookback", 5, 2, 5, 1 );
zBuyLevel = Optimize( "zBuyLevel", -1.1, -2, 0.5, 0.1 );
zSellIncrem = Optimize( "zSellIncrem", 2.3, 0, 4, 0.1 );

zSellLevel = zBuyLevel + zSellIncrem;

// Indicators
z = ZScore( C, zLookback );

// Buy and Sell rules
Buy = Cross( zBuyLevel, z );
Sell = Cross( z, zSellLevel );

// Plots
Plot( C, "C", colorBlack, styleCandle );
Plot( z, "zscore", colorRed, styleLine | styleownscale );

//////////////////////////// end ////////////////////
```

Figure 7.8 Z-score model listing

Model Development—Indicator-Based

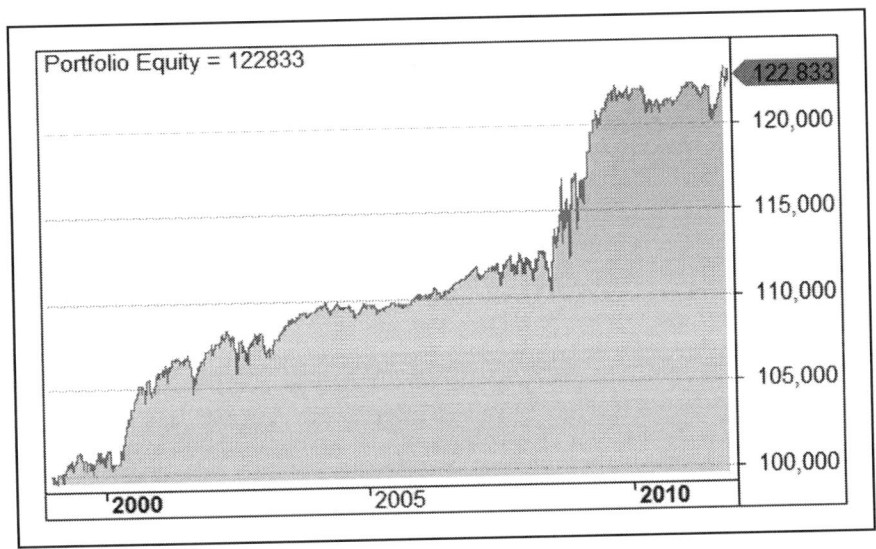

Figure 7.9 XLF with Z-score model

The summary of the ZScore system:
- Compute the z statistic using daily closing bars. Use a 5 day sequence, and simple moving average.
- Buy at the close of the daily bar when z-score crosses downward through -1.1. That is, buy when the close is 1.1 standard deviations below the mean, both of which are based on 5 days.
- Sell at the close of the daily bar when the 5-day z-score crosses upward through 1.2.
- There are 241 trades in 13 years.
- 69% are winners.
- Average gain per trade is 0.95%.
- Average holding period is 6.7 days.
- Total profit is $22,823.
- Is profitable for 50 of 50 of the list in Figure 7.3.
- Is profitable for 460 of the S&P 500.
- Is profitable for 533 of the S&P 600.

Position in range

Position in range indicators include many familiar indicators. The primary difference is the amount of smoothing and lag:
- slow stochastic
- fast stochastic
- unsmoothed stochastic (Williams %R)
- percent rank

```
//   PIRModel.afl
//
//   Disclaimer continues to apply
//
//   Copyright © 2014 Blue Owl Press, Inc
//
//   Signals are generated at the close of daily trading
//   for execution at the close of the same bar.
//
//   The indicator computed by this code is unsmoothed.

// Objective Function ObFnDemo1, from the Include directory
#include <ObFnDemo1.afl>;

// System settings
OptimizerSetEngine( "cmae" );
SetOption( "ExtraColumnsLocation", 1 );
SetBacktestMode( backtestRegular );
SetOption( "initialequity", 100000 );
MaxPos = 1;
SetOption( "maxopenpositions", MaxPos );
SetPositionSize( 10000, spsValue );
SetOption ( "CommissionMode", 3 );  // $ per share
SetOption( "CommissionAmount", 0.005 );
SetTradeDelays( 0, 0, 0, 0 );
BuyPrice = SellPrice = Close;

// Global variables and parameters

// User Functions
function PIR ( p, Lookback )
{
    //    Compute the position of the most
    //    recent value relative to the values
    //    in the lookback range.

    hh = HHV( p, Lookback );
    ll = LLV( p, Lookback );
    pp = 100.0 * ( p - ll ) / ( hh - ll );

    return pp;
}

//  Local variables, beginning with Param and Optimize
pirLookback = Optimize( "pirLookback", 10, 1, 99, 1 );
pirBuyLevel = Optimize( "pirBuyLevel", 10, 1, 99, 1 );
pirSellIncrem = Optimize( "pirSellIncrem", 36, 0, 50, 1 );

pirSellLevel = Min( pirBuyLevel + pirSellIncrem, 99 );


// Indicators
pp = PIR( C, pirLookback );

// Buy and Sell rules
Buy = Cross( pirBuyLevel, pp );
Sell = Cross( pp, pirSellLevel );

// Plots

Plot( C, "C", colorBlack, styleCandle );
```

Model Development—Indicator-Based

```
Plot( pp, "Position In Range", colorRed, styleLine
      | styleownscale );

///////////////////////////// end ////////////////
```

Figure 7.10 PIR model listing

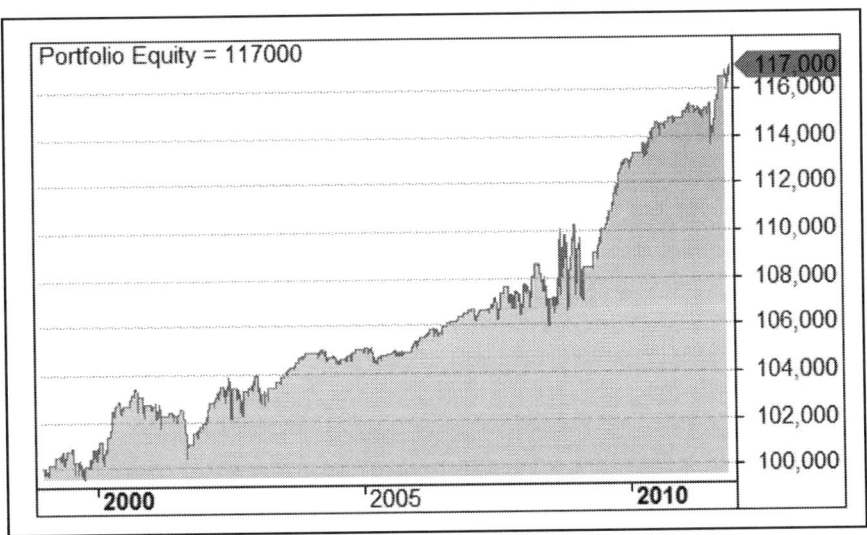

Figure 7.11 XLF with PIR model

The summary of the PIR system:
- Use daily closing prices. Note the highest close and lowest close for the past 10 days. Compute the range those values define. The PIR indicator is the percentage of the range the close of the final day is above the lowest value.
- Buy at the close of the daily bar when PIR crosses downward through 10.
- Sell at the close of the daily bar when the PIR crosses upward through 46.
- There are 201 trades in 13 years.
- 72% are winners.
- Average gain per trade is 0.85%.
- Average holding period is 5.6 days.
- Total profit is $17,000.
- Is profitable for 49 of 50 of the list in Figure 7.3.
- Is profitable for 442 of the S&P 500.
- Is profitable for 532 of the S&P 600.

Detrended price oscillator

DPO is the residual after removing a longer term trend from a price series. It is the output of a high-pass filter.

```
//  DPOModel.afl
//
//  Disclaimer continues to apply
//
//  Copyright © 2014 Blue Owl Press, Inc
//
//  Signals are generated at the close of daily trading
//  for execution at the close of the same bar.
//

// Objective Function ObFnDemo1, from the Include directory
#include <ObFnDemo1.afl>;

// System settings
OptimizerSetEngine( "cmae" );
SetOption( "ExtraColumnsLocation", 1 );
SetBacktestMode( backtestRegular );
SetOption( "initialequity", 100000 );
MaxPos = 1;
SetOption( "maxopenpositions", MaxPos );
SetPositionSize( 10000, spsValue );
SetOption ( "CommissionMode", 3 );  // $ per share
SetOption( "CommissionAmount", 0.005 );
SetTradeDelays( 0, 0, 0, 0 );
BuyPrice = SellPrice = Close;

// Global variables and parameters

// User Functions
function PIR ( p, Lookback )
{
    //    Compute the position of the most
    //    recent value relative to the values
    //    in the lookback range.

    hh = HHV( p, Lookback );
    ll = LLV( p, Lookback );
    pp = 100.0 * ( p - ll ) / ( hh - ll );

    return pp;
}

//  Local variables, beginning with Param and Optimize
MA1Length = Optimize( "MA1Length", 15, 1, 50, 1 );
pirLookback = Optimize( "pirLookback", 29, 2, 30, 1 );
pirBuyLevel = Optimize( "pirBuyLevel", 15, 10, 30, 1 );
pirSellIncrem = Optimize( "pirSellIncrem", 13, 0, 50, 1 );
HoldDays = Optimize( "HoldDays", 9, 1, 10, 1 );

pirSellLevel = Min( pirBuyLevel + pirSellIncrem, 99 );

// Indicators
MA1 = MA( C, MA1Length );
DPO = ( C - MA1 ) / MA1;
PIRDPO = PIR( DPO, PIRLookback );
```

Model Development—Indicator-Based

```
// Buy and Sell rules
Buy = Cross( pirBuyLevel, PIRDPO );
Sell = BarsSince( Buy ) >= HoldDays
          OR  Cross( PIRDPO, pirSellLevel );

// Plots
Plot( C, "C", colorBlack, styleCandle );
Plot( MA1, "MA1", colorBlue, styleLine | styleThick );
Plot ( PIRDPO, "PIRDPO", colorGreen, styleLine
          | styleOwnScale, 0, 100 );

///////////////////////////// end ////////////////
```

Figure 7.12 DPO model listing

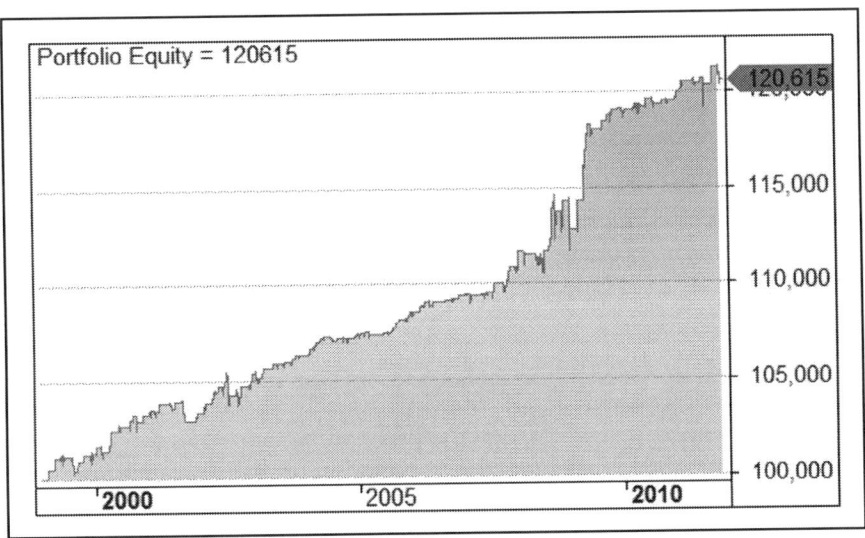

Figure 7.13 XLF with DPO model

The summary of the DPO system:
- Use closing prices of daily bars. The long term moving average is a 15 day simple moving average. Compute DPO as the percentage the current closing price is above or below the 15 day average. Use the PIR function to compute the position-in-range of the DPO within its 29 day range.
- Buy at the close of the daily bar when PIR of DPO crosses downward through 15.
- Sell at the close of the daily bar when the PIR of DPO crosses upward through 28 or on the 9th day of the trade.
- There are 173 trades in 13 years.
- 77% are winners.
- Average gain per trade is 1.19%.
- Average holding period is 3.9 days.

- Total profit is $20,615.
- Is profitable for 50 of 50 of the list in Figure 7.3.
- Is profitable for 440 of the S&P 500.
- Is profitable for 506 of the S&P 600.

Diffusion index

The Quantitative Trading Systems book[5] describes diffusion indexes. Diffusion indexes gather individual metrics from each of a set of members of a broad sector, weight each according to some measure of importance, combine them, normalize the result, and report a single value representing the broad sector. An example is an index computed as the number of new highs divided by the sum of the number of new highs plus the number of new lows for all stocks in a group. The index ranges between 0.0 when there are no new highs and 1.0 when there are no new lows.

The NYSE advance-decline statistic is a diffusion index. The effectiveness of a diffusion index depends on the purity of the index as it relates to the individual issues. If the set of issues used consists of similar individuals, the diffusion index acts in accordance with the central limit theorem. The consensus of the group reflects the broader category, and is very predictive. If the set is mixed, the resulting index has little predictive value. Our use of diffusion indexes is as a measure of overextension. Well defined diffusion indexes with lookback periods of a few days are mean reverting.

The AmiBroker function available for implementation of diffusion indexes at the time that book was written was the AddToComposite function (ATC). ATC is still available, and it is the best function for some uses.

Recent revisions of AmiBroker introduced some new functions—particularly Static Variables—that make diffusion indexes easier to code and use. Figure 7.14 is a program listing that computes a diffusion index based on daily RSI indicator. The broad sector is the financial sector of the US economy, with the S&P sector ETF XLF as the surrogate. The diffusion index is created from the ten largest components of the ETF.

The S&P web site lists the constituent members and their weightings.[6] There are two very evident problems.
- **Membership Bias**. Diffusion indexes are very susceptible to membership bias. The tests will be run over a period of some 13 years beginning in 1999. We can be fairly certain that there have been changes in the top ten constituents of XLF since 1999. Using data associated with the current list to test profit

---
5 http://www.quantitativetradingsystems.com/
6 http://www.sectorspdr.com/sectorspdr/sector/xlf/holdings

Model Development—Indicator-Based

and risk for a period in the past introduces a "survivorship" or "membership" bias. All of the major indexes readjust membership periodically. Some do it simply to help the index show regular and strong gains. Others do it to reflect changes in composition or importance among the constituent issues. Accurate results require that the list of issues correctly contain companies that are members as of the beginning of the period being tested. The S&P website does not provide a list of changes to the membership of XLF. Some data services, such as Norgate Premium Data, maintain historical membership for some indexes and provide tools for their use.[7] The data used with Figure 7.14 and this example has not been adjusted to avoid membership bias.

- **Near bankruptcy of AIG.** The share price of AIG is around $50 at the time of this writing. It had been below $10 in 2009 — down from $1200 in 2007. The drop in share price of 99 percent distorts everything.

  We have a subjective choice to make. Include it and live with the distortions? Or omit it and leave out one of the top ten holdings in the ETF? Since the list is not adjusted for membership, which already introduces a known bias, I will omit AIG, adding to the flaws. The purpose of the example is educational, so try both and use it as a learning experience.

For this example, the diffusion index is based on RSI of closing prices, with a 2 day lookback. There is nothing special about a 2 period RSI. Do your own research into other possible diffusion indicators. Trading results will vary depending on the choice of this indicator.

For clarity, this example uses two programs.

The first, Diffusion_CreateIndex.afl, shown in Figure 7.14, creates the diffusion index from the individual issues and stores it on disc. It uses a set of individual issues whose tickers are either in a list or a Watch-List. It opens each in turn, computes the RSI indicator, adds that value to the diffusion index under construction. XLF data is not used in this step. There is no buying or selling — only computation of the diffusion index.

```
// Diffusion_CreateIndex.afl
//
// Disclaimer continues to apply
//
// Copyright © 2014 Blue Owl Press, Inc
//

// System settings
SetBarsRequired( sbrAll, sbrAll );   // Require all data
```

---

7 http://www.premiumdata.net/products/premiumdata/ushistorical.php

```
// Global variables and parameters

//  Local variables, beginning with Param and Optimize
// The list could be hard coded in the program.
Tickerlist = "BRK.B,WFC,JPM,BAC,C,AXP,USB,GS,MET";
// Or it could be in a Watchlist
//ListNum = CategoryFind("ConstituentsOfXLF",categoryWatchli
          st);
//TickerList = GetCategorySymbols(categoryWatchlist,ListNum);

// Indicators
// Use SPY for dates and initialize to zero
XLFDiffIndex = 0 * Foreign( "SPY", "C" );

// Process the price data for each ticker in the list
for ( i = 0; ( sym = StrExtract( TickerList, i ) ) != ""; i++ )
{
    CS = Foreign( sym, "C" );
    RSIVal = RSIa( CS, 2 );
    XLFDiffIndex = XLFDiffIndex + RSIVal;
}

// Store the data on disc
StaticVarSet( "XLFDiffIndex", XLFDiffIndex, True );

//Plot(XLFDIffIndex,"DiffIndex",colorBlack,styleLine);

/////////////// end ///////////////
```

Figure 7.14 Create the diffusion index

Figure 7.15 shows the price data of XLF in the upper pane, the diffusion index, calculated by the Diffusion_CreateIndex program, in the lower pane.

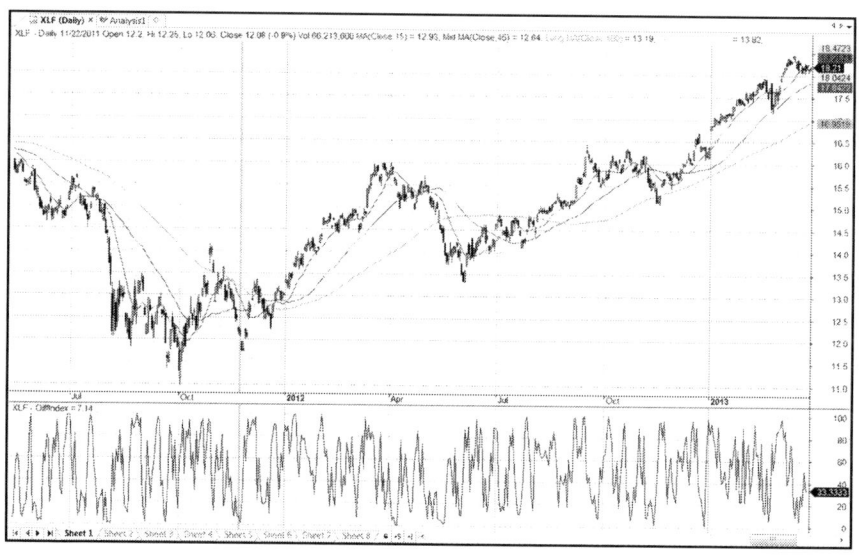

Figure 7.15 Plot of XLF and the diffusion index

Model Development—Indicator-Based

The second, Diffusion_UseIndex.afl, shown in Figure 7.16, reads the previously prepared diffusion index into a variable, and uses that variable as an indicator to trade XLF. Set the Current issue to XLF, the ETF that is the broad sector containing the issues used to create the diffusion index.

```
// Diffusion_UseIndex.afl
//
// Disclaimer continues to apply
//
// Copyright © 2014 Blue Owl Press, Inc
//

// Objective Function ObFnDemo1, from the Include directory
#include <ObFnDemo1.afl>;

// System settings
SetBarsRequired( sbrAll, sbrAll ); // Require all data
OptimizerSetEngine( "cmae" );
SetOption( "ExtraColumnsLocation", 1 );
SetBacktestMode( backtestRegular );
SetOption( "initialequity", 100000 );
MaxPos = 1;
SetOption( "maxopenpositions", MaxPos );
SetPositionSize( 10000, spsValue );
SetOption ( "CommissionMode", 3 ); // $ per share
SetOption( "CommissionAmount", 0.005 );
SetTradeDelays( 0, 0, 0, 0 );
BuyPrice = SellPrice = Close;

// Global variables and parameters
BuyLevel = Optimize( "BuyLevel", 31, 1, 99, 1 );
SellIncrem = Optimize( "SellIncrem", 18, 0, 50, 1 );

SellLevel = Min( BuyLevel + SellIncrem, 99 );

DiffIndex = StaticVarGet( "XLFDiffIndex" );

// Indicators
DIPR = PercentRank( DiffIndex, 126 );

// Buy and Sell rules
Buy = Cross( BuyLevel, DIPR );
Sell = Cross( DIPR, SellLevel );

// Plots
Plot( DIPR, "DiffIndex", colorBlack, styleLine );

///////////// end //////////////
```

Figure 7.16 Use the diffusion index

Figure 7.17 shows the results of trading XLF based on the diffusion index created using the program in Figure 7.14

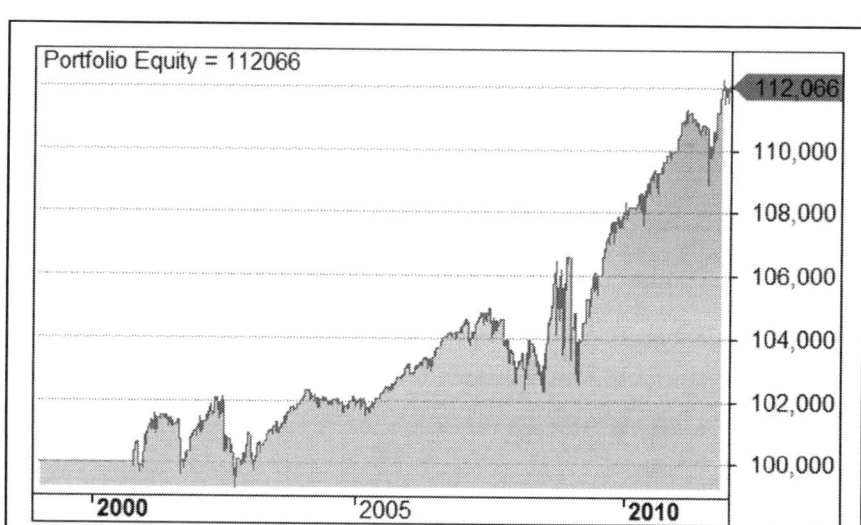

Figure 7.17 The equity curve from using the diffusion index

The summary of the Diffusion Index system:
- Compute the diffusion index as described above. Retrieve the index and compute its PercentRank over the lookback period of 6 months. Call the indicator DIPR.
- Buy at the close of the daily bar when DIPR crosses downward through 31.
- Sell at the close of the daily bar when the DIPR crosses upward through 49.
- There are 329 trades in 13 years.
- 66% are winners.
- Average gain per trade is 0.37%.
- Average holding period is 3.3 days.
- Total profit is $12,065.
- Is profitable for 49 of 50 of the list in Figure 7.3.
- Is profitable for 454 of the S&P 500.
- Is profitable for 500 of the S&P 600.

Chart Patterns

Patterns in the sequence and relationship of OHLC for a few bars are easily identified and sometimes reliably precede price changes.

For example, three consecutive lower closing prices are often followed by a rise in prices. Three consecutive higher closing prices are often followed by a fall in prices.

Chart patterns such as these are sometimes suggested as being predictive. Do test them. Be aware that patterns are highly susceptible to overfitting. Validation is particularly important for systems based on chart patterns.

Comments

The examples suggest the indicators that identify 24 cycles per year are essentially interchangeable. For a given data series, the differences between them are due as much to noise as to construction of the indicator. Pick one of these, or your own favorite. One is probably enough. Additional indicators add complexity, use degrees of freedom, and increase the likelihood of an overly curvefit model, but do not improve results.

None of the systems described have trailing exits or maximum loss exits (described in the next section). Testing them is left as an exercise.

Some data series respond better to one indicator than to others. That can be tested during development.

Double Down or Pyramiding

Most of the trades entered using the techniques described are immediately profitable and have short holding periods. They enter as the indicator drops through a critical level, caused by falling price. They often exit the next day. However, when one of these trades is wrong, it is often very wrong—being trapped in a trade where each day the indicator suggests that being long is more attractive than it was earlier.

One possible solution is to change the entry rule so the entry is made when the indicator is rising. Test that. The resulting systems may be safer. They may also be much less profitable because so many profitable trades are missed. You will not know if giving up the opportunity compensates for reducing risk until you have performed a thorough analysis.

A second possible solution is adding another position. I know, that is widely criticized as bad advice.

But it brings up a very important point about adding to open trades. Assume a system has two buy levels—one at 25, the second at 10. The system enters a long position when the indicator crosses downward through the first buy level on Tuesday with an indicator level of 20. On Wednesday, the indicator falls further, say to 8. Should a second position be added? My view is that the second position is the result of a different Buy rule than the first. As such, it constitutes a separate trading system. System A, call it, buys when the indicator drops through 25. System B buys when the indicator drops through 10. They must be developed, analyzed, traded, and managed as two separate systems.

The safe-f for System B may be higher or lower than for System A. We do not know which until after the analysis. Similarly, during live trading, one of the two systems may lose its edge while the other continues to be healthy. Develop them separately. Validate them separately. Manage them separately.

Entries

Given an entry signal, the entry happens at some *time*, such as the open or the close, or at some *price*, such as a limit order or a stop order.

Time

The pattern is recognized or condition met sometime during the bar. The signal is announced at or after the close of the bar. The entry takes place unconditionally (without restriction to price) at:
- The close of the bar or day that generated the signal. MOC. Market-on-Close.
- The open of the next day. NDO. Next Day Open.
- The close of the next day. As when trading mutual funds.

Price

The pattern is recognized and the signal generated at some specific price.

If the entry signal is associated with a higher price, the type of order placed with the broker is a "stop" order. For example, pre-compute the price, X, for the intra-day price that exceeds the highest of the previous five closing prices. Then place an order to "Buy at X, stop." If the intra-day price rises above X, the order will be filled at X or worse.

If the entry signal is associated with a lower price, the type of order placed is a "limit" order. For example:
- Precompute the closing price, W, that would cause the 3 day RSI to be below 20. Be prepared to enter a long position at the close if the closing price is W or lower using a Market On Close, Limit On Close, or Limit order.
- Precompute the intra-day price, X, that would cause the 5 day z-score using the sequence CCCCX to be below -1.0. Place an order to "buy at X, limit" to enter a long position intra-day if the price drops to X.

The price at which an indicator will have a given value can be pre-computed for almost any of the indicators we use. The requirements are:
- The computation depends on a single independent variable, usually price. This can be relaxed in some circumstances.
- The range of indicator values that are computed includes the desired specific value.

- The relationship is mathematically a function. For any given value of the independent variable, there is one and only one value of the indicator.

See Anticipating Signals in a later section of this chapter.

Exits

Once in a trade, there are five methods to exit. They are:
- logic
- profit target
- holding period
- trailing exit
- maximum loss

The model can have rules for any number of them, for all of them, or even for several of a specific method. Whichever rule is satisfied first causes the exit. Good modeling and simulation practice requires that each rule included in the model be used enough times to give statistically significant metrics of its effectiveness.

In pseudo-code, the entry and exit portion of the model have this form:
1. Initialize to no signals.

    ```
    Buy = 0;
    Sell = 0;
    ```

2. Buy and sell is typically based on logic, rules, indicators, and parameters.

    ```
    Buy = LogicBuy;
    Sell = LogicSell;
    ```

3. Sell based on one or more of the exit methods

    ```
    Sell = LogicSell OR ProfitSell OR HoldingPeriodSell
            OR TrailingSell OR MaximumLossSell;
    ```

Each sell condition is checked each bar, and is set to True when the conditions for it are met. The first in time to be "hit" causes an exit. If two or more become True at the same time, such as at the open of trading or at the close of trading, assume the worst case.

Each of the methods is illustrated with a simple example of that technique written out in "looping" code. AmiBroker has built-in functions that implement all of the four non-logic methods. They are variations of the ApplyStop function and are described later in this chapter. The looping code is provided to guide readers who are using platforms other than AmiBroker, and to allow the exit price to be plotted and printed.

Logic

Rules that recognize a pattern. Just as some pattern that precedes a price rise signaled entry, there may be a pattern that precedes a price drop that can be used to signal an exit. The exit rule does not need to be symmetric, or even to use the same indicator, as the entry rule. For example, the entry might be signalled by a low RSI, the exit by a moving average cross.

```
Buy = Cross(20,RSIa(C,2));
Sell = Cross(C,MA(C,5));
```

Profit target

Exit at a pre-computed price that results in a profit. The profit target can be a fixed percentage, such as 0.5% (or, for futures, a fixed number of points or dollars), or determined by volatility, such as 1.5 * ATR(3). For a long position, the profit target exit is above the entry and is a limit order.

Profit targets work well for systems expecting to hold trades for a short period of time, where large gains are not expected.

Figure 7.18 shows the code for a profit target exit. The buy and sell rules have been selected to illustrate the profit target exit. This is Not a good system—just a hopefully good illustration.

```
//  ProfitExit.afl
//
//  Disclaimer continues to apply
//
//  Copyright © 2014 Blue Owl Press, Inc
//

// Objective Function ObFnDemo1, from the Include directory
#include <ObFnDemo1.afl>;

// System settings
OptimizerSetEngine( "cmae" );
SetOption( "ExtraColumnsLocation", 1 );
SetBacktestMode( backtestRegular );
SetOption( "initialequity", 100000 );
MaxPos = 1;
SetOption( "maxopenpositions", MaxPos );
SetPositionSize( 10000, spsValue );
SetOption ( "CommissionMode", 3 ); // $ per share
SetOption( "CommissionAmount", 0.005 );
SetTradeDelays( 0, 0, 0, 0 );
BuyPrice = SellPrice = Close;

// Global variables and parameters

// User Functions

//  Local variables, beginning with Param and Optimize
ProfitTarget = 0.5;      // 0.5%
Long = 0 * Close; //    True when in a long position
```

Model Development—Indicator-Based

```
ProfitPrice = Close;      //Initialize array

// Indicators

// Buy and Sell rules

Buy = LogicBuy = Cross( 40, RSIa( C, 4 ) );
Sell = 0;
LogicSell = Cross( C, MA( C, 20 ) );

// Looping code for the profit target
// This is a mini-trading system simulator
// Process each bar, bar by bar, in time sequence.
// For each bar, process the Open, then intra-bar, then the
        Close.
// For each point in time, handle exits first, then entries,
// then adjustments

for ( i = 1; i < BarCount; i++ )
{
    if ( Long[i-1] )
    {
        // Coming into the bar in a long position

        if ( Open[i] > ProfitPrice[i-1] )
        {
            //    At the Open
            Sell[i] = 1;
            SellPrice[i] = Open[i];
            Long[i] = 0;
        }
        else
            if ( High[i] > ProfitPrice[i-1] )
            {
                //       Intra-bar
                Sell[i] = 1;
                SellPrice[i] = ProfitPrice[i-1];
                Long[i] = 0;
            }
            else
                if ( LogicSell[i] )
                {
                    //    At the close
                    Sell[i] = 1;
                    SellPrice[i] = Close[i];
                    long[i] = 0;
                }
                else
                {
                    //   Continuing Long
                    //   Adjust as necessary
                    ProfitPrice[i] = ProfitPrice[i-1];
                    Long[i] = 1;
                }
    }
    else
    {
        // Not Long coming into the bar
        if ( Buy[i] )
        {
            //    New Long position
            ProfitPrice[i] = Close[i]
                        * ( 1.00 + 0.01 * ProfitTarget );
```

```
                    Long[i] = 1;
            }
            else
            {
                //    Continue flat
                Long[i] = 0;
            }
        }
    }

    Plot( C, "C", colorBlack, styleCandle );

    shapes = IIf( Buy, shapeuparrow, IIf( sell, shapedownarrow,
            shapenone ) );
    shapecolors = IIf( Buy, colorgreen, IIf( sell, colorred,
            colorwhite ) );
    PlotShapes( shapes, shapecolors );

    ProfitColor = IIf( long, colorRed, colorWhite );
    Plot( ProfitPrice, "ProfitPrice", ProfitColor, styleDots
            | stylethick | styleNoLine, Null, Null, 0, 2 );

    // Explore

    Filter = 1;
    AddColumn( Open, "Open", 10.4 );
    AddColumn( High, "High", 10.4 );
    AddColumn( Low, "Low", 10.4 );
    AddColumn( Close, "Close", 10.4 );
    AddColumn( Buy, "Buy", 10.0 );
    AddColumn( BuyPrice, "BuyPrice", 10.4 );
    AddColumn( ProfitPrice, "ProfitPrice", 10.4 );
            //  Exit price for next day
    AddColumn( Sell, "Sell", 10.0 );
    AddColumn( SellPrice, "SellPrice", 10.4 );

    ///////////  end  /////////////
```

Figure 7.18 Looping code for profit target exit

Figure 7.19 illustrates the trade entry (shown by the up arrow), calculation of the profit target price (shown as dots), and the point at which the exit would have taken place (shown by the star burst).

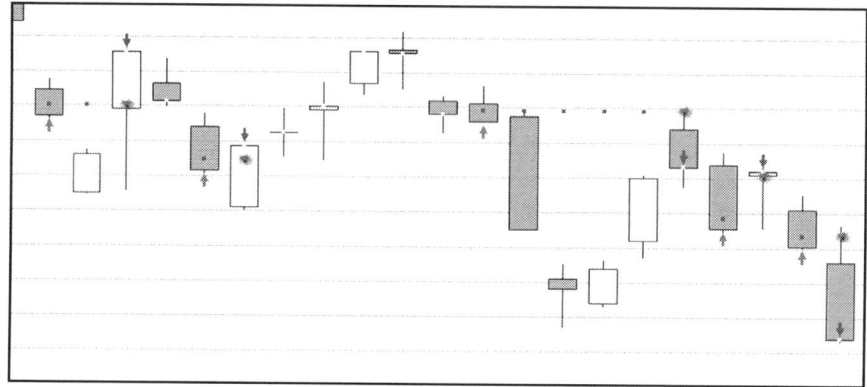

Figure 7.19 Chart of profit target exit

Model Development—Indicator-Based 235

Figure 7.20 shows the table created by the Explore statements in the program. The profitprice is shown in the third column from the right. This is the price at which a limit order would be placed with your broker for the next day's trade.

Ticker	Date/Time	Open	High	Low	Close	Buy	BuyPrice	ProfitPrice	Sell	SellPrice
XLF	9/7/2011	12.5800	12.9300	12.1100	12.9100	0	12.9100	12.9100	1	12.6027
XLF	9/8/2011	12.7300	12.8800	12.5900	12.6300	0	12.6300	12.6300	0	12.6300
XLF	9/9/2011	12.4800	12.5600	12.1800	12.2300	1	12.2300	12.2911	0	12.2300
XLF	9/12/2011	12.0200	12.3900	12.0000	12.3700	0	12.3700	12.3700	1	12.2911
XLF	9/13/2011	12.4500	12.5900	12.3100	12.4500	0	12.4500	12.4500	0	12.4500
XLF	9/14/2011	12.5800	12.7500	12.2900	12.6000	0	12.6000	12.6000	0	12.6000
XLF	9/15/2011	12.7400	12.9300	12.6700	12.9200	0	12.9200	12.9200	0	12.9200
XLF	9/16/2011	12.9300	13.0400	12.7000	12.9100	0	12.9100	12.9100	0	12.9100
XLF	9/19/2011	12.6400	12.6700	12.4500	12.5600	0	12.5600	12.5600	0	12.5600
XLF	9/20/2011	12.6200	12.7300	12.5200	12.5200	1	12.5200	12.5826	0	12.5200
XLF	9/21/2011	12.5500	12.5800	11.9000	11.9000	0	11.9000	12.5826	0	11.9000
XLF	9/22/2011	11.6200	11.7100	11.3400	11.5600	0	11.5600	12.5826	0	11.5600
XLF	9/23/2011	11.4800	11.7300	11.4600	11.6800	0	11.6800	12.5826	0	11.6800
XLF	9/26/2011	11.8400	12.2200	11.7400	12.2000	0	12.2000	12.5826	0	12.2000
XLF	9/27/2011	12.4800	12.6000	12.1500	12.2600	0	12.2600	12.2600	1	12.5826
XLF	9/28/2011	12.2800	12.3500	11.8900	11.9100	1	11.9100	11.9696	0	11.9100
XLF	9/29/2011	12.2200	12.3200	11.9100	12.2400	0	12.2400	12.2400	1	12.2200
XLF	9/30/2011	12.0200	12.1100	11.8000	11.8100	1	11.8100	11.8691	0	11.8100
XLF	10/3/2011	11.7200	11.9400	11.2600	11.2800	0	11.2800	11.2800	1	11.8691

Figure 7.20 Explore table showing profitprice for next day

Holding period

This method includes timed exits and inactivity exits. Either:
- The number of days (or bars) is determined before or immediately after entry. The trade is exited unconditionally, using an order such as Market on Close, after holding the specified number of bars.
- The profit or loss is analyzed while the trade is open, and a decision based on price action or profit of recent bars is made to exit the trade at the close (or open) of some day. The order is typically a market order for execution at the open (MOO) or at the close (MOC).

Holding periods work well for systems expecting to hold trades for a short period of time, where large gains are not expected.

Figure 7.21 shows the code for a holding period exit.

```
//  HoldingPeriodExit.afl
//
//  Disclaimer continues to apply
//
//  Copyright © 2014 Blue Owl Press, Inc
//

// Objective Function ObFnDemo1, from the Include directory
#include <ObFnDemo1.afl>;

// System settings
```

```
OptimizerSetEngine( "cmae" );
SetOption( "ExtraColumnsLocation", 1 );
SetBacktestMode( backtestRegular );
SetOption( "initialequity", 100000 );
MaxPos = 1;
SetOption( "maxopenpositions", MaxPos );
SetPositionSize( 10000, spsValue );
SetOption ( "CommissionMode", 3 ); // $ per share
SetOption( "CommissionAmount", 0.005 );
SetTradeDelays( 0, 0, 0, 0 );
BuyPrice = SellPrice = Close;

// Global variables and parameters

// User Functions

//  Local variables, beginning with Param and Optimize
HoldingPeriod = 5;        //5 days
// This code begins the count with the day of entry
// as does AmiAbroker.
// If there has been no other exit, on the close of
// the 5th day, exit Market on Close.
Long = 0 * Close; //      True when in a long position
// The number of bars the trade has been held.
BarsInTrade = 0 * Close;

// Indicators

// Buy and Sell rules

Buy = LogicBuy = Cross( 40, RSIa( C, 4 ) );
Sell = 0;
LogicSell = Cross( C, MA( C, 20 ) );

// Looping code for the holding period exit.
// This is a mini-trading system simulator
// Process each bar, bar by bar, in time sequence.
// For each bar, process the Open, then intra-bar, then the
         Close.
// For each point in time, handle exits first, then entries,
// then adjustments

for ( i = 1; i < BarCount; i++ )
{
    if ( Long[i-1] )
    {
        // Coming into the bar in a long position
        //  Nothing happens at open or intra-bar.

        if ( LogicSell[i]
            OR ( BarsInTrade[i-1] >= HoldingPeriod-1 ) )
        {
            //    At the close
            Sell[i] = 1;
            SellPrice[i] = Close[i];
            long[i] = 0;
        }
        else
        {
            //    Continuing Long
            //    Adjust as necessary
            BarsInTrade[i] = BarsInTrade[i-1] + 1;
            Long[i] = 1;
```

```
            }
        }
        else
        {
            // Not Long coming into the bar
            if ( Buy[i] )
            {
                //    New Long position
                BarsInTrade[i] = 1;
                Long[i] = 1;
            }
            else
            {
                //    Continue flat
                BarsInTrade[i] = 0;
                Long[i] = 0;
            }
        }
    }
    Plot( C, "C", colorBlack, styleCandle );

    shapes = IIf( Buy, shapeuparrow, IIf( sell, shapedownarrow,
                  shapenone ) );
    shapecolors = IIf( Buy, colorgreen, IIf( sell, colorred,
                       colorwhite ) );
    PlotShapes( shapes, shapecolors );

    // Explore

    ///////////  end  /////////////
```

Figure 7.21 Looping code for holding period exit

Trailing exit

A trailing exit requires calculation of a separate price series—call it "trailing price." At trade entry, the initial trailing price, lower than the entry price, is calculated, and assigned to the entry bar for use during the next bar. At the completion of each bar, a new trailing price is calculated, stored, and ready for reference during the next bar. The new trailing price is never lower than the previous value. Typically, it rises when the primary price rises and profit increases, and it stops rising, or at least slows the rate of rising, when the price stops rising and profit stops increasing.

The idea for the trailing exit is pretty simple:

```
If (Long)
   If (Low < TrailingPrice)   Exit
   Else   Adjust TrailingPrice
Else
   If (Buy)   Initialize TrailingPrice
   Else   Continue Flat
```

Execution is via a stop order. There may be slippage.

There are two commonly used trailing stop exit algorithms:
- **For the chandelier version**, imagine the trailing price hanging from the primary data series—a chandelier hanging from the ceiling. Either the high or the close can be used as the ceiling. Typically, the distance between the ceiling and the trailing price is a function of bar-to-bar volatility, such as standard deviation or average true range (ATR). The idea is to leave enough distance so that regularly experienced random price variation does not cause an exit, but a significant price drop associated with the end of the trend does cause an exit.

Figure 7.22 shows the code for a chandelier trailing exit.

```
//  ChandelierTrailingExit.afl
//
//  Disclaimer continues to apply
//
//  Copyright © 2014 Blue Owl Press, Inc
//

// Objective Function ObFnDemo1, from the Include directory
#include <ObFnDemo1.afl>;

// System settings
OptimizerSetEngine( "cmae" );
SetOption( "ExtraColumnsLocation", 1 );
SetBacktestMode( backtestRegular );
SetOption( "initialequity", 100000 );
MaxPos = 1;
SetOption( "maxopenpositions", MaxPos );
SetPositionSize( 10000, spsValue );
SetOption ( "CommissionMode", 3 ); // $ per share
SetOption( "CommissionAmount", 0.005 );
SetTradeDelays( 0, 0, 0, 0 );
BuyPrice = SellPrice = Close;

// Global variables and parameters

// User Functions

//  Local variables, beginning with Param and Optimize
Ceiling = High;    //      High or Close
TrailingPrice = Close;
HighInTrade = 0;
Slippage = 0.02;   // 2 cents per share
Long = 0 * Close; //      True when in a long position

// Indicators
TrailDistance = 5 * ATR( 10 );

// Buy and Sell rules

Buy = LogicBuy = Cross( MA( C, 50 ), MA( C, 200 ) );
Sell = 0;
LogicSell = Cross( MA( C, 200 ), MA( C, 50 ) );

// Looping code for the Chandelier trailing exit
// This is a mini-trading system simulator
// Process each bar, bar by bar, in time sequence.
```

Model Development—Indicator-Based

```
// For each bar, process the Open, then intra-bar, then the
        Close.
// For each point in time, handle exits first, then entries,
// then adjustments

for ( i = 1; i < BarCount; i++ )
{
    if ( Long[i-1] )
    {
        // Coming into the bar in a long position

        if ( Open[i] < TrailingPrice[i-1] )
        {
            //     At the Open
            Sell[i] = 1;
            SellPrice[i] = Open[i];
            Long[i] = 0;
        }
        else
            if ( Low[i] < TrailingPrice[i-1] )
            {
                //        Intra-bar
                Sell[i] = 1;
                SellPrice[i] = TrailingPrice[i-1] - Slippage;
                Long[i] = 0;
            }
            else
                if ( LogicSell[i] )
                {
                    //    At the close
                    Sell[i] = 1;
                    SellPrice[i] = Close[i];
                    long[i] = 0;
                }
                else
                {
                    //   Continuing Long
                    //   Adjust as necessary
                    if ( High[i] > HighInTrade )
                        HighInTrade = High[i];

                    TrailingPrice[i] = Max( HighInTrade -
                        TrailDistance[i],
                        TrailingPrice[i-1] );
                    Long[i] = 1;
                }
    }
    else
    {
        // Not Long coming into the bar
        if ( Buy[i] )
        {
            //    New Long position
            HighInTrade = High[i];
            TrailingPrice[i] = HighInTrade - TrailDistance[i];
            Long[i] = 1;
        }
        else
        {
            //    Continue flat
            Long[i] = 0;
        }
    }
}
```

```
Plot( C, "C", colorBlack, styleCandle );

shapes = IIf( Buy, shapeuparrow, IIf( sell, shapedownarrow,
              shapenone ) );
shapecolors = IIf( Buy, colorgreen, IIf( sell, colorred,
              colorwhite ) );
PlotShapes( shapes, shapecolors );

TrailColor = IIf( long, colorRed, colorWhite );
Plot( TrailingPrice, "TrailingPrice", TrailColor, styleDots
           | stylethick | styleNoLine, Null, Null, 0, 2
      );

// Explore

Filter = 1;
AddColumn( Open, "Open", 10.4 );
AddColumn( High, "High", 10.4 );
AddColumn( Low, "Low", 10.4 );
AddColumn( Close, "Close", 10.4 );
AddColumn( Buy, "Buy", 10.0 );
AddColumn( BuyPrice, "BuyPrice", 10.4 );
AddColumn( TrailingPrice, "TrailingPrice", 10.4 );//  Exit
           price for next day
AddColumn( Sell, "Sell", 10.0 );
AddColumn( SellPrice, "SellPrice", 10.4 );

///////////   end   //////////////ss
```

Figure 7.22 Chandelier trailing exit

- **For the parabolic version**, the trailing exit begins below some recent price considered to be safely below one day of random price change. With each passing day, the trailing exit moves upward. If the price moves upward quickly, the trailing exit follows quickly. If the upward movement of the price stagnates, the trailing exit continues to move upward, but more slowly. Figure 7.23 shows the code for the Parabolic Trailing Exit.

```
// ParabolicTrailingExit.afl
//
// Disclaimer continues to apply
//
// Copyright © 2014 Blue Owl Press, Inc
//

// Objective Function ObFnDemo1, from the Include directory
#include <ObFnDemo1.afl>;

// System settings
OptimizerSetEngine( "cmae" );
SetOption( "ExtraColumnsLocation", 1 );
SetBacktestMode( backtestRegular );
SetOption( "initialequity", 100000 );
MaxPos = 1;
SetOption( "maxopenpositions", MaxPos );
SetPositionSize( 10000, spsValue );
SetOption ( "CommissionMode", 3 ); // $ per share
```

```
SetOption( "CommissionAmount", 0.005 );
SetTradeDelays( 0, 0, 0, 0 );
BuyPrice = SellPrice = Close;

// Global variables and parameters

// User Functions

//  Local variables, beginning with Param and Optimize
Accel = 0;
AccelIncr = 0.005;       //Acceleration increment
AccelInit = 0.005;       //Acceleration initialization
AccelMax = 0.05;  //     Acceleration maximum
Slippage = 0.02;   // 2 cents per share
TrailInit = LLV( L, 10 );

TrailingPrice = Close;
Long = 0 * Close; //     True when in a long position

// Indicators

// Buy and Sell rules

Buy = LogicBuy = Cross( MA( C, 1 ), MA( C, 20 ) );
Sell = 0;
LogicSell = Cross( MA( C, 200 ), MA( C, 50 ) );

// Looping code for the Parabolic trailing exit
// This is a mini-trading system simulator
// Process each bar, bar by bar, in time sequence.
// For each bar, process the Open, then intra-bar, then the
         Close.
// For each point in time, handle exits first, then entries,
// then adjustments

for ( i = 1; i < BarCount; i++ )
{
    if ( Long[i-1] )
    {
        // Coming into the bar in a long position

        if ( Open[i] < TrailingPrice[i-1] )
        {
            //    At the Open
            Sell[i] = 1;
            SellPrice[i] = Open[i];
            Long[i] = 0;
        }
        else
            if ( Low[i] < TrailingPrice[i-1] )
            {
                //       Intra-bar
                Sell[i] = 1;
                SellPrice[i] = TrailingPrice[i-1] - Slippage;
                Long[i] = 0;
            }
            else
                if ( LogicSell[i] )
                {
                    //   At the close
                    Sell[i] = 1;
                    SellPrice[i] = Close[i];
                    long[i] = 0;
```

```
                    }
                    else
                    {
                        //   Continuing Long
                        //   Adjust as necessary
                        if ( High[i] > HighInTrade )
                        {
                            HighInTrade = High[i];
                            Accel = Min( Accel + AccelIncr, Accel-
            Max );
                        }

                        TrailingPrice[i] = TrailingPrice[i-1]
                            + Accel
                            * ( HighInTrade - TrailingPrice[i-1]
            );
                        Long[i] = 1;
                    }
            }
            else
            {
                // Not Long coming into the bar
                if ( Buy[i] )
                {
                    //   New Long position
                    HighInTrade = High[i];
                    TrailingPrice[i] = TrailInit[i];
                    Long[i] = 1;
                }
                else
                {
                    //   Continue flat
                    Long[i] = 0;
                }
            }
    }

    Plot( C, "C", colorBlack, styleCandle );

    shapes = IIf( Buy, shapeuparrow, IIf( sell, shapedownarrow,
            shapenone ) );
    shapecolors = IIf( Buy, colorgreen, IIf( sell, colorred,
            colorwhite ) );
    PlotShapes( shapes, shapecolors );

    TrailColor = IIf( long, colorRed, colorWhite );
    Plot( TrailingPrice, "TrailingPrice", TrailColor, styleDots
            | stylethick | styleNoLine, Null, Null, 0, 2 );

    // Explore

    Filter = 1;
    AddColumn( Open, "Open", 10.4 );
    AddColumn( High, "High", 10.4 );
    AddColumn( Low, "Low", 10.4 );
    AddColumn( Close, "Close", 10.4 );
    AddColumn( Buy, "Buy", 10.0 );
    AddColumn( BuyPrice, "BuyPrice", 10.4 );
    AddColumn( TrailingPrice, "TrailingPrice", 10.4 );//   Exit
            price for next day
    AddColumn( Sell, "Sell", 10.0 );
    AddColumn( SellPrice, "SellPrice", 10.4 );

    ////////////   end   //////////////
```

Figure 7.23 Parabolic trailing exit

Figure 7.24 shows the chart of price with the parabolic trailing price. Examine it carefully. The profit or loss is between the buy and sell arrows, not between the initial parabolic and final parabolic.

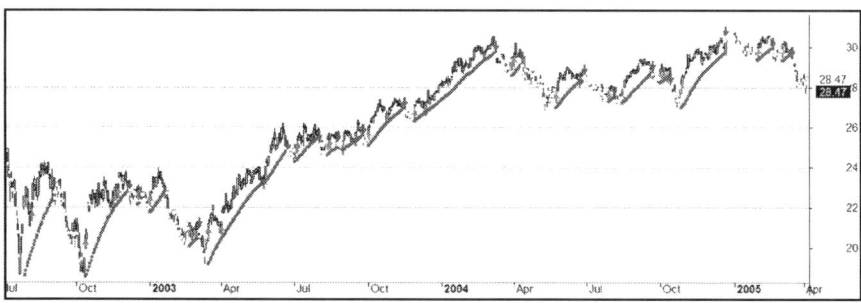

Figure 7.24 Parabolic trailing exit

With either algorithm, eventually the trailing price series and the primary data series will cross as the trailing price rises and / or the primary price falls. The exit takes place intra-bar (intra-day) as a stop order. Each day, or bar, the unexecuted previous exit order is cancelled and replaced with a new order, good for one bar, with a new exit price.

Trailing exits require several bars for the trailing price to catch up to the primary price. If both the primary data series and trailing prices are the same periodicity, trailing exits do not work well for trades held a small number of bars. Alternatively, trailing prices can be based on intra-day bars. Managing a trade where the trailing exit is based on intra-day bars requires action throughout the day as orders are cancelled and replaced.

Maximum loss exit

This is the infamous "money stop." A stop order is placed some distance below the entry price, hoping to prevent catastrophic loss.

A maximum loss exit seldom improves performance. That is not to say that your system should not have a maximum loss exit. It may be required for customer relations or for regulatory compliance. It is to say that you should expect performance to degrade when one is added.

Test your specific system with the following experiment. Develop the system with any entry and exit rules, but not including a maximum loss exit. Measure performance. Add a maximum loss exit with the exit distance so far below the entry price that it is never used. Make a series of test runs, gradually shortening the exit distance with each successive run. At each, measure performance. My experience is that the tighter the exit, the more the performance degrades.

Having a maximum loss exit rule in a system guarantees that any trade with a maximum adverse excursion at least as great as the loss level will be a losing trade. These trades will never have an opportunity to recover. Like any of the other exits, sound modeling principles require that this technique be the actual reason for trade exit enough times to show statistical significance.

Figure 7.25 shows the program listing for looping implementation of a maximum loss exit.

```
//  MaximumLossExit.afl
//
//  Disclaimer continues to apply
//
//  Copyright © 2014 Blue Owl Press, Inc
//

// Objective Function ObFnDemo1, from the Include directory
#include <ObFnDemo1.afl>;

// System settings
OptimizerSetEngine( "cmae" );
SetOption( "ExtraColumnsLocation", 1 );
SetBacktestMode( backtestRegular );
SetOption( "initialequity", 100000 );
MaxPos = 1;
SetOption( "maxopenpositions", MaxPos );
SetPositionSize( 10000, spsValue );
SetOption ( "CommissionMode", 3 ); // $ per share
SetOption( "CommissionAmount", 0.005 );
SetTradeDelays( 0, 0, 0, 0 );
BuyPrice = SellPrice = Close;

// Global variables and parameters

// User Functions

//  Local variables, beginning with Param and Optimize
MaxLoss = Optimize( "MaxLoss", 5, 1, 50, 1 );   // percent
HighSequence = Optimize( "HighSeq", 20, 1, 100, 1 );
LowSequence = Optimize( "LowSeq", 10, 1, 100, 1 );

Slippage = 0.02;   // 2 cents per share
MaxLossPrice = 0 * Close;
Long = 0 * Close; //      True when in a long position

// Indicators

// Buy and Sell rules

Buy = LogicBuy = C > Ref( HHV( C, HighSequence ), -1 );
Sell = 0;
LogicSell = C < Ref( LLV( C, LowSequence ), -1 );

//  Looping code for the Maximum Loss exit
//  This is a mini-trading system simulator
//  Process each bar, bar by bar, in time sequence.
//  For each bar, process the Open, then intra-bar, then the
         Close.
//  For each point in time, handle exits first, then entries,
//  then adjustments
```

```
for ( i = 1; i < BarCount; i++ )
{
    if ( Long[i-1] )
    {
        // Coming into the bar in a long position

        if ( Open[i] < MaxLossPrice[i-1] )
        {
            //    At the Open
            Sell[i] = 1;
            SellPrice[i] = Open[i];
            Long[i] = 0;
        }
        else
            if ( Low[i] < MaxLossPrice[i-1] )
            {
                //        Intra-bar
                Sell[i] = 1;
                SellPrice[i] = MaxLossPrice[i-1] - Slippage;
                Long[i] = 0;
            }
            else
                if ( LogicSell[i] )
                {
                    //    At the close
                    Sell[i] = 1;
                    SellPrice[i] = Close[i];
                    long[i] = 0;
                }
                else
                {
                    //    Continuing Long
                    //    Adjust as necessary
                    MaxLossPrice[i] = MaxLossPrice[i-1];
                    Long[i] = 1;
                }
    }
    else
    {
        // Not Long coming into the bar
        if ( Buy[i] )
        {
            //    New Long position
            MaxLossPrice[i] = ( 1 - 0.01 * MaxLoss ) *
          Close[i];
            Long[i] = 1;
        }
        else
        {
            //    Continue flat
            Long[i] = 0;
        }
    }
}

Plot( C, "C", colorBlack, styleCandle );

shapes = IIf( Buy, shapeuparrow, IIf( sell, shapedownarrow,
              shapenone ) );
shapecolors = IIf( Buy, colorgreen, IIf( sell, colorred,
              colorwhite ) );
PlotShapes( shapes, shapecolors );
```

```
        TrailColor = IIf( long, colorRed, colorWhite );
        Plot( MaxLossPrice, "MaxLossPrice", TrailColor, styleDots
                     | stylethick | styleNoLine, Null, Null, 0, 2
                );

        // Explore

        Filter = 1;
        AddColumn( Open, "Open", 10.4 );
        AddColumn( High, "High", 10.4 );
        AddColumn( Low, "Low", 10.4 );
        AddColumn( Close, "Close", 10.4 );
        AddColumn( Buy, "Buy", 10.0 );
        AddColumn( BuyPrice, "BuyPrice", 10.4 );
        AddColumn( MaxLossPrice, "MaxLossPrice", 10.4 );//  Exit price
                 for next day
        AddColumn( Sell, "Sell", 10.0 );
        AddColumn( SellPrice, "SellPrice", 10.4 );

        ///////////// end  /////////////
```

Figure 7.25 Maximum loss exit

Single statement exits

The looping code in the examples above is provided to:
- Illustrate how the trading simulator works.
- Give control over details of the exit methods.
- Plot exit prices.
- Compute and print a table of prices for tomorrow's trading.

Each of the four non-logic exits has a one-statement implementation in AmiBroker. They are variations of the ApplyStop function. Their names and parameters make them self-documenting. The statements corresponding to the four exits described above are:

```
        ApplyStop ( stopTypeProfit, stopModePercent, 5 );
        ApplyStop ( stopTypeNBar, stopModeBars, 5 );
        ApplyStop ( stopTypeTrailing, stopModePoint, 3*ATR(14) );
        ApplyStop ( stopTypeLoss, stopModePercent, 20 );
```

The ApplyStop implementations are much faster in execution and the program code is much less complex (and much less susceptible to errors).

Backtesting

Backtesting is the process of fitting the model to the data and observing the resulting performance.

The fitting can be done manually or programmatically.

Figure 7.26 shows the AmiBroker code for a method for doing it manually. Param statements let the developer change values of variables using slider controls. Indicators are recalculated and their plots redrawn. The equity curve is recalculated immediately and its plot shows the result.

```
// ManualEntryDesign.afl
//
// Disclaimer continues to apply
//
// Copyright © 2014 Blue Owl Press, Inc
//

// Objective Function ObFnDemo1, from the Include directory
#include <ObFnDemo1.afl>;

// System settings
OptimizerSetEngine( "cmae" );
SetOption( "ExtraColumnsLocation", 1 );
SetBacktestMode( backtestRegular );
SetOption( "initialequity", 100000 );
MaxPos = 1;
SetOption( "maxopenpositions", MaxPos );
SetPositionSize( 10000, spsValue );
SetOption ( "CommissionMode", 3 ); // $ per share
SetOption( "CommissionAmount", 0.005 );
SetTradeDelays( 0, 0, 0, 0 );
BuyPrice = SellPrice = Close;

// Global variables and parameters

// User Functions

//  Local variables, beginning with Param and Optimize
MALength1 = Param( "MALength1", 5, 1, 50, 1 );
MALength2 = Param( "MALength2", 50, 1, 50, 1 );
HoldDays = Param( "HoldDays", 10, 1, 50, 1 );

//MALength1 = optimize("MALength1",45,1,50,1);
//MALength2 = optimize("MALength2",1,1,50,1);
//HoldDays = optimize("HoldDays",1,1,50,1);

MA1 = MA( C, MALength1 );
MA2 = MA( C, MALength2 );

// Moving average crossover
// Poor system, but good illustration
Buy = Cross( MA1, MA2 );
Sell = BarsSince( Buy ) >= HoldDays;

// Remove extraneous buy and sell signals
Buy = ExRem( Buy, Sell );
Sell = ExRem( Sell, Buy );

e = Equity();

//  Plots
Plot( C, "C", colorBlack, styleCandle );
Plot( MA1, "MA1", colorGreen, styleLine );
Plot( MA2, "MA2", colorBlue, styleLine );
shapes = IIf( Buy, shapeUpArrow, IIf( Sell, shapeDownArrow,
              shapeNone ) );
shapecolors = IIf( Buy, colorGreen, IIf( Sell, colorRed,
              colorWhite ) );
```

```
    PlotShapes( shapes, shapecolors );
    Plot( e, "equity", colorGreen, styleLine | styleThick
                 | styleOwnScale );

////////////// end //////////////
```

Figure 7.26 Manual entry design program

Figure 7.27 shows the chart pane when this method is in operation.

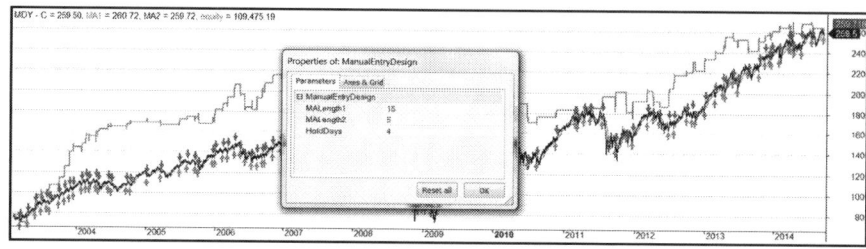

Figure 7.27 Manual entry design chart in operation

This is an excellent way to learn how a system idea responds to changes in parameters. In common with any non-programmatic system development, it suffers from these limitations:
- Only one variable is being modified at a time.
- The number of combinations that can be thoroughly tested is small.
- There are no statistical summaries.
- There are no trade details or trade lists.
- The results are not recorded.
- Selective recognition of patterns.
- Subjective interpretation of results.
- Non-repeatable.

The backtest is run programmatically through the Analysis dialogs. Test results are computed and can be saved for further analysis or comparison. Charts and statistical summaries are produced, as has been illustrated by the examples in this chapter.

Optimization

The program in Figure 7.26 has duplicated sets of statements defining the parameter values. Remove the comment marks from the Optimize statements, and add comment marks to the Param statements, then run the program as a **backtest**. When run as a backtest, the first of the four numeric arguments to the Optimize statement is used as a default value. The default values for the three variables are MALength1 of 45, MALength2 of 1, and HoldDays of 1.

Run the program again as an **optimize**. All of the combinations will be tested and ranked according to the value of the objective function. Note the three values for the model at the top of the list. For equities and equity ETFs, it is not the traditional configuration of a moving average crossover system.

While the word is optimize, the process is:
1. Choose some, usually many, alternative system configurations.
2. Run each as a single run backtest, evaluating the objective function for each, and entering the result into a list.
3. Sort the list according to objective function score.

Choosing alternatives is easy. The intelligence of an optimization is in the objective function used to rank the alternatives. Articles that discuss optimization should focus on the objective function, stationarity, and validation. All other aspects of optimization follow from those.

In-sample

The in-sample period, and the data associated with it, is the period examined, tested, and data mined in search for profitable patterns. As demonstrated, it takes very few iterations of a test run followed by model adjustment based on test results to fit the model to the in-sample data. All data series consist of valuable signal patterns and extraneous noise that appears to be signal patterns. In-sample testing fits the model to all of the signals that meet its rules — valuable ones and extraneous ones.

Out-of-sample

Whether the data contains valuable signals, and whether the model can identify them, can only be determined through a test of data that has not been used in the fitting process. Any data not used in fitting is called out-of-sample. It could be an earlier period of the same in-sample data, or an entirely different data series. But the out-of-sample data that provides the best test is a later period of the same series as the in-sample data.

All of the model ideas, indicator and parameter selection, searching, testing, and fitting are an attempt to build a mathematical model of a data series — a model of the reference class based on a sample of data believed to be representative.

The concepts of, and differences between, accuracy and precision were introduced in Chapter 6. If, as is typically the case, we do not have enough information about the reference class, we confuse precision with accuracy and assume out-of-sample results will be good (expecting high accuracy) because in-sample results are good (observing high precision). An example illustrates the danger.

Figures 7.28 and 7.29 each show a set of charts including the price of the primary data series and an equity curve. Figure 7.28 shows the results of in-sample development, testing, and parameter selection for three issues. The in-sample period was 1/1/1999 through 1/1/2010 for all three. The same rules were applied to all three, and the parameters adjusted to give the best results.

Any of the three could be the product of a system development project the end of the backtesting and optimization phase. They have roughly comparable risk and profit potential. Whether they have comparable value as systems for actual trading cannot be known without trading — or trading's surrogate, out-of-sample testing.

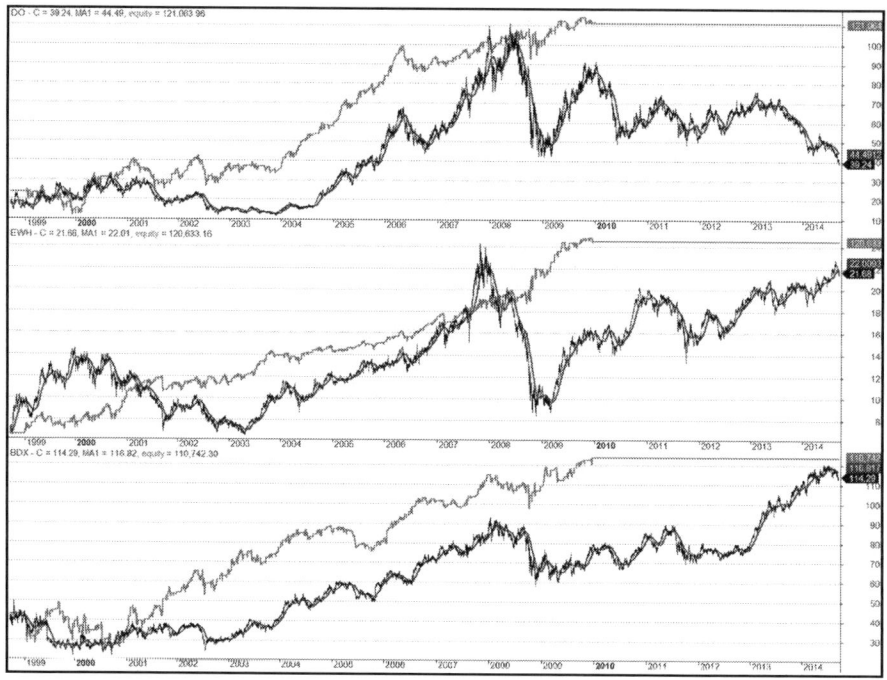

Figure 7.28 Three issues in-sample

Figures 7.29 extends the test through 2014. One continued to perform well, one returned little or no profit, the third is a loser. The point is that we were not able to judge out-of-sample performance until after out-of-sample testing.

Model Development—Indicator-Based

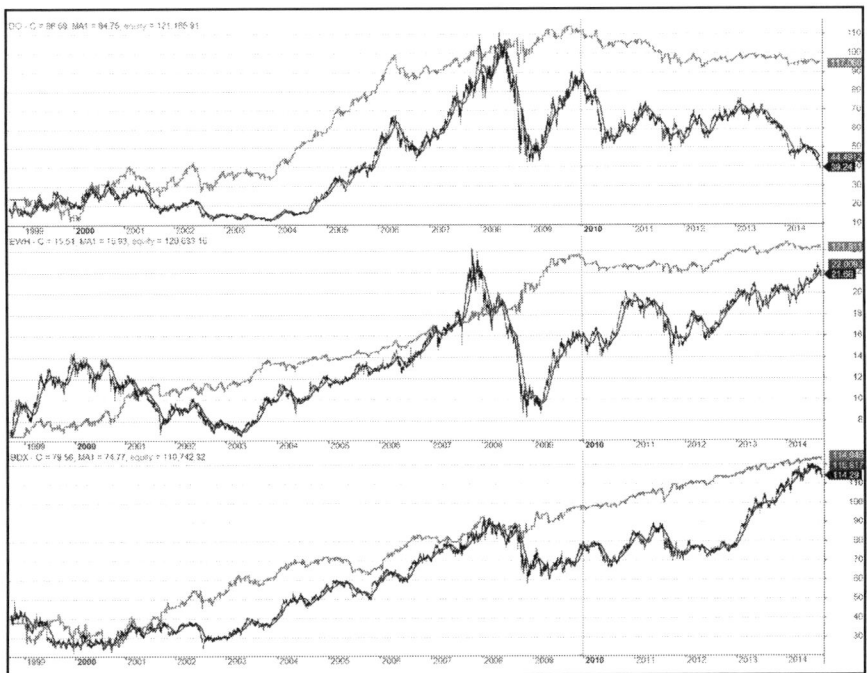

Figure 7.29 The same three issues out-of-sample

Walk Forward

Refer back to the goal of trading system development—that the developer / trader have confidence. Some people may feel that good in-sample performance is sufficient, or that out-of-sample testing using older data or other data series is sufficient. Others will think ahead to a time when the performance of the system being traded deteriorates and wonder how to re-validate it and return it to live trading. The walk forward process, discussed in general in Chapter 6, is an automated technique for validating and re-validating a trading system.

AmiBroker has excellent walk forward features. Figure 7.30 shows the walk forward settings dialog. It can be found using the Analysis > Settings menus, then choosing the Walk-Forward tab. The key meta-variables are:
- Start date of the first in-sample period.
- Length of the in-sample period (by setting the end date of the first in-sample period.
- Step size.
- Objective function (Optimization target).

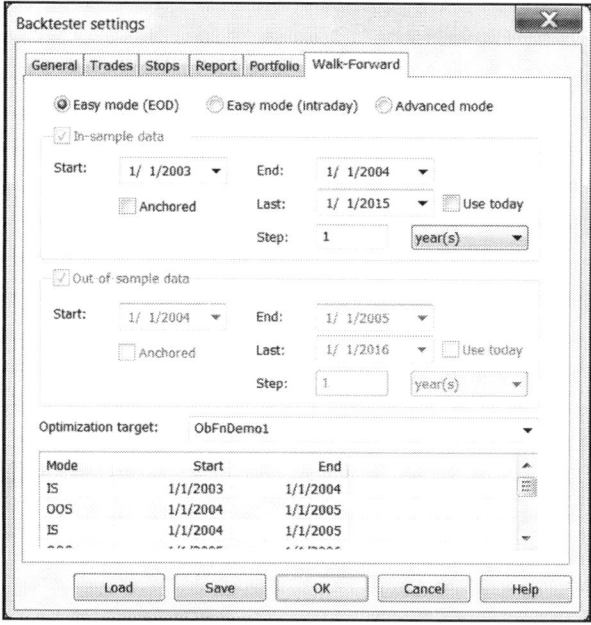

Figure 7.30 Walk forward settings dialog

A walk forward test run begins with selection of the issue to test. Make it the "current" issue, so it is displayed in the main pane of the chart window.

Select the model to use. One way is to open the afl file in the Formula Editor, then Send to Analysis Window. On the Analysis tab, verify the name of the formula in the box in the top line, as shown in Figure 7.31.

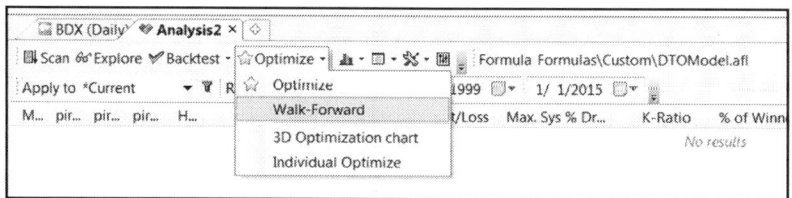

Figure 7.31 Walk forward selection

Using the Analysis tab, use the Optimize pull-down menu, see Figure 7.31, and click Walk Forward. The run will begin. It is a sequence of in-sample optimizations and out-of-sample tests. Beginning with an in-sample optimization, the results for each test period are displayed on the Results List tab as they are calculated. When the optimization has finished, the list is sorted by objective function score. The param-

Model Development—Indicator-Based

eter values of the top-ranked result are used for a one-time test of the out-of-sample period that immediately follows the in-sample period just examined. Those two results are displayed on the Walk Forward tab, as shown in Figure 7.32. The periods step forward and the next analysis begins automatically.

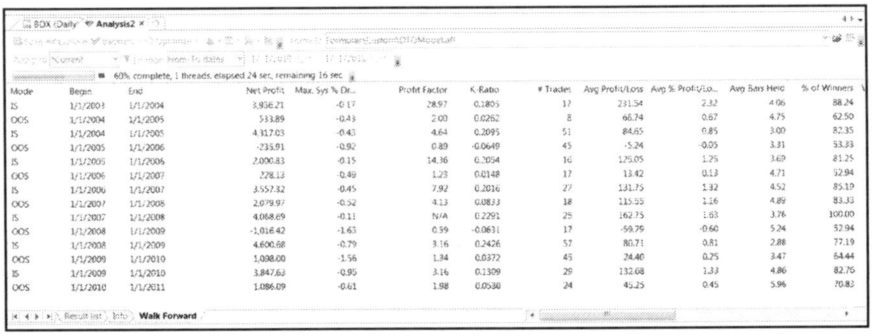

Figure 7.32 Walk forward results in progress

When the entire walk forward sequence is complete, use the Report Explorer to open the report for the combined out-of-sample tests. As shown in Figure 7.33, use the Report icon's pull down menu and click Report Explorer.

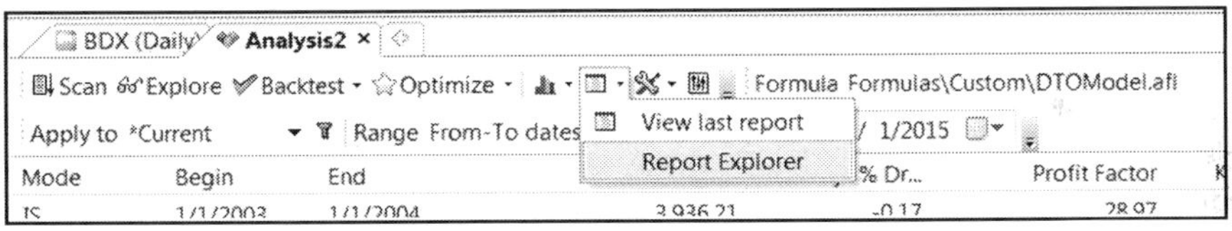

Figure 7.33 Opening the Report Explorer

The individual reports are in order by the date of the test. Scroll down to the end and double click the entry with the code PS in the Type column. See Figure 7.34.

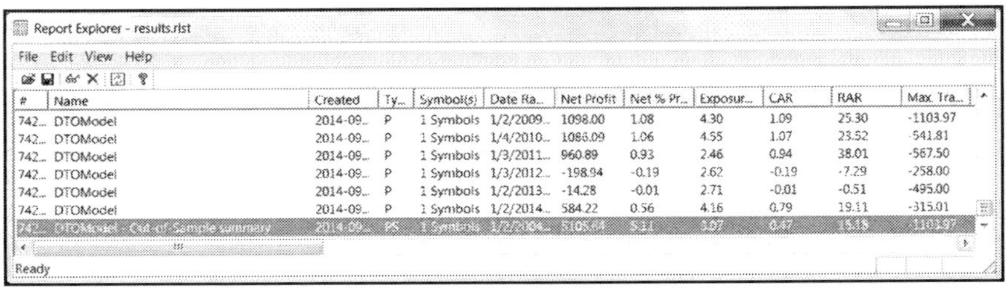

Figure 7.34 Opening the out-of-sample report

The familiar Summary Report will open, as shown in Figure 7.35. The results reported are all out-of-sample. The equity curve is formed by concatenating the curves for the individual periods together. The statistics are a compilation of all the OOS periods—added or averaged, as is appropriate.

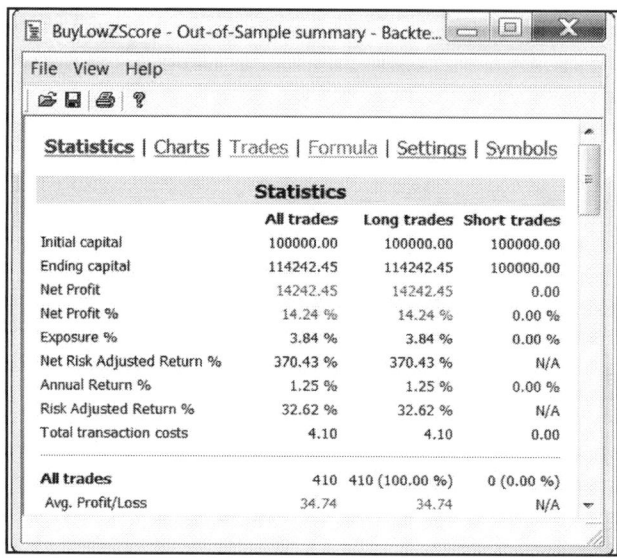

Figure 7.35 Out-of-sample summary report

The trade list, shown in Figure 7.36, is all of the out-of-sample trades, and only out-of-sample trades. This is the "best estimate" set of trades that can be used to analyze risk, determine safe-f, and estimate profit. Select the entire trade list (Control-A), copy it to the clip board (Control-C), and paste it in Excel. If it doesn't work the first time, try again.

Model Development—Indicator-Based

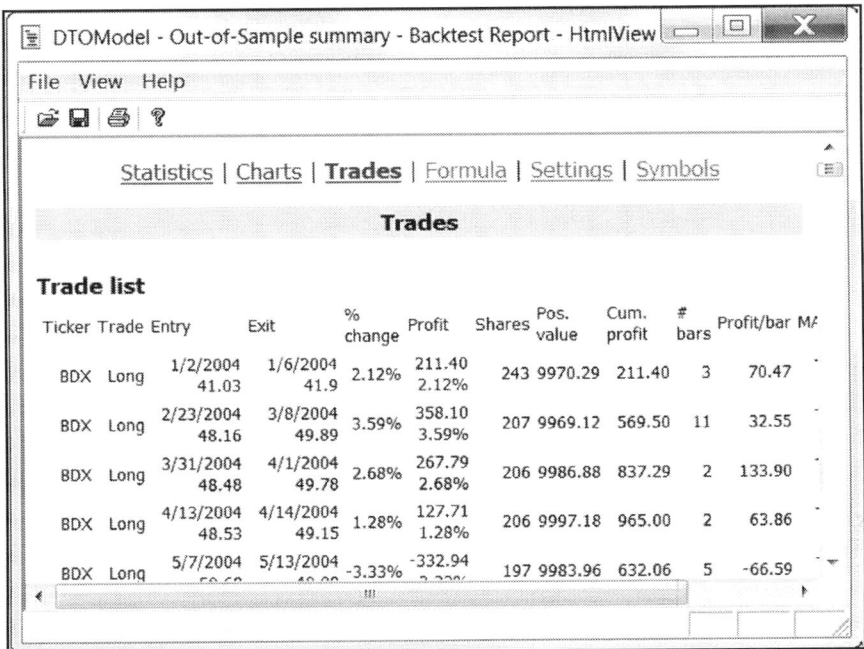

Figure 7.36 Out-of-sample trade list

Discovering Tradable Systems

There is some subjectivity, and it will require some experimentation on your part, to determine the best lengths to use for in-sample and out-of-sample periods. For the issues and models described, try one year out-of-sample and one, two, four, or six year in-sample periods. Adjust as you learn the characteristics of the system. The lengths that work depend on the strength of the trading signal within the data's noise, stationarity of the signal, and robustness of the model to changes in synchronization.

The length of the out-of-sample period is the amount of time you expect good system performance beyond the in-sample period. It is also the resynchronization period. I recommend the out-of-sample period be short enough that it is a realistic interval for trading management. If the out-of-sample period is too long, and the system loses synchronization, that will cause uncertainty about how to manage the system as performance fluctuates.

Every out-of-sample period should have several complete trades in it. Shortening the out-of-sample length too much will leave periods with no trades.

However long you decide to make the periods, I recommend having several years out-of-sample. During a walk forward run, many alternative systems are tested, and a choice made from among them. It is important that the alternatives are comparable. To compare period-length alternatives, fix the total out-of-sample length at, say, six years. Six one-year or 12 six-month periods. Do this by using one single date throughout the testing as the end date of the first in-sample period. Adjusting the length of the in-sample period is then done by setting the start date of the first in-sample period accordingly. Adjusting the length of the individual out-of-sample periods is done by choosing the desired length for the pull down menu. The total time period covered by the out-of-sample testing will be constant throughout.

Many optimizations are confined to rules and parameters. But the domain is potentially broader. The ultimate objective is maximum gain for a defined and limited risk. Consider alternative data series using the same time periods. But be aware of subjectivity as they are chosen.

The purpose of the walk forward phase is several-fold:
- Each walk forward step is a practice step showing the transition from development to trading. We get to see the out-of-sample performance of systems whose rules and parameters were chosen objectively.
- Every time actual trading performance is poor and the system is taken offline, it must be re-validated before resuming trading. Each walk forward step is an example of a re-validation.
- The set of trades produced by the out-of-sample portions of the process are the best estimate of future performance. This set of trades is so important that it is called "the best estimate" and is used to estimate risk, establish maximum safe positions size, and estimate profit.
- The concatenated out-of-sample equity curve gives early warning that a system may be losing its edge. Watch for an upward sloping curve to begin to flatten.

Validated Systems

A few of the models described in this chapter were applied to a few of the tickers listed. The objective function used was the one listed in Figure 7.2, or a slight variation of it. The out-of-sample period was set to 1 year; in-sample 1 year to 6 years. These are simplistic models—daily data, at most one action per day, a single entry rule, a single exit rule, no filters, no profit target, timed, trailing, or maximum loss exits.

A majority of the results were, if not immediately tradable, very promising. A few examples are shown. Each is a chart of the out-of-sample equity curve and a summary of the statistics. The caption to each documents the symbol and model. Test them yourself. Use your objective function. Determine the length of the in-sample and out-of-sample periods. Your results will not be exactly the same as these, but they should be close.

The equity curves shown are completely out-of-sample. The model used for each out-of-sample period was chosen automatically. It is the model that scored highest over the in-sample optimization.

These examples clearly show:
- There are identifiable and profitable trades with the characteristics we hoped to find.
    * Trade frequently
    * Trade accurately
    * Hold a short period
- There are persistent patterns that precede the trades.
- Any of several indicators recognize these patterns.
- The patterns exist in many data series.
- We can develop models using automated processes that do not rely on decisions made from examination of out-of-sample data.

A system using the RSI model.

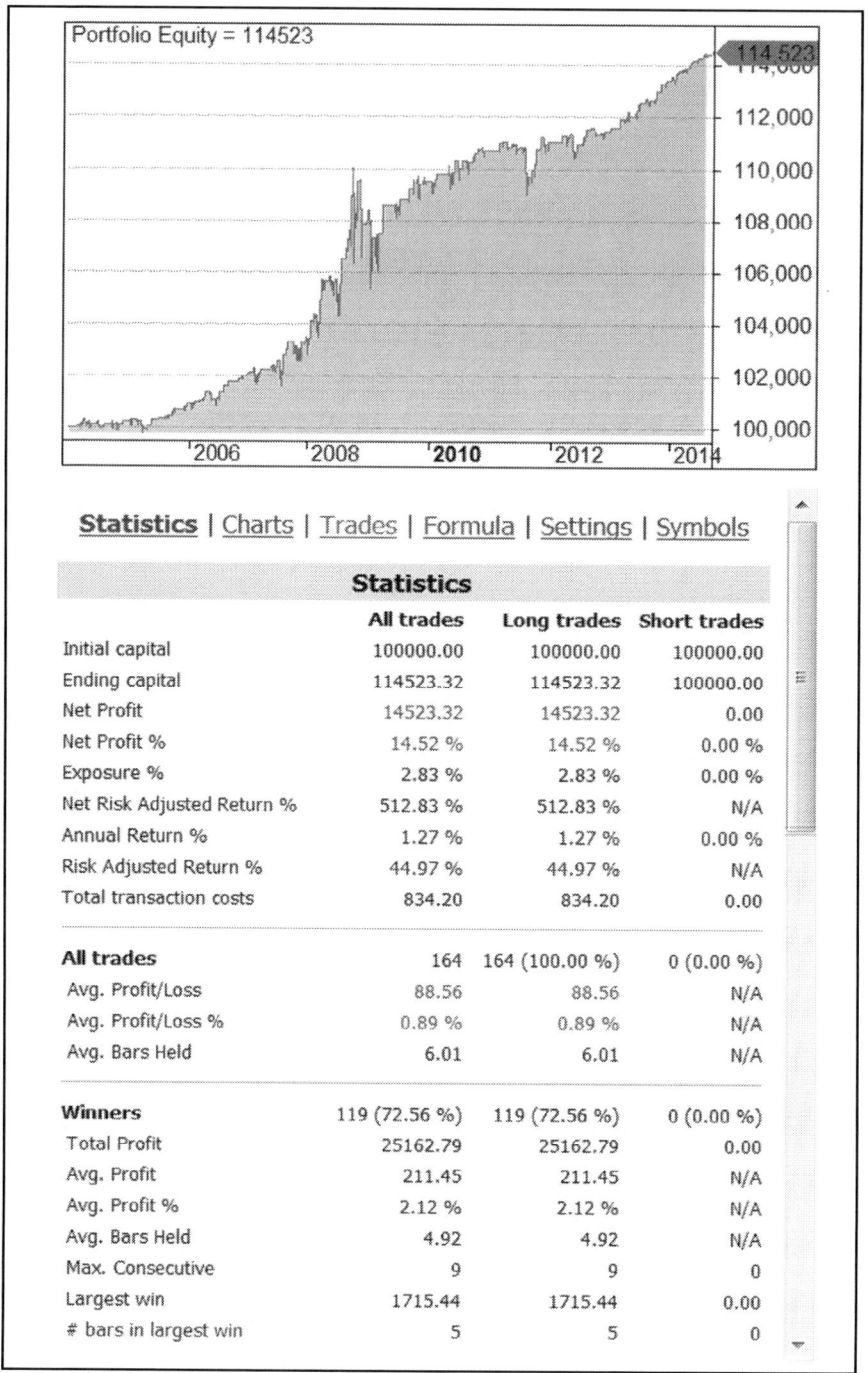

Figure 7.37 *XLF with RSI Model walk forward out-of-sample*

Model Development—Indicator-Based

A system using the low z-score model.

Figure 7.38 AZO with z-score Model walk forward out-of-sample

Summary

The development process is complete. The phases were:
- Develop a statement of personal risk tolerance.
- Analyze potential data series to determine the risk and profit potential in each. Select a few issues that are known to have the right risk and potential for further testing.
- Using relatively simple entry rules, develop and backtest a series of models to see if those issues have profitable trades that follow persistent patterns.
- Using an objective function to rank alternative systems, use the walk forward process to objectively choose systems.
- The final result is a set of trades, produced as objectively as possible, that are the best estimate of future performance of the system.

Review the flowchart in Chapter 1 and on this book's cover. The best estimate set of trades is the connection between system development and trading management. Development is complete. Turn to Chapter 9, Trading Management.

Anticipating Signals

A simple example is used for clarity of instruction. The concept and technique apply to almost any price you wish to anticipate.

Assume we are using a system that enters a long position when an indicator falls through a critical level. The indicator is based on the closing price of end-of-day data. The system is currently flat. If the next closing price is low enough, there will be a signal. We want to know what that price will be early enough so we can trade at the closing price of the bar that causes the signal. **Call this "action at the close of the signal bar."** For discussion, call the price at which the signal will be generated the "signal price."

Assume the system is based on crossover of two moving averages, such as the detrended price oscillator. Both averages use daily closing prices. One has a lookback length of 3 days, the other 10 days. On Figure 7.39, if the day at the vertical line has closed, we want to know what closing price the next day would cause a crossing and buy signal.

We could feed real-time transaction prices near the close to the program and let it sound an alert, flash a message on the monitor, or send an e-mail announcing the signal. Instead, this technique uses the trading system development platform and data available to provide the answer a full day earlier.

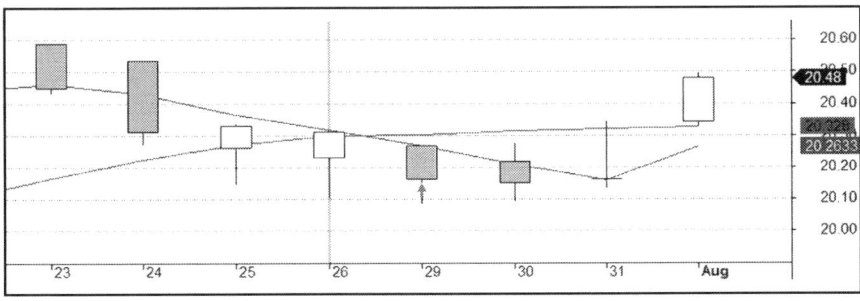

Figure 7.39 Closing price and moving averages

Figure 7.40 shows a spreadsheet with the data we have and the value we are looking for.

Date	7/23/2013	7/24/2013	7/25/2013	7/26/2013	7/29/2013
Close	20.45	20.31	20.33	20.31	What value here
MA3	20.460	20.430	20.363	20.317	Makes these two equal?
MA10	20.163	20.224	20.269	20.298	

Figure 7.40 Value we are looking for

When the two moving averages are equal, their difference is zero. Hence the name of the process as well as its description—find the zero of a function.

$$MA(C,3) = MA(C,10)$$
$$f = MA(C,3) - MA(C,10) = 0$$

Given all the closing prices except the final one, f is a function of the final price. Call that final, as yet unknown, value of the closing price series, Cest. When it is eventually determined, Cest is the signal price.

Since the MA(C,3) term is more sensitive to the final value than the MA(C,10) term, MA(C,3) will be greater than MA(C,10) for some Cest and less for some other value. The two will be equal at one and only one value of Cest.

In this case, the function is simple and has a closed form solution. We could solve the algebra and write a formula to compute Cest. But, that will usually not be the case. Any change to the model would require new algebra and a new formula. What is a simple trading system change from a simple moving average to an exponential or adaptive moving average would require different algebra and produce a considerably different formula. Still more complex indicators do not have closed form definitions or are transformed from other indicators and are not reversible.

The platform already has the formulas needed to compute averages and other indicators for any series of closing prices. We will use the platform and the following binary search algorithm to find the value computationally for any function of a single variable (usually price for our application) of any complexity.

1. Pick a very large value, call it CestHigh, that makes the function MA(C,3)-MA(C,10) greater than zero. Two times the highest of the previous 10 known closes should work.
2. Pick a very small value, call it CestLow, that makes the function less than zero. $0.01 should work.
3. Repeatedly, adjust CestHigh and CestLow until they are close to the same value.
   A. Compute CestMid to be the average of CestHigh and CestLow.

B. Evaluate the function MA(C,3)-MA(C,10) using CestMid as the final value.
C. If the result is positive, CestMid is on the same side of Cest as CestHigh, so replace CestHigh with CestMid; Otherwise replace CestLow with CestMid.

When the difference between CestHigh and CestLow is less than one tick, they are equal for our purpose. They have converged to Cest, the price we want to know, the signal price. Any close lower than the signal price will create a buy order.

Mathematically, the process is root finding, or solving for the zero of a function of one variable. In order for it to work:
- There must be a functional relationship.
  * One independent variable. In this case, it is the closing price that is the final price of the moving average series.
  * One dependent variable. The value of the function, f.
  * Given a value for the independent variable, call it Cguess, the value of the dependent variable, call it Fest, is unique.
- There is at least one value of Cguess where Fest is less than 0.
- There is at least one value of Cguess where Fest is greater than 0.
- There is one and only one value of Cguess where Fest equals 0.

The implementation steps depend on the platform you are using.

Because of the way AmiBroker handles data structures, we need a trick. In AmiBroker, all arrays are exactly the same length—the number of bars in the primary data series—defined as BarCount. AmiBroker is zero-based, so the index runs from 0 to BarCount-1. We want to calculate a value for the next close. It does not yet exist, so its data element in the array does not yet exist. If it were possible, we would just extend the close, the two moving averages, and whatever working arrays are needed by 1 element to make room for the next close. It would be element BarCount. However, doing that would cause AmiBroker to experience a fatal subscript-out-of-range error at run time. To trick AmiBroker into letting us do the calculation, we shift all the array data back one index position. Figure 7.41 illustrates.

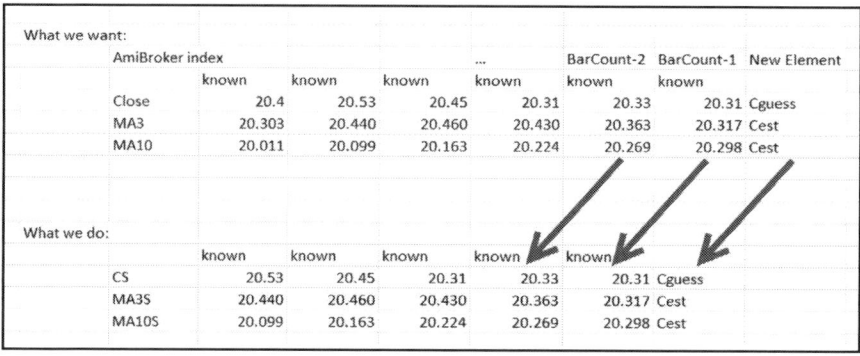

Figure 7.41 Shifting data to accommodate AmiBroker

The code is:

```
CS = Ref ( Close, 1);
```

This appears to introduce a future leak, and the Check function will flag it as such. But it is not a future leak, it is only an artifact of our trick.

Element BarCount-1 of the new array, CS, is now empty and undefined. (The original array, Close, is unaffected.) AmiBroker will allow us to use CS to compute the indicators, just as Close was used. We have created room for the trial values of the next close.

Figure 7.42 shows the AmiBroker code to compute the price at which the moving averages cross.

```
//  AnticipateMACross.afl
//
//  Anticipating moving average crossover
//
//  Disclaimer continues to apply
//
//  Copyright © 2014 Blue Owl Press, Inc
//

// Objective Function ObFnDemo1, from the Include directory
#include <ObFnDemo1.afl>;

// System settings
OptimizerSetEngine( "cmae" );
SetOption( "ExtraColumnsLocation", 1 );
SetBacktestMode( backtestRegular );
SetOption( "initialequity", 100000 );
MaxPos = 1;
SetOption( "maxopenpositions", MaxPos );
SetPositionSize( 10000, spsValue );
SetOption ( "CommissionMode", 3 ); // $ per share
SetOption( "CommissionAmount", 0.005 );
SetTradeDelays( 0, 0, 0, 0 );
BuyPrice = SellPrice = Close;

// Global variables and parameters
```

```
// User Functions
function FunctionToZero ( p, LB1, LB2 )
{
    f = MA( p, LB1 ) - MA( p, LB2 );
    return f;
}

// Local variables
AccuracyTolerance = 0.003;
LB1 = 3;
LB2 = 10;

// Indicators
MA1 = MA( C, LB1 );
MA2 = MA( C, LB2 );

// Buy and Sell Rules
Buy = Cross( MA2, MA1 );
Sell = Cross( MA1, MA2 );

// Anticipate Signal Price
CS = Ref( C, 1 );
LastIndex = BarCount - 1;
HighValue = 2 * HHV( C, 10 );
CestHigh = HighValue[LastIndex];
CS[LastIndex] = CestHigh;
FestHigh = FunctionToZero( CS, LB1, LB2 );
SignHigh = sign( FestHigh[LastIndex] );
CestLow = 0.01;
CS[LastIndex] = CestLow;
FestLow = FunctionToZero( CS, LB1, LB2 );
SignLow = sign( FestLow[LastIndex] );
CestDiff = CestHigh - CestLow;

itercount = 0;

while ( abs( CestDiff ) > AccuracyTolerance AND itercount < 100
          )
{
    CestMid = ( CestHigh + CestLow ) / 2;
    CS[LastIndex] = CestMid;
    FestMid = FunctionToZero( CS, LB1, LB2 );
    SignMid = sign( FestMid[LastIndex] );

    if ( SignMid == SignHigh )
        CestHigh = CestMid;
    else
        CestLow = CestMid;

    CestDiff = CestHigh - CestLow;

    itercount = itercount + 1;
}

SignalPrice = CestMid;

// Plots
Plot( C, "C", colorBlack, styleCandle );
Plot( MA1, "MA1", colorBlue, styleLine );
Plot( MA2, "MA2", colorRed, styleLine );

shapes = IIf( Buy, shapeUpArrow, IIf( Sell, shapeDownArrow,
              shapenone ) );
```

```
shapecolors = IIf( Buy, colorGreen, IIf( Sell, colorRed,
            colorWhite ) );
PlotShapes( shapes, shapecolors );

// Explore

Filter = 1;

AddColumn( SignalPrice, "SignalPrice", 10.4 );
AddColumn( itercount, "Iterations Needed", 10.0 );

////////////// end //////////////
```

Figure 7.42 Estimate close for moving average cross

Figure 7.43 shows the results of the Exploration, giving the signal price—the price below which there will be a trading signal.

Ticker	Date/Time	SignalPrice	Iterations Needed
XLF	7/26/2013	20.3170	14

Figure 7.43 Exploration

The signal price is 20.317. Any close of $20.31 or lower will cause a buy signal to be issued.

Summary

The technique described is a binary search for the zero of a function. It enables you to compute the price at which some condition will be true.

The example shown is the price at which two simple moving averages cross. The algebra to determine that price is easy, and an explicit formula could be written that would directly compute the answer and eliminate the looping code.

Changing from the cross of two simple moving averages, replacing one of the simple averages with an exponential average, makes the algebra unwieldy. But, using this technique, the new function is accommodated by changing a single line in the FunctionToZero from:

```
f = MA( p, LB1 ) - MA( p, LB2 );
```

to:

```
f = EMA( p, LB1 ) - MA( p, LB2 );
```

Chapter 8
Model Development Machine Learning

Kevin Murphy defines machine learning as "a set of methods that can automatically detect patterns in data, and then use the uncovered patterns to predict future data."[1]

Python as a Development Platform

Python is well suited to be the platform for machine learning based trading system development. We will be using this configuration:
- Anaconda Spyder
- NumPy
- SciPy
- Pandas
- MatPlotLib
- Scikit-learn

Before we can begin working with machine learning, we need support for Python-based traditional trading systems. We need to be able to do using Python what we can already do using AmiBroker. Recall the order of program elements in an AmiBroker trading system program:
1. Comments documenting the program
2. System settings
3. Global variables
4. Functions

---

[1] Murphy, Kevin, *Machine Learning: A Probabilistic Perspective*, MIT Press, 2012.

5. Local variables
6. Indicators
7. Rules
8. Signals
9. (Evaluation of signals)
10. Plots
11. Explorations

The evaluation of signals step was performed by AmiBroker—by the trading system development platform. It happened when Backtest was chosen from the Analysis menu. Or when the single statement

```
e = equity();
```

was executed.

AmiBroker is, and all trading system development platforms are, a special purpose computer program with a language specifically designed to be used for trading system development. It has the functions required to handle time series data, and to evaluate trading signals, built in to it.

Python is a general purpose language. If we want to use it as a trading system development platform, we need to provide the functions specific to trading ourselves. There are two functions that require special attention:
- Data and date ranges
- Evaluation of signals

Data and Date Ranges

AmiBroker automatically handles the separation of data, loading whatever amount of data is necessary for the tests, initializing the variables and indicators, testing the rules over the date range specified, and formatting the results.

Those same functions must be performed in the Python program. The Python program is given a date range to load and a date range to test, as shown in Figure 8.1.

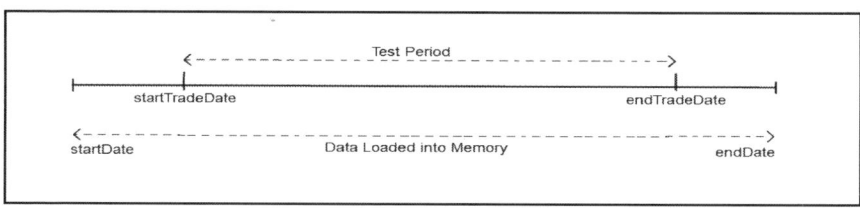

Figure 8.1 Defining the test period

Figure 8.2 shows the python code for a template program that reads end-of-day data from Yahoo Finance and uses dates to define an operational range. You will be doing this when you read a long price history, but want to restrict the period processed or tabulated.

```python
"""
DateIndexing.py

Using dates to define a time period

Disclaimer continues to apply

Copyright  2014 Blue Owl Press, Inc
Dr. Howard Bandy
October 2014

"""

from datetime import datetime
from pandas.io.data import DataReader

ticker = "XLV"
source = "yahoo"

#   Define the date range to be loaded
startDate = datetime(2012,1,4)
endDate = datetime(2014,3,1)

qt = DataReader(ticker, source, startDate, endDate)

print " "
print "Ticker:              ", ticker
print "Data source:         ", source
print "First date retrieved: ", startDate
print "Last date retrieved: ", endDate

nrows = qt.shape[0]
print "Rows of data:        ", nrows

qt.columns = ['Open','High','Low','Close','Vol','AdjClose']
qtC = qt.AdjClose

#   Define the date range to be tested
startTradeDate = datetime(2013,1,3)
endTradeDate = datetime(2013,2,4)

print "startTradeDate:      ", startTradeDate, "Value: ",
        qtC[startTradeDate]
print "endTradeDate:        ", endTradeDate,   "Value: ",
        qtC[endTradeDate]
print "---------------- Data within date range --------"
for i in range(nrows):
    dt = qtC.index[i]
    datesPass = dt >= startTradeDate and dt <= endTradeDate
    if datesPass:
        print "i, Date, Close: ", i, dt, qtC[i]
print "---------------- Done ----------------------"

############   end   ##########
```

Figure 8.2 Using dates to define a time period in Python

Figure 8.3 shows the output.

```
Ticker:                 XLV
Data source:            yahoo
First date retrieved:   2012-01-04 00:00:00
Last date retrieved:    2014-03-01 00:00:00
Rows of data:           541
startTradeDate:         2013-01-03 00:00:00 Value:  39.6
endTradeDate:           2013-02-04 00:00:00 Value:  41.6
----------------- Data within date range --------
i, Date, Close:   250 2013-01-03 00:00:00 39.6
i, Date, Close:   251 2013-01-04 00:00:00 39.78
i, Date, Close:   252 2013-01-07 00:00:00 39.9
i, Date, Close:   253 2013-01-08 00:00:00 39.91
i, Date, Close:   254 2013-01-09 00:00:00 40.35
i, Date, Close:   255 2013-01-10 00:00:00 40.63
i, Date, Close:   256 2013-01-11 00:00:00 40.62
i, Date, Close:   257 2013-01-14 00:00:00 40.66
i, Date, Close:   258 2013-01-15 00:00:00 40.61
i, Date, Close:   259 2013-01-16 00:00:00 40.53
i, Date, Close:   260 2013-01-17 00:00:00 40.89
i, Date, Close:   261 2013-01-18 00:00:00 41.02
i, Date, Close:   262 2013-01-22 00:00:00 41.14
i, Date, Close:   263 2013-01-23 00:00:00 41.09
i, Date, Close:   264 2013-01-24 00:00:00 41.35
i, Date, Close:   265 2013-01-25 00:00:00 41.67
i, Date, Close:   266 2013-01-28 00:00:00 41.53
i, Date, Close:   267 2013-01-29 00:00:00 41.98
i, Date, Close:   268 2013-01-30 00:00:00 41.85
i, Date, Close:   269 2013-01-31 00:00:00 41.73
i, Date, Close:   270 2013-02-01 00:00:00 42.06
i, Date, Close:   271 2013-02-04 00:00:00 41.6
----------------- Done -------------------------
```

Figure 8.3 Output from DateIndexing.py

There will be circumstances when you prefer to define a range of data based on dates, then copy the data in that range to a new variable for further processing. Figure 8.4 shows the python code for a template program that does this. Note that the dates used to define the start and end of the range are not required to be present in the source. The bdate function specifies business days.

```
"""
DateRange.py

Using a range of dates to define a time period

Disclaimer continues to apply

Copyright  2014 Blue Owl Press, Inc
Dr. Howard Bandy
October 2014

"""

import pandas
from datetime import datetime
from pandas.io.data import DataReader

ticker = "XLV"
source = "yahoo"

#    Define the date range to be loaded
startDate = datetime(2012,1,4)
endDate = datetime(2014,3,1)

qt = DataReader(ticker, source, startDate, endDate)

print " "
print "Ticker:                 ", ticker
print "Data source:            ", source
print "First date retrieved: ", startDate
print "Last date retrieved:  ", endDate

nrows = qt.shape[0]
print "Rows of data:           ", nrows

qt.columns = ['Open','High','Low','Close','Vol','AdjClose']
qtC = qt.AdjClose

#    Define the date range to be tested
startTradeDate = datetime(2013,1,1)
endTradeDate = datetime(2013,2,4)

#    Use business days
workingDateRange = pandas.bdate_range(startTradeDate,
               endTradeDate)

workingData = qtC[workingDateRange]
nrows = workingData.shape[0]
print "nrows in workingData: ", nrows

print workingData

print "----------------- Done -----------------------"

############    end   ##########
```

Figure 8.4 Copying a section of data using a date range

Figure 8.5 shows the output.

```
Ticker:                    XLV
Data source:               yahoo
First date retrieved:      2012-01-04 00:00:00
Last date retrieved:       2014-03-01 00:00:00
Rows of data:              541
nrows in workingData:      25
2013-01-01        NaN
2013-01-02      39.55
2013-01-03      39.60
2013-01-04      39.78
2013-01-07      39.90
2013-01-08      39.91
2013-01-09      40.35
2013-01-10      40.63
2013-01-11      40.62
2013-01-14      40.66
2013-01-15      40.61
2013-01-16      40.53
2013-01-17      40.89
2013-01-18      41.02
2013-01-21        NaN
2013-01-22      41.14
2013-01-23      41.09
2013-01-24      41.35
2013-01-25      41.67
2013-01-28      41.53
2013-01-29      41.98
2013-01-30      41.85
2013-01-31      41.73
2013-02-01      42.06
2013-02-04      41.60
Freq: B, Name: AdjClose, dtype: float64
----------------- Done ------------------------
```

Figure 8.5 Output from DateRange.py

Evaluation of Signals

Through a combination of some system settings and some functionality built in to every trading system development platform, a series of buy and sell signals is combined with a primary data series, resulting in a series of trades.

To use Python, we must provide that functionality and all of its details.

The code to evaluate signals and manage positions follows the activities of the trader through a time period—say, a day. Positions are entered and exited, and status variables are maintained. The flow is:
1. Action at the open.
    A. Market on open exit.

    B. Market on open entry.
    C. Update status variables.
2. Action intra-day.
    A. Stop order exit.
    B. Limit order exit.
    C. Stop order entry.
    D. Limit order entry.
    E. Arbitrating conflicting orders.
    F. Update status variables.
3. Action at the close.
    A. Market on close exit.
    B. Market on close entry.
    C. Update status variables.

Status variables keep track of current information on a bar-by-bar or day-by-day basis, as well as historical information related to closed trades on a trade-by-trade basis. Variables include:
- Current—day-by-day.
    * Account balance. Cash plus share equity.
    * Cash.
    * Shares.
    * Entry date and time.
    * Entry price.
    * Open trade equity.
    * Indicator values.
    * Price for limit orders.
    * Price for stop orders.
    * Bar count for timed exits.
- Historical—trade-by-trade.
    * Shares
    * Dollars
    * Entry date and price.
    * Exit date and price.
    * Profit.
    * Maximum favorable excursion.
    * Maximum adverse excursion.

Whichever of these are necessary for a system must be defined, initialized, updated, and reported by the Python code. The complexity is reduced considerably when the system is trading a single issue long / flat, which will be the case for the examples in this book. It is reduced still more if all actions are at the same time, such as market-on-close of the signal bar, which is the case for the first examples, but is relaxed later.

Translation to Python

To illustrate the use of Python as a trading system development platform, the RSI model discussed in Chapter 7 is translated to Python. It enters a long position at the close of trading on the day when the short-lookback RSI crosses down through a critical level, exits at the close of trading when that same indicator crosses up through a different level. In these first examples, both the AmiBroker and Python versions use impulse signals and trade MOC of the signal bar. In an effort to focus on the translation of the trading-related components, the listing has been edited to the essential code and much of the overhead has been removed. Figure 8.6 lists the AmiBroker program and Figure 8.10 lists the equivalent Python program.

Expecting comparable output begins with providing identical input. Currently, there is not a Python API to the Norgate database used by AmiBroker. However, both platforms can use Yahoo data.

A Yahoo database was set up and loaded with historical end-of-day data for use by AmiBroker.

It is possible to create a local database for use by Python, download the desired historical data in ASCII format, store it in the database, and have the Python program read that data.

Instead, for this example, the data is read on-the-fly. That is, the Python program downloads a fresh copy directly into a program variable as the program executes. For this example, the data used is XLV, the S&P Healthcare Sector ETF. The period tested is 1/4/2002 through 1/3/2012. Data is loaded from 1/1/1999 to allow for initialization of indicators.

```
//  RSIModel.afl
//
//  Disclaimer continues to apply
//
//  Copyright © 2014 Blue Owl Press, Inc
//
//  Signals are generated at the close of daily trading
//  for execution at the close of the same bar.

// System settings
OptimizerSetEngine( "cmae" );
SetOption( "ExtraColumnsLocation", 1 );
SetBacktestMode( backtestRegular );
SetOption( "initialequity", 100000 );
MaxPos = 1;
SetOption( "maxopenpositions", MaxPos );
SetPositionSize( 10000, spsValue );
SetOption ( "CommissionMode", 3 );  // $ per share
SetOption( "CommissionAmount", 0.005 );
SetTradeDelays( 0, 0, 0, 0 );
BuyPrice = SellPrice = Close;
```

```
// User Functions
function RSI_Custom( p, Lambda )
{
    //     p == series having its RSI computed
    //     lambda == weight given to latest value
    UpMove = Max( p - Ref( p, -1 ), 0 );
    DnMove = Max( Ref( p, -1 ) - p, 0 );

    //     Initialze arrays
    UpMoveSm = 0 * p;
    DnMoveSm = 0 * p;

    for ( i = 1;i < BarCount;i++ )
    {
        UpMoveSm[i] = Lambda * UpMove[i] +
                    ( 1.0 - Lambda ) * UpMoveSM[i-1];
        DnMoveSm[i] = Lambda * DnMove[i] +
                    ( 1.0 - Lambda ) * DnMoveSM[i-1];
    }

    Numer = UpMoveSm;

    Denom = UpMoveSm + DnMoveSm;
    return ( 100 * IIf( Denom <= 0, 0.5, Numer / Denom ) );
}

// Local variables, beginning with Param and Optimize
Lambda = Optimize( "Lambda", 0.74, 0.20, 0.80, 0.01 );
RSIBuyLevel = Optimize( "RSIBuyLevel", 33, 1, 99, 1 );
RSISellIncrem = Optimize( "RSISellIncrem", 46, 0, 60, 1 );

RSISellLevel = Min( RSIBuyLevel + RSISellIncrem, 99 );

// Indicators
RSI_C = RSI_Custom( C, Lambda );

// Buy and Sell rules
Buy = Cross( RSIBuyLevel, RSI_C );
Sell = Cross( RSI_C, RSISellLevel );

// Plots
Plot( C, "C", colorBlack, styleCandle );
shapes = IIf( Buy, shapeUpArrow,
            IIf( Sell, shapeDownArrow, shapenone ) );
shapecolors = IIf( Buy, colorGreen,
            IIf( Sell, colorRed, colorWhite ) );
PlotShapes( shapes, shapecolors );

Plot( RSI_C, "RSICustom", colorGreen,
        styleLine | styleOwnScale, 0, 100 );

// Explore

Filter = 1;
AddColumn( C, "C", 10.4 );
AddColumn( RSI_C, "RSI_C", 10.4 );

///////////////////////////// end ////////////////
```

Figure 8.6 RSI model using impulse signals (AmiBroker)

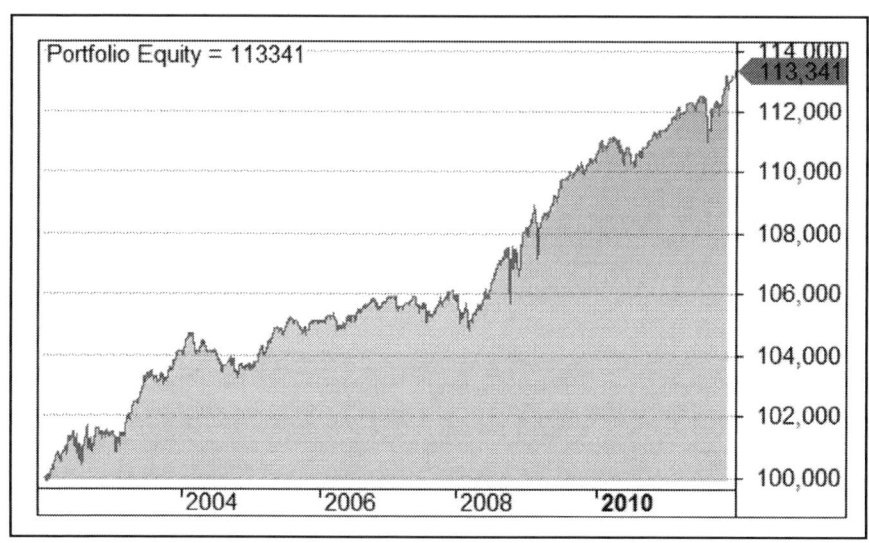

Figure 8.7 Equity curve from RSI model using AmiBroker

Statistics | Charts | Trades | Formula | Settings | Symbols

Statistics

	All trades	Long trades	Short trades
Initial capital	100000.00	100000.00	100000.00
Ending capital	113340.99	113340.99	100000.00
Net Profit	13340.99	13340.99	0.00
Net Profit %	13.34 %	13.34 %	0.00 %
Exposure %	4.95 %	4.95 %	0.00 %
Net Risk Adjusted Return %	269.35 %	269.35 %	N/A
Annual Return %	1.26 %	1.26 %	0.00 %
Risk Adjusted Return %	25.44 %	25.44 %	N/A
Total transaction costs	1487.54	1487.54	0.00
All trades	389	389 (100.00 %)	0 (0.00 %)
Avg. Profit/Loss	34.30	34.30	N/A
Avg. Profit/Loss %	0.34 %	0.34 %	N/A
Avg. Bars Held	4.42	4.42	N/A
Winners	281 (72.24 %)	281 (72.24 %)	0 (0.00 %)
Total Profit	31247.85	31247.85	0.00
Avg. Profit	111.20	111.20	N/A
Avg. Profit %	1.11 %	1.11 %	N/A
Avg. Bars Held	3.30	3.30	N/A
Max. Consecutive	10	10	0
Largest win	895.50	895.50	0.00
# bars in largest win	4	4	0
Losers	108 (27.76 %)	108 (27.76 %)	0 (0.00 %)
Total Loss	-17906.86	-17906.86	0.00
Avg. Loss	-165.80	-165.80	N/A
Avg. Loss %	-1.66 %	-1.66 %	N/A
Avg. Bars Held	7.35	7.35	N/A
Max. Consecutive	4	4	0
Largest loss	-1534.06	-1534.06	0.00
# bars in largest loss	13	13	0

Figure 8.8 Statistics from RSI model using AmiBroker

Since this system trades a single issue, and always trades at the close of the signal bar at the closing price, the logic is simple. The trading system simulator used to evaluate the system is also very simple. Each day within the range of trading days is processed using the flowchart shown in Figure 8.9.

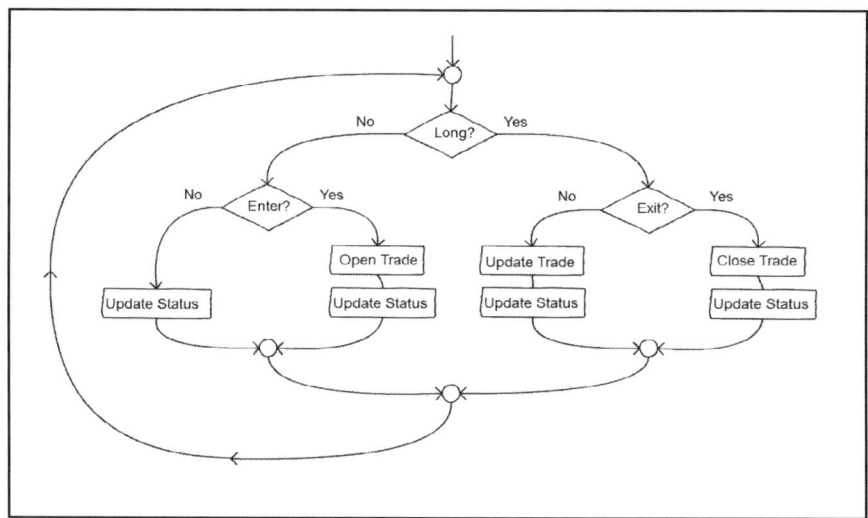

Figure 8.9 Flowchart of Python trading system program

The following skeleton illustrates the date ranges and the program flow. The "pass" statement is a placeholder.

```
#   Initialize status variables
#   Calculate the RSI indicator using all data loaded
RSIC = ...
#   Use the RSI indicator to generate
#   Buy and Sell impulse signals.
buy = ...
sell = ...
#   Loop over all the days loaded
for i in range(1, ndays):
    #   Extract the date
    dt = qtC.index[i]
    #   Check the date
    datesPass = dt>=startTradeDate and dt<=endTradeDate
    if datesPass:
        iTradeDate = iTradeDate + 1
        if sharesHeld[iTradeDate-1] > 0:
            #   In a long position
            if sell[i]:
                #   Exit -- close the trade
                pass
            else:
                #   Continue long
                pass
```

```
            else:
                #   Flat
                If buy[i]:
                    #   Enter a new position
                    pass
                else:
                    #   Continue flat
                    pass

    #   Format and print results
    #######   end   ######
```

Figure 8.10 shows the Python program equivalent to the AmiBroker program in Figure 8.6. It also uses impulse signals, and enters and exits based on the same indicator. Each element of the status variable arrays is one trading day. Mark-to-market accounting is updated after the close of trading and all transactions for the day have been completed. Trades are stored in an array sized to accommodate a trade every day. The list of closed trades contains percentage gain.

```
"""
RSIModel_ImpulseSignals.py

Translation of RSIModel.afl
from AmiBroker to Python

Disclaimer continues to apply

Copyright  2014 Blue Owl Press, Inc
Dr. Howard Bandy
October 2014

Signals are Buy and Sell impulse signals
generated at the close of daily trading
for execution at the close of the same bar.

All trades fixed size of $10,000

"""

#   System settings

from datetime import datetime
import matplotlib.pyplot as plt
from scipy import stats
import numpy as np
import pandas as pd
import math

from pandas import Series, DataFrame, DatetimeIndex
from pandas.io.data import DataReader

#   User functions
def RSI_Custom ( p, lam):
    nrows = p.shape[0]

    upMoveSm = np.zeros(nrows)
    dnMoveSm = np.zeros(nrows)
    numer = np.zeros(nrows)
    denom = np.zeros(nrows)
    RSISeries = np.zeros(nrows)
```

```python
#       pChg = p.pct_change()
        pChg = p - p.shift(1)
        upMove = np.where(pChg>0, pChg, 0)
        dnMove = np.where(pChg<0, -pChg, 0)
        
        for i in range (nrows):
            upMoveSm[i] = lam*upMove[i] + (1.0-lam)*upMoveSm[i-1]
            dnMoveSm[i] = lam*dnMove[i] + (1.0-lam)*dnMoveSm[i-1]
            numer[i] = upMoveSm[i]
            denom[i] = upMoveSm[i] + dnMoveSm[i]
            if (denom[i]<=0):
                RSISeries[i] = 50.0
            else:
                RSISeries[i] = 100.0 * numer[i] / denom[i]
        
        return (RSISeries)

#   Define and load data

ticker = "XLV"
source = "yahoo"

#   Define the date range to load
startDate = datetime(1999,1,4)
endDate = datetime(2015,1,1)

qt = DataReader(ticker, source, startDate, endDate)

ndays = qt.shape[0]
print ndays

qt.columns = ['Open','High','Low','Close','Vol','AdjClose']
qtC = qt.AdjClose

#   Define the date range to trade
startTradeDate = datetime(2002,1,4)
print startTradeDate
endTradeDate = datetime(2012,1,3)

print qtC[startTradeDate]
print qtC[endTradeDate]
print qtC.index

#   Local variables for trading system

initialEquity = 100000
fixedTradeDollars = 10000
commission = 0.005      #  Dollars per share per trade

lam = 0.01*74
RSIBuyLevel = 33
RSISellIncr = 46
RSISellLevel = min(RSIBuyLevel + RSISellIncr,99)

#   Indicators

RSIC = Series(RSI_Custom(qtC, lam))
#           print RSIC.head()
#           print RSIC.tail()

#RSIC.plot()
```

```python
#  Buy and Sell rules

buy = np.zeros(ndays)
sell = np.zeros(ndays)
for i in range (1, ndays):
    if RSIC[i-1]>=RSIBuyLevel and RSIC[i]<RSIBuyLevel:
        buy[i] = 1
    if RSIC[i-1]<RSISellLevel and RSIC[i]>=RSISellLevel:
        sell[i] = 1

#buyPlot = Series(buy)
#buyPlot.plot()

#sellPlot = Series(sell)
#sellPlot.plot()

#  Evaluation of signals

print "Starting single run"

#  Status variables

#  These are scalar and apply to the current conditions

entryPrice = 0
exitPrice = 0

#  These have an element for each day loaded
#  Some will be unnecessary

accountBalance = np.zeros(ndays)
cash = np.zeros(ndays)
sharesHeld = np.zeros(ndays)
tradeGain = np.zeros(ndays)
openTradeEquity = np.zeros(ndays)

iTradeDay = 0
iTradeNumber = 0

#  Day 0 contains the initial values
accountBalance[0] = initialEquity
cash[0] = accountBalance[0]
sharesHeld[0] = 0

#  Loop over all the days loaded
for i in range (1,ndays):
    #  Extract the date
    dt = qtC.index[i]
    #  Check the date
    datesPass = dt>=startTradeDate and dt<=endTradeDate
    if datesPass:
        iTradeDay = iTradeDay + 1
        if sharesHeld[iTradeDay-1] > 0:
            #  In a long position
            if sell[i]:
                #  Exit -- close the trade
                exitPrice = qtC[i]
                grossProceeds = sharesHeld[iTradeDay-1] *
                        exitPrice
                commissionAmount = sharesHeld[iTradeDay-1] *
                        commission
```

```python
                    netProceeds = grossProceeds - commissionAmount
                    cash[iTradeDay] = cash[iTradeDay-1] + 
                            netProceeds
                    accountBalance[iTradeDay] = cash[iTradeDay]
                    sharesHeld[iTradeDay] = 0
                    iTradeNumber = iTradeNumber+1
                    tradeGain[iTradeNumber] = (exitPrice / 
                            (1.0 * entryPrice))
                    pass
                else:
                    #   Continue long
                    sharesHeld[iTradeDay] = sharesHeld[iTradeDay-1]
                    cash[iTradeDay] = cash[iTradeDay-1]
                    MTMPrice = qtC[i]
                    openTradeEquity = sharesHeld[iTradeDay] * 
                            MTMPrice
                    accountBalance[iTradeDay] = cash[iTradeDay] + 
                            openTradeEquity
                    pass
            else:
                #   Flat
                if buy[i]:
                    #   Enter a new position
                    entryPrice = qtC[i]
                    sharesHeld[iTradeDay] = int(fixedTradeDollars/
                            (entryPrice+commission))
                    shareCost = sharesHeld[iTradeDay]*
                            (entryPrice+commission)
                    cash[iTradeDay] = cash[iTradeDay-1] - shareCost
                    openTradeEquity = sharesHeld[iTradeDay]*
                            entryPrice
                    accountBalance[iTradeDay] = cash[iTradeDay] + 
                            openTradeEquity
                    pass
                else:
                    #   Continue flat
                    cash[iTradeDay] = cash[iTradeDay-1]
                    accountBalance[iTradeDay] = cash[iTradeDay]
                    pass

    #   Format and print results

    finalAccountBalance = accountBalance[iTradeDay]
    print "Final account balance:", finalAccountBalance
    numberTradeDays = iTradeDay
    numberTrades = iTradeNumber
    print "Number of trades:", numberTrades

    #print "equity: ", equity

    Sequity = Series(accountBalance[0:numberTradeDays-1])

    Sequity.plot()

    ############   end   ################
```

Figure 8.10 RSI model using impulse signals (Python)

The two versions of the system have the same number of trades—389. The final equity reported from AmiBroker is $113,341. From Python it is $113,335. Figure 8.11 shows the equity curve from the Python program. Compare with Figure 8.7.

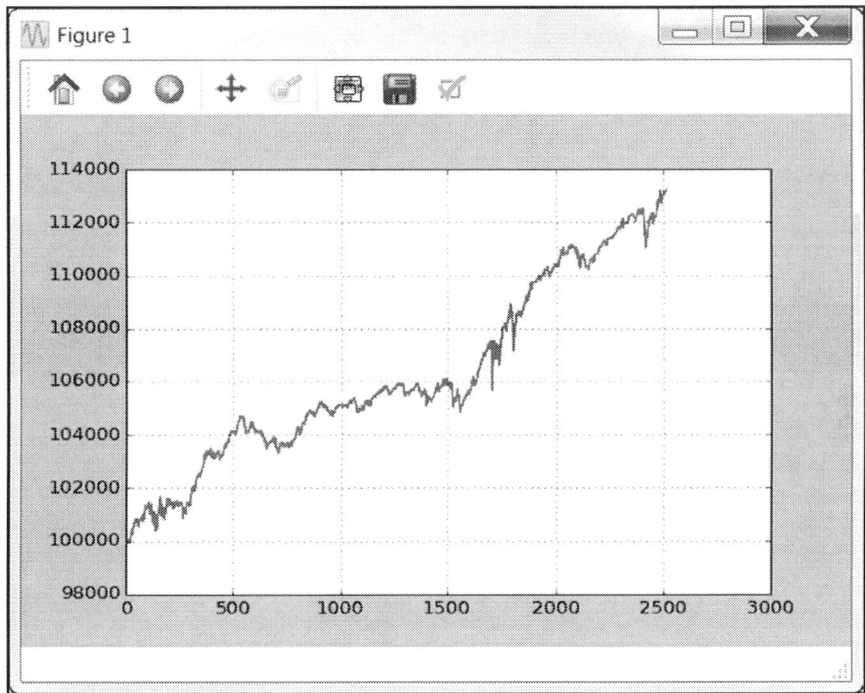

Figure 8.11 Equity curve from Python RSI model using impulse signals

Convert Impulse Signals to State Signals

Later, as indicators are searched for patterns using machine learning techniques, each day must be a completely self-contained data point. Rather than using impulse signals to enter one day and exit some number of days later, each day has a state signal associated with it. That state signal indicates the position to be held from the current day's close to the next close.

To convert from impulse signals to state signals in AmiBroker, replace these lines:

```
// Buy and Sell rules

Buy = Cross( RSIBuyLevel, RSI_C );
Sell = Cross( RSI_C, RSISellLevel );
```

with these lines:

```
// Buy and Sell rules

BuySignal = Cross( RSIBuyLevel, RSI_C );
SellSignal = Cross( RSI_C, RSISellLevel );

Buy = Flip( BuySignal, SellSignal );
Sell = Flip( SellSignal, BuySignal );
```

This creates a sequence of single-day Buy and Sell commands, each stored in an array variable of its own, one element for each day. Exactly one of the daily Buy/Sell array pair will have a value of 1. The other will be 0. When already in a long position, subsequent Buy signals cause continuation of the long position with no transactions and no commission cost.

For our use in Python, there will be two states for the state variable. We describe them using the labels *beLong* and *beFlat*. The state will be used as the target for the classification learning, so we want a single variable with two values. The variable will be named *target*, with a value of +1 representing beLong, and -1 representing beFlat.

In AmiBroker, the code to assign values to target using the state variables resulting from the Flip statements above would be:

```
target = iif(Buy, 1, -1);
```

In Python, given two arrays of impulse variables, Buy and Sell, target is assigned the proper state using the following code.

```
#   Buy and Sell rules

buy = np.zeros(ndays)
sell = np.zeros(ndays)
for i in range (1, ndays):
    if RSIC[i-1]>=RSIBuyLevel and RSIC[i]<RSIBuyLevel:
        buy[i] = 1
    if RSIC[i-1]<RSISellLevel and RSIC[i]>=RSISellLevel:
        sell[i] = 1

#   Convert to state signals

target = np.zeros(ndays)
if buy[0]:
    target[0] = 1
else:
    target[0] = -1
for i in range(1,ndays):
    if buy[i]:
        target[i] = 1
    elif sell[i]:
        target[i] = -1
    else:
        target[i] = target[i-1]
```

Figure 8.12 shows the entire program to implement the RSI system using state signals in Python.

```
"""
RSIModel_StateSignals.py

Translation of RSIModel.afl
from AmiBroker to Python

Disclaimer continues to apply

Copyright  2014 Blue Owl Press, Inc
Dr. Howard Bandy
October 2014

Signals begin as Buy and Sell impulse signals
generated at the close of daily trading
for execution at the close of the same bar.
They are converted into state signals
prior to being interpreted in the trading system.

All trades fixed size of $10,000

"""

#   System settings

from datetime import datetime
import matplotlib.pyplot as plt
from scipy import stats
import numpy as np
import pandas as pd
import math

from pandas import Series, DataFrame, DatetimeIndex
from pandas.io.data import DataReader

#   User functions
def RSI_Custom ( p, lam):
    nrows = p.shape[0]

    upMoveSm = np.zeros(nrows)
    dnMoveSm = np.zeros(nrows)
    numer = np.zeros(nrows)
    denom = np.zeros(nrows)
    RSISeries = np.zeros(nrows)

#      pChg = p.pct_change()
    pChg = p - p.shift(1)
    upMove = np.where(pChg>0, pChg, 0)
    dnMove = np.where(pChg<0, -pChg, 0)

    for i in range (nrows):
        upMoveSm[i] = lam*upMove[i] + (1.0-lam)*upMoveSm[i-1]
        dnMoveSm[i] = lam*dnMove[i] + (1.0-lam)*dnMoveSm[i-1]
        numer[i] = upMoveSm[i]
        denom[i] = upMoveSm[i] + dnMoveSm[i]
        if (denom[i]<=0):
            RSISeries[i] = 50.0
        else:
            RSISeries[i] = 100.0 * numer[i] / denom[i]
```

```python
    return (RSISeries)

# Define and load data

ticker = "XLV"
source = "yahoo"

# Define the date range to load
startDate = datetime(1999,1,4)
endDate = datetime(2015,1,1)

qt = DataReader(ticker, source, startDate, endDate)

ndays = qt.shape[0]
print ndays

qt.columns = ['Open','High','Low','Close','Vol','AdjClose']
qtC = qt.AdjClose

# Define the date range to trade
startTradeDate = datetime(2002,1,4)
print startTradeDate
endTradeDate = datetime(2012,1,3)

print qtC[startTradeDate]
print qtC[endTradeDate]
print qtC.index

# Local variables for trading system

initialEquity = 100000
fixedTradeDollars = 10000
commission = 0.005      # Dollars per share per trade

lam = 0.01*74
RSIBuyLevel = 33
RSISellIncr = 46
RSISellLevel = min(RSIBuyLevel + RSISellIncr,99)

# Indicators

RSIC = Series(RSI_Custom(qtC, lam))
#           print RSIC.head()
#           print RSIC.tail()

#RSIC.plot()

# Buy and Sell rules

buy = np.zeros(ndays)
sell = np.zeros(ndays)
for i in range (1, ndays):
    if RSIC[i-1]>=RSIBuyLevel and RSIC[i]<RSIBuyLevel:
        buy[i] = 1
    if RSIC[i-1]<RSISellLevel and RSIC[i]>=RSISellLevel:
        sell[i] = 1

# Convert to state signals

target = np.zeros(ndays)
if buy[0]:
```

```
            target[0] = 1
    else:
            target[0] = -1
    for i in range(1,ndays):
        if buy[i]:
            target[i] = 1
        elif sell[i]:
            target[i] = -1
        else:
            target[i] = target[i-1]


    #   Evaluation of signals

    print "Starting single run"

    #   Status variables

    #   These are scalar and apply to the current conditions

    entryPrice = 0
    exitPrice = 0

    #   These have an element for each day loaded
    #   Some will be unnecessary

    accountBalance = np.zeros(ndays)
    cash = np.zeros(ndays)
    sharesHeld = np.zeros(ndays)
    tradeGain = np.zeros(ndays)
    openTradeEquity = np.zeros(ndays)

    iTradeDay = 0
    iTradeNumber = 0

    #   Day 0 contains the initial values
    accountBalance[0] = initialEquity
    cash[0] = accountBalance[0]
    sharesHeld[0] = 0

    #   Loop over all the days loaded
    for i in range (1,ndays):
        #   Extract the date
        dt = qtC.index[i]
        #   Check the date
        datesPass = dt>=startTradeDate and dt<=endTradeDate
        if datesPass:
            iTradeDay = iTradeDay + 1
            if sharesHeld[iTradeDay-1] > 0:
                #   In a long position
                if target[i]<0:
                    #   target is -1 -- beFlat
                    #   Exit -- close the trade
                    exitPrice = qtC[i]
                    grossProceeds = sharesHeld[iTradeDay-1] *
                            exitPrice
                    commissionAmount = sharesHeld[iTradeDay-1] *
                            commission
                    netProceeds = grossProceeds - commissionAmount
                    cash[iTradeDay] = cash[iTradeDay-1] +
                            netProceeds
                    accountBalance[iTradeDay] = cash[iTradeDay]
```

```python
                    sharesHeld[iTradeDay] = 0
                    iTradeNumber = iTradeNumber+1
                    tradeGain[iTradeNumber] = (exitPrice /
                            (1.0 * entryPrice))
                    pass
                else:
                    #   target is +1 -- beLong
                    #   Continue long
                    sharesHeld[iTradeDay] = sharesHeld[iTradeDay-1]
                    cash[iTradeDay] = cash[iTradeDay-1]
                    MTMPrice = qtC[i]
                    openTradeEquity = sharesHeld[iTradeDay] *
                            MTMPrice
                    accountBalance[iTradeDay] = cash[iTradeDay] +
                            openTradeEquity
                    pass
            else:
                #   Currently flat
                if target[i]>0:
                    #   target is +1 -- beLong
                    #   Enter a new position
                    entryPrice = qtC[i]
                    sharesHeld[iTradeDay] = int(fixedTradeDollars/
                            (entryPrice+commission))
                    shareCost = sharesHeld[iTradeDay]*
                            (entryPrice+commission)
                    cash[iTradeDay] = cash[iTradeDay-1] - shareCost
                    openTradeEquity = sharesHeld[iTradeDay]*
                            entryPrice
                    accountBalance[iTradeDay] = cash[iTradeDay] +
                            openTradeEquity
                    pass
                else:
                    #   target is -1 -- beFlat
                    #   Continue flat
                    cash[iTradeDay] = cash[iTradeDay-1]
                    accountBalance[iTradeDay] = cash[iTradeDay]
                    pass

    #   Format and print results


    finalAccountBalance = accountBalance[iTradeDay]
    print "Final account balance:", finalAccountBalance
    numberTradeDays = iTradeDay
    numberTrades = iTradeNumber
    print "Number of trades:", numberTrades

    #print "equity: ", equity

    Sequity = Series(accountBalance[0:numberTradeDays-1])

    Sequity.plot()

    ############   end   ################
```

Figure 8.12 RSI model using state signals (Python)

Results from the Python program using state signals are identical to those from the Python program using impulse signals, as the equity curve shown in Figure 8.13 demonstrates. Compare with Figures 8.7 and 8.11.

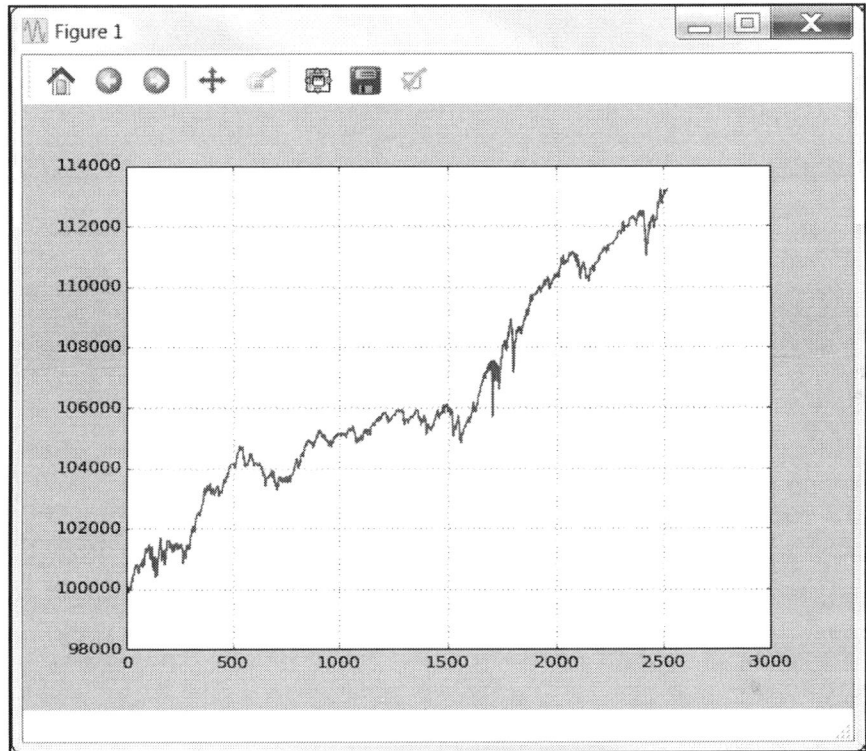

Figure 8.13 Equity curve from Python RSI model using state signals

The opening sections of this chapter have demonstrated that Python can be used as a trading system development platform. Also that state signals are equivalent to impulse signals.

For the remainder of this chapter, systems will use state signals and be marked to market daily at the close.

We will often be able to assign +1 or -1 to target directly during the data preparation phase for machine learning.

Machine Learning—Generalities

Machine learning is an excellent tool for quantitative technical analysis.

The goal of machine learning is to:
- find patterns in the data.
- develop mathematical models that describe the patterns.
- use those models to make predictions about yet-unseen data.

The goal of quantitative technical analysis is to:
- find patterns in historical price and volume trading data that precede profitable trading opportunities.
- develop mathematical models that describe the patterns.
- use those models to make predictions about yet-unseen price changes.

Supervised Learning

There are two general broad machine learning techniques—supervised and unsupervised.

Supervised learning provides a *target* with each data point. While the target can be either a number or a text string, it is essentially a label that identifies the category to which the data point belongs. The success of learning is related to the ability of the model to predict the correct value of the target for previously unseen data.

Unsupervised learning does not provide a target. Rather, its purpose is to identify to which of several groups of data a particular data point belongs.

We will focus exclusively on supervised learning.

The learning process is multiple iterations of:
- extensive data mining.
- model modification.
- model evaluation.

Machine learning relies on:
- a large number of independent data points.
- consistent relationships throughout the data—stationarity.

Each data point must be self-contained. The data points will be examined and evaluated individually. They may and will be randomized and reordered. If there is a relationship between successive data points as they occur in their native setting, that relationship must be included with each data point.

The patterns we are looking for in financial time series data definitely do require information about successive data points. For example, the signal to enter a long position in the RSI model depends on knowing both the current value of the RSI indicator and the previous value.

Model Development - Machine Learning

When working with trading system development platforms, previous values, known as lagged values, are readily available through functions that refer to earlier values. As shown in Figure 8.14, there is one value for the RSI indicator for every day. The rules defining the buy signal refer to the previous day's value. The system requires that the data remain in its original time sequence. The result of comparing RSI on 1/13 with Ref(RSI,-1)—the value on 1/12—results in a buy signal on 1/13.

Ticker	Date/Time	Close	RSI	Buy	Sell	GainAhead
XLV	1/4/2012	33.31	40.77	0	0	0.30
XLV	1/5/2012	33.41	75.11	0	0	0.15
XLV	1/6/2012	33.46	88.23	0	1	0.18
XLV	1/9/2012	33.52	96.57	0	0	0.75
XLV	1/10/2012	33.77	99.72	0	0	0.09
XLV	1/11/2012	33.80	99.81	0	0	0.30
XLV	1/12/2012	33.90	99.96	0	0	-0.44
XLV	1/13/2012	33.75	17.94	1	0	0.62

Figure 8.14 RSI data used by trading system development platform

When working with machine learning, previous values must be precomputed and explicitly stored as additional data fields. As shown in Figure 8.15, additional variables have been defined to store previous values of important data. The learning algorithm will use all of the data for 1/13, including GainAhead as the target value for that day, to learn that is a good day to buy.

Ticker	Date/Time	Ref(Close,-2)	Ref(Close,-1)	Close	Ref(RSI,-3)	Ref(RSI,-2)	Ref(RSI,-1)	RSI	GainAhead	Buy	Sell
XLV	1/4/2012	undef	undef	33.31	undef	undef	undef	40.77	0.30	0	0
XLV	1/5/2012	undef	33.31	33.41	undef	undef	40.77	75.11	0.15	0	0
XLV	1/6/2012	33.31	33.41	33.46	undef	40.77	75.11	88.23	0.18	0	1
XLV	1/9/2012	33.41	33.46	33.52	40.77	75.11	88.23	96.57	0.75	0	0
XLV	1/10/2012	33.46	33.52	33.77	75.11	88.23	96.57	99.72	0.09	0	0
XLV	1/11/2012	33.52	33.77	33.80	88.23	96.57	99.72	99.81	0.30	0	0
XLV	1/12/2012	33.77	33.80	33.90	96.57	99.72	99.81	99.96	-0.44	0	0
XLV	1/13/2012	33.80	33.90	33.75	99.72	99.81	99.96	17.94	0.62	1	0

Figure 8.15 RSI data used by machine learning

Imagine all of the data loaded into a single spreadsheet, each day in a row, sorted by date. Each column holds the data for a variable. There is one special variable, called the *target*, and all of the other variables are used to predict the target. In traditional statistics, particularly regression, those would be called the dependent variable and the set of independent variables, respectively. Many people working with machine learning in a time series context prefer the term *predictor variable* to the term independent variable because there is very often dependence among the predictor variables.

If it is important to know the value of a predictor variable at an earlier time, say yesterday, then yesterday's value must be explicitly computed and included as a separate predictor variable.

Trading system development platforms use a relatively small number of columns, require that the time sequence be maintained, and refer to previous values using on-the-fly formulas.

Machine learning requires that previous values be computed and provides a column for each, resulting in many columns, and removing the restriction on time sequence.

Classification

Supervised learning is further divided into classification and regression.

When the target is a category, such as which species of plant a flower comes from, the model is classification. When the target is a numeric value, such as the number of bushels of corn per acre, the model is regression.

Our model could be either classification or regression.

Classification if the target corresponds to brokerage orders to buy and sell. When modeling one-day close to close holding, we define the two categories as beLong and beFlat, respectively.

Regression if the target is the one-day-ahead price change. An additional step of comparing the predicted change to a threshold is required to determine the proper order.

In both these options, the position size is left to be handled by a second model, the dynamic position sizing model, in the trading management phase. Because many traders will be using trading system development platforms to generate buy and sell signals, and position size cannot be properly performed within the TSDP system, the remainder of this discussion treats the machine learning as a classification. Consequently, whether the trades come from a TSDP system or a machine learning system, they are compatible with dynamic position sizing.

> Position sizing can be properly addressed within a Python-based trading system. It is possible to develop a single model where the target is safe-f—the position size for the next trade. The program has two sections. The first develops the trading system, passing intermediate results to the second which develops the trading management system. That is left as an exercise.

To be clear. Machine learning has many more options than are being discussed here, but we will focus on those that are best suited to trading system development. For the remainder of this chapter, the discussion is of supervised learning applied to classification problems.

Machine Learning—Examples using Iris

Before beginning work on a trading model, we will review a famous, and easily replicated, classification problem—Iris.

Sir Ronald Fisher dominated statistics in the early to mid twentieth century. In 1935, Edgar Anderson compiled the iris data set. The dataset consists of 150 data points, 50 each from three species of flowers—Iris setosa, Iris virginica, and Iris versicolor. Each data point includes four measurements from the sample flower—length and width of the sepal, and length and width of the petal. In 1936, Fisher published an analysis of the dataset using discriminant analysis, and it has been known as Fisher's Iris Data since. The data can be downloaded from the University of California Irvine Machine Learning Repository.[2] The data is in csv format in a file named iris.data. Figure 8.16 shows a portion of the data. Save the data file as iris.data on your hard drive.

```
5.1,3.5,1.4,0.2,Iris-setosa
4.9,3.0,1.4,0.2,Iris-setosa
4.7,3.2,1.3,0.2,Iris-setosa
4.6,3.1,1.5,0.2,Iris-setosa
5.0,3.6,1.4,0.2,Iris-setosa
7.0,3.2,4.7,1.4,Iris-versicolor
6.4,3.2,4.5,1.5,Iris-versicolor
6.9,3.1,4.9,1.5,Iris-versicolor
5.5,2.3,4.0,1.3,Iris-versicolor
6.5,2.8,4.6,1.5,Iris-versicolor
6.3,3.3,6.0,2.5,Iris-virginica
5.8,2.7,5.1,1.9,Iris-virginica
7.1,3.0,5.9,2.1,Iris-virginica
6.3,2.9,5.6,1.8,Iris-virginica
6.5,3.0,5.8,2.2,Iris-virginica
```

Figure 8.16 A portion of the Iris dataset

---

[2] http://archive.ics.uci.edu/ml/

Sidebar—Python file directories

We will be programming Python to read and write disk files. Knowing which path and directory Python is using is sometimes confusing.

For Anaconda Spyder, select the Tools menu, then Preferences.

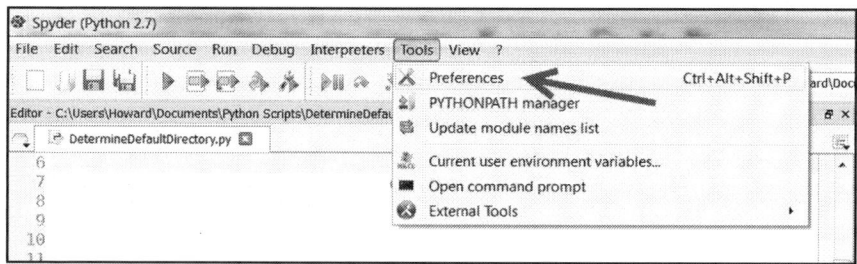

Select Global Working Directory. The directories currently defined are listed. If desired, they can be changed from this menu.

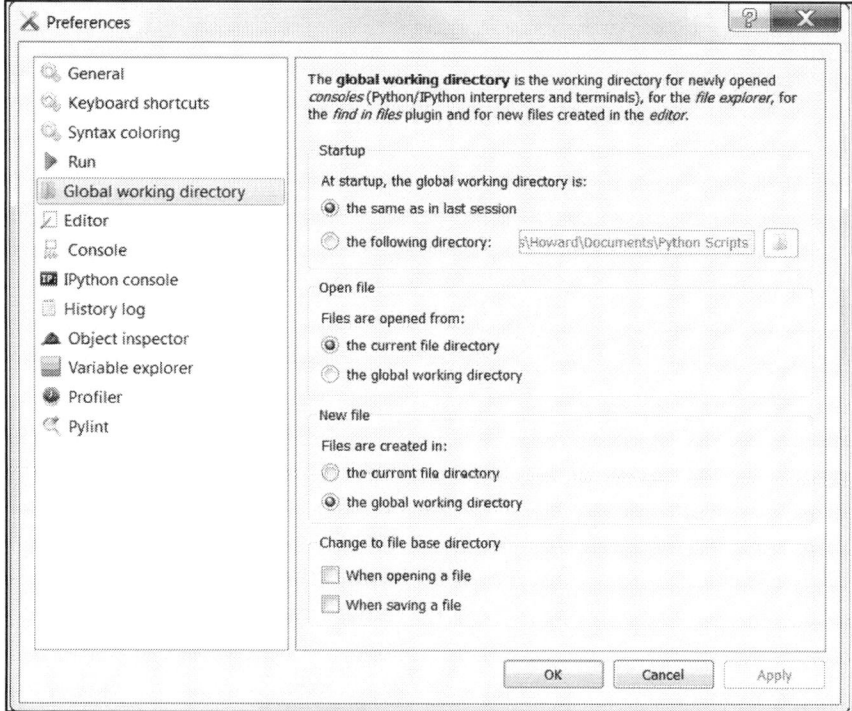

My working directory is \Document\Python Scripts. By default, when I request that Python open a program file, it will look in this directory. When a file is written to disk with only a file name, the disk file will be created in this directory. When a Python program opens a file specified only by its file name, it is expected to be in this directory. Specifying a full path overrides the defaults. Figure 8.17 shows a Python program that writes a disk file using only a file name. The purpose of the program is to provide a file with a known name for use when using Windows Explorer to search.

```
"""
DetermineDefaultDirectory.py

The purpose of this program is to
determine the default directory used by Python.

After running the program, use Windows Explorer
to locate the file named dump.csv.

Disclaimer continues to apply

Copyright  2014 Blue Owl Press, Inc
Dr. Howard Bandy
October 2014

"""

import pandas.io.data as web
from datetime import datetime

ticker = "spy"
source = "google"
start_date = datetime(2014,1,1)
end_date = datetime(2014,5,15)

qt = web.DataReader(ticker, source, start_date, end_date)

print "\nReading data for " + ticker + " from " + source
print "shape of the data array:     ",  qt.shape

#   Remember the number of rows
nrows = qt.shape[0]
print "number of rows:               ", nrows

#   Remember the number of columns
ncols = qt.shape[1]
print "number of columns:            ", ncols

print "Writing to disk in csv format"
qt.to_csv("dump.csv")

print "\nThe purpose of this program is to"
print "determine the default directory used by Python."
print "After running the program, use Windows Explorer"
print "to locate the file named dump.csv."

#  /////  end  /////
```

Figure 8.17 Determine default directory

end of sidebar

Figure 8.18 shows the petals and sepals of the iris flower.

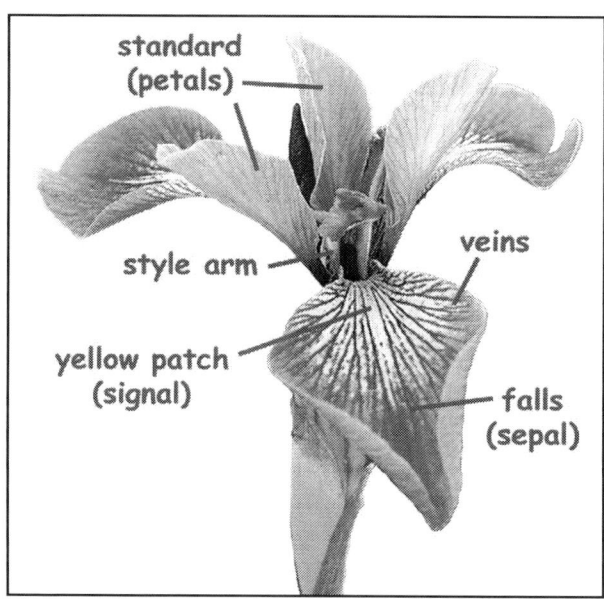

Figure 8.18 Iris flower

Figure 8.19 shows the Python program that reads the iris data from the disk, defines names for the variables, and prints the first and last 5 lines of the file. Figure 8.20 shows the output. Note that the data structure, irisdata, into which the pd.read_csv function stores the data, is a Pandas DataFrame, created automatically by the function.

```
"""
ReadIrisData.py

This program:
  Reads the iris data file from the hard drive.
  Assigns names to the variables.
  Prints the first and last lines of data.

Disclaimer continues to apply

Copyright  2014 Blue Owl Press, Inc
Dr. Howard Bandy
"""
import pandas as pd

print "\nReading iris data from hard drive"

irisdata = pd.read_csv('iris.data',index_col=False,
                  names=['Sepal Length','Sepal Width',\
                      'Petal Length','Petal Width',\
                      'Species'])
print type(irisdata)
```

```
    print "First rows\n", irisdata[:5]
    print "Last rows\n", irisdata[-5:]

    print "end of run"

    ###########   end   ############
```

Figure 8.19 Read iris data

```
Reading iris data from hard drive
<class 'pandas.core.frame.DataFrame'>
First rows
    SepalLength  SepalWidth  PetalLength  PetalWidth      Species
0           5.1         3.5          1.4         0.2  Iris-setosa
1           4.9         3.0          1.4         0.2  Iris-setosa
2           4.7         3.2          1.3         0.2  Iris-setosa
3           4.6         3.1          1.5         0.2  Iris-setosa
4           5.0         3.6          1.4         0.2  Iris-setosa

[5 rows x 5 columns]
Last rows
     SepalLength  SepalWidth  PetalLength  PetalWidth         Species
145          6.7         3.0          5.2         2.3  Iris-virginica
146          6.3         2.5          5.0         1.9  Iris-virginica
147          6.5         3.0          5.2         2.0  Iris-virginica
148          6.2         3.4          5.4         2.3  Iris-virginica
149          5.9         3.0          5.1         1.8  Iris-virginica

[5 rows x 5 columns]
end of run
```

Figure 8.20 Output from program 8.19

The first step in any data analysis is always visual inspection. Plot each column. Figure 8.21 shows the Python program to plot one column, and Figure 8.22 the output. Modify it as required to plot all four of them.

```
"""
PlotIrisData.py

This program:
  Reads the iris data file from the hard drive.
  Assigns names to the variables.
  Plots one of the columns.

Disclaimer continues to apply

Copyright  2014 Blue Owl Press, Inc
Dr. Howard Bandy
"""
import pandas as pd

print "\nReading iris data from hard drive"

irisdata = pd.read_csv('iris.data',index_col=False,
                names=['Sepal Length','Sepal Width',\
```

```
                            'Petal Length','Petal Width',\
                            'Species'])

    columnToPlot = irisdata['Sepal Length'].plot(title='Sepal
            Length')

    print "end of run"
    ###########   end   ###########
```

Figure 8.21 Plot iris data

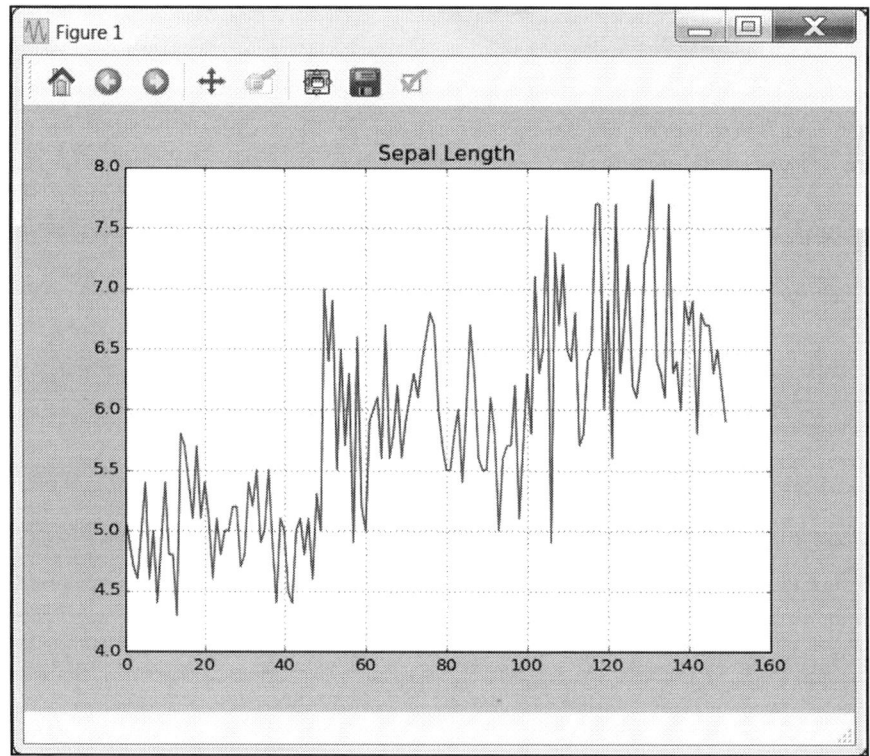

Figure 8.22 Output from PlotData.py

The purpose of the classification is to identify some characteristics that uniquely identify each category. Plotting each of the pairs of predictor variables might reveal information. Figure 8.23 shows the Python program that creates such a plot. Figure 8.24 shows the output.

```
"""
IrisPlotPairsData.py

The purpose of this program is to
plot the pairwise relationships between
predictor variables for the Iris data.

Disclaimer continues to apply

Copyright   2014 Blue Owl Press, Inc
Dr. Howard Bandy

"""

import numpy as np
from pandas import Series, DataFrame
import pandas as pd
import matplotlib.pyplot as plt

iris_df = DataFrame()

iris_data_path = 'C:\Users\Howard\Documents\Python Scripts\
        IrisData.csv'

iris_df = pd.read_csv(iris_data_path,
            index_col=False,header=None,encoding='utf-8')

iris_df.columns=['sepal length','sepal width','petal length',
            'petal width','class']

print iris_df.columns.values
print iris_df.head()
print iris_df.tail()
irisX = irisdata[['sepal length','sepal width','petal length',
            'petal width']]
print irisX.tail()
irisy = irisdata['class']
print irisy.head()
print irisy.tail()

colors = ['red','green','blue']
markers = ['o','>','x']

irisyn = np.where(irisy=='Iris-setosa',0,\
        np.where(irisy=='Iris-virginica',2,1))

Col0 = irisdata['sepal length']
Col1 = irisdata['sepal width']
Col2 = irisdata['petal length']
Col3 = irisdata['petal width']

plt.figure(num=1,figsize=(16,10))
plt.subplot(2,3,1)
for i in range(len(colors)):
    xs = Col0[irisyn==i]
    xy = Col1[irisyn==i]
    plt.scatter(xs,xy,color=colors[i],marker=markers[i])
plt.legend( ('Iris-setosa', 'Iris-versicolor',
            'Iris-virginica') )
plt.xlabel(irisdata.columns[0])
plt.ylabel(irisdata.columns[1])
```

```
plt.subplot(2,3,2)
for i in range(len(colors)):
    xs = Col0[irisyn==i]
    xy = Col2[irisyn==i]
    plt.scatter(xs,xy,color=colors[i],marker=markers[i])
plt.xlabel(irisdata.columns[0])
plt.ylabel(irisdata.columns[2])

plt.subplot(2,3,3)
for i in range(len(colors)):
    xs = Col0[irisyn==i]
    xy = Col3[irisyn==i]
    plt.scatter(xs,xy,color=colors[i],marker=markers[i])
plt.xlabel(irisdata.columns[0])
plt.ylabel(irisdata.columns[3])

plt.subplot(2,3,4)
for i in range(len(colors)):
    xs = Col1[irisyn==i]
    xy = Col2[irisyn==i]
    plt.scatter(xs,xy,color=colors[i],marker=markers[i])
plt.xlabel(irisdata.columns[1])
plt.ylabel(irisdata.columns[2])

plt.subplot(2,3,5)
for i in range(len(colors)):
    xs = Col1[irisyn==i]
    xy = Col3[irisyn==i]
    plt.scatter(xs,xy,color=colors[i],marker=markers[i])
plt.xlabel(irisdata.columns[1])
plt.ylabel(irisdata.columns[3])

plt.subplot(2,3,6)
for i in range(len(colors)):
    xs = Col2[irisyn==i]
    xy = Col3[irisyn==i]
    plt.scatter(xs,xy,color=colors[i],marker=markers[i])
plt.xlabel(irisdata.columns[2])
plt.ylabel(irisdata.columns[3])
plt.show()

###########   end   ############
```

Figure 8.23 Plot iris pairs data

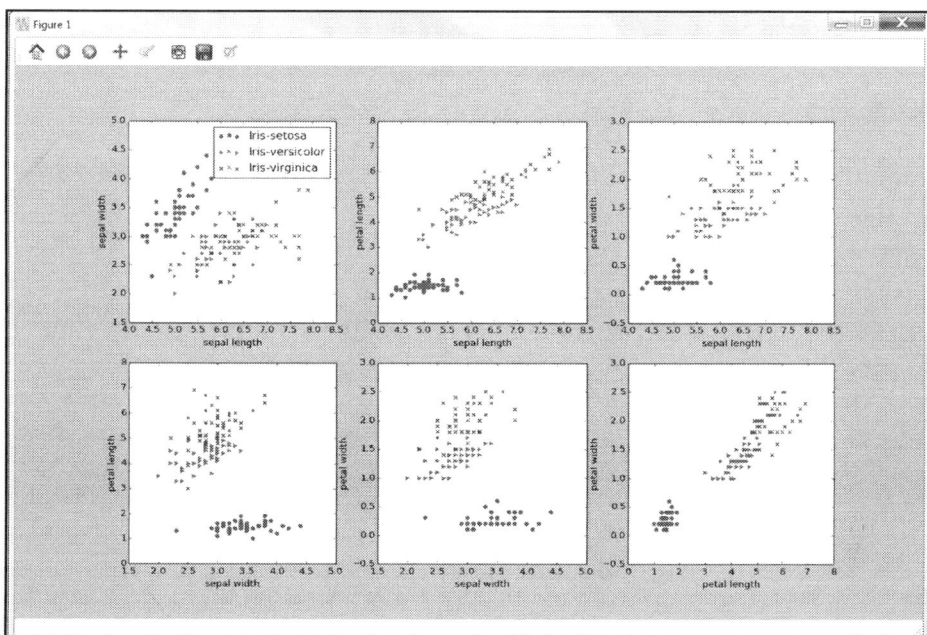

Figure 8.24 The six pairwise scatter plots

As can be seen in the three plots that show petal length, petal length separates Iris-setosa from the other two species. The maximum petal length of any Iris-setosa example is 1.9 cm; the minimum petal length of any other example is 3.0 cm. Drawing a horizontal line across the upper-middle or lower-left plot, or a vertical line in the lower-right plot, anywhere between 1.9 and 3.0 cm perfectly separates the round symbols from the others. Removing Iris-setosa converts a three-category classification to a two-category classification. This demonstrates one important and powerful technique used in rule-based learning. It is known as the *sequential covering algorithm.*

The sequential covering algorithm is repeated application of:
1. Learn one rule with high accuracy.
2. Remove positive examples covered by this rule.

There are several methods and metrics for deciding which rule is best, including accuracy and entropy. The machine learning library gives options for specifying which to use. We will return to this later.

Having removed Iris-setosa, the remaining two species cannot be separated by a horizontal or vertical line. No matter which of the six subplots is examined, no matter where a horizontal or vertical line is drawn, no single straight line separates the 'x' characters from the triangles. The best is a line at petal width of 1.6. If petal width is greater than 1.6, classify the example as Iris-virginica; if less, classify it as

Iris-versicolor. Classification is about 94 percent correct. Accuracy is defined to be the result of dividing the number of elements correctly identified, 94, by the total number evaluated, 100.

In this case 94% accuracy is respectable. There are two cautions:
1. The 100 elements being tested were equally balanced by species / class—50 of each. Random assignment would result in about 50% accuracy, so 94% is a big improvement. If the split had been 95 of one class and 5 of the other, simply always predicting the majority class would have resulted in 95% accuracy, so 94% would not be seen as a success.
2. The result is entirely in-sample. Iris data is stationary, the data points are independent, and there is no time sequence. Even so, if the model's intended use is prediction, we need evidence of its ability to accurately classify specimens not used to develop the model.

We need to be particularly aware of both points as we develop trading models because:
- We often have unbalanced classes.
- We know that an unbiased estimate of future trading performance requires out-of-sample testing.

If two categories can be separated by a straight line—a straight line drawn at any angle—those categories are said to be linearly separable. Iris-setosa is linearly separable from the two other species. However, no straight line, even one drawn at an angle, perfectly separates Iris-virginica and Iris-versicolor. They are not linearly separable.

Note that when we use a trading system development platform to code rules for a trading system, much of what we are doing is drawing straight lines that are horizontal or vertical. A rule such as RSI(2) < 20 is a straight line separating those data points where the RSI value is less than 20 from those where it is more.

Cross Validation

Cross validation is a technique used to estimate out-of-sample performance. The method described here is "K-fold cross validation", where there are K partitions.

The data is divided into several groups, known as folds or partitions. Say five for this example. Five model-fitting runs are made. For each run, one of the folds is designated to be the out-of-sample data and is held out. The other four are used as in-sample data to develop a model, which is tested on the one group that was held out.

After all five runs, the five out-of-sample results are summarized to estimate performance on previously unseen data.

Figure 8.25 illustrates division of the data into five partitions, and the five model-fitting runs.

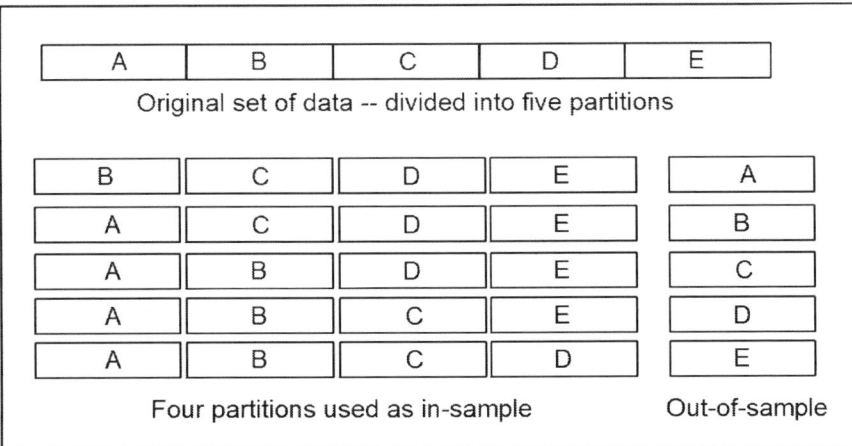

Figure 8.25 Creating five cross validation partitions

Figure 8.26 lists a Python program that performs a five partition cross validation of the iris data.

```
"""
IrisCrossValidation.py

This program:
  Reads the iris data file from the UCI repository.
  Divides it into five cross validation partitions.
  Runs a support vector model five times --
    each of the five partitions is out-of-sample
    for one of the runs.
  Prints the five accuracy scores.

Disclaimer continues to apply

Copyright  2014 Blue Owl Press, Inc
Dr. Howard Bandy

"""
from sklearn import cross_validation
from sklearn import datasets
from sklearn import svm

#  Load iris data from the UCI repository.
#  Split the columns into predictor variables
#  and target variable using the definitions
#  contained in the dataset file
iris = datasets.load_iris()

#  Use a support vector model with a linear kernel
clf = svm.SVC(kernel='linear',C=1)

#  Divide the rows into five partitions.
#  Make five model fitting runs.
```

```
#  For each run, set aside one partition
#  as out-of-sample test data.
#  Use the other four as in-sample train data.
#  Compute the accuracy score for each run.
scores = cross_validation.cross_val_score(
    clf, iris.data, iris.target, cv=5)

print "Accuracy scores for the five partitions: ", scores

#############   end   ###################
```

Figure 8.26 Creating five cross validation partitions

Figure 8.27 shows the output from the program. Each of the five values is the accuracy score for a test of 30 examples that were not used to fit the model.

```
Accuracy scores for the five partitions:
        [ 1.000  0.967  0.900  0.967  1.000 ]
```

Figure 8.27 Output from the five cross validation partitions

Cross Validation Recommendations

Studies of the bias associated with validation[3] suggest *stratified* cross validation is preferable to any of unstratified K-fold, leave-one-out (jackknife), or bootstrap cross validation. The minimum number of folds suggested is ten. For cross validation to provide an accurate estimate, the data must be stationary across all partitions.

Using stratified sampling is particularly important when classes are unbalanced to ensure that each class is proportionally represented in each fold.

As we will see in an example to follow, our target will often be unbalanced. Assume 10% of the data is positive class and we are using daily data. Using ten folds, the average number of examples of the class of interest per fold will be two to three per year. Without stratified sampling, some folds would have no instances of the smaller class.

When the scikit-learn function
    cross_validation.cross_val_score()
is called, and a target is supplied, the default fold construction method is StratifiedKFold.[4] We do not need to do anything other than use the default in order to be using the preferred method.

---

[3] Kohavi, Ron, *A Study of Cross-Validation and Bootstrap Accuracy Estimation and Model Selection*, Stanford University, 1995. http://ai.stanford.edu/~ronnyk/accEst.pdf

[4] http://scikit-learn.org/stable/modules/cross_validation.html

That said, there will probably be circumstances where you want to change the order of the data, say randomize, prior to fitting the model. Figure 8.28 lists a program that shuffles the 150 elements into random order before creating the cross validation partitions.

```
"""
IrisShuffleBeforePartitioning.py

This program:
  Reads the iris data file from the UCI repository.
  Creates an array of integers with as many rows
    as the data, and shuffles them into random order.
  Creates copies of the data and target arrays
    reordered by the shuffled array.
  Divides it into five cross validation partitions.
  Runs a support vector model five times --
    each of the five partitions is out-of-sample
    for one of the runs.
  Prints the five accuracy scores.

Disclaimer continues to apply

Copyright  2014 Blue Owl Press, Inc
Dr. Howard Bandy

"""

import numpy as np
from sklearn import cross_validation
from sklearn import datasets
from sklearn import svm

irisdata = datasets.load_iris()

#  Learn the number of rows
nrows = irisdata.data.shape[0]

#  Create an array in shuffled order
randomIndex = np.random.permutation(nrows)

#  Copy the original data into shuffled order
newIrisX = irisdata.data[randomIndex]
newIrisY = irisdata.target[randomIndex]

#  Use a support vector model with a linear kernel
clf = svm.SVC(kernel='linear')

#  Divide the rows into five partitions.
#  Make five model fitting runs.
#  For each run, set aside one partition
#  as out-of-sample test data.
#  Use the other four as in-sample train data.
#  Compute the accuracy score for each run.
scores = cross_validation.cross_val_score(
    clf, newIrisX, newIrisY, cv=5)

print "Accuracy scores for the five partitions: ", scores

print "end of run"

###########   end   ############
```

Figure 8.28 Shuffle before partitioning

Figure 8.29 shows the output from five successive runs of the program. As before, each of the values is the accuracy score for a test of 30 examples that were not used to fit the model.

```
Accuracy scores for the five partitions:
            [ 0.967  1.000  0.967  1.000  0.967 ]
            [ 0.967  1.000  1.000  0.967  1.000 ]
            [ 0.967  0.967  1.000  0.967  1.000 ]
            [ 0.967  1.000  0.967  1.000  0.967 ]
            [ 0.967  1.000  0.933  1.000  0.933 ]
```

Figure 8.29 Output from the shuffled five cross validation partitions

Confusion Matrix

Earlier chapters have discussed the attractiveness of using CAR25 as an objective function. At some points in the trading system development process, we will be able to do that. However, sometimes it will be more convenient, or necessary, to use the metrics provided by the machine learning tools.

One of those metrics is the confusion matrix. Figure 8.30 shows a confusion matrix for a binary classification—typical of our application.

A binary classification divides data elements according to the two values of the target variable. One of the target values will be coded +1, the other -1. Although these are numbers, they are treated more as labels. The variable coded +1 is the positive variable, and data elements with the +1 label are the positive class, category, condition, or set.

Whether balanced or unbalanced, the positive class is usually the class of primary interest. This is true even when being positive is undesirable—as in testing positive for a serious disease.

The model, and the metrics of the model, are from the perspective of the positive class.

A confusion matrix can be computed using the results of the model's evaluation of any set of data—training (in-sample) or testing (out-of-sample). We are most interested in the results of applying the model to the test data.

The two axes of the matrix represent:
- The prediction of the model (the columns), and
- The set the element actually belongs in (the rows).

The two columns are labeled "predicted positive" and "predicted negative." The two rows are labeled "actual positive" and "actual negative."

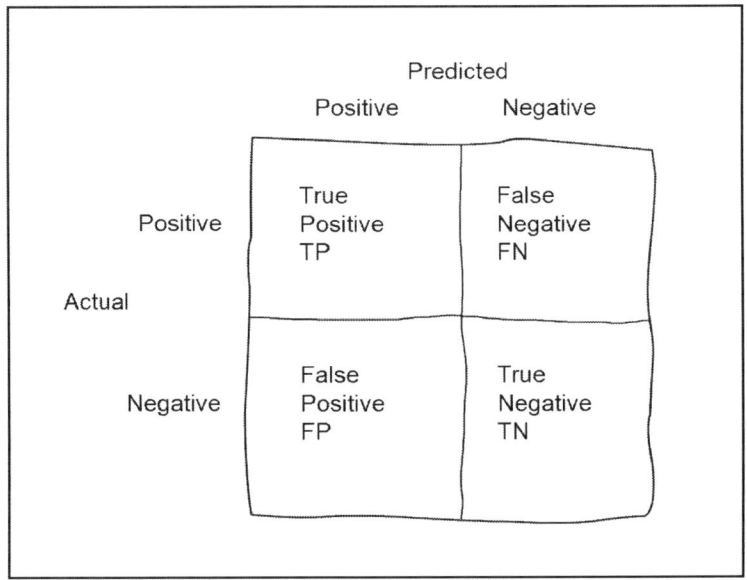

Figure 8.30 Confusion matrix for binary classification

Each data element tested is actually a member of one class and is predicted to be a member of one class. It belongs in one of the four cells. Which one depends on the element's actual membership and its predicted membership.

The matrix is best seen as a metric of prediction of the positive class. An element that is actually positive, but predicted to be negative, is described as a false negative. It is falsely predicted to be negative. The four combinations are:
- True positive. Abbreviated as TP. Actually positive, correctly predicted to be positive.
- False negative. FN. Actually positive, incorrectly predicted to be negative. Also known as a Type II error.[5]

---

5 Some suggest, tongue-in-cheek, additional error types:

Type III error is:
* Giving the right answer to the wrong question.
* Using the wrong null hypothesis.
* Correctly rejecting the null hypothesis for the wrong reason.

Type IV error is:
* Choosing the test to suit the data.
* Solving the right problem, too late.

- False positive. FP. Actually negative, incorrectly predicted to be positive. Also known as a Type I error.
- True negative. TN. Actually negative, correctly predicted to be negative.

Several metrics are computed from the counts in the four cells.

Accuracy = (TP + TN) / (TP + FN + TP + TN)
: The proportion of data points that are correctly predicted—the ratio of the sum of the diagonal to the total number of data points.
We want accuracy to be high.

True Positive Rate = TP / (TP + FN)
: Also called Sensitivity or Recall.
The proportion of positive data points that are predicted to be positive—the ratio of the top row.
Used as the vertical axis of the Receiver Operating Characteristic (ROC) plot.
We want this to be high.

True Negative Rate = TN / (TN + FP)
: We want this to be high.

False Positive Rate = FP / (FP + TN)
: The proportion of positive data points that are predicted to be negative—the ratio of the bottom row.
Used as the horizontal axis of the ROC plot.
We want this to be low.

False Negative Rate = FN / (FN + TP)
: We want this to be low.

Precision = TP / (TP + FP)
: The proportion of data points that are predicted to be positive that actually are positive—the ratio of the left column.

Perfect prediction would result in all entries being on the diagonal—positive elements all predicted to be positive and negative elements all predicted to be negative. Accuracy would be perfect. Errors in prediction result in off-diagonal entries.

Predictions that fall into TP and TN are always desirable. Think of them as contributing a profit or gain. The off-diagonal cells have costs. Margineantu shows that any confusion / cost matrix that has non-zero values in any of the diagonal cells can be converted to one that has all zeros on the diagonal. So we will proceed as is standard, assume or specify zero cost for each diagonal element, and specify a positive cost for each misclassified off-diagonal element.

The cost of a model is the sum of the cost associated with each of the four cells times the number of occurrences of each. It is the objective function by which machine learning algorithms measure the fit of the model to the data. The model resulting in the minimum cost is the best model.

If the algorithm does not accept or explicitly use a cost matrix, all diagonal costs have a value of 0, and all off-diagonal costs are assumed to have a value of 1. The sum of all costs—which equals the sum of all off-diagonal results—is the misclassification cost of the model.

False negative and false positive are both undesirable. But which is worse depends on the situation.
- **False negative is expensive.** Assume positive is having a life threatening, but treatable, disease. Missing the diagnosis, a false negative, results in death, while treating an individual who is not afflicted, a false positive, is inconvenient. The "cost" associated with the false negative cell is high, and the cost associated with the false positive cell is low.
- **False positive is expensive.** Assume the positive category is being guilty of a crime. Wrongly convicting an innocent person, a false positive, has very serious consequences for that person, while allowing a guilty person to remain unpunished, a false negative, may be less serious. The cost associated with a false positive is high, and the cost associated with a false negative is low.

Improving one of the off-diagonal entries usually comes at the expense of the worsening the other off-diagonal entry.

When classes are unbalanced, or when the costs of Type I and Type II errors are very different, and when the function is able to use it, a cost matrix can be used to guide the model toward solutions that balance not just the numbers of errors, but their costs. Since the algorithm has no understanding of the problem being modeled, setting the costs requires judgement, based on domain knowledge, from the model developer.

Overview with Diagrams

Using the notation of matrix algebra, supervised machine learning algorithms are solving the equation:

$AX = y$

where:

A is the array of coefficients that represent the fitted model.

X is the array of predictor variables.

y is the vector of target variables.

Train / Test Split

Prior to calling the fitting function, the data, such as irisData, is split into four sets by a function whose job it is to split the original data into a set that will be used to train the model and a set that will be used to test the fitted model. See Figure 8.31.

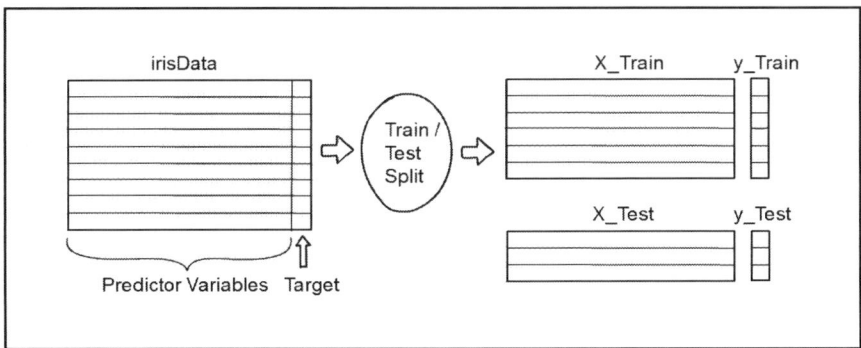

Figure 8.31 The train / test split procedure

IrisData is a 150 row by 5 column array. The "train / test split" function, which in the case of the program that is illustrated in the next section is *StratifiedShuffleSplit*, produces four new data arrays. Assume that two-thirds of the data will be used for training, one-third reserved for testing (as is standard procedure). The four arrays are:

X_Train. A 100 row by 4 column array that has only values for the predictor variables.

y_Train. A 100 row by 1 column array that has values for the target variable.

X_Test. A 50 row by 4 column array that has only values for predictor variables.

y_Test. A 50 row by 1 column array that has values for the target variable.

X_Train and X_Test are similar in that they have columns for the same predictor variables in the same sequence. The data in X_Train is in-sample data. It is used to compute the solution to the matrix equation.

Model Fitting

Whenever the machine learning fitting procedure makes reference to a particular row of the X_Train array, the corresponding row of y_Train is the target value used to guide the fitting. Figure 8.32 shows a diagram of the model fitting process.

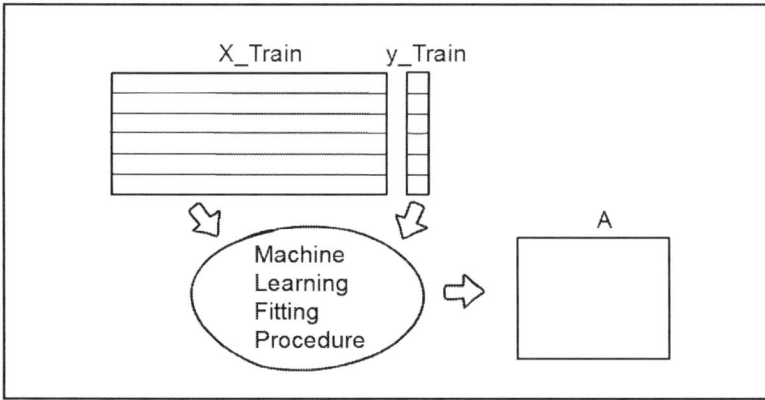

Figure 8.32 The model fitting process

The fitted model consists of two components:
- The rules, functions, and equations that define the specific model, such as linear regression or support vector.
- The array A that contains the coefficients of the equations, chosen as best for this specific X_Train.

Model Prediction

In order to assess whether the fitted model has identified general patterns in the data, the array A is used together with the predictor variables in the X_Test array to predict the 50 values of the target. X_Test is out-of-sample data. The result will be a 50 row by 1 column array; call it y_Predict. Figure 8.33 shows a diagram of the prediction procedure.

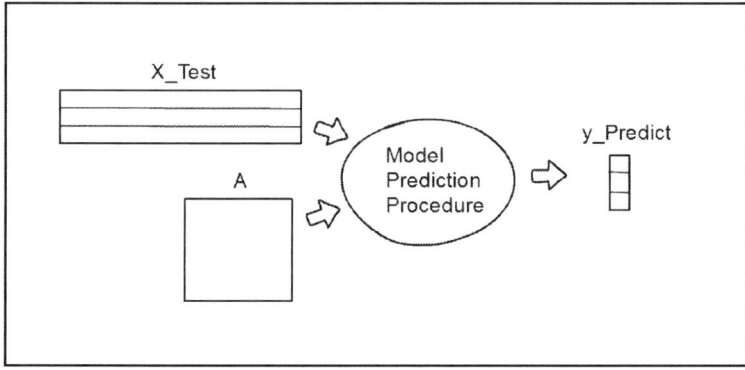

Figure 8.33 The model prediction procedure

Model Evaluation

Comparing the known targets, y_Test, with the predicted targets, y_Predict, produces the goodness of fit metrics, including the confusion matrix. Figure 8.34 shows a diagram of the procedure.

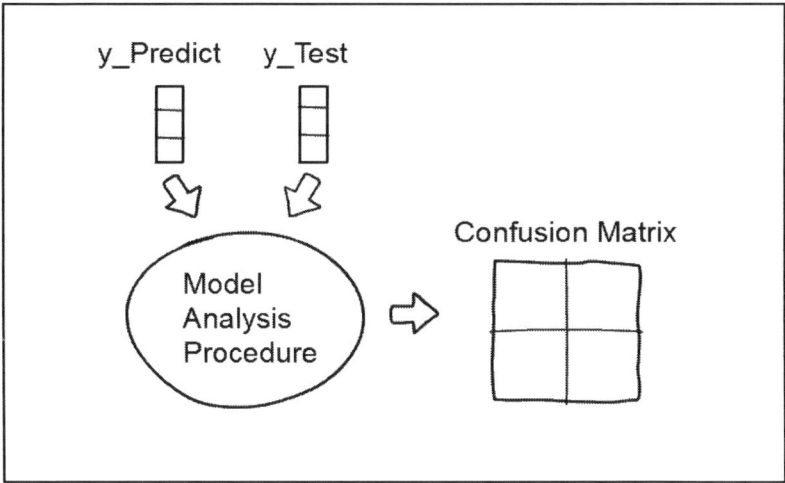

Figure 8.34 The model evaluation procedure

The confusion matrix gets the predicted values from y_Predict and the actual values from y_Test.

Stratified Shuffle Split

To work with trading data and trading models, we will use the method of splitting the data between training and testing just described.

The *StratifiedShuffleSplit* function from scikit-learn[6] splits a set of data into two subsets, keeping the two sets balanced in proportion to the percentage of each target class in the data. The split is two sets of integers, each integer representing an index value, each set a subset of the original data. One set, *train*, identifies those elements that will be used as the training data. The other set, *test*, identifies those elements that will be used as test data. No individual element is in both sets. Stratified sampling ensures that the proportion of target classes in both the train set and the test set are the same as in the original data. Sampling is done with replacement, resulting in some elements occurring more than once and some not being used at all for any specific split. Following the random subsampling procedure recommended by Japkowicz

---

6 http://scikit-learn.org/stable/modules/generated/sklearn.cross_validation.StratifiedShuffleSplit.html

and Shah,[7] about two-thirds of the data set is used to train the model, one-third to test. The process is repeated many times, say 50 or 100. Each split is unique. Each time a split is made, a model is fit to the training set, then evaluated using the test set. The confusion matrix entries from each of the 50 or 100 runs are accumulated and an average reported. Figure 8.35 lists a program that illustrates the procedure.

```
"""
IrisStratifiedShuffleSplit.py

This program:
  Reads the iris data file from the UCI repository.
  Sets the target to +1 for Iris-virginica, -1 for all other
  Repeatedly:
    Divides the data using StratifiedShuffleSplit.
    Runs a learning algorithm.
    Evaluates the test data.
  Prints the combined confusion matrix.

Disclaimer continues to apply

Copyright  2014 Blue Owl Press, Inc
Dr. Howard Bandy

"""

import numpy as np
from sklearn.cross_validation import StratifiedShuffleSplit
from sklearn import datasets
from sklearn import svm
from sklearn.metrics import confusion_matrix

irisdata = datasets.load_iris()

#   Assign target values
#   In the iris dataset, Iris-Virginica has value 2
irisy = np.where(irisdata.target==2,1,-1)

#   Predictor variables are raw data -- no scaling
irisX = irisdata.data

iterations = 100

#   Algorithm is support vector machine with linear kernel
learner = svm.SVC(kernel='linear',class_weight='auto')

#   Make 'iterations' index vectors for the train-test split
sss = StratifiedShuffleSplit(irisy,iterations,test_size=0.33,
                    random_state=None)

#   Initialize the confusion matrix
cm_sum = np.zeros((2,2))

#   For each entry in the set of splits, fit and predict
for train_index,test_index in sss:
    X_train, X_test = irisX[train_index], irisX[test_index]
```

---

7 Japkowicz, Nathalie and Mohak Shah, *Evaluating Learning Algorithms*, Cambridge, 2011.

```
            y_train, y_test = irisy[train_index], irisy[test_index]
            y_pred = learner.fit(X_train, y_train).predict(X_test)
            # Compute confusion matrix
            cm = confusion_matrix(y_test, y_pred)
            cm_sum = cm_sum + cm

        print "\n\nConfusion matrix for %i randomized tests" %
                iterations
        print '     predicted'
        print '      pos neg'

        print 'pos:  %i   %i' % (cm_sum[1,1], cm_sum[1,0])
        print 'neg:  %i   %i' % (cm_sum[0,1], cm_sum[0,0])

        print "\nend of run"

    ###########   end   ############
```

Figure 8.35 Using StratifiedShuffleSplit to create train and test sets

Figure 8.36 Shows the result.

```
Confusion matrix for 100 randomized tests
     predicted
      pos neg
pos:  1695   5
neg:  113   3187

end of run
```

Figure 8.36 Output from previous program

Data Preparation

Refer to Dorian Pyle[8] for an excellent book-length discussion of data preparation.

We have been working with the iris data in the form as it comes from the UCI repository. The data is so well behaved, as you have seen in the plots, that very little data preparation is needed. Typically, and certainly when working with financial data, some data preparation is helpful, and perhaps necessary. The primary data series used as input to our technical systems are typically price and volume. Additionally, auxiliary data may include price and volume of other tradable issues or indexes, or counts such as the number of advancing issues, or ratios such as the percentage of issues traded that made new highs.

Element Independence

There is a data element, a row in the dataset, for every day. Each and every data element must be self contained. If lagged values, such as

---

8 Pyle, Dorian, *Data Preparation for Data Mining*, Morgan Kaufmann, 1999.

yesterday's value, are required, there must be a separate field for each lag. For example, if the model will be using current RSI and the RSI value from each of the previous two days, there must be three RSI variables—perhaps named RSI, RSIY1, and RSIY2—representing the current value, yesterday's value, and the value previous to yesterday. The data elements will be randomized during learning. There are no links from any individual data element to any of its predecessors.

Time and date alignment

Whenever more than one data series is used, the times and dates of all the data series must be synchronized. Pick a time zone that will be convenient during signal generation and trade execution, and adjust all dates and times to that. Either the time zone of the exchange or the time zone of the trader are good choices.

Missing data

The preferred option for missing data is to copy the last known data value forward. If the data value is allowed to remain "missing," the program must have some way to first recognize that it is missing, then some reasonable way to handle missing data.

An alternative is to delete that entire data entry. Which means there is no prediction for that day.

Interpolation is not an option. That introduces a future leak.

Outliers

Outliers are data points well beyond the expected high or low. Begin with a visual inspection. If a data point is an outlier, it could be either legitimately an extreme value, such as the "flash crash" of May 6, 2010, or an erroneous value—a "bad tick."

If you have the ability to change the data, as you would when using a local database, and performing database maintenance yourself, your first decision is whether to change the data or not. Then, if you decide to change it, determining what value to change it to.

If you do not have the ability to change the data, as would be the case when retrieving data on-the-fly, or when a data service maintains the database, the program must handle the outlier gracefully. There are several possible actions:
- Delete the outlying data point and treat it as missing.
- Winzorize the outlying data point and set it to some predetermined value at the edge of the expected range. A drawback to Winzoring is that relative order is lost. All outliers are given the same value.

- Transform the distribution of the data stream so that outliers are brought into a reasonable range while retaining relative order. Perhaps using the softmax function.

Target definition

The target for our models will be binary. Strings, such as 'Iris-setosa', may be acceptable. Or the model may prefer or require numeric data. +1 and -1 are usually safe choices. When numeric labels are used, take the preference of the specific model into account and assign the label +1 to the category that is of primary interest—the positive category.

Transformations

Transformations are mathematical functional relationships, defined over a set of inputs called the function's *domain*. Given a specific input value, there is a single, unique output value. The set of output values is called the *range* of the function.

As we use each of them, the purpose of a transformation is to change the distribution of the data to which it is applied.

Transformations are well suited to implementation as program functions in the language of the platform. The RSI indicator described in earlier chapters is a good example.

For time series, all transformations should be done using a sliding window. It is important that all calculations refer only to data knowable as of the time of the data element. Including any data more recent than that introduces a future leak. Even seemingly innocuous computations, such as computing the mean of an entire spreadsheet column or data series, even if it is thought to be stationary, introduces an unfavorable bias.

Many machine learning algorithms work better, or even require, data to conform to a defined distribution. Two transformations are particularly important in data preparation for machine learning—standardization and normalization.

Standardization

Standardization has a special meaning for data preparation. It is a transformation that results in a distribution with a mean of 0.0 and a standard deviation of 1.0. Computing the z-score is a standardizing transformation. Many models, such as support vector machines, perform better when the predictor variables have been standardized. Scikit-learn has a standardization function[9] that can be used when the data is stationary. When used with time series data, it introduces an unfavorable bias, so an explicit sliding window should be used.

---

9 http://scikit-learn.org/stable/modules/generated/sklearn.preprocessing.StandardScaler.html

Normalization

Normalization also has a special meaning for data preparation. It refers to any transformation that results in all values being in the range of 0.0 to 1.0. Some models, such as neural networks, prefer, or even require, predictor variables be normalized prior to calling the fitting function. Scikit-learn has a normalization function[10] that can be used when the data is stationary. As with standardization, allowing the function to use all of the data along a time-series axis introduces a future leak and an unfavorable bias. Again, an explicit sliding window should be used.

Normalization into a range of 0 to 1 does not necessarily imply that the distribution will be uniform within that range. If you want the distribution to be uniform, use an additional binning and distribution transformation, such as percentrank.

One function that performs normalization is linear scaling. Linear scaling maps the maximum and minimum values of the input data to 1.0 and 0.0, respectively. It maps all input data points into the 0 to 1 range, maintaining their proportional position. It does not change the distribution. If the domain had a concentration toward high values, the range will also have a concentration toward high values.

Another normalizing transformation is percentrank. Using a sliding window with a lookback period of, say six months or one year, sort all data points within the window into ascending order and distribute them as uniformly as possible into 100 bins. The lowest values are assigned bin 1, the highest bin 100. The value assigned for the data point being transformed is the bin number, or rank, of that data point. (Divide the bin number by 100, giving 0.0 to 1.0.) Percentrank not only scales, but also changes the distribution, making it nearly uniform.

A third is a logistic transformation. I recommend the version of the logistic transformation known as softmax. Softmax has a linear central section that contains most of the data with minimal distortion, but squeezes outliers into the extremes. It has the advantage of maintaining the relative order of all data points. If the distribution resulting from the linear transformation into the central section is not satisfactory, follow softmax with whatever other transformation is desired. The formula for softmax is:

$$a = \frac{x - \mu}{\frac{\lambda \sigma}{2 \pi}}$$

$$y(t) = \frac{1}{1 + e^{-a}}$$

---

10 http://scikit-learn.org/stable/modules/generated/sklearn.preprocessing.normalize.html

where:
- e = 2.71828
- π = 3.14159
- x = value being transformed
- l = length of the sliding window
- μ = mean of values within the sliding window
- σ = standard deviation of values within the sliding window
- λ = the number of standard deviations to be kept linear
- y = the transformed value

Figure 8.37 shows the softmax function for a lambda of 6, which is a typical value. The section of linearity is about 3 standard deviations on each side of the mean. If the distribution prior to applying softmax is approximately Normal, the six standard deviations will capture nearly all of the data. Many technical analysis indicators, such as RSI using a short lookback, are bimodal rather than Normal, so visually check the transformed data to be certain it has the distribution you intend.

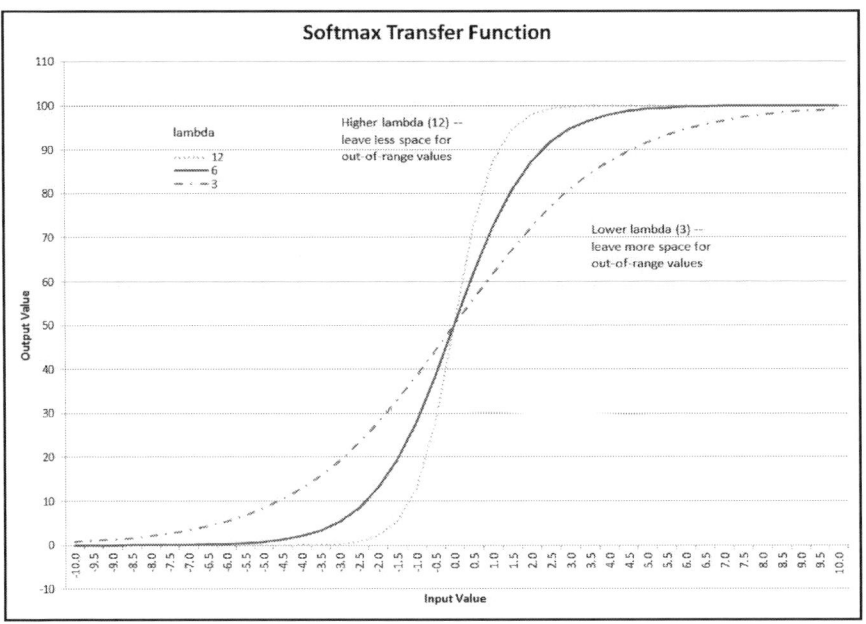

Figure 8.37 Softmax function

See Chapter 5 of my Mean Reversion book for a more complete discussion of transformations.[11]

---

11 Bandy, Howard, *Mean Reversion Trading Systems*, Blue Owl Press, 2013.

Examples of Learning Algorithms

A number of techniques have been developed to fit models to data. A complete discussion of the characteristics, capabilities, and limitations of the many machine learning models that might produce profitable trading systems is beyond the scope of this book. Please refer to one or more of the excellent books by Peter Harrington,[12] Willi Richert,[13] Peter Flach,[14] or Yaser Abu-Mostafa[15] for overview, general discussion, and application examples. Examples in the Harrington and Richert books are in Python. Also visit the online sites of scikit-learn[16] for complete reference and many tutorial examples.

The next sections show examples of use of several of the learning algorithms. For the most part, the only difference between these examples is in the definition of the model. The data preparation, call to fit, and evaluation use exactly the same lines of code in all examples.

All models, no matter how they are defined, have model-specific parameters. These are described as hyper-parameters or meta-parameters. Some have only a few, others many. Some apply to the data, such as how the data is split into training and testing, others apply to the model, such as a sensitivity variable. The example programs that follow are intended to illustrate how to set up, call, and evaluate each machine learning model. No attempt has been made to explore the options beyond those illustrated. The specific meta-parameter settings have not been tuned to create the best model.

Do not draw comparison of results from these examples. Do use them as templates for your own analysis, which will include study of meta-parameters.

Each of the following sections lists a complete program that attempts to predict whether an individual flower is Iris-virginica or not. All 150 data elements of the iris data set are used. There are only two target categories—Iris-virginica, given the value +1, and not-Iris-virginica, given the value -1.

---

12 Harrington, Peter, *Machine Learning in Action*, Manning, 2012
13 Richert, Willi, et al, *Building Machine Learning Systems with Python*, Packt, 2013.
14 Flach, Peter, *Machine Learning: The Art and Science of Algorithms that Make Sense of Data*, Cambridge, 2012.
15 Abu-Mostafa, Yaser, et al, *Learning from Data*, AML Books, 2012.
16 http://scikit-learn.org/stable/

Ada boost

```
"""
IrisExample_Adaboost.py

Example of classification
Model is Ada Boost

This program:
  Reads the iris data file from the UCI repository.
  Sets the target to +1 for Iris-virginica, -1 for all other
  Repeatedly:
    Divides the data using StratifiedShuffleSplit.
    Runs a learning algorithm.
    Evaluates the test data.
  Prints the combined confusion matrix.

Disclaimer continues to apply

Copyright  2014 Blue Owl Press, Inc
Dr. Howard Bandy

"""

import numpy as np
from sklearn.cross_validation import StratifiedShuffleSplit
from sklearn import datasets
from sklearn.ensemble import AdaBoostClassifier
from sklearn.metrics import confusion_matrix

irisdata = datasets.load_iris()

#   Assign target values
#   In the iris dataset, Iris-Virginica has value 2
irisy = np.where(irisdata.target==2,1,-1)

#   Predictor variables are raw data -- no scaling
irisX = irisdata.data

iterations = 10

#   Algorithm is Ada Boost
model = AdaBoostClassifier(n_estimators=100)

#   Make 'iterations' index vectors for the train-test split
sss = StratifiedShuffleSplit(irisy,iterations,test_size=0.33,
                             random_state=None)

#   Initialize the confusion matrix
cm_sum = np.zeros((2,2))

#   For each entry in the set of splits, fit and predict
for train_index,test_index in sss:
    X_train, X_test = irisX[train_index], irisX[test_index]
    y_train, y_test = irisy[train_index], irisy[test_index]
    model.fit(X_train, y_train)
    y_pred = model.predict(X_test)
    # Compute confusion matrix
    cm = confusion_matrix(y_test, y_pred)
    cm_sum = cm_sum + cm
```

```
    print "\n\nLearning algorithm is Ada Boost"
    print "\nConfusion matrix for %i randomized tests" % iterations
    print '      predicted'
    print '       pos neg'

    print 'pos:  %i   %i' % (cm_sum[1,1], cm_sum[1,0])
    print 'neg:  %i   %i' % (cm_sum[0,1], cm_sum[0,0])

    print "\nend of run"

###########   end   ############
```

Figure 8.38 Ada Boost classification — Python code

```
Learning algorithm is Ada Boost

Confusion matrix for 10 randomized tests
      predicted
       pos neg
pos:   156  14
neg:   11   319

end of run
```

Figure 8.39 Ada Boost classification — output

For more information, refer to the scikit-learn webpage.[17]

---

17 http://scikit-learn.org/stable/modules/generated/sklearn.ensemble.AdaBoostClassifier.html

Decision tree

```
"""
IrisExample_DecisionTree.py

Example of classification
Model is Decision Tree

This program:
  Reads the iris data file from the UCI repository.
  Sets the target to +1 for Iris-virginica, -1 for all other
  Repeatedly:
    Divides the data using StratifiedShuffleSplit.
    Runs a learning algorithm.
    Evaluates the test data.
  Prints the combined confusion matrix.

Disclaimer continues to apply

Copyright  2014 Blue Owl Press, Inc
Dr. Howard Bandy

"""

import numpy as np
from sklearn.cross_validation import StratifiedShuffleSplit
from sklearn import datasets
from sklearn.tree import DecisionTreeClassifier
from sklearn.metrics import confusion_matrix

irisdata = datasets.load_iris()

#  Assign target values
#  In the iris dataset, Iris-Virginica has value 2
irisy = np.where(irisdata.target==2,1,-1)

#  Predictor variables are raw data -- no scaling
irisX = irisdata.data

iterations = 10

#  Algorithm is Decision Tree
model = DecisionTreeClassifier()

#  Make 'iterations' index vectors for the train-test split
sss = StratifiedShuffleSplit(irisy,iterations,test_size=0.33,
                             random_state=None)

#  Initialize the confusion matrix
cm_sum = np.zeros((2,2))

#  For each entry in the set of splits, fit and predict
for train_index,test_index in sss:
    X_train, X_test = irisX[train_index], irisX[test_index]
    y_train, y_test = irisy[train_index], irisy[test_index]
    model.fit(X_train, y_train)
    y_pred = model.predict(X_test)
    # Compute confusion matrix
    cm = confusion_matrix(y_test, y_pred)
    cm_sum = cm_sum + cm
```

```
    print "\n\nLearning algorithm is Decision Tree"
    print "\nConfusion matrix for %i randomized tests" % iterations
    print '     predicted'
    print '      pos neg'

    print 'pos:  %i   %i' % (cm_sum[1,1], cm_sum[1,0])
    print 'neg:  %i   %i' % (cm_sum[0,1], cm_sum[0,0])

    print "\nend of run"

########### end ############
```

Figure 8.40 Decision tree classification — Python code

```
Learning algorithm is Decision Tree

Confusion matrix for 10 randomized tests
     predicted
      pos neg
pos:  162  8
neg:  8   322

end of run
```

Figure 8.41 Decision Tree classification — output

For more information, refer to the scikit-learn webpage.[18]

---

18 http://scikit-learn.org/stable/modules/tree.html

Gradient boost

```
"""
IrisExample_GradientBoost.py

Example of classification
Model is Gradient Boost

This program:
  Reads the iris data file from the UCI repository.
  Sets the target to +1 for Iris-virginica, -1 for all other
  Repeatedly:
    Divides the data using StratifiedShuffleSplit.
    Runs a learning algorithm.
    Evaluates the test data.
  Prints the combined confusion matrix.

Disclaimer continues to apply

Copyright  2014 Blue Owl Press, Inc
Dr. Howard Bandy

"""

import numpy as np
from sklearn.cross_validation import StratifiedShuffleSplit
from sklearn import datasets
from sklearn.ensemble import GradientBoostingClassifier
from sklearn.metrics import confusion_matrix

irisdata = datasets.load_iris()

#   Assign target values
#   In the iris dataset, Iris-Virginica has value 2
irisy = np.where(irisdata.target==2,1,-1)

#   Predictor variables are raw data -- no scaling
irisX = irisdata.data

iterations = 10

#   Algorithm is Gradient Boost
model = GradientBoostingClassifier(n_estimators=100)

#   Make 'iterations' index vectors for the train-test split
sss = StratifiedShuffleSplit(irisy,iterations,test_size=0.33,
                   random_state=None)

#   Initialize the confusion matrix
cm_sum = np.zeros((2,2))

#   For each entry in the set of splits, fit and predict
for train_index,test_index in sss:
    X_train, X_test = irisX[train_index], irisX[test_index]
    y_train, y_test = irisy[train_index], irisy[test_index]
    model.fit(X_train, y_train)
    y_pred = model.predict(X_test)
    # Compute confusion matrix
    cm = confusion_matrix(y_test, y_pred)
    cm_sum = cm_sum + cm
```

```
    print "\n\nLearning algorithm is Gradient Boost"
    print "\nConfusion matrix for %i randomized tests" % iterations
    print '     predicted'
    print '      pos neg'

    print 'pos:  %i   %i' % (cm_sum[1,1], cm_sum[1,0])
    print 'neg:  %i   %i' % (cm_sum[0,1], cm_sum[0,0])

    print "\nend of run"

########### end ############
```

Figure 8.42 Gradient Boost classification — Python code

```
Learning algorithm is Gradient Boost

Confusion matrix for 10 randomized tests
      predicted
       pos neg
pos:   158  12
neg:   14   316

end of run
```

Figure 8.43 Gradient Boost classification — output

For more information, refer to the scikit-learn webpage.[19]

---

19 http://scikit-learn.org/stable/modules/generated/sklearn.ensemble.GradientBoostingClassifier.html

Linear discriminant analysis

```
"""
IrisExample_LinearDiscrim.py

Example of classification
Model is Linear Discriminant Analysis

This program:
  Reads the iris data file from the UCI repository.
  Sets the target to +1 for Iris-virginica, -1 for all other
  Repeatedly:
    Divides the data using StratifiedShuffleSplit.
    Runs a learning algorithm.
    Evaluates the test data.
  Prints the combined confusion matrix.

Disclaimer continues to apply

Copyright  2014 Blue Owl Press, Inc
Dr. Howard Bandy

"""

import numpy as np
from sklearn.cross_validation import StratifiedShuffleSplit
from sklearn import datasets
from sklearn.lda import LDA
from sklearn.metrics import confusion_matrix

irisdata = datasets.load_iris()

#  Assign target values
#  In the iris dataset, Iris-Virginica has value 2
irisy = np.where(irisdata.target==2,1,-1)

#  Predictor variables are raw data -- no scaling
irisX = irisdata.data

iterations = 10

#  Algorithm is Linear Discriminant Analysis
model = LDA()

#  Make 'iterations' index vectors for the train-test split
sss = StratifiedShuffleSplit(irisy,iterations,test_size=0.33,
                             random_state=None)

#  Initialize the confusion matrix
cm_sum = np.zeros((2,2))

#  For each entry in the set of splits, fit and predict
for train_index,test_index in sss:
    X_train, X_test = irisX[train_index], irisX[test_index]
    y_train, y_test = irisy[train_index], irisy[test_index]
    model.fit(X_train, y_train)
    y_pred = model.predict(X_test)
    # Compute confusion matrix
    cm = confusion_matrix(y_test, y_pred)
    cm_sum = cm_sum + cm
```

```
    print "\n\nLearning algorithm is Linear Discriminant Analysis"
    print "\nConfusion matrix for %i randomized tests" % iterations
    print '      predicted'
    print '       pos neg'

    print 'pos:   %i   %i' % (cm_sum[1,1], cm_sum[1,0])
    print 'neg:   %i   %i' % (cm_sum[0,1], cm_sum[0,0])

    print "\nend of run"

########### end ############
```

Figure 8.44 Linear discriminant classification — Python code

```
Learning algorithm is Linear Discriminant Analysis

Confusion matrix for 10 randomized tests
      predicted
       pos neg
pos:   155  15
neg:    22 308

end of run
```

Figure 8.45 Linear discriminant classification — output

For more information, refer to the scikit-learn webpage.[20]

---

[20] http://scikit-learn.org/stable/modules/generated/sklearn.lda.LDA.html

Logistic regression

```
"""
IrisExample_LogisticRegression.py

Example of classification
Model is Logistic Regression

This program:
  Reads the iris data file from the UCI repository.
  Sets the target to +1 for Iris-virginica, -1 for all other
  Repeatedly:
    Divides the data using StratifiedShuffleSplit.
    Runs a learning algorithm.
    Evaluates the test data.
  Prints the combined confusion matrix.

Disclaimer continues to apply

Copyright  2014 Blue Owl Press, Inc
Dr. Howard Bandy

"""

import numpy as np
from sklearn.cross_validation import StratifiedShuffleSplit
from sklearn import datasets
from sklearn import linear_model
from sklearn.metrics import confusion_matrix

irisdata = datasets.load_iris()

#  Assign target values
#  In the iris dataset, Iris-Virginica has value 2
irisy = np.where(irisdata.target==2,1,-1)

#  Predictor variables are raw data -- no scaling
irisX = irisdata.data

iterations = 10

#  Algorithm is Logistic Regression
model = linear_model.LogisticRegression()

#  Make 'iterations' index vectors for the train-test split
sss = StratifiedShuffleSplit(irisy,iterations,test_size=0.33,
                            random_state=None)

#  Initialize the confusion matrix
cm_sum = np.zeros((2,2))

#  For each entry in the set of splits, fit and predict
for train_index,test_index in sss:
    X_train, X_test = irisX[train_index], irisX[test_index]
    y_train, y_test = irisy[train_index], irisy[test_index]
    model.fit(X_train, y_train)
    y_pred = model.predict(X_test)
    # Compute confusion matrix
    cm = confusion_matrix(y_test, y_pred)
    cm_sum = cm_sum + cm
```

```
    print "\n\nLearning algorithm is Logistic Regression"
    print "\nConfusion matrix for %i randomized tests" % iterations
    print '      predicted'
    print '     pos neg'

    print 'pos:  %i  %i' % (cm_sum[1,1], cm_sum[1,0])
    print 'neg:  %i  %i' % (cm_sum[0,1], cm_sum[0,0])

    print "\nend of run"

############    end    ############
```

Figure 8.46 Logistic regression classification — Python code

```
Learning algorithm is Logistic Regression

Confusion matrix for 10 randomized tests
      predicted
        pos neg
pos:    170  0
neg:    10  320

end of run
```

Figure 8.47 Logistic regression classification — output

For more information, refer to the scikit-learn webpage.[21]

---

21 http://scikit-learn.org/stable/modules/generated/sklearn.linear_model.LogisticRegression.html

Naive Bayes — Gaussian

```
"""
IrisExample_NaiveBayes_Gaussian.py

Example of classification
Model is Gaussian Naive Bayes

This program:
  Reads the iris data file from the UCI repository.
  Sets the target to +1 for Iris-virginica, -1 for all other
  Repeatedly:
    Divides the data using StratifiedShuffleSplit.
    Runs a learning algorithm.
    Evaluates the test data.
  Prints the combined confusion matrix.

Disclaimer continues to apply

Copyright  2014 Blue Owl Press, Inc
Dr. Howard Bandy

"""

import numpy as np
from sklearn.cross_validation import StratifiedShuffleSplit
from sklearn import datasets
from sklearn.naive_bayes import GaussianNB
from sklearn.metrics import confusion_matrix

irisdata = datasets.load_iris()

#  Assign target values
#  In the iris dataset, Iris-Virginica has value 2
irisy = np.where(irisdata.target==2,1,-1)

#  Predictor variables are raw data -- no scaling
irisX = irisdata.data

iterations = 10

#  Algorithm is Gaussian Naive Bayes
model = GaussianNB()

#  Make 'iterations' index vectors for the train-test split
sss = StratifiedShuffleSplit(irisy,iterations,test_size=0.33,
                             random_state=None)

#  Initialize the confusion matrix
cm_sum = np.zeros((2,2))

#  For each entry in the set of splits, fit and predict
for train_index,test_index in sss:
    X_train, X_test = irisX[train_index], irisX[test_index]
    y_train, y_test = irisy[train_index], irisy[test_index]
    model.fit(X_train, y_train)
    y_pred = model.predict(X_test)
    # Compute confusion matrix
    cm = confusion_matrix(y_test, y_pred)
    cm_sum = cm_sum + cm
```

```
    print "\n\nLearning algorithm is Gaussian Naive Bayes"
    print "\nConfusion matrix for %i randomized tests" % iterations
    print '      predicted'
    print '      pos neg'

    print 'pos:  %i  %i' % (cm_sum[1,1], cm_sum[1,0])
    print 'neg:  %i  %i' % (cm_sum[0,1], cm_sum[0,0])

    print "\nend of run"

########### end ############
```

Figure 8.48 Naive Bayes - Gaussian — Python code

```
Learning algorithm is Gaussian Naive Bayes

Confusion matrix for 10 randomized tests
     predicted
      pos neg
pos:  166  4
neg:  29  301

end of run
```

Figure 8.49 Naive Bayes - Gaussian — output

For more information, refer to the scikit-learn webpage.[22]

---

22 http://scikit-learn.org/stable/modules/generated/sklearn.naive_bayes.GaussianNB.html

Naive Bayes — multinomial

```
"""
IrisExample_NaiveBayes_Multinomial.py

Example of classification
Model is Multinomial Naive Bayes

This program:
  Reads the iris data file from the UCI repository.
  Sets the target to +1 for Iris-virginica, -1 for all other
  Repeatedly:
    Divides the data using StratifiedShuffleSplit.
    Runs a learning algorithm.
    Evaluates the test data.
  Prints the combined confusion matrix.

Disclaimer continues to apply

Copyright  2014 Blue Owl Press, Inc
Dr. Howard Bandy

"""

import numpy as np
from sklearn.cross_validation import StratifiedShuffleSplit
from sklearn import datasets
from sklearn.naive_bayes import MultinomialNB
from sklearn.metrics import confusion_matrix

irisdata = datasets.load_iris()

#  Assign target values
#  In the iris dataset, Iris-Virginica has value 2
irisy = np.where(irisdata.target==2,1,-1)

#  Predictor variables are raw data -- no scaling
irisX = irisdata.data

iterations = 10

#  Algorithm is Multinomial Naive Bayes
model = MultinomialNB()

#  Make 'iterations' index vectors for the train-test split
sss = StratifiedShuffleSplit(irisy,iterations,test_size=0.33,
                    random_state=None)

#  Initialize the confusion matrix
cm_sum = np.zeros((2,2))

#  For each entry in the set of splits, fit and predict
for train_index,test_index in sss:
    X_train, X_test = irisX[train_index], irisX[test_index]
    y_train, y_test = irisy[train_index], irisy[test_index]
    model.fit(X_train, y_train)
    y_pred = model.predict(X_test)
    # Compute confusion matrix
    cm = confusion_matrix(y_test, y_pred)
    cm_sum = cm_sum + cm
```

```
    print "\n\nLearning algorithm is Multinomial Naive Bayes"
    print "\nConfusion matrix for %i randomized tests" % iterations
    print '        predicted'
    print '        pos neg'

    print 'pos:   %i   %i' % (cm_sum[1,1], cm_sum[1,0])
    print 'neg:   %i   %i' % (cm_sum[0,1], cm_sum[0,0])

    print "\nend of run"

########### end ############
```

Figure 8.50 Naive Bayes - multinomial — Python code

```
Learning algorithm is Multinomial Naive Bayes

Confusion matrix for 10 randomized tests
       predicted
        pos neg
pos:   127   43
neg:    1   329

end of run
```

Figure 8.51 Naive Bayes - multinomial — output

For more information, refer to the scikit-learn webpage.[23]

---

23 http://scikit-learn.org/stable/modules/generated/sklearn.naive_bayes.MultinomialNB.html

Nearest neighbor

```
"""
IrisExample_Neighbors.py

Example of classification
Model is K Nearest Neighbors

This program:
  Reads the iris data file from the UCI repository.
  Sets the target to +1 for Iris-virginica, -1 for all other
  Repeatedly:
    Divides the data using StratifiedShuffleSplit.
    Runs a learning algorithm.
    Evaluates the test data.
  Prints the combined confusion matrix.

Disclaimer continues to apply

Copyright  2014 Blue Owl Press, Inc
Dr. Howard Bandy

"""

import numpy as np
from sklearn.cross_validation import StratifiedShuffleSplit
from sklearn import datasets
from sklearn import neighbors
from sklearn.metrics import confusion_matrix

irisdata = datasets.load_iris()

#   Assign target values
#   In the iris dataset, Iris-Virginica has value 2
irisy = np.where(irisdata.target==2,1,-1)

#   Predictor variables are raw data -- no scaling
irisX = irisdata.data

iterations = 10

#   Algorithm is K Nearest Neighbors
model = neighbors.KNeighborsClassifier(n_neighbors=15,
         weights='distance')
#   Make 'iterations' index vectors for the train-test split
sss = StratifiedShuffleSplit(irisy,iterations,test_size=0.33,
                            random_state=None)

#   Initialize the confusion matrix
cm_sum = np.zeros((2,2))

#   For each entry in the set of splits, fit and predict
for train_index,test_index in sss:
    X_train, X_test = irisX[train_index], irisX[test_index]
    y_train, y_test = irisy[train_index], irisy[test_index]
    model.fit(X_train, y_train)
    y_pred = model.predict(X_test)
    # Compute confusion matrix
    cm = confusion_matrix(y_test, y_pred)
    cm_sum = cm_sum + cm
```

```
    print "\n\nLearning algorithm is K Nearest Neighbors"
    print "\nConfusion matrix for %i randomized tests" % iterations
    print '      predicted'
    print '      pos neg'

    print 'pos:  %i   %i' % (cm_sum[1,1], cm_sum[1,0])
    print 'neg:  %i   %i' % (cm_sum[0,1], cm_sum[0,0])

    print "\nend of run"

########### end ############
```

Figure 8.52 Nearest neighbor — Python code

```
Learning algorithm is K Nearest Neighbors

Confusion matrix for 10 randomized tests
      predicted
        pos neg
pos:    166  4
neg:     9  321

end of run
```

Figure 8.53 Nearest neighbor — output

For more information, refer to the scikit-learn webpage.[24]

---

24 http://scikit-learn.org/stable/modules/generated/sklearn.neighbors.KNeighborsClassifier.html

Passive aggressive

```
"""
IrisExample_PassiveAggressive.py

Example of classification
Model is Perceptron

This program:
  Reads the iris data file from the UCI repository.
  Sets the target to +1 for Iris-virginica, -1 for all other
  Repeatedly:
    Divides the data using StratifiedShuffleSplit.
    Runs a learning algorithm.
    Evaluates the test data.
  Prints the combined confusion matrix.

Disclaimer continues to apply

Copyright   2014 Blue Owl Press, Inc
Dr. Howard Bandy

"""

import numpy as np
from sklearn.cross_validation import StratifiedShuffleSplit
from sklearn import datasets
from sklearn.linear_model import PassiveAggressiveClassifier
from sklearn.metrics import confusion_matrix

irisdata = datasets.load_iris()

#   Assign target values
#   In the iris dataset, Iris-Virginica has value 2
irisy = np.where(irisdata.target==2,1,-1)

#   Predictor variables are raw data -- no scaling
irisX = irisdata.data

iterations = 10

#   Algorithm is PassiveAggressiveClassifier
model = PassiveAggressiveClassifier(n_iter=500)

#   Make 'iterations' index vectors for the train-test split
sss = StratifiedShuffleSplit(irisy,iterations,test_size=0.33,
                             random_state=None)

#   Initialize the confusion matrix
cm_sum = np.zeros((2,2))

#   For each entry in the set of splits, fit and predict
for train_index,test_index in sss:
    X_train, X_test = irisX[train_index], irisX[test_index]
    y_train, y_test = irisy[train_index], irisy[test_index]
    model.fit(X_train, y_train)
    y_pred = model.predict(X_test)
    # Compute confusion matrix
    cm = confusion_matrix(y_test, y_pred)
    cm_sum = cm_sum + cm
```

```
    print "\n\nLearning algorithm is PassiveAggressiveClassifier"
    print "\nConfusion matrix for %i randomized tests" % iterations
    print '     predicted'
    print '      pos neg'

    print 'pos:  %i  %i' % (cm_sum[1,1], cm_sum[1,0])
    print 'neg:  %i  %i' % (cm_sum[0,1], cm_sum[0,0])

    print "\nend of run"

########### end ############
```

Figure 8.54 Passive aggressive — Python code

```
Learning algorithm is PassiveAggressiveClassifier

Confusion matrix for 10 randomized tests
     predicted
      pos neg
pos:  163  7
neg:  10  320

end of run
```

Figure 8.55 Passive aggressive — output

For more information, refer to the scikit-learn webpage.[25]

---

25 http://scikit-learn.org/stable/modules/generated/sklearn.linear_model.PassiveAggressiveClassifier.html

Perceptron

```
"""
IrisExample_Perceptron.py

Example of classification
Model is Perceptron

This program:
  Reads the iris data file from the UCI repository.
  Sets the target to +1 for Iris-virginica, -1 for all other
  Repeatedly:
    Divides the data using StratifiedShuffleSplit.
    Runs a learning algorithm.
    Evaluates the test data.
  Prints the combined confusion matrix.

Disclaimer continues to apply

Copyright  2014 Blue Owl Press, Inc
Dr. Howard Bandy

"""

import numpy as np
from sklearn.cross_validation import StratifiedShuffleSplit
from sklearn import datasets
from sklearn.linear_model import Perceptron
from sklearn.metrics import confusion_matrix

irisdata = datasets.load_iris()

#  Assign target values
#  In the iris dataset, Iris-Virginica has value 2
irisy = np.where(irisdata.target==2,1,-1)

#  Predictor variables are raw data -- no scaling
irisX = irisdata.data

iterations = 10

#  Algorithm is Perceptron
model = Perceptron(n_iter=500)

#  Make 'iterations' index vectors for the train-test split
sss = StratifiedShuffleSplit(irisy,iterations,test_size=0.33,
                             random_state=None)

#  Initialize the confusion matrix
cm_sum = np.zeros((2,2))

#  For each entry in the set of splits, fit and predict
for train_index,test_index in sss:
    X_train, X_test = irisX[train_index], irisX[test_index]
    y_train, y_test = irisy[train_index], irisy[test_index]
    model.fit(X_train, y_train)
    y_pred = model.predict(X_test)
    # Compute confusion matrix
    cm = confusion_matrix(y_test, y_pred)
    cm_sum = cm_sum + cm
```

```
    print "\n\nLearning algorithm is Perceptron"
    print "\nConfusion matrix for %i randomized tests" % iterations
    print '     predicted'
    print '      pos neg'

    print 'pos:  %i  %i' % (cm_sum[1,1], cm_sum[1,0])
    print 'neg:  %i  %i' % (cm_sum[0,1], cm_sum[0,0])

    print "\nend of run"

########### end ############
```

Figure 8.56 Perceptron — Python code

```
Learning algorithm is Perceptron

Confusion matrix for 10 randomized tests
     predicted
      pos neg
pos:  157  13
neg:  17   313

end of run
```

Figure 8.57 Perceptron — output

For more information, refer to the scikit-learn webpage.[26]

---

[26] http://scikit-learn.org/stable/modules/generated/sklearn.linear_model.Perceptron.html

Quadradic discriminant analysis

```
"""
IrisExample_QuadraticDiscrim.py

Example of classification
Model is Quadratic Discriminant Analysis

This program:
  Reads the iris data file from the UCI repository.
  Sets the target to +1 for Iris-virginica, -1 for all other
  Repeatedly:
    Divides the data using StratifiedShuffleSplit.
    Runs a learning algorithm.
    Evaluates the test data.
  Prints the combined confusion matrix.

Disclaimer continues to apply

Copyright   2014 Blue Owl Press, Inc
Dr. Howard Bandy

"""

import numpy as np
from sklearn.cross_validation import StratifiedShuffleSplit
from sklearn import datasets
from sklearn.qda import QDA
from sklearn.metrics import confusion_matrix

irisdata = datasets.load_iris()

#   Assign target values
#   In the iris dataset, Iris-Virginica has value 2
irisy = np.where(irisdata.target==2,1,-1)

#   Predictor variables are raw data -- no scaling
irisX = irisdata.data

iterations = 10

#   Algorithm is Quadratic Discriminant Analysis
model = QDA()

#   Make 'iterations' index vectors for the train-test split
sss = StratifiedShuffleSplit(irisy,iterations,test_size=0.33,
                             random_state=None)

#   Initialize the confusion matrix
cm_sum = np.zeros((2,2))

#   For each entry in the set of splits, fit and predict
for train_index,test_index in sss:
    X_train, X_test = irisX[train_index], irisX[test_index]
    y_train, y_test = irisy[train_index], irisy[test_index]
    model.fit(X_train, y_train)
    y_pred = model.predict(X_test)
    #  Compute confusion matrix
    cm = confusion_matrix(y_test, y_pred)
    cm_sum = cm_sum + cm
```

```
print "\n\nLearning algorithm is Quadratic Discriminant
        Analysis"
print "\nConfusion matrix for %i randomized tests" % iterations
print '     predicted'
print '      pos neg'

print 'pos:  %i   %i' % (cm_sum[1,1], cm_sum[1,0])
print 'neg:  %i   %i' % (cm_sum[0,1], cm_sum[0,0])

print "\nend of run"

########### end ############
```

Figure 8.58 Quadratic discriminant classification — Python code

```
Learning algorithm is Quadratic Discriminant Analysis

Confusion matrix for 10 randomized tests
     predicted
       pos neg
pos:   163  7
neg:    7  323

end of run
```

Figure 8.59 Quadratic discriminant classification — output

For more information, refer to the scikit-learn webpage.[27]

---

27 http://scikit-learn.org/stable/modules/generated/sklearn.qda.QDA.html

Random forests

```
"""
IrisExample_RandomForest.py

Example of classification
Model is Random Forest

This program:
  Reads the iris data file from the UCI repository.
  Sets the target to +1 for Iris-virginica, -1 for all other
  Repeatedly:
    Divides the data using StratifiedShuffleSplit.
    Runs a learning algorithm.
    Evaluates the test data.
  Prints the combined confusion matrix.

Disclaimer continues to apply

Copyright  2014 Blue Owl Press, Inc
Dr. Howard Bandy

"""

import numpy as np
from sklearn.cross_validation import StratifiedShuffleSplit
from sklearn import datasets
from sklearn.ensemble import RandomForestClassifier
from sklearn.metrics import confusion_matrix

irisdata = datasets.load_iris()

#  Assign target values
#  In the iris dataset, Iris-Virginica has value 2
irisy = np.where(irisdata.target==2,1,-1)

#  Predictor variables are raw data -- no scaling
irisX = irisdata.data

iterations = 10

#  Algorithm is Random Forest
model = RandomForestClassifier(n_estimators=30)

#  Make 'iterations' index vectors for the train-test split
sss = StratifiedShuffleSplit(irisy,iterations,test_size=0.33,
                    random_state=None)

#  Initialize the confusion matrix
cm_sum = np.zeros((2,2))

#  For each entry in the set of splits, fit and predict
for train_index,test_index in sss:
    X_train, X_test = irisX[train_index], irisX[test_index]
    y_train, y_test = irisy[train_index], irisy[test_index]
    model.fit(X_train, y_train)
    y_pred = model.predict(X_test)
    # Compute confusion matrix
    cm = confusion_matrix(y_test, y_pred)
    cm_sum = cm_sum + cm
```

```
    print "\n\nLearning algorithm is Random Forest"
    print "\nConfusion matrix for %i randomized tests" % iterations
    print '      predicted'
    print '       pos neg'

    print 'pos:  %i   %i' % (cm_sum[1,1], cm_sum[1,0])
    print 'neg:  %i   %i' % (cm_sum[0,1], cm_sum[0,0])

    print "\nend of run"

###########   end   ############
```

Figure 8.60 Random forest classification — Python code

```
Learning algorithm is Random Forest

Confusion matrix for 10 randomized tests
      predicted
       pos neg
pos:  151  19
neg:   13 317

end of run
```

Figure 8.61 Random forest classification — output

For more information, refer to the scikit-learn webpage.[28]

---

[28] http://scikit-learn.org/stable/modules/generated/sklearn.ensemble.RandomForestClassifier.html

Support vector machine with linear kernel

```
"""
IrisExample_SVC_Linear.py

Example of classification
Model is Support Vector Classification with Linear Kernel

This program:
  Reads the iris data file from the UCI repository.
  Sets the target to +1 for Iris-virginica, -1 for all other
  Repeatedly:
    Divides the data using StratifiedShuffleSplit.
    Runs a learning algorithm.
    Evaluates the test data.
  Prints the combined confusion matrix.

Disclaimer continues to apply

Copyright  2014 Blue Owl Press, Inc
Dr. Howard Bandy

"""

import numpy as np
from sklearn.cross_validation import StratifiedShuffleSplit
from sklearn import datasets
from sklearn import svm
from sklearn.metrics import confusion_matrix

irisdata = datasets.load_iris()

#   Assign target values
#   In the iris dataset, Iris-Virginica has value 2
irisy = np.where(irisdata.target==2,1,-1)

#   Predictor variables are raw data -- no scaling
irisX = irisdata.data

iterations = 10

#   Algorithm is support vector machine with linear kernel
model = svm.SVC(kernel='linear',class_weight='auto')

#   Make 'iterations' index vectors for the train-test split
sss = StratifiedShuffleSplit(irisy,iterations,test_size=0.33,
                    random_state=None)

#   Initialize the confusion matrix
cm_sum = np.zeros((2,2))

#   For each entry in the set of splits, fit and predict
for train_index,test_index in sss:
    X_train, X_test = irisX[train_index], irisX[test_index]
    y_train, y_test = irisy[train_index], irisy[test_index]
    model.fit(X_train, y_train)
    y_pred = model.predict(X_test)
    # Compute confusion matrix
    cm = confusion_matrix(y_test, y_pred)
    cm_sum = cm_sum + cm
```

```
    print "\n\nLearning algorithm is Support Vector Classification"
    print "  with linear kernel"
    print "\nConfusion matrix for %i randomized tests" % iterations
    print '     predicted'
    print '     pos neg'

    print 'pos:  %i   %i' % (cm_sum[1,1], cm_sum[1,0])
    print 'neg:  %i   %i' % (cm_sum[0,1], cm_sum[0,0])

    print "\nend of run"

    ###########   end   ############
```

Figure 8.62 Support vector classification - linear kernel — Python code

```
Learning algorithm is Support Vector Classification
  with linear kernel

Confusion matrix for 10 randomized tests
     predicted
     pos neg
pos:  170  0
neg:  12  318

end of run
```

Figure 8.63 Support vector classification - linear kernel — output

For more information, refer to the scikit-learn webpage.[29]

---

[29] http://scikit-learn.org/stable/modules/generated/sklearn.svm.SVC.html

Support vector machine with polynomial kernel

```
"""
IrisExample_SVC_Poly.py

Example of classification
Model is Support Vector Classification with Polynomial Kernel

This program:
  Reads the iris data file from the UCI repository.
  Sets the target to +1 for Iris-virginica, -1 for all other
  Repeatedly:
    Divides the data using StratifiedShuffleSplit.
    Runs a learning algorithm.
    Evaluates the test data.
  Prints the combined confusion matrix.

Disclaimer continues to apply

Copyright  2014 Blue Owl Press, Inc
Dr. Howard Bandy

"""

import numpy as np
from sklearn.cross_validation import StratifiedShuffleSplit
from sklearn import datasets
from sklearn import svm
from sklearn.metrics import confusion_matrix

irisdata = datasets.load_iris()

#  Assign target values
#  In the iris dataset, Iris-Virginica has value 2
irisy = np.where(irisdata.target==2,1,-1)

#  Predictor variables are raw data -- no scaling
irisX = irisdata.data

iterations = 10

#  Algorithm is support vector machine with polynomial kernel
model = svm.SVC(kernel='poly',degree=2,class_weight='auto')

#  Make 'iterations' index vectors for the train-test split
sss = StratifiedShuffleSplit(irisy,iterations,test_size=0.33,
                             random_state=None)

#  Initialize the confusion matrix
cm_sum = np.zeros((2,2))

#  For each entry in the set of splits, fit and predict
for train_index,test_index in sss:
    X_train, X_test = irisX[train_index], irisX[test_index]
    y_train, y_test = irisy[train_index], irisy[test_index]
    model.fit(X_train, y_train)
    y_pred = model.predict(X_test)
    # Compute confusion matrix
    cm = confusion_matrix(y_test, y_pred)
    cm_sum = cm_sum + cm
```

```
    print "\n\nLearning algorithm is Support Vector Classification"
    print "   with polynomial kernel"
    print "\nConfusion matrix for %i randomized tests" % iterations
    print '     predicted'
    print '     pos neg'
    print 'pos:  %i   %i' % (cm_sum[1,1], cm_sum[1,0])
    print 'neg:  %i   %i' % (cm_sum[0,1], cm_sum[0,0])

    print "\nend of run"

########### end ############
```

Figure 8.64 Support vector classification - polynomial kernel — Python code

```
Learning algorithm is Support Vector Classification
  with polynomial kernel

Confusion matrix for 10 randomized tests
      predicted
      pos neg
pos:  170  0
neg:  13   317

end of run
```

Figure 8.65 Support vector classification - polynomial kernel — output

For more information, refer to the scikit-learn webpage.[30]

---

[30] http://scikit-learn.org/stable/modules/generated/sklearn.svm.SVC.html

Support vector machine with radial basis kernel

```
"""
IrisExample_SVC_RBF.py

Example of classification
Model is Support Vector Classification with Radial Basis Kernel

This program:
  Reads the iris data file from the UCI repository.
  Sets the target to +1 for Iris-virginica, -1 for all other
  Repeatedly:
    Divides the data using StratifiedShuffleSplit.
    Runs a learning algorithm.
    Evaluates the test data.
  Prints the combined confusion matrix.

Disclaimer continues to apply

Copyright  2014 Blue Owl Press, Inc
Dr. Howard Bandy

"""

import numpy as np
from sklearn.cross_validation import StratifiedShuffleSplit
from sklearn import datasets
from sklearn import svm
from sklearn.metrics import confusion_matrix

irisdata = datasets.load_iris()

#  Assign target values
#  In the iris dataset, Iris-Virginica has value 2
irisy = np.where(irisdata.target==2,1,-1)

#  Predictor variables are raw data -- no scaling
irisX = irisdata.data

iterations = 10

#  Algorithm is support vector machine with radial basis kernel
model = svm.SVC(kernel='rbf',degree=3,gamma=0.1,
        class_weight=None)

#  Make 'iterations' index vectors for the train-test split
sss = StratifiedShuffleSplit(irisy,iterations,test_size=0.33,
                random_state=None)

#  Initialize the confusion matrix
cm_sum = np.zeros((2,2))

#  For each entry in the set of splits, fit and predict
for train_index,test_index in sss:
    X_train, X_test = irisX[train_index], irisX[test_index]
    y_train, y_test = irisy[train_index], irisy[test_index]
    model.fit(X_train, y_train)
    y_pred = model.predict(X_test)
    # Compute confusion matrix
    cm = confusion_matrix(y_test, y_pred)
    cm_sum = cm_sum + cm
```

```
    print "\n\nLearning algorithm is Support Vector Classification"
    print "  with radial basis kernel"
    print "\nConfusion matrix for %i randomized tests" % iterations
    print '     predicted'
    print '      pos neg'

    print 'pos:  %i   %i' % (cm_sum[1,1], cm_sum[1,0])
    print 'neg:  %i   %i' % (cm_sum[0,1], cm_sum[0,0])

    print "\nend of run"

    ########### end #############ss
```

Figure 8.66 Support vector classification - radial basis kernel — Python code

```
Learning algorithm is Support Vector Classification
  with radial basis kernel

Confusion matrix for 10 randomized tests
     predicted
      pos neg
pos:  164  6
neg:  8    322

end of run
```

Figure 8.67 Support vector classification - radial basis kernel — output

For more information, refer to the scikit-learn webpage.[31]

---

31 http://scikit-learn.org/stable/modules/generated/sklearn.svm.SVC.html

Balancing Class Membership

When the two classes are unevenly represented by membership count, say 5% and 95%, two conditions arise:
- A prospective model earns a high score by simply predicting the majority class.
- There will be test sets with very few elements from the smaller class.

If it is necessary to bring the membership into more equal balance, that must be done prior to the train - test split. There are two options:
- Remove some elements from the larger class.
- Add elements to the smaller class.

From the perspective of both the person developing the model and the logic of the model itself, the information value of all data points is identical. Removal would be at random, possibly removing data elements with high signal content. The preferable adjustment is to add enough copies of the smaller set to the original dataset to balance membership count.

Adjusting Misclassification Costs

A similar condition exists when the costs of Type I and Type II errors are different.

The goodness of fit metric we have been using is the confusion matrix. (While our ultimate metric is CAR25 for a given level of risk, that cannot be computed during model fitting.) Our working metric during development is the number of misclassified predictions. These are shown as off-diagonal entries, they have different costs, and we want to reduce their total cost.

Scikit-learn has many scoring and goodness of fit metrics, of which confusion matrix is one.[32] Whichever is used, scoring is reporting. The scoring function is performed after the model has been fit — after data preparation, splitting, training, and testing. Improving the confusion matrix can only be done by improving the fit of the model.

Depending on the default options of the model being fit, and lacking a cost matrix created with knowledge of the problem, the fitting algorithm (from the perspective of a confusion matrix) either:
- Treats all off-diagonal errors as equally costly.
- Sets the ratio of misclassification costs of the classes to be the inverse of the ratio of class membership count.

If costs are mildly different, say 2:1, adding copies of the class that has higher cost when misclassified might be helpful. The class that

---

[32] http://scikit-learn.org/stable/modules/model_evaluation.html

occurs less frequently is usually the class whose errors are more costly, in which case adding copies of its elements improves the balance of both class membership and misclassification cost. But when costs are highly different, say 1000:1, adding enough copies to balance costs both is not practical and would create a dataset that is highly unbalanced in membership.

Depending on the machine learning model, the following parameters might be helpful. Visit the scikit-learn websites for detailed explanations of which parameters are accepted for which models, and how they are interpreted. Some of the options include:

- A *class_weight* parameter that assigns user-specified weight to all members of given classes. This works with:
  * AdaBoost.
  * Logistic regression.
  * Perceptron.
  * Support vector machine.

  The default cost of any off-diagonal error is 1. To help reduce the number of false negative errors, the following statement sets the cost of errors made in predicting class 1 to be 500:

  ```
  model = svm.SVC(kernel='linear',class_weight={1: 500})
  ```

  Similarly, setting the cost of errors in class -1 to be more expensive reduces the number of false positive errors.

- A *sample_weight* parameter that assigns user-specified weight to individual dataset elements. This works with:
  * Naive Bayes.
  * Passive aggressive classifier.
  * Perceptron.
  * Random forests.
  * Support vector machine.

- A *weights* parameter that determines the method of measuring the distance metric when measuring distances. This works with:
  * KNeighborsClassifier.

  ```
  model = neighbors.KNeighborsClassifier(n_neighbors=15,
  weights='distance')
  ```

A Confusion Matrix for AmiBroker

The main topic of this chapter is machine learning. Most of the discussion involves use of the classification algorithms as implemented in Python. This section is a short side discussion.

A trading system development platform system is also a classifier—usually using the decision tree algorithm. It makes predictions when it generates buy and sell signals. When those are state signals to beLong or beFlat, there is a prediction for each and every day. There is a corresponding actual result for each and every day. At its simplest, it is whether the direction of the prediction was correct. Indeed, the reason we recommend using state signals is to provide daily reporting and daily opportunity for trade management. Recall the comparison in Chapter 2 of impulse signals and trade-by-trade management with state signals and mark-to-market management. Comparative equity curves are shown in Figures 2.13 and 2.14 respectively.

For a system that is long / flat and is marked to market daily, there are 252 data points in each year. Each has a prediction and an actual result. Figure 8.68 shows the confusion matrix. The numbers are hypothetical and reflect a very profitable year.

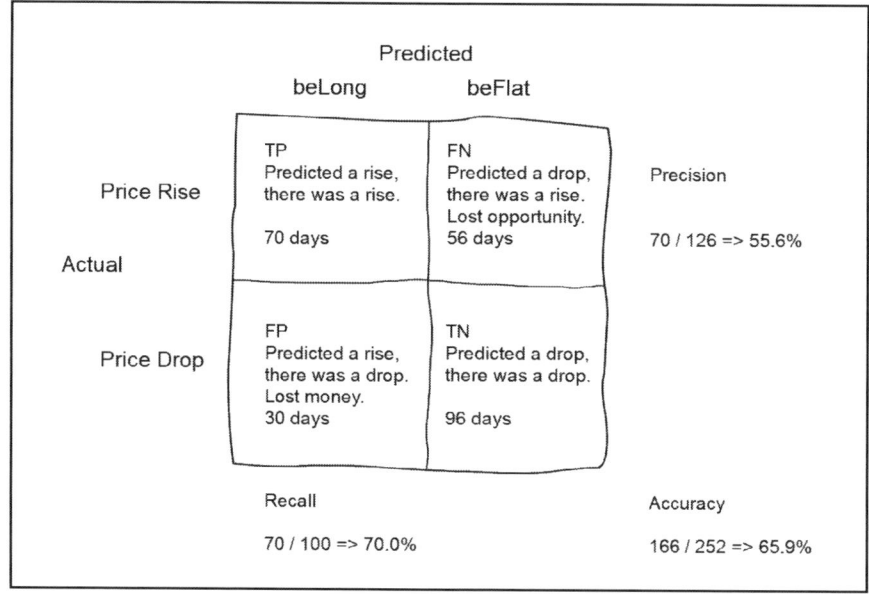

Figure 8.68 Confusion matrix for one year

100 days were predicted to have price rise worth being long (the left column), 152 were predicted to be not safe or not worthwhile to hold a long position (the right column). The price actually rose 126 days, and fell 126 days (the two rows).

Precision is the ratio of the top row. 70 of 126 days where the price rose were correctly predicted to be days when a long position gained.

Recall is the ratio of the left column. 70 of 100 days where the prediction was to be long saw a price rise.

Accuracy is the ratio of the main diagonal. 166 of 252 days were correctly predicted.

For this model, false positive is the expensive error. False positive days occur when the system predicts a price rise and gives a signal to beLong, but the price actually drops. Of the three metrics displayed, false positive is a factor in recall. We want recall to be high. There are two ways to obtain high recall. One is increasing true positives relative to false positives. The other is reducing false positives. False positives are reduced when fewer signals to beLong are given. That might be a good idea, or might not.

Conceptually, the model computes indicators and summarizes them to a single value that has a range from favorable to unfavorable. Testing shows there is a fuzzy relationship (at best) between favorableness of the indicator at today's close and the price change from today's close to tomorrow's close. As illustrated in Figure 8.69.

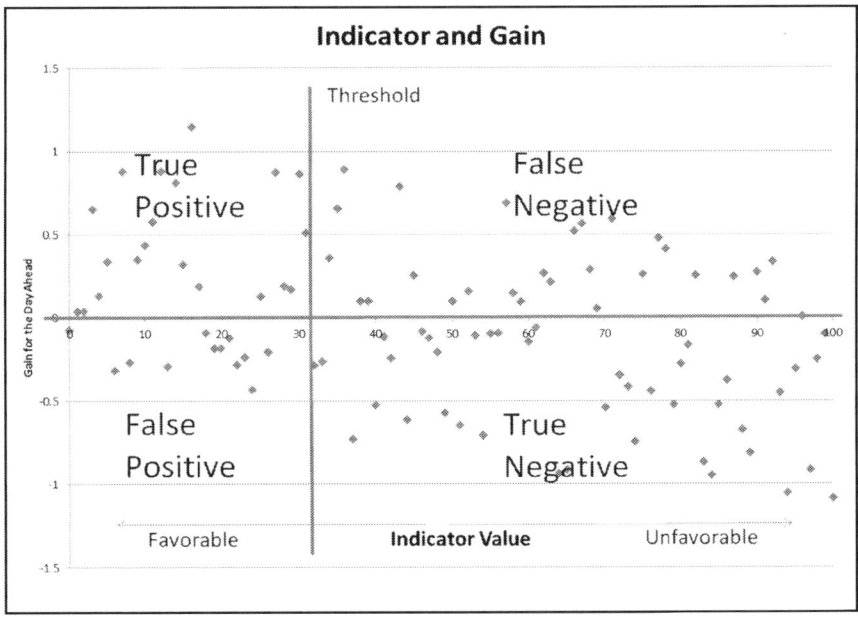

Figure 8.69 Indicator and price change

The area of the plot is divided into four by the two heavy straight lines. The rules of the system compare the value of the indicator with a threshold. The value of the threshold is represented by the position of the vertical line. On one side of the threshold — the left in this diagram — the prediction is for a price gain and the signal is beLong. On the other side, the signal is beFlat. The heavy horizontal line divides the price change for the day ahead into gain — above the line — and loss. The four areas of the chart correspond directly to the four areas of the confusion matrix.

In both Figures 8.68 and 8.69, each data point is a marked-to-market daily change recorded as either a winning trade or a losing trade.

Adjusting the threshold adjusts the portion of days to be long. If the relationship is well formed, those trades taken will be fewer but better as the threshold is moved to the left, or more frequent but weaker as the threshold is moved to the right. Placement of the threshold during development depends heavily on the objective function being used. Optimal placement of the threshold requires calculation of risk-normalized profit potential. The only way to completely avoid false positives is to move the threshold all the way to the left—to not trade at all.

In-sample Out-of-sample

A confusion matrix can be developed from any set of trades. If the data is stationary, applying the trained model to any subsets of the data result in confusion matrices that are about the same—the same within the statistical variation of the data. We relied on that a few pages ago when the classification procedures were demonstrated, with the results being the sum of ten runs, each a different split of the iris data. One of the practical tests of whether a set of data is stationary or not is the variation between models fitted to different sets of data chosen from different times.

To illustrate, we compute two confusion matrices, both using the RSI2 model described earlier applied to XLV for the period 1/1/2008 through 1/1/2012.

The first, Figure 8.70, is the result of optimizing the four year period, then reporting those results, which are completely in-sample.

		Predict			
		beLong	beFlat	Sum	Precision
Actual	gain	304	212	516	0.59
	drop	252	241	493	
	Sum	556	453	1009	
	Recall	0.55			0.54
		52			

Figure 8.70 RSI system confusion matrix 4 years in-sample

Recall is 55%, precision is 59%, accuracy is 54%. Of the 556 days predicted to be long, 304 had gains, 252 had losses, a net of 52 winning days. Gains on winning days were slightly greater than losses on losing days (not shown), so the terminal wealth is 2.09, a gain of 109% over the four years.

The second, Figure 8.71, is the result of walk forward validation runs. The in-sample period was set to one year, out-of-sample also to one year. The results reported are the accumulation of four one-year out-of-sample periods, spanning 1/1/2008 through 1/1/2012.

		Predict		Sum	Precision
		beLong	beFlat		
Actual	gain	239	277	516	0.46
	drop	213	280	493	
	Sum	452	557	1009	
	Recall	0.53			0.51
		26			

Figure 8.71 RSI system confusion matrix 4 years out-of-sample

Recall is 53%, precision is 46%, accuracy is 51%. Of the 452 days predicted to be long, 239 had gains, 213 had losses, a net of 26 winning days. Terminal wealth is 1.61, a gain of 61% over the four years.

The large drop in performance from in-sample to out-of-sample is an indication that the system is not stationary, and that in-sample results are not reliable estimates of future performance.

Machine Learning—Trading

We return to the Python environment.

As of this writing, data preparation for machine learning for trading requires working with two data structures—pandas dataframes and numpy arrays. Pandas dataframes are excellent for two reasons—their power and flexibility for "data wrangling" tasks, and because they are the data structure returned by the Quandl data provider which many of you will be using.

The machine learning libraries were developed before publication of pandas. The primary data structure they expect for data passed to them is numpy arrays. As more machine learning procedures are revised, enabling them to accept and process pandas dataframes, this inconvenience may pass.

The major steps in model development, expanded to include machine learning, and extended to include trading, are:

For Development:
1. Select a primary data series. Its datetime field will be used to establish the index for all data elements. There will be at least one price series—one that provides the transaction prices.

Depending on the data provider and the specific data series, it will be named the *close* or *settle* price. For the discussion in this book, that series will be called the *close of the primary data series*. There may be other prices for the primary series, typically open, high, and low, sometimes volume, sometimes open interest.

Close of the primary data series is being traded. The *target*—the price changes we want to learn to predict—comes from this series. Look into the future to compute the target, naming it *target*. The target variable will be one of two classes or categories—+1 for the positive class, beLong, -1 for the negative class, beFlat. Where to set the threshold is one of your decisions, implemented as a system parameter.

2. Select whatever predictor variables using the primary data series you want to compute. Examples include technical analysis and statistical indicators and transformations such as RSI, MACD, ATR, moving average, standard deviation, and z-score.

   Set the necessary parameters as program variables. Use sliding windows with defined lookback periods to avoid future leaks.

3. The final step for each variable is normalization or standardization, whichever is required by the machine learning procedure being called. Note there is not a universal choice. Some machine learning procedures can work with raw data, some require standardization where all values are z-scores having both positive and negative values centered on zero, while others require normalization where all values are in the range of 0.0 to 1.0. Refer to the documentation for requirements and examples.

   Think ahead to live trading. New data will arrive bar-by-bar and must be transformed and added to the existing data. Be certain that no matter what value the new data has, it will be processed correctly and consistently.

4. One by one, load auxiliary data series, using pandas dataframes to handle alignment by datetime. Select desired indicators and transformations, set their parameter values, and compute the predictor variables they create.

5. Make copies of lagged variables, creating quasi-independent elements for every day.

6. Drop unneeded variables.

7. Copy from pandas dataframe to numpy array in preparation of creating the target and predictor sets, and training and testing sets.

8. Set the meta-parameters, including date ranges.
   This is an important step, and will require some experimentation. The success of the system depends not only

on choosing good predictor variables and good parameters for those variables. It also depends on choosing a length for the date period used for learning over which the system is stationary. Whether you use cross-validation or train-test-split, the relationship between predictor variables and target must be consistent over the entire date range used. That is, it must be stationary, and in this step you determine the length of stationarity.

Do not proceed until you thoroughly understand how your system behaves related to the length of the train-test period.

Most of your system development effort will be spent in the tasks list above this paragraph. The remaining development tasks are relatively mechanical.

9. Split the data into a training set and a testing set.
10. Select a machine learning technique for the model.
11. Fit the model to the data of the training set.
12. Evaluate the predictions made by the fitted model for the test data set.
13. Report the fit as a confusion matrix.
14. Validate the model to your satisfaction. Walk forward, if possible.
15. Save the best estimate set of trades.
16. Save the model.

Thinking ahead to trading the system, prepare for these steps:
17. Update all data series to current.
18. Apply the transformations.
19. Retrieve the previously fitted model.
20. Retrieve or regenerate the best estimate set of trades.
21. Generate the new signal and append it to the best estimate set.
22. Apply dynamic position sizing to calculate safe-f.
23. Given safe-f, calculate CAR25.
24. Decide whether to take the signal or take the system offline.

Dealing with Dimensionality

Invariably, we want the predictor variables to include many possible combinations and variations. Many auxiliary data series. Many indicators. A wide range of lookback lengths. A wide range of critical levels.

Soon, the data array or spreadsheet has more columns (parameters) than rows (observations). This is described in statistical and modeling literature as *p greater than n*.[33] It is an example of the curse of dimensionality.[34]

---

33 http://arxiv.org/abs/math.ST/0506081
34 http://en.wikipedia.org/wiki/Curse_of_dimensionality

The problem is sometimes relieved by dimension reduction or feature extraction. The purpose of dimension reduction and feature selection is to reduce the number of variables without substantially reducing the information.

Although the topic is too broad to be covered in detail in this book, scikit-learn includes some techniques that can be applied to the problem:
- Some models are relatively immune to p greater than n, including:
  * AdaBoost[35] (but beware of overlapping classes and conflicting data points, which we have in abundance).[36]
  * Support Vector Machine (SVM).[37]
- Regularization—penalizing complexity.
  * Support Vector Machines have a regularization parameter.
- Dimension reduction, such as that performed by:
  * Principal Component Analysis (PCA).[38]
  * Linear Discriminant Analysis (LDA).[39]
  * Manifold Learning.[40]
- Feature selection, such as that performed by:
  * Random forest classifier. It does feature selection automatically as part of its algorithm.[41]
  * SelectFpr (False Positive Rate).[42]
  * SelectKBest.[43]
  * SelectPercentile.[44]
  * Recursive Feature Elimination (RFE).[45]
  * Recursive Feature Elimination with Cross Validation (RFECV).[46]

---

35 http://scikit-learn.org/stable/modules/generated/sklearn.ensemble.AdaBoostClassifier.html
36 http://groups.inf.ed.ac.uk/calvin/hp_avezhnev/Pubs/AvoidingBoostingOverfitting.pdf
37 http://scikit-learn.org/stable/modules/svm.html
38 http://scikit-learn.org/stable/modules/generated/sklearn.decomposition.PCA.html#sklearn.decomposition.PCA
39 http://scikit-learn.org/stable/modules/generated/sklearn.lda.LDA.html
40 http://scikit-learn.org/stable/auto_examples/manifold/plot_compare_methods.html
41 http://scikit-learn.org/stable/modules/generated/sklearn.ensemble.RandomForestClassifier.html
42 http://scikit-learn.org/stable/modules/generated/sklearn.feature_selection.SelectFpr.html
43 http://scikit-learn.org/stable/modules/generated/sklearn.feature_selection.SelectKBest.html
44 http://scikit-learn.org/stable/modules/generated/sklearn.feature_selection.SelectPercentile.html
45 http://scikit-learn.org/stable/auto_examples/plot_rfe_digits.html#example-plot-rfe-digits-py
46 http://scikit-learn.org/stable/auto_examples/plot_rfe_with_cross_validation.html#example-plot-rfe-with-cross-validation-py

Model Development - Machine Learning

Before applying any of these techniques, do enough research into the technique to understand it, and refer to the scikit-learn documentation of the function.

There is some thought that performing feature selection prior to fitting a support vector machine is counterproductive.[47]

Setting Dates and Test Period Lengths

Select a *pivot date*. The pivot date is the date at the beginning of the first out-of-sample period. Say 1/1/2006. Fixing the pivot date for all tests that will be compared helps in two ways:
- Select a length for the in-sample period. Say four years. That length becomes a meta-parameter.
  The starting date of the first IS period is computed by subtracting the IS length from the pivot date.
- Select a length for the out-of-sample period beyond the train-test period. Say one year. It is also a meta-parameter.
  No matter what the length of the individual OOS periods are, the total of all OOS periods will be the same for all runs.

Stationarity and Validation

Moving from a trading system development platform to machine learning does not change the need to consider stationarity. Figure 8.72 shows the relationship in time of the final model fitting train-and-test run, and live trading.

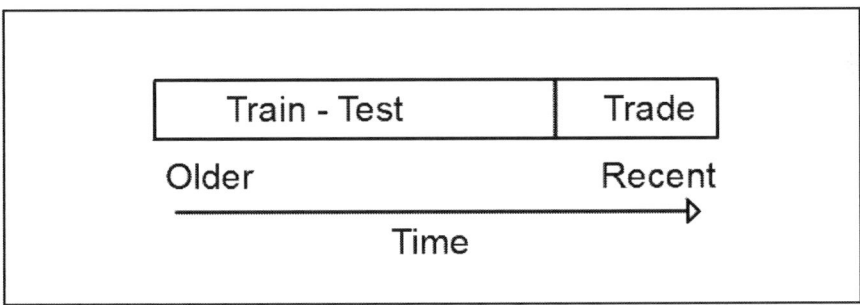

Figure 8.72 Model fitting and live trading

For trading to be profitable when real money is at stake, the model must fit the data for the trading period. To estimate the performance as accurately as possible, we recommend using three sets of data throughout development—train and test, both of which are in-sample, and a separate out-of-sample. Not only does this provide continuity from

---

47 http://stats.stackexchange.com/questions/35276/
svm-overfitting-curse-of-dimensionality

development to trading, it also fits well into the walk forward validation process.

Validation

Is the model identifying profitable signals? Or fitting to random noise? Is the system good enough to trade?

Backtest results are excellent. But we know that a single set of in-sample results by themselves have no value in estimating future performance. We need confidence that this performance will continue into trading with real money.

The goal of validation is increasing confidence. This section describes four validation tests intended to test the quality of the signal that can help answer these questions and build confidence. They are all performed during development. A substantial ingredient of confidence is personal preference and you will be making some subjective decisions.
- Perturb the data.
- Perturb the parameters.
- Test other data.
- Walk forward.

Perturb the data

The model is identifying patterns that precede profitable trades in the training data. Are the patterns persistent in as-yet-unseen data? Or are they random, but lucky?

The data is a combination of signal plus noise. What constitutes signal is specific to the trading system. Anything not explicitly identified as signal is noise, even if it contains profitable patterns that can be identified by some other model.

This test increases the amount of noise in the data:

```
NoisyData = OriginalData + AddedNoise
```

Define AddedNoise with a distribution. It could be Gaussian, uniform, bimodal, or anything you can imagine.

Using a Monte Carlo simulation, make a series of tests with increasing levels of added noise. Note the relationship between added noise and system performance. Use that information to compare alternative systems.

Perturb the parameters

Indicators have parameters such as the length of the lookback. Rules have parameters such as the indicator level at which a signal is generated. Systems have parameters, such as the type of order used to enter a trade.

Identify the parameters. Decide which should be tested. Decide on a set or range of values to test. Use a Monte Carlo technique with those parameters that have a distribution. Use a list of values with those parameters that are binary or have a limited number of alternatives. Note the relationship between parameter value and system performance.

Look for robustness and stability. Prefer plateaus to spikes.

Test other data

If development was done using data from one sector ETF, test other sector ETFs or the individual components of the ETF.

If developed using one currency pair, test other currency pairs.

If developed using one common stock, test other common stocks.

Expect models to have similar performance on similar data series. But do not expect, or require, a system to be universal.

Portfolios

The systems this book describes trade a single issue long / flat.

If you want to trade several issues, I recommend developing a system for each. Those systems may be similar, or they may be an attempt to provide some diversification. In either event, each should be developed, tested, validated, funded, and traded on its own. The result is a portfolio of single-issue systems rather than a portfolio of issues traded as a single system.

Walk forward

The gold standard of validation is walk forward testing, as described in Chapter 6.

Pipeline

Pipeline is a scikit-learn utility that can be used to chain together multiple estimators into a single statement. One of its features is automatic grid search of several sets of parameters, similar to the search done during an exhaustive optimization.

Refer to the scikit-learn website[48] for current documentation and examples.

---

[48] http://scikit-learn.org/stable/modules/pipeline.html

Save the Model — Pickle and Joblib

Going through the development process, including validation, the model that was eventually chosen was produced by:

```
model.fit
```

The predictions of that model were made by:

```
model.predict
```

The *fit* function produced the "A" array and stored it in local variables within the model. During development, those two statements were sequential in the same program. Nothing happened to change anything within the model's local variables between the time the model was created and subsequently used. In order to make predictions with new data in a different portion of a Python program, and in particular in a different program some hours or days after the model was created, it must be stored in some location after fitting and retrieved later when needed. The *pickle* and *joblib* functions handle storing and reloading.

Pickle stores the model in a Python variable, then retrieves it in the same program, using the following sequence:

```
import pickle
model.fit(X,y)
s = pickle.dumps(model)
#  Other processing
model2 = pickle.loads(s)
newy = model2.predict(newX)
print newy
```

Joblib stores the model to a disk file, using the following sequences:

Fit a model, then save it:

```
from sklearn.externals import joblib
model.fit(X,y)
joblib.dump(model, 'modelFile.pkl')
```

At some later time, probably in some other Python program, retrieve the model and use it to predict:

```
from sklearn.externals import joblib
model2 = joblib.load('modelFile.pkl')
newy = model2.predict(newX)
print newy
```

No further training is required. The "A" array was retrieved by the load function. But the data must be consistent throughout.

Save Best Estimate

Decide what trades from the system—daily marked-to-market changes in the price of the primary data series, augmented by whatever additional trades you feel make the result a better estimate of future performance—will be saved as the *best estimate* set of results. Save these to a disk file, from which they will be read by the trading management routines as discussed in Chapter 9. If you plan to forecast two years ahead, begin with a best estimate set of at least four years.

Toxic Trades—Two Modeling Phases

In Chapter 2 we saw the importance of avoiding large losing trades. Call them *toxic trades*. Rather than just dividing days into two classes, long and flat, you might want to identify and model three classes of days—toxic, long, and flat.

Maximum growth suggests taking many profitable trades. Minimizing risk suggests avoiding toxic trades. We could set up a multiple classification, such as the original iris problem. Instead, we will invoke sequential coverage and model in two phases:

Phase 1 Avoid toxic trades.

Phase 2 Discover profitable trades.

Phase 1—Avoid toxic trades
- A. Define toxic trades.
- B. Treat toxic as the positive class. Label all days as either *toxic*, +1, or *benign*, -1.
- C. Develop a model that predicts toxic.
- D. False negative is the expensive error. Minimize the number of days that are falsely predicted to be benign, but are actually toxic.
- E. Be willing to miss some winners to eliminate serious losers.
- F. Remove all days predicted to be toxic from further analysis and modeling.
- G. Create a new data array that has records for only those days predicted to be benign. Pass this array to phase 2. Phase 2 will not even see the days that were removed.

A prediction to be toxic is not necessarily a signal to be short. For example, the model may associate being toxic with being volatile, recognize a period of high volatility, and predict a day to be toxic when it is not. Our research indicates we should gladly suffer some loss of opportunity in order to avoid serious loss of money. It is only by working through the complete sequence of creating the best estimate set, estimating risk, determining safe-f, estimating profit, and determining CAR25, that we can judge where to set the tradeoff boundary.

The confusion matrix associated with predicting toxic or benign is shown in Figure 8.73. We hope to eliminate false negatives, the upper right off-diagonal cell. Those errors occur when the prediction is for a benign day when it is actually toxic. Every remaining false negative is an error that allows a toxic day to pass to the second phase.

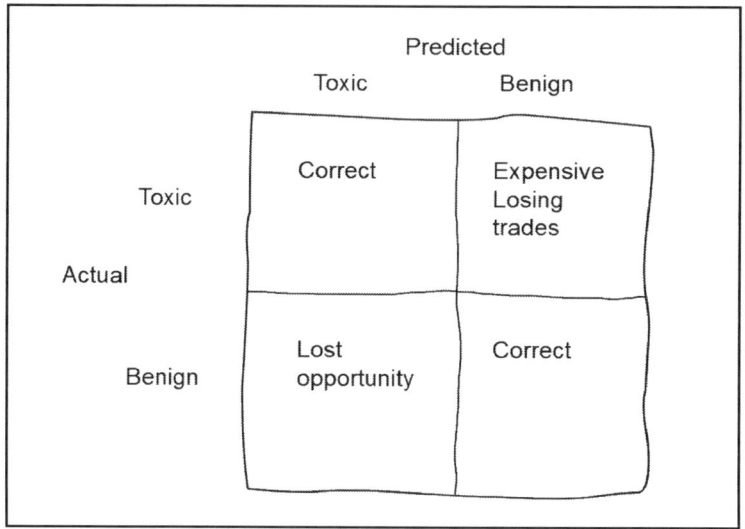

Figure 8.73 Confusion matrix for predicting toxic or benign

Phase 2—Discover profitable trades, as was previously described
   A. Define profitable trades.
   B. Treat being long as the positive class. Label all days as either *beLong*, +1, or *beFlat*, -1.
   C. Develop a model that predicts beLong.
   D. False positive is the expensive error. Minimize the number of days that are actually losers, but were predicted to be winners.

The confusion matrix associated with predicting beLong or beFlat is shown in Figure 8.74. We hope to eliminate false positives, the lower left off-diagonal cell. Those errors occur when the prediction is for a rising price, generating a signal to be long, when a falling price actually occurs and the correct classification is to go flat or remain flat.

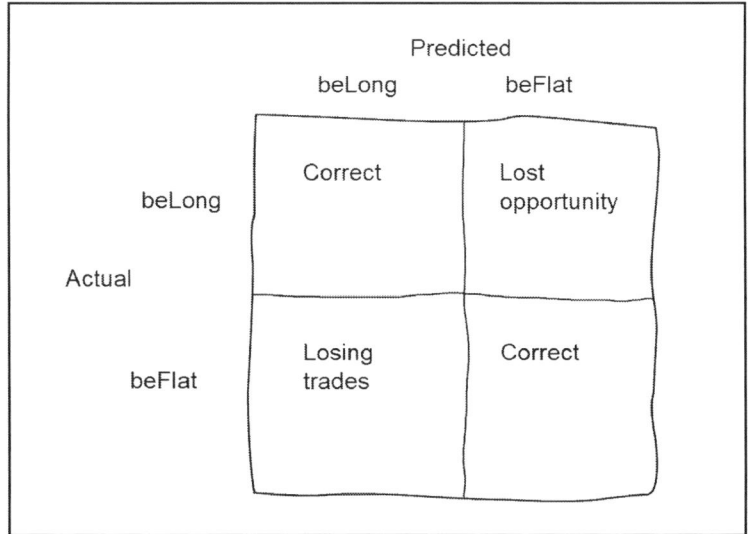

Figure 8.74 Confusion matrix for predicting beLong or beFlat

If you do decide to model toxic / benign, it does not require a separate program. It can be done as preliminary in the same program that models beLong /beFlat. Whether it is worth doing depends on the distribution of losing trades in the false positive quadrant of the beLong / beFlat model's confusion matrix. Work through the risk-normalized profit potential of the alternatives to decide.

If you are planning a hybrid trading system using both trading system development platform and machine learning models, identifying toxic trades is an excellent task for the machine learning component. Replace Phase 2 described here with a TSDP model. Entering a long trade requires a beLong or Buy signal from the TSDP model, along with a confirming prediction of benign from the machine learning model.

Example Trading System in Python

The Python program that follows in Figure 8.75 is approximately equivalent to the RSI2 program used for previous example. The primary data series is XLV, and the date range tested is 2008 through 2011. Data is obtained from Quandl.

Several functions are defined, but not used. If you will not need them, they can be removed.

The main program begins at the double dashed line about half way through the listing.

Where practical, program variables and meta-variables are gathered into one section of the listing and assigned as variables with names. You may wish to automate searches over some of these.

The Quandl authorization token listed will work for limited testing. Register with Quandl[49] to receive a token of your own which will increase the limits.

Note that several predictor variables were defined, computed, tested, and are being omitted from this run. They have been left in place, but commented out. Adding predictor variables to the model and removing them from the model is as easy as removing or adding the single comment character.

Data is prepared and stored in pandas dataframes through the construction of the target variable and predictor variables. When those steps are complete, the data is copied to numpy arrays, then split into train and test data sets using stratified shuffle split.

Two confusion matrices are prepared and initialized—one for the in-sample results, the other for out-of-sample.

The model is fit, then tested, for however many iterations were requested. Multiple iterations give an estimate of robustness. After each fitting and testing, the confusion matrices are updated. After all iterations, the two confusion matrices are printed and the run is complete.

The confusion matrices that are produced by this example are shown in Figure 8.76, following the listing.

To be clear. This is an example. A template. Within a few hours of copying it into your own Python environment, changing the primary data series, adding predictor variables, and modifying parameters, you will have different and probably much better results.

```
"""
QTA_Chapter8_Template.py

Disclaimer continues to apply

Copyright  2014 Blue Owl Press, Inc
Dr. Howard Bandy

"""

import math
import numpy as np
import pandas as pd
import Quandl
from sklearn.cross_validation import StratifiedShuffleSplit
from sklearn.linear_model import LogisticRegression
from sklearn.metrics import confusion_matrix
```

---

[49] https://www.quandl.com/

```python
#   -------------------------------
#   Define functions.
#   These are retained in the template for reference and
#   use when needed.

def RSI(p,lb):
    # RSI technical indicator.
    # p, the series having its RSI computed.
    # lb, the lookback period, does not need to be integer.
    #     typical values in the range of 1.5 to 5.0.
    # Return is a numpy array with values in the range 0.0 to 1.0.
    nrows = p.shape[0]
    lam = 2.0 / (lb + 1.0)
    UpMove = np.zeros(nrows)
    DnMove = np.zeros(nrows)
    UpMoveSm = np.zeros(nrows)
    DnMoveSm = np.zeros(nrows)
    Numer = np.zeros(nrows)
    Denom = np.zeros(nrows)
    pChg = np.zeros(nrows)
    RSISeries = np.zeros(nrows)
    # Compute pChg in points using a loop.
    for i in range (1,nrows):
        pChg[i] = p[i] - p[i-1]
    # Compute pChg as a percentage using a built-in method.
#       pChg = p.pct_change()
    UpMove = np.where(pChg>0,pChg,0)
    DnMove = np.where(pChg<0,-pChg,0)
    
    for i in range(1,nrows):
        UpMoveSm[i] = lam*UpMove[i] + (1.0-lam)*UpMoveSm[i-1]
        DnMoveSm[i] = lam*DnMove[i] + (1.0-lam)*DnMoveSm[i-1]
        Numer[i] = UpMoveSm[i]
        Denom[i] = UpMoveSm[i] + DnMoveSm[i]
        if Denom[i] <= 0:
            RSISeries[i] = 0.5
        else:
            RSISeries[i] =  Numer[i]/Denom[i]
    return(RSISeries)
#   -------------------------------

def ROC(p,lb):
    # Rate of change technical indicator.
    # p, the series having its ROC computed.
    # lb, the lookback period.  Typically 1.
    # Return is a numpy array with values as decimal fractions.
    # A 1% change is 0.01.
    nrows = p.shape[0]
    r = np.zeros(nrows)
    for i in range(lb, nrows):
        r[i] = (p[i]-p[i-lb])/p[i-lb]
    return(r)
#   -------------------------------

def zScore(p,lb):
    # z score statistic.
    # p, the series having its z-score computed.
    # lb, the lookback period, an integer.
    #     the length used for the average and standard deviation.
    #     typical values 3 to 10.
    # Return is a numpy array with values as z-scores centered on 0.0.
```

```python
        nrows = p.shape[0]
        st = np.zeros(nrows)
        ma = np.zeros(nrows)
        # use the pandas sliding window functions.
        st = pd.rolling_std(p,lb)
        ma = pd.rolling_mean(p,lb)
        z = np.zeros(nrows)
        for i in range(lb,nrows):
            z[i] = (p[i]-ma[i])/st[i]
        return(z)
    #   --------------------------------

    def softmax(p,lb,lam):
        # softmax transformation.
        # p, the series being transformed.
        # lb, the lookback period, an integer.
        #     the length used for the average and standard deviation.
        #     typical values 20 to 252.  Be aware of ramp-up requirement.
        # lam, the length of the linear section.
        #     in standard deviations.
        #     typical value is 6.
        # Return is a numpy array with values in the range 0.0 to 1.0.
        nrows = p.shape[0]
        a = np.zeros(nrows)
        ma = np.zeros(nrows)
        sd = np.zeros(nrows)
        sm = np.zeros(nrows)
        sq = np.zeros(nrows)
        y = np.zeros(nrows)
        for i in range(lb,nrows):
            sm[i] = sm[i]+p[i]
        ma[i] = sm[i] / lb
        for i in range(lb,nrows):
            sq[i] = (p[i]-ma[i])*(p[i]-ma[i])
        sd[i] = math.sqrt(sq[i]/(nrows-1))
        for i in range(lb,nrows):
            a[i] = (p[i]-ma[i])/((lam*sd[i])/(2.0*math.pi))
            y[i] = 1.0 / (1.0 + math.e**a[i])
        return(y)

    #   -----------------------------


    def DPO(p,lb):
        # Detrended price oscillator.
        # A high pass filter.
        # p, the series being transformed.
        # lb, the lookback period, a real number.
        # Uses pandas ewma function.
        # Return is a numpy array with values centered on 0.0.
        nrows = p.shape[0]
        ma = pd.ewma(p,span=lb)
        d = np.zeros(nrows)
        for i in range(1,nrows):
            d[i] = (p[i]-ma[i])/ma[i]
        return(d)
    #   --------------------------------
```

```python
def numberZeros(p):
    # Counts the number of zero crossings.
    # p, the series being counted.
    # Return is an integer.
    # The number of times p crosses up through 0.0.
    nrows = p.shape[0]
    nz = 0
    for i in range(1,nrows):
        if (p[i-1]<0 and p[i]>=0):
            nz = nz+1
    return(nz)

def gainAhead(p):
    # Computes change in the next 1 bar.
    # p, the base series.
    # Return is a numpy array of changes.
    # A change of 1% is 0.01
    # The final value is unknown.  Its value is 0.0.
    nrows = p.shape[0]
    g = np.zeros(nrows)
    for i in range(0,nrows-1):
        g[i] = (p[i+1]-p[i])/p[i]
    return(g)

def ATR(ph,pl,pc,lb):
    # Average True Range technical indicator.
    # ph, pl, pc are the series high, low, and close.
    # lb, the lookback period.  An integer number of bars.
    # True range is computed as a fraction of the closing
            price.
    # Return is a numpy array of floating point values.
    # Values are non-negative, with a minimum of 0.0.
    # An ATR of 5 points on a issue closing at 50 is
    #    reported as 0.10.
    nrows = pc.shape[0]
    th = np.zeros(nrows)
    tl = np.zeros(nrows)
    tc = np.zeros(nrows)
    tr = np.zeros(nrows)
    trAvg = np.zeros(nrows)
    
    for i in range(1,nrows):
        if ph[i] > pc[i-1]:
            th[i] = ph[i]
        else:
            th[i] = pc[i-1]
        if pl[i] < pc[i-1]:
            tl[i] = pl[i]
        else:
            tl[i] = pc[i-1]
        tr[i] = th[i] - tl[i]
    for i in range(lb,nrows):
        trAvg[i] = tr[i]
        for j in range(1,lb-1):
            trAvg[i] = trAvg[i] + tr[i-j]
        trAvg[i] = trAvg[i] / lb
        trAvg[i] = trAvg[i] / pc[i]
    return(trAvg)

# ---------------------------------
```

```
def priceChange(p):
    nrows = p.shape[0]
    pc = np.zeros(nrows)
    for i in range(1,nrows):
        pc[i] = (p[i]-p[i-1])/p[i-1]
    return pc

#   ------------------------------------------------------
#   ------------------------------------------------------

#   Download data
print "\nReading data from Quandl "

ticker = "GOOG/NYSE_XLV"
dataLoadStartDate = "1998-12-22"
dataLoadEndDate = "2016-01-04"
testFirstYear = "2008"
testFinalYear = "2011"
iterations = 100

RSILookback = 1.0
zScoreLookback = 10
ATRLookback = 5
beLongThreshold = 0.0

model = LogisticRegression()

qt = Quandl.get(ticker, trim_start=dataLoadStartDate,
                trim_end=dataLoadEndDate,
             authtoken="abc123")

print "Successfully retrieved Primary"

dataSet = qt
dataSet['Pri'] = qt.Close
dataSet['Pri_RSI'] = RSI(dataSet.Pri,RSILookback)
#dataSet['Pri_ATR'] = zScore(ATR(qt.High,qt.Low,
#                    qt.Close,ATRLookback),
#                    zScoreLookback)
#dataSet['Pri_ATR_Y1'] = dataSet['Pri_ATR'].shift(1)
#dataSet['Pri_ATR_Y2'] = dataSet['Pri_ATR'].shift(2)
#dataSet['Pri_ATR_Y3'] = dataSet['Pri_ATR'].shift(3)
#dataSet['priceChange'] = priceChange(dataSet['Pri'])
#dataSet['priceChangeY1'] = dataSet['priceChange'].shift(1)
#dataSet['priceChangeY2'] = dataSet['priceChange'].shift(2)
#dataSet['priceChangeY3'] = dataSet['priceChange'].shift(3)
dataSet['Pri_RSI_Y1'] = dataSet['Pri_RSI'].shift(1)
dataSet['Pri_RSI_Y2'] = dataSet['Pri_RSI'].shift(2)
dataSet['Pri_RSI_Y3'] = dataSet['Pri_RSI'].shift(3)
#dataSet['Pri_RSI_Y4'] = dataSet['Pri_RSI'].shift(4)

dataSet['gainAhead'] = gainAhead(dataSet.Close)
dataSet['beLong'] = np.where(dataSet.gainAhead>beLongThreshold,1,-1)

mData = dataSet.drop(['Open','High','Low','Close',
                      'Volume','Pri','gainAhead'],
                     axis=1)

#   Select the date range to test
mmData = mData.ix[testFirstYear:testFinalYear]
```

```
datay = mmData.beLong
mmData = mmData.drop(['beLong'],axis=1)
dataX = mmData

#  Copy from pandas dataframe to numpy arrays
dy = np.zeros_like(datay)
dX = np.zeros_like(dataX)

dy = datay.values
dX = dataX.values

#  Make 'iterations' index vectors for the train-test split
sss = StratifiedShuffleSplit(dy,iterations,test_size=0.33,
                             random_state=None)

#  Initialize the confusion matrix
cm_sum_is = np.zeros((2,2))
cm_sum_oos = np.zeros((2,2))

#  For each entry in the set of splits, fit and predict
for train_index,test_index in sss:
    X_train, X_test = dX[train_index], dX[test_index]
    y_train, y_test = dy[train_index], dy[test_index]

#  fit the model to the in-sample data
    model.fit(X_train, y_train)

#  test the in-sample fit
    y_pred_is = model.predict(X_train)
    cm_is = confusion_matrix(y_train, y_pred_is)
    cm_sum_is = cm_sum_is + cm_is

#  test the out-of-sample data
    y_pred_oos = model.predict(X_test)
    cm_oos = confusion_matrix(y_test, y_pred_oos)
    cm_sum_oos = cm_sum_oos + cm_oos

tpIS = cm_sum_is[1,1]
fnIS = cm_sum_is[1,0]
fpIS = cm_sum_is[0,1]
tnIS = cm_sum_is[0,0]
precisionIS = tpIS/(tpIS+fpIS)
recallIS = tpIS/(tpIS+fnIS)
accuracyIS = (tpIS+tnIS)/(tpIS+fnIS+fpIS+tnIS)
f1IS = (2.0 * precisionIS * recallIS) / (precisionIS+recallIS)

tpOOS = cm_sum_oos[1,1]
fnOOS = cm_sum_oos[1,0]
fpOOS = cm_sum_oos[0,1]
tnOOS = cm_sum_oos[0,0]
precisionOOS = tpOOS/(tpOOS+fpOOS)
recallOOS = tpOOS/(tpOOS+fnOOS)
accuracyOOS = (tpOOS+tnOOS)/(tpOOS+fnOOS+fpOOS+tnOOS)
f1OOS = (2.0 * precisionOOS * recallOOS) /
           (precisionOOS+recallOOS)

print "\n\nSymbol is ", ticker
print "Learning algorithm is Logistic Regression"
print "Confusion matrix for %i randomized tests" % iterations
print "for years ", testFirstYear, " through ", testFinalYear
```

```
    print "\nIn sample"
    print "     predicted"
    print "      pos neg"
    print "pos:  %i   %i   %.2f" % (tpIS, fnIS, recallIS)
    print "neg:  %i   %i" % (fpIS, tnIS)
    print "      %.2f         %.2f " % (precisionIS, accuracyIS)
    print "f1:   %.2f" % f1IS

    print "\nOut of sample"
    print "     predicted"
    print "      pos neg"
    print "pos:  %i   %i   %.2f" % (tpOOS, fnOOS, recallOOS)
    print "neg:  %i   %i" % (fpOOS, tnOOS)
    print "      %.2f         %.2f " % (precisionOOS, accuracyOOS)
    print "f1:   %.2f" % f1OOS

    print "\nend of run"

#   ////   end   ////
```

Figure 8.75 Python trading system template

```
Reading data from Quandl
Token abc123 activated and saved for later use.
Returning Dataframe for  GOOG/NYSE_XLV
Successfully retrieved Primary


Symbol is  GOOG/NYSE_XLV
Learning algorithm is Logistic Regression
Confusion matrix for 100 randomized tests
for years  2008  through  2011

In sample
     predicted
       pos neg
pos:  22058  12942   0.63
neg:  18306  15194
       0.55          0.54
f1:    0.59

Out of sample
     predicted
       pos neg
pos:  10424   6776   0.61
neg:   9401   7199
       0.53          0.52
f1:    0.56

end of run
```

Figure 8.76 Python trading system output

Train / Test / Validate

StratifiedShuffleSplit, or StratifiedKFold, divides a set of data into two subsets. One, *train*, is used to fit the model—to compute the "A" matrix. The second, *test*, is used to test the fit. For both sets, the correct value of the target is known. For the train set, the target provides the right-hand-side of the equations being solved. The model predicts the value for the data in the test set, and the scoring algorithm compares the known target with the predicted target. Review Figures 8.31 through 8.34.

As you read machine learning literature, the result of the scoring algorithm, such as the confusion matrix's *recall* metric, is used to decide whether the fit is adequate. As part of the model development process, you will try many combinations of predictor variables, parameters, and meta-parameters. Many model.fit / model.predict / score runs are made, modifying the system based on the score. At the end of that process, the score is high. Fit and predict agree. The *test* data was used not only to test the fit, but also to guide the fit. It may have started out as out-of-sample data, but by the end of the model fitting process it is in-sample data.

If the purpose of the model is explanatory, or predictive of a stationary system, that causes little concern. As I have pointed out several times, predicting financial time series data is different. We need evidence that the system will predict accurately for data that has not been used in development. The validation process serves that purpose. Figure 8.77 illustrates.

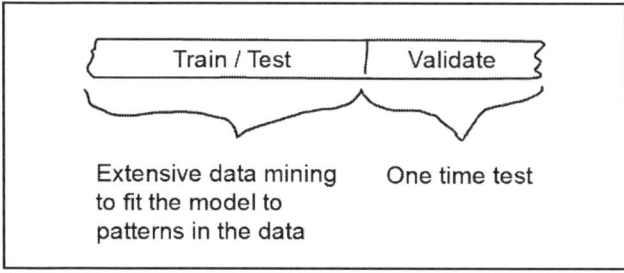

Figure 8.77 Relationship of validation data to train and test data

It is precisely the relationship shown in Figure 6.15, relabeled to the terminology of this chapter's material. And when the train / test / validate is stepped forward, it corresponds with the walk forward process described in Chapter 6 with Figures 6.18 through 6.21.

Figure 8.78 shows the use of the validation set, following and building on the schematic flow shown in Figures 8.31 through 8.34. Specifically, the validation data is processed in the same way the X_Test data was processed in Figure 8.33. The *Model Prediction Procedure* generates an array, named y_Validate in both the figure following and the program following, where each row is a prediction to beLong or beFlat. The gain is known. Those days that are predicted to beLong are days a long position would have been held, and the gainAhead of the primary data series is credited to the trading account. Those days that are predicted to beFlat, the account would earn risk-free interest, which we assume to be zero. The result is a set of out-of-sample marked-to-market one day holding trades, the *best estimate* set of trades, and the equity curve created by them. These daily trades are the same as those produced by a trading system development platform system.

Model Development - Machine Learning

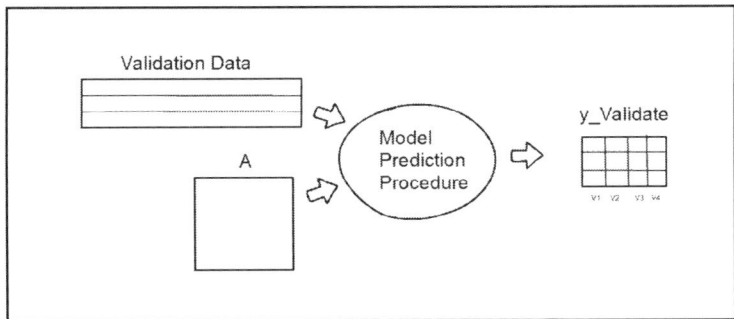

Figure 8.78 Schematic of using the validation data set

y_Validate is conceptually a composite of four vectors, each with as many rows as the validation data has.
- V1 is the prediction generated by the model. It's entries are either beLong or beFlat.
- V2 is the gain for the next day—gainAhead. The amounts are known for all days except the final day.
- V3 is the realized gain. When the prediction is beLong, the account changes by the amount in gainAhead. When the prediction is beFlat, the account grows by the risk-free amount, which for this analysis is we assume to be zero.
- V4 is the cumulative equity. When plotted, it is the equivalent of the equity curve shown in Figure 7.37 or 7.38—an equity curve produced from the out-of-sample trades of a walk forward process.

The out-of-sample marked-to-market daily gain is the *best estimate* of future performance of this system.

Note that, just as with the TSDP system, repeated generation of out-of-sample results followed by modification of any part of the system erodes the out-of-sampleness. Strictly speaking, you only get one bite at this apple. Be conservative when considering modifying the system based on OOS results.

Figure 8.79 lists a program that computes the out-of-sample marked-to-market trades for a single validation period.

```
"""
QTA_Chapter8_Validate.py

Disclaimer continues to apply

Copyright  2014 Blue Owl Press, Inc
Dr. Howard Bandy

"""
```

```python
import math
import matplotlib.pyplot as plt
import numpy as np
import pandas as pd
import Quandl
from sklearn.cross_validation import StratifiedShuffleSplit
from sklearn.linear_model import LogisticRegression
from sklearn.metrics import confusion_matrix

# --------------------------------
# Define functions.
# These are retained in the template for reference and
# use when needed.

def RSI(p,lb):
    # RSI technical indicator.
    # p, the series having its RSI computed.
    # lb, the lookback period, does not need to be integer.
    #     typical values in the range of 1.5 to 5.0.
    # Return is a numpy array with values in the range 0.0 to
    #      1.0.
    nrows = p.shape[0]
    lam = 2.0 / (lb + 1.0)
    UpMove = np.zeros(nrows)
    DnMove = np.zeros(nrows)
    UpMoveSm = np.zeros(nrows)
    DnMoveSm = np.zeros(nrows)
    Numer = np.zeros(nrows)
    Denom = np.zeros(nrows)
    pChg = np.zeros(nrows)
    RSISeries = np.zeros(nrows)
    # Compute pChg in points using a loop.
    for i in range (1,nrows):
        pChg[i] = p[i] - p[i-1]
    # Compute pChg as a percentage using a built-in method.
#     pChg = p.pct_change()
    UpMove = np.where(pChg>0,pChg,0)
    DnMove = np.where(pChg<0,-pChg,0)

    for i in range(1,nrows):
        UpMoveSm[i] = lam*UpMove[i] + (1.0-lam)*UpMoveSm[i-1]
        DnMoveSm[i] = lam*DnMove[i] + (1.0-lam)*DnMoveSm[i-1]
        Numer[i] = UpMoveSm[i]
        Denom[i] = UpMoveSm[i] + DnMoveSm[i]
        if Denom[i] <= 0:
            RSISeries[i] = 0.5
        else:
            RSISeries[i] =  Numer[i]/Denom[i]
    return(RSISeries)
# --------------------------------

def zScore(p,lb):
    # z score statistic.
    # p, the series having its z-score computed.
    # lb, the lookback period, an integer.
    #     the length used for the average and standard
    #        deviation.
    #     typical values 3 to 10.
    # Return is a numpy array with values as z-scores centered
    #      on 0.0.
    nrows = p.shape[0]
    st = np.zeros(nrows)
```

```python
    ma = np.zeros(nrows)
    # use the pandas sliding window functions.
    st = pd.rolling_std(p,lb)
    ma = pd.rolling_mean(p,lb)
    z = np.zeros(nrows)
    for i in range(lb,nrows):
        z[i] = (p[i]-ma[i])/st[i]
    return(z)
# ---------------------------------

def gainAhead(p):
    # Computes change in the next 1 bar.
    # p, the base series.
    # Return is a numpy array of changes.
    # A change of 1% is 0.01
    # The final value is unknown.  Its value is 0.0.
    nrows = p.shape[0]
    g = np.zeros(nrows)
    for i in range(0,nrows-1):
        g[i] = (p[i+1]-p[i])/p[i]
    return(g)

def ATR(ph,pl,pc,lb):
    # Average True Range technical indicator.
    # ph, pl, pc are the series high, low, and close.
    # lb, the lookback period.  An integer number of bars.
    # True range is computed as a fraction of the closing
    #       price.
    # Return is a numpy array of floating point values.
    # Values are non-negative, with a minimum of 0.0.
    # An ATR of 5 points on a issue closing at 50 is
    #     reported as 0.10.
    nrows = pc.shape[0]
    th = np.zeros(nrows)
    tl = np.zeros(nrows)
    tc = np.zeros(nrows)
    tr = np.zeros(nrows)
    trAvg = np.zeros(nrows)
    
    for i in range(1,nrows):
        if ph[i] > pc[i-1]:
            th[i] = ph[i]
        else:
            th[i] = pc[i-1]
        if pl[i] < pc[i-1]:
            tl[i] = pl[i]
        else:
            tl[i] = pc[i-1]
        tr[i] = th[i] - tl[i]
    for i in range(lb,nrows):
        trAvg[i] = tr[i]
        for j in range(1,lb-1):
            trAvg[i] = trAvg[i] + tr[i-j]
        trAvg[i] = trAvg[i] / lb
        trAvg[i] = trAvg[i] / pc[i]
    return(trAvg)
# ---------------------------------
```

```python
def priceChange(p):
    nrows = p.shape[0]
    pc = np.zeros(nrows)
    for i in range(1,nrows):
        pc[i] = (p[i]-p[i-1])/p[i-1]
    return pc

#  -----------------------------------------------
#  -----------------------------------------------

#  Download data
print "\nReading data from Quandl "


ticker = "GOOG/NYSE_XLV"
dataLoadStartDate = "1998-12-22"
dataLoadEndDate = "2016-01-04"
testFirstYear = "2000"
testFinalYear = "2009"
validationFirstYear = "2010"
validationFinalYear = "2014"
iterations = 1

RSILookback = 1.5
zScoreLookback = 10
ATRLookback = 15
beLongThreshold = 0.0

model = LogisticRegression()

qt = Quandl.get(ticker, trim_start=dataLoadStartDate,
                trim_end=dataLoadEndDate,
                authtoken="abc123")

print "Successfully retrieved Primary"

dataSet = qt
dataSet['Pri'] = qt.Close
dataSet['Pri_RSI'] = RSI(dataSet.Pri,RSILookback)
dataSet['Pri_ATR'] = zScore(ATR(qt.High,qt.Low,qt.
        Close,ATRLookback),
                  zScoreLookback)
dataSet['Pri_ATR_Y1'] = dataSet['Pri_ATR'].shift(1)
dataSet['Pri_ATR_Y2'] = dataSet['Pri_ATR'].shift(2)
dataSet['Pri_ATR_Y3'] = dataSet['Pri_ATR'].shift(3)
dataSet['priceChange'] = priceChange(dataSet['Pri'])
dataSet['priceChangeY1'] = dataSet['priceChange'].shift(1)
dataSet['priceChangeY2'] = dataSet['priceChange'].shift(2)
dataSet['priceChangeY3'] = dataSet['priceChange'].shift(3)
dataSet['Pri_RSI_Y1'] = dataSet['Pri_RSI'].shift(1)
dataSet['Pri_RSI_Y2'] = dataSet['Pri_RSI'].shift(2)
dataSet['Pri_RSI_Y3'] = dataSet['Pri_RSI'].shift(3)
dataSet['Pri_RSI_Y4'] = dataSet['Pri_RSI'].shift(4)

dataSet['gainAhead'] = gainAhead(dataSet['Pri'])
dataSet['beLong'] = np.where(dataSet.
        gainAhead>beLongThreshold,1,-1)

nrows = dataSet.shape[0]
gainArray = np.zeros(nrows)
```

```python
mData = dataSet.drop(['Open','High','Low','Close',
                      'Volume','Pri','gainAhead'],
                     axis=1)
validationData = dataSet.drop(['Open','High','Low','Close',
                      'Volume','Pri'],
                     axis=1)

#  Select the date range to test
mmData = mData.ix[testFirstYear:testFinalYear]

datay = mmData.beLong
mmData = mmData.drop(['beLong'],axis=1)
dataX = mmData

#  Copy from pandas dataframe to numpy arrays
dy = np.zeros_like(datay)
dX = np.zeros_like(dataX)

dy = datay.values
dX = dataX.values


#  Make 'iterations' index vectors for the train-test split
sss = StratifiedShuffleSplit(dy,iterations,test_size=0.33,
                             random_state=None)

#  Initialize the confusion matrix
cm_sum_is = np.zeros((2,2))
cm_sum_oos = np.zeros((2,2))

#  For each entry in the set of splits, fit and predict
for train_index,test_index in sss:
    X_train, X_test = dX[train_index], dX[test_index]
    y_train, y_test = dy[train_index], dy[test_index]

#   fit the model to the in-sample data
    model.fit(X_train, y_train)

#   test the in-sample fit
    y_pred_is = model.predict(X_train)
    cm_is = confusion_matrix(y_train, y_pred_is)
    cm_sum_is = cm_sum_is + cm_is

#   test the out-of-sample data
    y_pred_oos = model.predict(X_test)
    cm_oos = confusion_matrix(y_test, y_pred_oos)
    cm_sum_oos = cm_sum_oos + cm_oos

tpIS = cm_sum_is[1,1]
fnIS = cm_sum_is[1,0]
fpIS = cm_sum_is[0,1]
tnIS = cm_sum_is[0,0]
precisionIS = tpIS/(tpIS+fpIS)
recallIS = tpIS/(tpIS+fnIS)
accuracyIS = (tpIS+tnIS)/(tpIS+fnIS+fpIS+tnIS)
f1IS = (2.0 * precisionIS * recallIS) / (precisionIS+recallIS)

tpOOS = cm_sum_oos[1,1]
fnOOS = cm_sum_oos[1,0]
fpOOS = cm_sum_oos[0,1]
tnOOS = cm_sum_oos[0,0]
precisionOOS = tpOOS/(tpOOS+fpOOS)
```

```
    recallOOS = tpOOS/(tpOOS+fnOOS)
    accuracyOOS = (tpOOS+tnOOS)/(tpOOS+fnOOS+fpOOS+tnOOS)
    f1OOS = (2.0 * precisionOOS * recallOOS) / (precisionOOS+recallOOS)

    print "\n\nSymbol is ", ticker
    print "Learning algorithm is Logistic Regression"
    print "Confusion matrix for %i randomized tests" % iterations
    print "for years ", testFirstYear, " through ", testFinalYear

    print "\nIn sample"
    print "       predicted"
    print "        pos neg"
    print "pos:   %i  %i  %.2f" % (tpIS, fnIS, recallIS)
    print "neg:   %i  %i" % (fpIS, tnIS)
    print "       %.2f         %.2f " % (precisionIS, accuracyIS)
    print "f1:    %.2f" % f1IS

    print "\nOut of sample"
    print "       predicted"
    print "        pos neg"
    print "pos:   %i  %i  %.2f" % (tpOOS, fnOOS, recallOOS)
    print "neg:   %i  %i" % (fpOOS, tnOOS)
    print "       %.2f         %.2f " % (precisionOOS, accuracyOOS)
    print "f1:    %.2f" % f1OOS

    #  ----------------------------------------------
    #  Validation
    #
    #  Validation data has not been used in development
    #
    #  The validationData dataFrame was created from
    #    the dataSet dataFrame
    #
    #  Select the date range
    print "\nBeginning validation of period " , validationFirstYear,\
          "through ", validationFinalYear

    #  Leave validationData intact to allow testing other date ranges
    vDataRange = validationData.ix[validationFirstYear: 
                   validationFinalYear]

    valRows = vDataRange.shape[0]
    print "There are %i data points" % valRows

    #  Data passed to predict must be the same format as dX
    #  Create a new variable, retaining the gainAhead field
    #    in vDataRange for creation of best estimate set
    #    and equity curve
    vData = vDataRange.drop(['gainAhead','beLong'],axis=1)

    #  test the validation data
    y_validate = model.predict(vData)

    #  Create the best estimate set of trades
    bestEstimate = np.zeros(valRows)

    #  You may need to adjust for the first and / or final entry
    for i in range(valRows-1):
    #    print newData.gainAhead.iloc[i], newy[i], equity[i-1]
        if y_validate[i] > 0.0:
            bestEstimate[i] = vDataRange.gainAhead.iloc[i]
        else:
            bestEstimate[i] = 0.0
```

```
#  Create and plot the equity curve
equity= np.zeros(valRows)
equity[0] = 1.0
for i in range(1,valRows):
    equity[i] = (1+bestEstimate[i])*equity[i-1]

print "\nTerminal wealth: ", equity[valRows-1]
plt.plot(equity)

print "\nend of run"
print

#  /////  end  /////ss
```

Figure 8.79 Program to create a best estimate set of trades

```
Reading data from Quandl
Token a   activated and saved for later use.
Returning Dataframe for  GOOG/NYSE_XLV
Successfully retrieved Primary


Symbol is  GOOG/NYSE_XLV
Learning algorithm is Logistic Regression
Confusion matrix for 1 randomized tests
for years  2000  through   2009

In sample
     predicted
       pos neg
pos:   421  422   0.50
neg:   395  451
       0.52          0.52
f1:    0.51

Out of sample
     predicted
       pos neg
pos:   197  219   0.47
neg:   199  218
       0.50          0.50
f1:    0.49

Beginning validation of period  2010 through  2014
There are 1259 data points

Terminal wealth:   2.43627036107

end of run
```

Figure 8.80 Output from program to create a best estimate set of trades

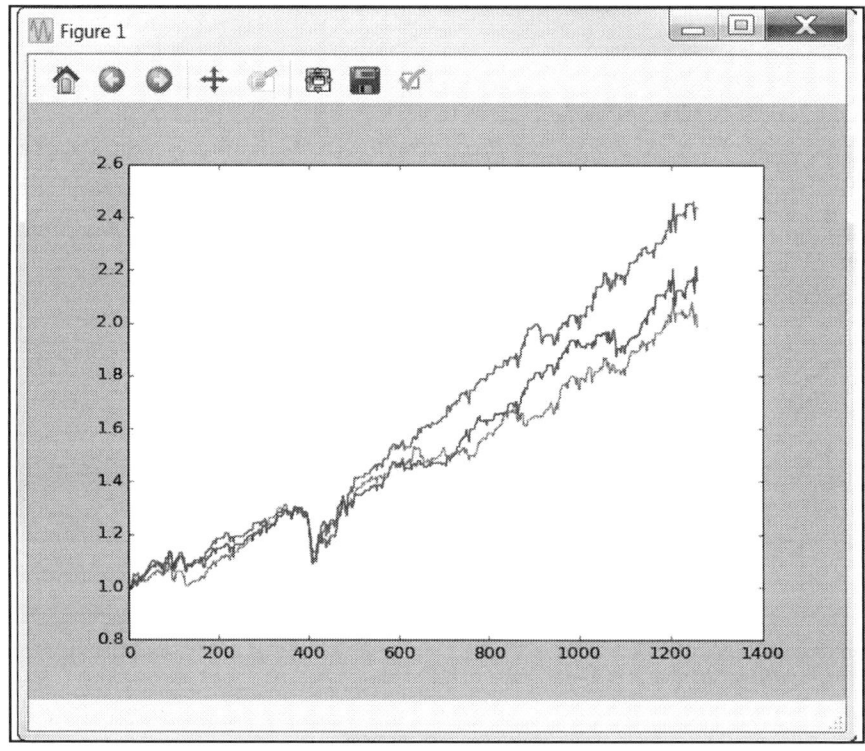

Figure 8.81 Equity curves for validation period—three separate runs

Caution

Do not begin the validation phase until you are as satisfied with the system as you can be based on the fit / predict / score of single sets of train / test data. When you begin validation, you should consider the modeling phase complete. You will probably examine some meta-parameters, such as the length of the train / test period and the length of the validation period. But try to refrain from changing predictor variables or their parameters.

Coordination with a TSDP

There is no need to abandon your trading system development platform. If you are using, or want to use, a data provider who maintains the database you use (such as Norgate) and a trading system platform (such as AmiBroker) to calculate indicators and display charts, use a two-platform machine learning solution.

The logical transition is after data acquisition and preprocessing. The initial processing is done in the TSDP. It reads data, computes indicators, displays charts, and tests trading system ideas—all as usual. When you want to add the machine learning component, write a disk file in csv format that has everything needed by the Python program. Switch to Python, read the csv file (into one of the dataSet, mData, or dX and dy variables) and continue.

If you are in the development phase, continuation will be train / test split, then fit and score.

If you are in the trading phase, continuation will be retrieval of the model, retrieval or regeneration of the best estimate set, then calculation of safe-f and CAR25.

Coordination through the csv file is key.
- Decide which functions you want in your technical analysis program and which in Python.
- Decide what you want in the csv file. What fields and what format.
- Write and test the code required to write the file from your technical analysis program.
- Write and test the code required to read the file into the Python program and store it in the proper variables.

If necessary, or simply if you prefer, you can do data acquisition and preprocessing in both and combine them in the Python program. You might want to do this if you need a one-off data series that your database supplied does not provide, but an on-the-fly supplier, such as Quandl, does. If you do this, use of pandas dataframes will ease data alignment.

Transition to Trading

At this point, the trading system has been developed and validated. The best estimate set of trades will be used to determine the risk and profit potential. The model has been saved and can be retrieved and used to generate new signals and new trades from current data.

Since the evaluation of trades, determination of safe-f, estimate of CAR25, and decision to trade the system or take it off line will be made as a daily trading management activity, those functions are discussed in Chapter 9, Trading Management.

At the completion of validation, you have a system—a combination of a model and data—and you have a set of out-of-sample marked-to-market trades. These trades are the best estimate of future performance. Continuing to add one value to this set every day, and using it to determine the size of the position to hold, are functions of trading management. We go there next.

Summary—Calibrate Your Expectations

We are developing a practical business application, not solving a theoretical problem, not writing an academic paper.

Lower your expectations. Accuracy in the ninety percent range might be achievable when classifying plant species, but not when classifying trading signals.

Wanting a profitable system does not guarantee finding one, or even that one exists. The techniques and programs in this book should be seen as guides and templates, rather than solutions.

Our goal is maximum account growth for a defined level of risk. Our objective function is CAR25 estimated on out-of-sample data.

The profitability and tradability of the final model depends on successfully identifying, interpreting, and modeling many factors. Some are related to the markets, some to the trader, some to the modeling and simulation process, and some to selection of predictor variables.

Those readers who have experience using trading system development platforms know how easy it is to develop flawed systems.

Scikit-learn alone (there are other machine learning libraries) has expanded your options from that one technique to well over twenty. Without careful attention to good modeling and simulation practices, it will be 20 times easier to develop bad systems. If this happens, do not blame the tools.

Chapter 9
Trading Management

Trading management is all about position size. We regularly hear how important proper position size is to trading. I agree. I am one of the people advising traders to manage trading by managing position size.

If you were certain the issue you are trading would rise, you would take a large-sized long position. If that dusty lamp you found at a garage sale came with a genie who could read tomorrow's newspaper in his crystal ball with perfect accuracy, you could "bet the farm" taking a large long position when the genie predicted a rise, and remain flat when he predicted a drop. If his accuracy was less than perfect, but still good, you could still take a long position when he predicted a rise, relying on gains to exceed losses.

For a given distribution of price changes and genie accuracy, there is an optimal position size. If you have a different risk tolerance than I do, optimal for you will be different than optimal for me. But there is an optimal for each of us.

Provided the future distribution of price changes always matches the past distribution of price changes, one computation of optimal position size is sufficient. It will never change. That does not mean that account equity will not have drawdowns. It does mean that the shape of the equity curve going forward is the same no matter what the recent results.

The optimal position size depends on:
- The future distribution of price changes.
- The genie's accuracy.
- Your risk tolerance.

The game changes when either:
- The genie's crystal ball gets hazy and predictions are less accurate. Perhaps due to an increase in the noise relative to the signal in the data.
- The distribution of price changes changes. Perhaps due to changes in the economy, the business sector, the company, or whatever factors affect the issue being traded.

Either can happen quickly. We need tools that can help detect such a change so that we can react accordingly. The change, and our reaction to it, is recognition that the system is not stationary. Safe-f will drop in response to losing trades. CAR25 will drop as safe-f drops.

When CAR25 of the trading system is below the CAR25 of a risk-free alternative use of funds, the system is broken. Treat it as broken, not as a challenge to your resolve, not as an opportunity to bet big because the recovery is "due." It is irrational to believe that all drawdowns are temporary and your equity will always be restored.

The only data going into this decision is recent trade results. Your trading system model did not change. The patterns in the data series being processing changed. Why? For how long? Whether the explanations the news anchors tell us are accurate or not, the only measurable data we have is recent trades.

If the trading system results were stationary, trading management would be easy. We would have known the value of safe-f following the first in-sample test many hours of development effort ago. All four options for weighting the best estimate set would lead to the same safe-f and CAR25. (See the section on weights later in this chapter.) A single risk assessment based on the trades resulting from optimization of in-sample data, followed by computation of safe-f with respect to your personal risk tolerance, would identify the position size that could be used forever. There would be no need for further analysis. Losing periods would not matter. Systems would never fail. Every drawdown would be an opportunity to increase position size anticipating a rapid recovery.

If you, or your advisor, always stay the course, trade through adversity, use a predetermined position size, or include position size within the trading system, you are acting as if the system is stationary. If the degree of synchronization ever changes, your position size will be wrong. It will either be too high and you will go bankrupt, or too low and you will not achieve the account growth possible.

Developers, and article writers, who stop after in-sample testing are, incorrectly, assuming a stationary process.

It is because system performance ebbs and flows that dynamic position sizing is necessary. Figure 9.1 shows a summary of 4000 one-day trade results from one of the systems tested earlier. The 16 year sequence has been divided into 64 periods, each 63 trading days (3 months) long. The average daily gain for those days that were signaled to be long was computed for each period. The line and dots show the average gain, the bars at the bottom show how many of those 63 days have a signal to be long.

Mean and count do not provide sufficient information to estimate risk and determine position size. But they are sufficient to demonstrate that the performance of a trading system is not stationary. There must be a process to recognize changes in performance and modify position size in response. That process must act quickly enough to avoid losing money during unfavorable periods.

The size of your next trade is related to your confidence that it will be profitable. It is analogous to the weather forecast. When the radar shows a front approaching and the forecaster states there is a 90% chance of rain, you take your umbrella with you. The probability of rain is not based on repeated trials of the same experiment. It is a statement of confidence. (Given an opportunity for repeated trials, the statement of confidence and result of repeated trials will converge and agree.) The more (justifiably) confident you are that the next trade will be a winner, the higher your position size can, and should, be. As your confidence drops, your position size should also drop. If the system appears to be broken, the position size should be zero. You should take it offline and stop trading it until it demonstrates that it has recovered.

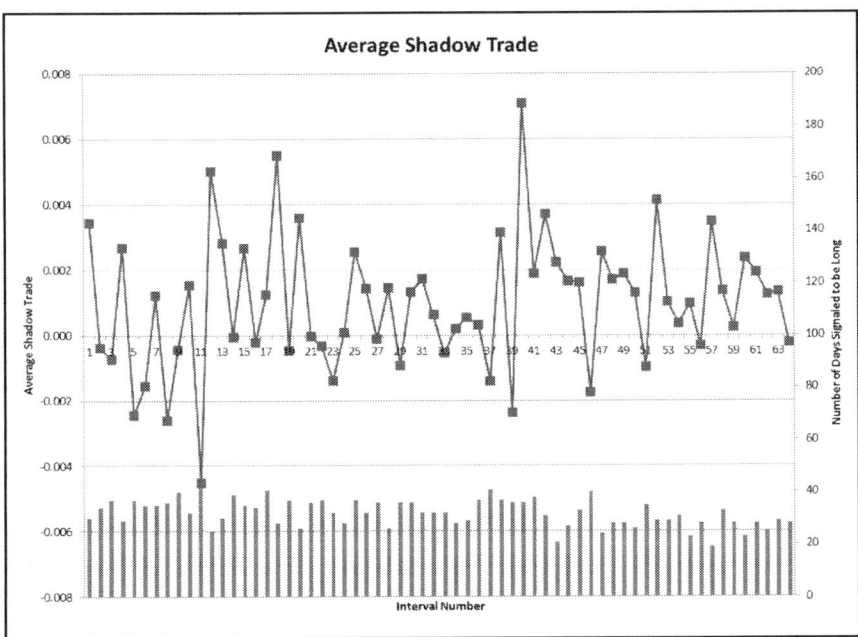

Figure 9.1 Synchronization between the model and the data is not stationary

The process depends on having a baseline distribution against which to compare new data. We want to detect when the new data is unlikely to have come from the same distribution. In the terminology of Bayesian analysis, the baseline is called the *prior distribution* or *probability*. The new data is the *likelihood*. The Statisticat website[1] has some excellent explanations.

After receiving new data, our confidence, our new estimate of the probability, may change. It is called the *posterior distribution*.

As with frequentist statistical analysis, confidence increases as the number of data points increases and the variability of the data decreases. Data quality matters. Having an unbiased and representative prior is important. For our analysis, the initial prior distribution is the best estimate set of trades from development's validation. As live trades are made, they will gradually replace the simulated trades. They arrive one-by-one and they have a time order. The trading management system's model must evaluate them one-by-one and in the order they arrive.

The technique for assessing the current health of the system is called *sequential learning*.[2][3] Jim Albert, Bowling Green State University Professor of Mathematics and Statistics, has a blog post[4] that illustrates the use of sequential learning in industrial quality control. Shigezumi's paper discusses Bayesian sequential learning in the context of classifying EEG data.[5] Our trading management approach is very similar. The Lopes *Particle Learning* paper[6] might be interesting to mathematically inclined readers. A set of lecture slides presented by Professor James Rawlings[7] describes the use of *Moving Horizon Estimation* for process control. Taken together, the process is called *empirical Bayesian analysis*, described in a Wikipedia article.[8]

Sidebar—Bet Sequencing

Position sizing for trading systems shares background, terminology, and techniques with both gambling and information theory.

Many of the position sizing techniques mentioned in trading literature were developed from betting methods used in gambling.

---

1   http://www.bayesian-inference.com/likelihood
2   http://web.engr.oregonstate.edu/~tgd/publications/mlsd-ssspr.pdf
3   http://webdocs.cs.ualberta.ca/~greiner/R/seq.html
4   http://learnbayes.wordpress.com/
5   http://cdn.intechopen.com/pdfs-wm/44183.pdf
6   https://www0.gsb.columbia.edu/faculty/mjohannes/PDFpapers/CLJP2.pdf
7   http://jbrwww.che.wisc.edu/home/jbraw/stuttgart2011/ch4-stuttgart-2011-jbr.pdf
8   http://en.wikipedia.org/wiki/Empirical_Bayes_method

Many of the techniques assume individual outcomes are independent. That is, independent of each other—the distribution of results for the next trial does not change as a result of earlier trials. If the game has a *memory* of previous play, outcomes are not independent.

A fair roulette game clearly has independent outcomes—neither the wheel nor the ball has a memory of the previous outcomes.

In blackjack, the probability of winning or losing changes based on cards previously played. Blackjack has a memory and hands are not independent.

Acting as if the outcomes are not independent when they are independent is called the *gambler's fallacy*. You will hear it expressed in statements such as "Red has come up seven times in a row. Bet heavy on black. Black is overdue."

There are two broadly defined bet sequencing techniques—Martingale and anti-Martingale.

Martingale

When using a Martingale technique, bet size is increased after losses.

As a betting system, the Martingale appears to guarantee a profit in the long run.

Begin with an original bet of some size, say $1.00. Wait for the outcome of the game. If you win, withdraw your winnings, and begin again with a $1.00 bet. If you lose, double your bet and play again.

Eventually you will win, recovering all of your losses plus one original bet.

This will work provided you are able to fund every bet you might have to make. Your bet size doubles with every loss. Your first bet is $1. After one loss, your second bet is $2. If you lose again, after two consecutive losses your third bet is $4. And so forth. Your bet after n losses is $2 ^ n. After a sequence of 10 losing bets you will be required to bet $1,024. Every winning play returns a net gain of $1 for the series. The system fails because you are eventually required to place a bet larger than you can afford, are willing to place, or are permitted to place. You fall behind the series, and can never catch up.

Casinos ensure that eventuality through use of table limits. A table might have a minimum bet of $5 and a maximum bet of $5,000. The maximum is 1000 times the minimum. Even if you come into the casino with enough money to fund bets larger than $5,000, when the Martingale system requires you to bet $5,120 after the 10th loss (1024 times $5), the table limit limits your bet to $5,000. Even if you win, instead of being $1 ahead for the series, you are $120 behind.

All casino games have unequal odds, with the house having the edge. In roulette, in addition to the 18 red and 18 black pockets, it has 2 that are green. What would be an even money bet, such as red / black or odd / even, is always a loser when the ball falls into a green pocket. This changes the odds from 50% probability of winning to 47.4% of winning. The player reaches the table limit of one thousand times the initial bet once every 613 sequences, rather than once every 1024 sequences for an event that happens 50% of the time.

In the short term, gamblers using a Martingale system will be winners of small amounts. In the long term, gamblers using a Martingale system will be losers of large amounts. The table limit, or its equivalent, will cause an eventual net loss to any player using a Martingale, even if the advantage is in his favor. If the player won all green pocket events, his probability of winning would be 52.6%, and he would have an advantage over the house. He still loses whenever his bet exceeds the table limit, which will happen once every 1758 plays. And he is still a long term loser.

Betting systems based on increasing bet size after a loss are called negative progression systems and all suffer the same disadvantage of the Martingale system.

Anti-Martingale

As you might suspect from its name, anti-Martingale systems increase bet size after wins rather than after losses. Anti-Martingale betting schemes assume that wins occur in streaks—that there is serial correlation—which is in violation of outcomes being independent. If either there is serial correlation or the player has an advantage, then anti-Martingale schemes can be profitably used. (But still beware of the table limit.)

We only trade when our trading system has a positive expectation—an advantage to the player. We act as though there is serial correlation. We *bet the run of the table*.

Dynamic position sizing is an anti-martingale. In response to a series of losing trades, it reduces position size. In response to a series of winning trades, it increases position size.

It recognizes periods of favorable performance and increases position size to take advantage of them.

Note that dynamic position sizing gives variable control over position size. Compare with filters that take long trades only when the close is above its moving average; or equity curve filters that take long trades only when the equity curve is above its shadow equity curve. Those are binary—permit or block.

End of sidebar

Development went well. You designed a system that fits your requirements. Validation tests are promising. Risk is within your tolerance. There is enough profit potential that you think the system is tradable. You begin making trades in the market with real money. You note variation in profits—periods that match those of the validation, and periods of underperformance.

How do you manage trading day-by-day? The model you developed recognizes the patterns and issues the signals. You follow the signals, buying and selling. Has the system performance changed? How healthy is it? Are you getting the best performance for the risk you are willing to take? How do you know when to change position size, and to what new value?

If your development was rigorous, then there is a chance that real trade results are similar to validation results. If your development used poor technique and allowed biases and unreasonable assumptions into the system, then real trade results will be very different.

Most of the time, bad systems lose money fast and good systems make money slowly. Sometimes bad systems get lucky, and sometimes good systems get unlucky.

Poor performance might be because the logic and the data are temporarily out of sync, but the system is a good one and it will eventually recover. Or it might be because the system is bad—either never was good and test results were based on unachievable assumptions, or the data has changed permanently and the logic is no longer able to recognize profitable trades. You may not be able to tell the difference. If trading results are poor, you cannot tell a temporary drawdown from the start of a permanent failure.

The trading system reads the data, recognizes the patterns you helped it learn, and issues the signals. The price and volume data do not have enough information to determine what the best position size should be.

It is the task of the trading management system to deal with the signals and trade results. It has only one purpose—deciding the position size for the next trade.

The technique is *dynamic position sizing*. This chapter explains how it works.

Two Systems

Assuming daily data, price and volume data are inspected, and signals to be long or be flat are issued, daily. Equity is marked-to-market daily, system health is evaluated daily, and the appropriate position size is computed daily. All of this happens at the same time relative to the trading day, but using two distinct systems.

When we think of a trading system, we think of trades following patterns in price and volume. That certainly is a major component, but it is one of two. Figure 9.2, a repeat of Figure 1.1, shows the flowchart for the complete trading process. It has two columns. Each represents one of the components.

The left column is that portion where patterns in data are recognized, and buy and sell signals issued. Call it the *trading system*.

The right column is that portion where trading is managed. Call it the *trading management system*.

They are connected through the *best estimate* set of trades.

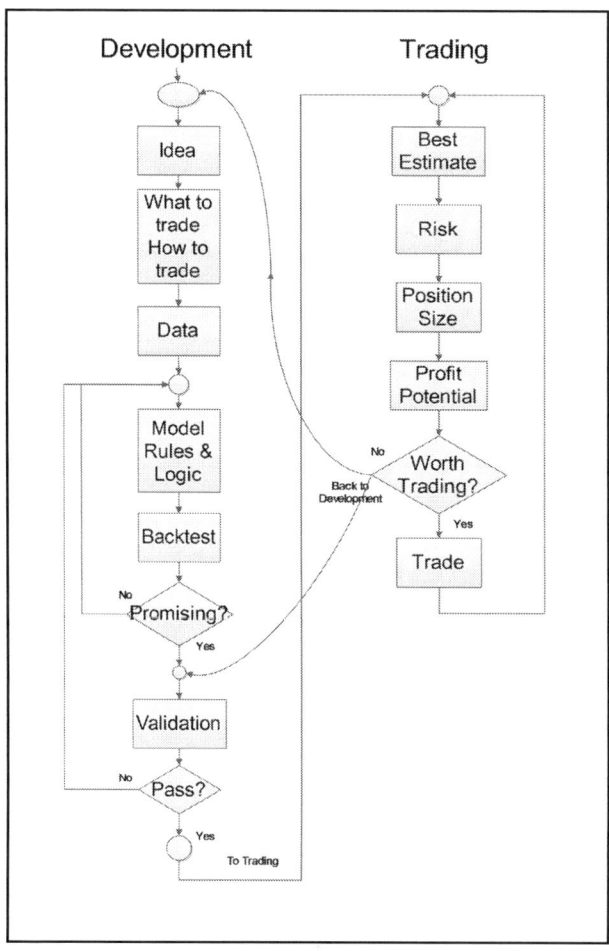

Figure 9.2 Flowchart of a trading system showing two components. On the left, the trading system; on the right, the trading management system.

Trading System

You have a trading system that you are confident is identifying profitable trades. The trading system accepts price and volume data as its input and produces buy and sell signals and a trade list as its output. The system could have been developed using a traditional trading system development platform, as in Chapter 7, a machine learning classification program, as in Chapter 8, or a set of rules based on your personal experience. To the trading management process, it makes no difference which technique was used. The trade list we have named the *best estimate* set of trades is the final result—the output. Figure 9.3, a repeat of Figure 1.2, shows a block diagram of the trading system.

The model portion of the trading system is a *classifier*. It evaluates a series of prices—transaction data—and produces a series of trade signals. At each evaluation point, the output of the system is a binary variable. Either *beLong* or *beFlat*. These signals are applied to the primary data series, resulting in a list of trades.

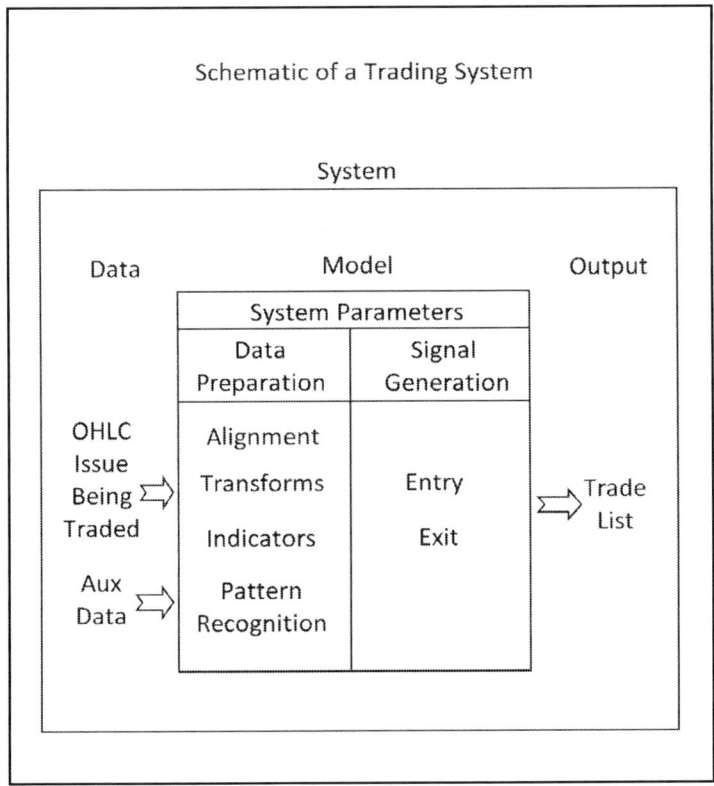

Figure 9.3 Block diagram of trading system

Trading Management System

Figure 9.4 shows a block diagram of the trading management system.

The price and volume data has been transformed by the functions of the trading system into the set of trades. Price and volume are not used in trading management. If you do refer to price and volume prior to making the trade, and use that information to modify the signal, whatever rules you use belong to the trading system. Return here when the trading system has all the rules and you are confident in following the signals without further reference to price and volume.

The system's input is the sequence of trades from the *best estimate*. Its output is *safe-f*, the position size used for the next trade. The trading management system implements *dynamic position sizing*.

The model portion of the trading management system is an *estimator*. It evaluates a series of individual trades in time order resulting from the *beLong* and *beFlat* signals. At each evaluation point, the output of the trading management system is a number—safe-f—the fraction of the trading account to use as the position size for the next trade.

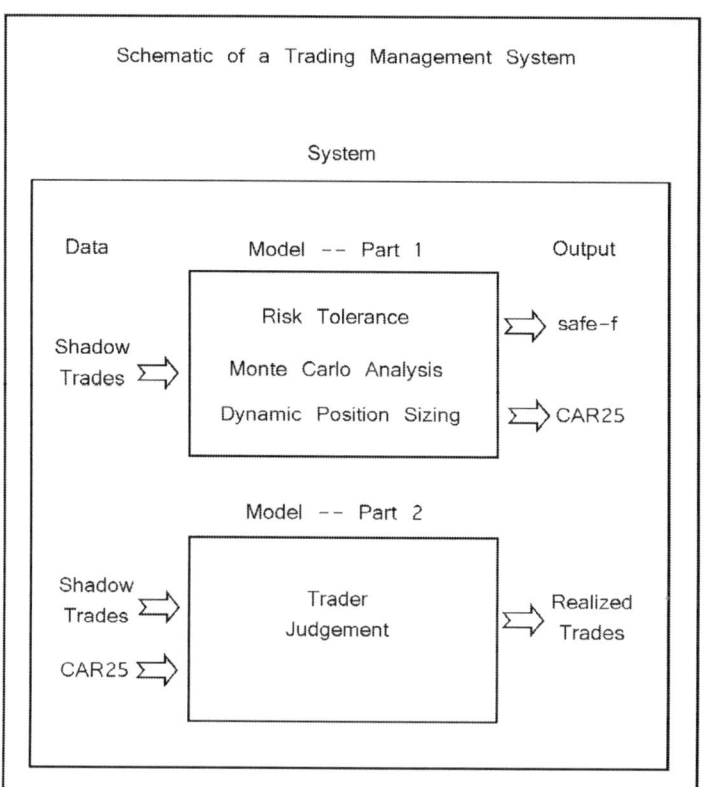

Figure 9.4 Block diagram of trading management system

The purpose of this system is to estimate system health, risk, and profit potential. It has two subsystems that run in sequence.

Part 1

Input to the first subsystem is all trades signaled by the trading system. Call these *shadow trades*. They are analyzed using a combination of sequential learning, empirical Bayesian analysis, and Monte Carlo analysis. The trader's personal risk tolerance is coded into the model. The output of the first subsystem is a pair of numbers that represent the degree of synchronization between the trading system's pattern recognition logic and the price series it processes. It gives an on-the-fly, trade-by-trade, estimate of:
- Safe-f. The dynamic position size. The fraction of the trading account that is allocated to this system to use for the next trade.
- CAR25. The risk-normalized profit potential of the trading system.

The first subsystem has its own development process of fitting a model to data. You have already seen it. The logic of the risk assessment and position size calculation have been well defined in the early chapters of this book, and in my Modeling book.[9]

For development of the trading management system, and immediately prior to making every trade, you have these data items to work with:
- The historical sequence of signals and shadow trades from the trading system. These are fed into the best estimate set of trades.
- The current signal.

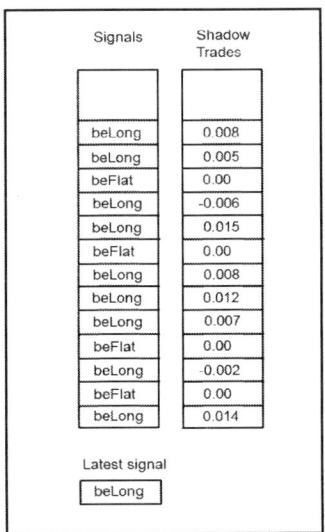

Figure 9.5 Current signal and previous shadow trades

---

9   Bandy, Howard, *Modeling Trading System Performance*, Blue Owl Press, 2011.

Best Estimate and Weights

Refer again to the right side of Figure 9.2. The trading management system uses the best estimate set of trades to establish a baseline. At the time the trading system is moved from development to trading, the best estimate set contains the trades produced by the validation phase. It was this set of trades that provided the confidence that the trading system was worth trading. It will be augmented with each and every shadow trade, including trades with gains of zero that result from signals to be flat.

There is a system development decision to make. How to handle the best estimate set as it grows? There are two options:
- Keep and use the entire trade history.
- Use a sliding window of the most recent trade results.

Each has two sub-options:
- Give equal weight to all trades.
- Give more weight to more recent results.

Figure 9.6 shows the four.

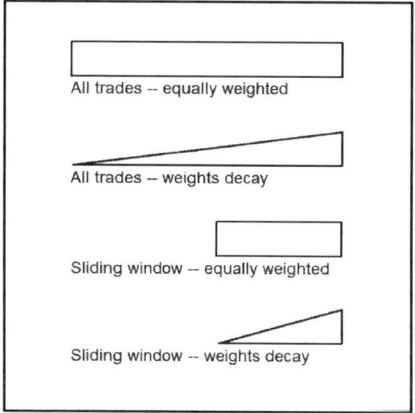

Figure 9.6 Weighting alternatives for the best estimate set

In addition to how many trades to keep and how to weight them, decide the risk tolerance. That is your personal choice. Following examples in earlier chapters, we will continue to use 5% / 20% / 2 years in this chapter.

Two years of daily signals is about 500 daily data points. Each day has an associated shadow trade. If the signal is beFlat, the shadow trade is 0.0. If the signal is beLong, the shadow trade is the change in the primary data series for the day ahead.

The best estimate set provides the pool from which the trades will be drawn. Its size determines how quickly the system responds to changes, and how long it remembers previous trades. Test using periods as short as a few months to as long as twice your forecast horizon. Try four years (1000 trades) to start. This is a metaparameter whose value you will need to determine for your own system. As mentioned, initially these come from the validation's out-of-sample tests.

I recommend using a sliding window with a fixed number of trades rather than all trades. As each new shadow trade is produced, it is added to the current end of the moving window and the oldest trade still remaining in the window is dropped. This lets the system forget a period of poor trades. You hope that is a good thing, and testing the length of the moving window will help determine whether it is. This also provides a mechanism for replacing the simulated trades from development, and whatever bias they contain, with real trades.

I recommend decaying weights. This gives recent performance more weight. And it avoids sudden changes as large trades leave the best estimate set. Robins and Frean discuss advantages and disadvantages of *catastrophic forgetting*,[10] the immediate removal of an older data point as a new data point is added to a sliding window where all elements are equally weighted. The more elegant weighting is exponential decay. Triangular is more practical and is regularly used in simulations. I recommend it. Each weight is proportional to the index of that trade's entry in the moving window.

Part 1 of the dynamic position sizing process is shown in Figure 9.7. It shows the triangular weighting scheme (the third column) that would be used for a 12 trade moving window. For this, or any weighting scheme where the weights are not uniform, it will be necessary to make extra draws from the best estimate set. Whether you decide to use uniform weights or decaying weights, enough data points must be drawn for the simulation so the total of the weights is equal to the desired length of the simulation. Each time a trade is drawn:
1. The shadow trade is multiplied by its weight, reducing its importance if decaying weights are being used.
2. That resulting reduced trade is added to the series as if it was a normal, unmodified trade.
3. The weight is added to a running sum of weights for that series.

When the sum of weights reaches the desired length-equivalent, say 500 for a two year simulation, the series is complete and can be analyzed. Using triangular weighting, the series will have about twice the number of entries, 1000, as the forecast period has days, 500.

The Monte Carlo simulation is run to compute safe-f and CAR25. The direction and amount of the change in safe-f depends on the value of the newest shadow trade, and on the change that creates in the set of

---

10 http://www.cs.otago.ac.nz/staffpriv/anthony/publications/pdfs/RobinsFrean98.pdf

trades used for the simulation. Note that a sequence of beFlat signals with shadow trades of zero can result in a change in the trade decision as previous trades lose influence.

The dynamic position sizing algorithm uses only shadow trades resulting from signals to be long. As such, it rewards true positives and penalizes false positives. It has no awareness of either true negatives or false negatives. It cannot estimate lost opportunity. A signal to be flat results in a shadow trade of zero, which is included as a data point in the list of shadow trades.

Safe-f and CAR25 for the next trade can be calculated as soon as the most recent trade result is known.

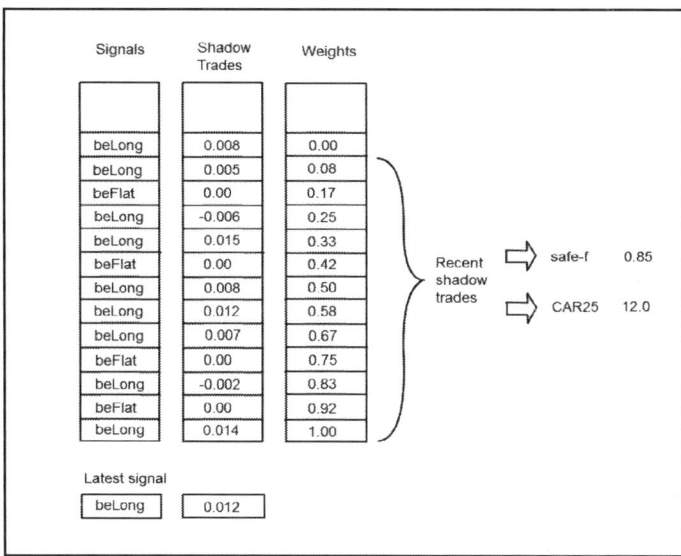

Figure 9.7 Dynamic position sizing process — Part 1

Part 2

The second subsystem relies on the trader's judgement and consideration of other uses for the funds. Its input is the sequence of shadow trades, a beLong or beFlat signal to take a long position or not, and the value of CAR25 from the first subsystem. The trader decides, by comparing CAR25 for this system with CAR25 of alternative systems, including risk-free notes, whether to take the trade or not. If the trade is taken, it is taken with a position size of safe-f and becomes a realized trade with a gain or loss. If the trade is not taken, the realized trade is zero. Figure 9.8 shows that process.

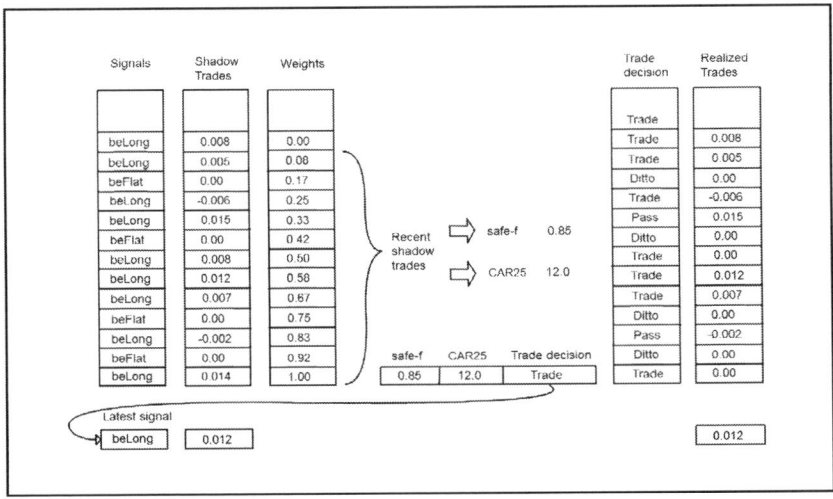

Figure 9.8 Dynamic position sizing — Part 2

The weights are used only for the calculation of safe-f and CAR25. If the signal is beLong and the decision is to Trade, the shadow trade is taken as a real trade with that same percentage gain or loss, but at a position size adjusted by safe-f.

Figure 9.8 shows the trade decision for only the latest signal. That is what is done daily as part of trading. Prior to trading, as part of the development process, it will have been carried out for every day. Figure 9.9 shows how the position size carries through to trades and to the account equity.

Signals	Realized Trades	safe-f	CAR25	Trade decision	Trade gain / loss	Account equity
				Trade		100000
beLong	0.008	0.75	10.1	Trade	600	100600
beLong	0.005	0.78	10.2	Trade	392	100992
beFlat	0.00	0.78	10.2	Ditto	0	100992
beLong	-0.006	0.70	9.4	Trade	-424	100568
beLong	0.015	0.82	11.6	Pass	1237	101805
beFlat	0.00	0.82	11.6	Ditto	0	101805
beLong	0.00	0.82	11.6	Trade	0	101805
beLong	0.012	0.86	12.1	Trade	1051	102856
beLong	0.007	0.87	12.2	Trade	626	103482
beFlat	0.00	0.87	12.2	Ditto	0	103482
beLong	-0.002	0.85	12.0	Pass	-176	103306
beFlat	0.00	0.85	12.0	Ditto	0	103306
beLong	0.00	0.85	12.0	Trade	0	103306
beLong	0.012				1054	104360

Figure 9.9 Dynamic position sizing and account equity

The change in the dollar amount of your account equity is the product of three numbers:
- The previous account equity in dollars.
- The percent of that equity used to take the trade, safe-f.
- The percent gained from that trade, realized trade.

The overall output is an equity curve comprised of realized trades taken with a fraction of the funds for that system—the fraction specified daily by safe-f.

This is part of the validation of the trading management system. Once the system has been accepted, the calculation is needed only for the current day.

Algorithms and Programs

This is a system. It has both a model and data. There are parameters you can set to control how the model interprets the data and guides your trading. The examples in this section use the assumptions and values described earlier. They are listed again as the programs that use them are described.

As we have seen with trading systems, system development is a process of multiple iterations of design, test, and adjustment of the model, followed by a limited number of validation tests. Testing alternatives in-sample, validating out-of-sample—techniques you know well.

Data

You may wish to use one program to compute the historical data needed to populate the best estimate set's moving window and write it to a file on disk. Then read that data with a second program that continues on with the trading management process.

Chapter 4 has examples of the code needed to write such a disk file. For AmiBroker, see Figure 4.3. For Python, see Figure 4.11. The file will be read by a Python program. See Figure 4.12 for the generic example, and the code that follows for specifics.

An alternative to reading a disk file is to regenerate the best estimate data on-the-fly in the program that computes safe-f and CAR25. This option puts all of the steps in a single program which:
- Reads all of the data series. Enough historical data to generate the required number of data points to populate the best estimate set's moving window. All the way through the current data required to determine today's signal and position size.
- Computes the signal and gainAhead data and stores it in an array. Depending on the length of the moving window, the length of the resynchronization cycle, and the recentness of the

changes to parameters, it may be necessary to use two or more sets of parameters.

For the examples in this chapter, the signals and shadow trades are read from a data file in csv format. The file would have been written by a trading system program, perhaps with manual updates for recent trades or to introduce some desired bias.

For this example, the data is in a file named QTA_Chapter9.csv. It can be downloaded and saved to your hard disk. It has about 3000 rows, each representing one day. Each record has three fields:
- date
- signal
- gainAhead

Figure 9.10 shows the first few and last few rows.

	A	B	C	D
1	Date	signal	gainAhead	
2	1/2/2003	-1	0.010286	
3	1/3/2003	-1	0.011067	
4	1/6/2003	-1	-0.01445	
5	1/7/2003	1	-0.00755	
6	1/8/2003	1	0.010295	
...	...	1	,,139	
3019	12/26/2014	-1	0.003472	
3020	12/29/2014	-1	-0.00432	
3021	12/30/2014	1	-0.00999	
3022	12/31/2014	1	0	
3023				

Figure 9.10 The first and last rows of the csv file

As will be demonstrated, the date field can be used to create the index of the dataframe, enabling easy selection of ranges of data by date.

The signal field has two values:
    1 — beLong
    -1 — beFlat

GainAhead is the change in price of the primary data series from the current close to the next close. A gain of 1% is 0.01.

Figure 9.11 lists the Python program that reads the file, creating a pandas dataframe, and storing the data into it. The result is similar to that shown in Figure 9.5.

```
"""
ReadSignalsCSV.py

Disclaimer continues to apply

Copyright  2014 Blue Owl Press, Inc
Dr. Howard Bandy
"""

import matplotlib.pyplot as plt
import numpy as np
import pandas as pd

#  Set the path for the csv file
path = 'C:\Users\Howard\Documents\Python Scripts\
            QTA_Chapter9.csv'

#  Use pandas to read the csv file,
#  creating a pandas dataFrame
sst = pd.read_csv(path)
print type(sst)

#  Print the column labels
print sst.columns.values
print sst.head()
print sst.tail()

#  Count the number of rows in the file
nrows = sst.shape[0]
print 'There are %0.f rows of data' % nrows

#  Compute cumulative equity for all days
equityAllSignals = np.zeros(nrows)
equityAllSignals[0] = 1
for i in range(1,nrows):
    equityAllSignals[i] = \
            (1+sst.gainAhead[i])*equityAllSignals[i-1]

print 'TWR for all signals is %0.3f' %  \
        equityAllSignals[nrows-1]

#  Compute cumulative equity for days with beLong signals
equityBeLongSignals = np.zeros(nrows)
equityBeLongSignals[0] = 1
for i in range(1,nrows):
    if (sst.signal[i] > 0):
        equityBeLongSignals[i] = \
            (1+sst.gainAhead[i])*equityBeLongSignals[i-1]
    else:
        equityBeLongSignals[i] = equityBeLongSignals[i-1]

print 'TWR for all days with beLong signals is %0.3f' % \
        equityBeLongSignals[nrows-1]

#  Plot the two equity streams
plt.plot(equityBeLongSignals, '.')
plt.plot(equityAllSignals, '--')
plt.show()

#  /////   end   /////
```

Figure 9.11 Program to read the csv signal and shadow trade data

Figure 9.12 is the output of the program.

```
>>> runfile('C:/Users/Howard/Documents/Python Scripts/ReadSignalsCSV.py
cuments/Python Scripts')
<class 'pandas.core.frame.DataFrame'>
['Date' 'signal' 'gainAhead']
       Date  signal   gainAhead
0   1/2/2003      -1    0.010286
1   1/3/2003      -1    0.011067
2   1/6/2003      -1   -0.014448
3   1/7/2003       1   -0.007552
4   1/8/2003       1    0.010295

[5 rows x 3 columns]
            Date  signal   gainAhead
3016  12/24/2014       1    0.007139
3017  12/26/2014      -1    0.003472
3018  12/29/2014      -1   -0.004325
3019  12/30/2014       1   -0.009990
3020  12/31/2014       1    0.000000

[5 rows x 3 columns]
There are 3021 rows of data
TWR for all signals is 3.027
TWR for all days with beLong signals is 4.553
>>>
```

Figure 9.12 Output of the program that reads the csv file and computes cumulative equity

Figure 9.13 shows the chart produced by the program.

The lighter weight dashed line is the cumulative equity for all days. It is essentially the chart of the closing price.

The heavier line is the cumulative equity for those days when the signal is beLong. It is the equity curve that would be realized if all funds were used to take a position for every beLong signal. That is, traded at full fraction, or f = 1.00.

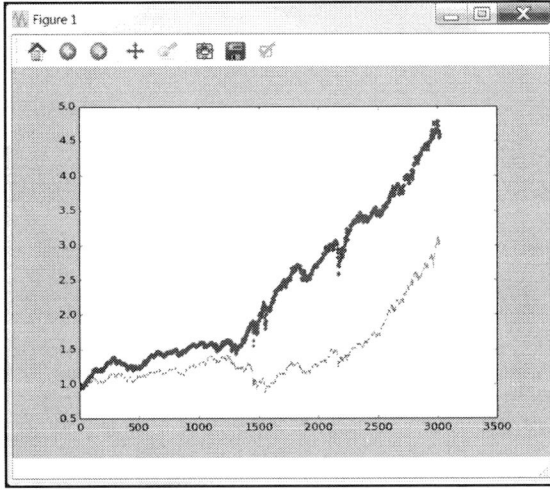

Figure 9.13 Chart showing equity curves for all days and days when the signal is beLong

Given the data, as in Figure 9.5, and triangular weighting, as in Figure 9.6, we can calculate values of safe-f and CAR25 following every trade, as in Figure 9.7. Together, they represent the health of the trading system and the desirability of taking the next trade. Figure 9.14 illustrates for the day with index i.

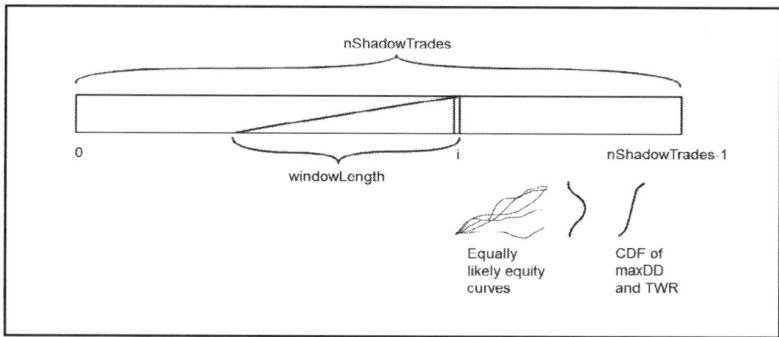

Figure 9.14 Data used to analyze the day with index i

We begin by outlining the algorithm for the calculation for a single day. Later that is expanded for a longer sequence of days.

The algorithm to compute safe-f and CAR25 for day i is:

    Parameters:
        forecastHorizon = 500
        ddTolerance = 0.20
        tailRiskPct = 95
        windowLength = 2 * forecastHorizon
        nCurves = 50
    Variables:
        fraction = 1.00
        dd95 = 2 * ddTolerance
    Computation:
        Repeat until dd95 is close to ddTolerance:

            Generate nCurves equity curves, storing the values of maxDD and TWR in arrays nCurves long. See the algorithm for a single equity curve in Figure 9.16, below.

            Compute dd95 (maxDD at tailRiskPct percentile)

            if dd95 ~= ddTolerance:
                safe-f = fraction
                exit
            else:
                fraction = fraction * ddTolerance / dd95
                continue

Figure 9.15 Algorithm to calculate safe-f for day i

Given the value of safe-f for day i, the value of CAR25 for that day comes from the array of TWR values that were computed and stored. TWR25 is the value of final equity at the 25th percentile.

> The relationship between CAR25 and TWR25 is:
> $(1+CAR25)^N = TWR25$
> The computation of CAR25, given TWR25, is:
> $CAR25 = e \wedge (\ln(TWR25)/N) - 1.0$
> For example, if TWR25 is 1.30, and assuming a forecast horizon of 2 years:
> $CAR25 = e \wedge (\ln(1.30)/2) - 1.0 = 0.14 = 14\%$

The algorithm for the calculation of a single equity curve, which is performed in the repeated section above for each of nCurves.

```
Parameters:
    forecastHorizon = 500
    windowLength = 2 * forecastHorizon
    initialEquity = 100000
Variables:
    curves(nCurves)
    equity = 0
    maxEquity = 0
    drawdown = 0
    maxDrawdown = 0
    horizonSoFar = 0
    fraction
Computation:
    Repeat until horizonSoFar >= forecastHorizon:
        j = randomInteger (0, windowLength)
        weightJ = 1 - j/windowLength
        horizonSoFar = horizonSoFar + weightJ
        signalJ = signal[i-j]
        if signalJ > 0:
            tradeJ = gainAhead[i-j] * weightJ
        else:
            tradeJ = 0
        thisTrade = fraction * tradeJ * equity
        equity = equity + thisTrade
        maxEquity = max (equity, maxEquity)
        drawdown = maxEquity - equity
        maxDrawdown = max(drawdown, maxDrawdown)
    TWR[] = equity
    maxDD[] = maxDrawdown
```

Figure 9.16 Algorithm to calculate a single equity curve

Robustness

The dynamic position sizing process is very robust. There are several parameters that you can tune to help fit the operation of the program to your trading operation. Some small tests illustrate results as parameters are varied through a range of values.

Statement of risk tolerance

As you have seen, the statement of risk tolerance we are using is:

I am trading a $100,000 account, forecasting ahead 2 years. I want to hold the probability of a drawdown greater than 20% to a chance of less than 5%.

That statement has four parameters:
- Initial equity—$100,000
- Forecast horizon—2 years
- Drawdown tolerance—20%
- Tail risk—5%

That statement is represented in the program by four variables. You code your risk tolerance into the simulator by stating values for:
- forecastHorizon = 500
- initialEquity = 100000
- ddTolerance = 0.20
- tailRiskPct = 95

The size of the moving window can be specified either as a specific value, say 1000, or as a multiple of the forecast period, such as:
- windowLength = 2 * forecastHorizon

Outliers

The dynamic position sizing technique cannot protect against outliers. The simulation draws shadow trades from the moving window to estimate future drawdown. If / when a large loss is encountered in a short period of trading, such as October 1987 or October 2008, and there are no similar trades in the moving window, the drawdown experienced can, and probably will, exceed the stated tolerance. Protecting against them requires:
- Accurately estimating the number and depth of the outlier losing trades.
- Keeping shadow trades similar to the outliers in the moving window.

The result will be overly conservative most of the time.

Alternatively, use a fudge-factor. If you anticipate that a period such as October 2008 could happen again, and you want to always be prepared for it:

- Run the dynamic position sizing without allowing for outliers. Say your ddTolerance is 20%.
- Include October 2008 in the range.
- Note the maximum drawdown. Say it is 35%.
- Compute the ratio of 20 to 35 == 57%.
- Reduce whatever safe-f the simulation suggests by multiplying it by 0.57.

You will be prepared for another October 2008, at the cost of underperformance during rising prices.

Sensitivity

Models are sensitive to changes in parameters. Your modeling tasks include determining the best values for the parameters of the models taking the specific data into account.

For a given system, are safe-f and CAR25 sensitive to those parameters?

Beginning with a system that is safe and profitable, each of those four parameters is varied, and the effect on safe-f and CAR25 noted.

The base, used as the midpoint of each of the tests, is a system that trades XLV long / flat, holds 3 days, is 70 percent accurate.

Figure 9.17 shows a table

		initial equity	maximum drawdown	safe-f	CAR25
Initial Equity	10000	10,000	20%	0.98	45
	100000	100,000	20%	0.94	44
	1000000	1,000,000	20%	0.97	45
Drawdown Tolerance	10%	100,000	10%	0.49	22
	20%	100,000	20%	0.94	44
	30%	100,000	30%	1.48	75
	40%	100,000	40%	2.09	121
Tail Risk	2%	100,000	20%	0.84	39
	5%	100,000	20%	0.94	44
	10%	100,000	20%	1.11	53
Forecast Horizon	252	100,000	20%	1.14	48
	504	100,000	20%	0.94	44
	1008	100,000	20%	0.85	42

Figure 9.17 Sensitivity to the statement of risk tolerance

Each of the four segments of the table has the results for the base statement.

Initial Equity. Position size, safe-f, and profit potential, CAR25, are not affected by the initial account balance.

Drawdown Tolerance. The drawdown tolerance parameter is the limit to maximum drawdown—20% in the base. The tail risk parameter is held at 5% for all four of these test runs. Being willing to accept higher drawdown increases the fraction of the account that can be used for each trade, and increases profit potential. The way the dynamic position sizing works, telling the algorithm to allow deeper drawdowns guarantees you will experience deeper drawdowns. Do this only if you have high confidence that the system is sound and will recover.

Tail Risk. The tail risk is the probability you are willing to accept the maximum drawdown—5% in the base. Tightening the tail risk to 2% implies moving the point of the CDF where risk is controlled from the 95th percentile to the 98th percentile. The CDF curve is highly non-linear in the tail region. Tightening the tail risk forces more conservative position sizing, lowering safe-f and lowering CAR25.

Forecast Horizon. Drawdown increases in proportion to the square root of holding period. The simulation suffers an increase in uncertainty as the distance increases, just as regression models or any forecasting models do. A longer horizon implies deeper drawdowns. To hold the expected drawdown to within the 5% / 20% limits, safe-f decreases and CAR25 decreases.

How many equity curves?

Monte Carlo techniques are useful because they approximate expected actual results through multiple simulated trials. The algorithm in Figure 9.15 shows that 50 individual simulated equity curves will be formed, then sorted into ascending order so the value at the 95th percentile can be reported. Is that the right number? The minimum seems to be 20, where the 19th largest is at the 95th percentile. As the number is increased to 50, 100, 200, or even 1000, the value reported is more precise, but at increasing computational cost. What level of accuracy is a reasonable compromise between accuracy and cost? Figure 9.18 contains a table organized by length of moving window (columns) and number of equity curves (rows). Each cell shows the mean and standard deviation of safe-f computed for 100 trials at the values for that cell's pair.

		safe-f, mean, forecast horizon of 2 years				
		windowLength -- Days				
		20	50	100	500	1000
	20	2.97	3.60	3.32	2.72	2.33
nCurves	50	2.83	3.37	3.11	2.57	2.20
	100	2.80	3.36	3.06	2.54	2.19
	200	2.79	3.33	3.04	2.52	2.15

		safe-f, standard deviation, forecast horizon of 2 years				
		windowLength -- Days				
		20	50	100	500	1000
	20	0.27	0.32	0.35	0.30	0.25
nCurves	50	0.20	0.22	0.22	0.20	0.16
	100	0.14	0.19	0.18	0.14	0.12
	200	0.11	0.14	0.12	0.13	0.11

Figure 9.18 Estimate of safe-f related to number of equity curves created

There is an increase in precision with 50 equity curves compared to 20. Above that, the standard deviation tightens, but the mean does not change much. Keep in mind that this is a simulation intended to guide the trader. There are many sources of uncertainty, so increase in precision is of limited value. In my opinion, 50 equity curves is a reasonable number.

Window length influences how quickly the estimate of safe-f changes as performance changes. A short window, say 20 days, reacts quickly. That is good when avoiding falling prices. But bad when seeking stability in operations. Our tests found a 20 day window was too short and often unstable. You will need to do some experimentation with your specific trade history. Figure 9.19 shows the closing price for a period in 2007. The value of safe-f is computed for the six day period for points in the dotted box for several window lengths and shown in Figure 9.20.

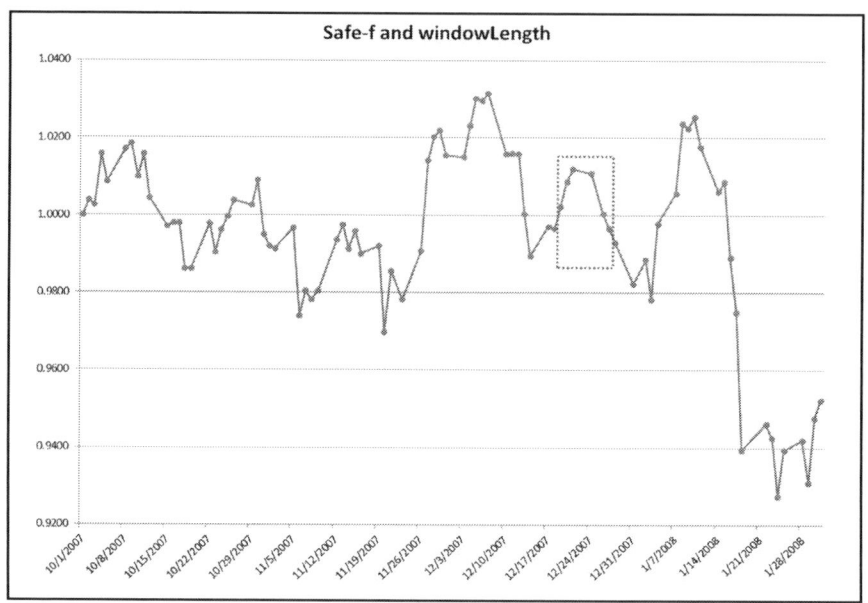

Figure 9.19 Closing price for a several month period

Figure 9.20 safe-f related to window length for the period in the dotted box

Shortening the window means fewer trade records are in the memory of the process, and older trades drop out more quickly. Safe-f adapts more quickly. This is very similar to computing a moving average. Longer window length implies a smoother safe-f series and an associated longer lag. The optimal length depends very much on the series being modeled. There is no universal correct length. You will need to do some experimenting.

Update frequency is another metaparameter. The examples shown in Figures 9.18 and 9.20 updated daily. The program code has a variable that allows you to update less frequently. Our testing indicates that updating once a week, or whenever a new position is taken, does not hurt performance and will make implementation less burdensome. When in a position and marking to market daily, be alert to losing trades and recompute safe-f after losses. But do not make minor changes in position intra-trade. Instead, recalculate safe-f in preparation for taking a new position after the system has gone flat. If your holding period is longer than one week, consider rebalancing position size once a week.

Extending the period between rebalancing risks holding too large a position as a trade enters a drawdown. Extending the period between recomputation of safe-f to several months or years creates a system that acts if it is stationary.

Action thresholds

During development, you will want to test parameters such as the threshold at which you take the system offline. For example, you might want to take the system offline when safe-f falls below 0.70, or when CAR25 falls below 6%. Testing these would be inconvenient if done using multiple Python runs, but easily done in a spreadsheet. To accomodate spreadsheet analysis, two disk files are written. The code for both these is at the bottom of the program listing. When you have moved from development to trading, either comment out or ignore the disk files and set the date range to just the past week or two. The program displays the most recent portion of the data structure that has the latest signal, safe-f, and CAR25.

Data structure

The program does not store the trade-by-trade equity and drawdown. If you want those for some additional analysis, allocate arrays to hold values. The length of each trade sequence will depend on the specific trades drawn and their specific weights. In accordance with the central limit theorem, the number of trades needed will be Normally distributed. Using triangular weighting, the average is twice the length of the forecast horizon, and the standard deviation is about 0.80 times the square root of the average. For a 500 day forecast, the number of trades required will be an average of 1000 with a standard deviation of about 25. Assuming the number of trades in any single equity curve will seldom exceed six standard deviations, declaring the array to have a length of 1150 should be sufficient. Have your program test before attempting to store into a non-existent location.

Listing

The Python program that implements dynamic position sizing is listed in Figure 9.21. In addition to the variables already discussed, you can vary the date range. When you are verifying that the technique and program work for your trading system, you will want to specify a large number of trades covering a long period of time. That data is written to a disk file and displayed in a chart. Execution time is proportional to the number of calculations of safe-f. The examples shown below processed 3000 end-of-day data points, updated daily, for a total of 3000 calculations. This run takes a few hours. A test of one year, updating weekly, would be 52 calculations, and takes a few minutes. When you have moved to operation, you receive the buy and sell signals from the trading system and the position size from this program. Only a few of the most recent data periods are needed, and that calculation takes only a few seconds. You will probably comment out the sections of code that write to the disk and display the chart.

Note that there are many lines of code commented out in this listing. They can be reactivated to help understand the program and the process, or deleted to shorten the code.

```
"""
DynamicPositionSizing.py

Disclaimer continues to apply

Copyright  2014 Blue Owl Press, Inc
Dr. Howard Bandy
"""
from __future__ import division
import matplotlib.pyplot as plt
import numpy as np
import pandas as pd
from scipy import stats
import datetime as dt
from pandas.core import datetools
import time


#  Set the path for the csv file
path = 'C:\Users\Howard\Documents\Python Scripts\
            QTA_Chapter9.csv'

#  Use pandas to read the csv file,
#  creating a pandas dataFrame
sst = pd.read_csv(path)
#print type(sst)

#  Print the column labels
#print sst.columns.values
#print sst.head()
#print sst.tail()

#  Count the number of rows in the file
nrows = sst.shape[0]
#print 'There are %0.f rows of data' % nrows

#  Compute cumulative equity for all days
#equityAllSignals = np.zeros(nrows)
#equityAllSignals[0] = 1
#for i in range(1,nrows):
#    equityAllSignals[i] = (1+sst.gainAhead[i])*
                     equityAllSignals[i-1]
#
```

```
#print 'TWR for all signals is %0.3f' %  
            equityAllSignals[nrows-1]

#  Compute cumulative equity for days with beLong signals
#equityBeLongSignals = np.zeros(nrows)
#equityBeLongSignals[0] = 1
#for i in range(1,nrows):
#    if (sst.signal[i] > 0):
#        equityBeLongSignals[i] = (1+sst.gainAhead[i])*
                    equityBeLongSignals[i-1]
#    else:
#        equityBeLongSignals[i] = equityBeLongSignals[i-1]
#
#print 'TWR for all days with beLong signals is %0.3f' %
            equityBeLongSignals[nrows-1]

#  Plot the two equity streams
#plt.plot(equityBeLongSignals, '.')
#plt.plot(equityAllSignals, '--')
#plt.show()

sst = sst.set_index(pd.DatetimeIndex(sst['Date']))
sst=sst.drop('Date', axis=1)
sst['safef'] = 0.0
sst['CAR25'] = 0.0

#print sst.columns.values
#print sst.head()
#print sst.tail()

# create a range of times
#   start date is inclusive
#start = dt.datetime(2010,1,4)
start = dt.datetime(2014,1,3)
#   end date is inclusive
end = dt.datetime(2014,12,31)
updateInterval = 1

forecastHorizon = 500
initialEquity = 100000
ddTolerance = 0.20
tailRiskPct = 95
windowLength = 1000
nCurves = 50

years_in_forecast = forecastHorizon / 252.0

#  Work with the index rather than the date
iStart = sst.index.get_loc(start)
iEnd = sst.index.get_loc(end)

for i in range(iStart, iEnd+1, updateInterval):
    print sst.index[i], sst.signal[i], sst.gainAhead[i]

#  Initialize variables
    curves = np.zeros(nCurves)
    numberDraws = np.zeros(nCurves)
    TWR = np.zeros(nCurves)
    maxDD = np.zeros(nCurves)

    fraction = 1.00
    dd95 = 2 * ddTolerance
```

```python
        while (abs(dd95-ddTolerance)>0.03):
            #  Generate nCurve equity curves
            print "  Fraction ", fraction
            
            for nc in range(nCurves):
        #        print "working on curve ", nc
                equity = initialEquity
                maxEquity = equity
                drawdown = 0
                maxDrawdown = 0
                horizonSoFar = 0
                nd = 0
                while (horizonSoFar < forecastHorizon):
                    j = np.random.randint(0,windowLength)
        #            print j
                    nd = nd + 1
                    weightJ = 1.00 - j/windowLength
        #            print weightJ
                    horizonSoFar = horizonSoFar + weightJ
                    signalJ = sst.signal[i-j]
                    if signalJ > 0:
                        tradeJ = sst.gainAhead[i-j] * weightJ
                    else:
                        tradeJ = 0.0
                    thisTrade = fraction * tradeJ * equity
                    equity = equity + thisTrade
                    maxEquity = max(equity,maxEquity)
                    drawdown = (maxEquity-equity)/maxEquity
                    maxDrawdown = max(drawdown,maxDrawdown)
        #           print "equity, maxDD, ndraws:", equity,
                                maxDrawdown, nd
                TWR[nc] = equity
                maxDD[nc] = maxDrawdown
                numberDraws[nc] = nd
            
            #  Find the drawdown at the tailLimit-th percentile
            dd95 = stats.scoreatpercentile(maxDD,tailRiskPct)
        #    print "  DD %i: %.3f " % (tailRiskPct, dd95)
            fraction = fraction * ddTolerance / dd95
            TWR25 = stats.scoreatpercentile(TWR,25)
            CAR25 = 100*(((TWR25/initialEquity) **
                    (1.0/years_in_forecast))-1.0)
    
        print fraction, CAR25
        sst.safef[i]=fraction
        sst.CAR25[i] = CAR25
    
#print maxDD
#print numberDraws

print sst.tail(60)
diskPath = "C:\Users\Howard\Documents\Python Scripts\
            DynamicRunPartA.csv"
print "Writing to disk in csv format"
sst.to_csv(diskPath)

# ----------------------------------------
#    
#  compute equity, maximum equity, drawdown, and maximum
        drawdown
```

```
sst['trade'] = 0.0
sst['fract'] = 0.0
sst['equity'] = 0.0
sst['maxEquity'] = 0.0
sst['drawdown'] = 0.0
sst['maxDD'] = 0.0

initialEquity = 100000

sst.safef[0] = 1.0
sst.CAR25[0] = 10.0
sst.equity[0] = initialEquity

for i in range(1,nrows):
    if (sst.safef[i]==0 and sst.CAR25[i]==0):
        sst.safef[i] = sst.safef[i-1]
        sst.CAR25[i] = sst.CAR25[i-1]
        sst.fract[i] = sst.safef[i]
        sst.equity[i] = sst.equity[i-1]
    else:
        sst.fract[i] = sst.safef[i]
        sst.equity[i] = sst.equity[i-1]

for i in range(iStart, iEnd):
    if (sst.signal[i] > 0):
        sst.trade[i] = sst.fract[i-1] * sst.equity[i-1] * \
                        sst.gainAhead[i]
    else:
        sst.trade[i] = 0.0
    sst.equity[i] = sst.equity[i-1] + sst.trade[i]
    sst.maxEquity[i] = max(sst.equity[i],sst.maxEquity[i-1])
    sst.drawdown[i] = (sst.maxEquity[i]-sst.equity[i]) /
                    sst.maxEquity[i]
    sst.maxDD[i] = max(sst.drawdown[i],sst.maxDD[i-1])

print sst.tail(60)

#  Plot the equitycurve and drawdown
plt.subplot(2,1,1)
plt.plot(sst.equity)
plt.subplot(2,1,2)
plt.plot(sst.drawdown)
plt.show

diskPath = "C:\Users\Howard\Documents\Python Scripts\
                DynamicRunPartB.csv"
print "Writing to disk in csv format"
sst.to_csv(diskPath)

#  /////  end  /////
```

Figure 9.21 Program to compute dynamic position size

Output

During development, your first interest is probably in the charts. Figure 9.22 shows the equity curve and drawdown for a 3000 day period. The terminal wealth is about 600,000 — TWR of 6.0 and CAR of 16.1%. Compare with Figure 9.13 where the TWR of buy and hold is abut 3.0 (CAR of 9.6%), and the TWR taking all beLong signals at fraction 1.0 is about 4.6 (CAR of 13.6%). There is a year-long drawdown in the early period that reaches about 25% for a short time, but less than 5% of the time. Otherwise drawdown is held below 20%.

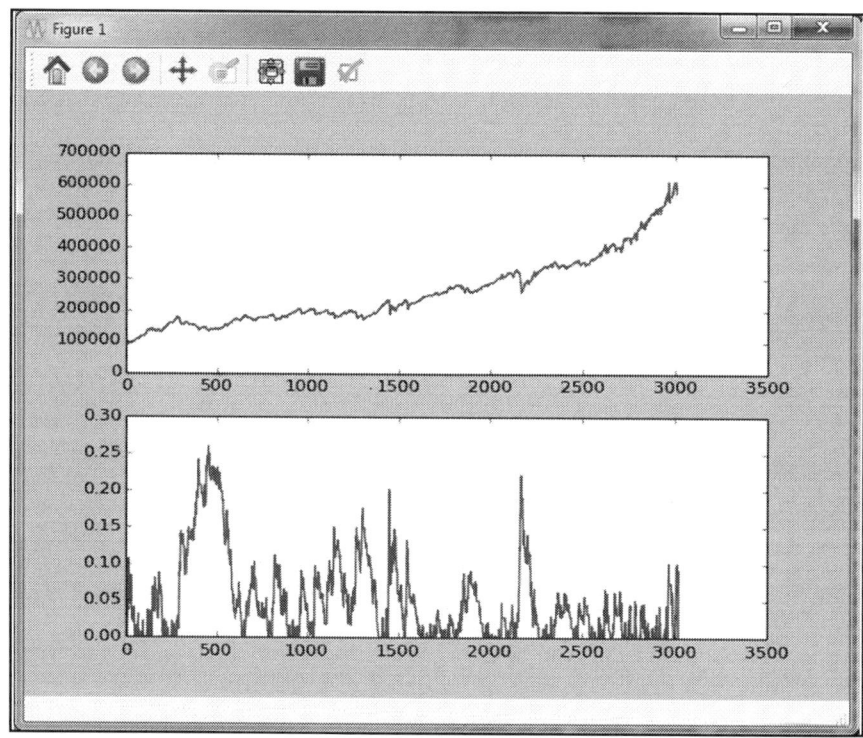

Figure 9.22 Equity curve and drawdown using safe-f. Update frequency is daily, length of the moving window is 1000 trades.

Figures 9.23 and 9.24 show the equity and drawdown for two variations of the size of the moving window. While the final equity for the 100 day window is higher, the early period suffered five years of flat performance with drawdown reaching 30%.

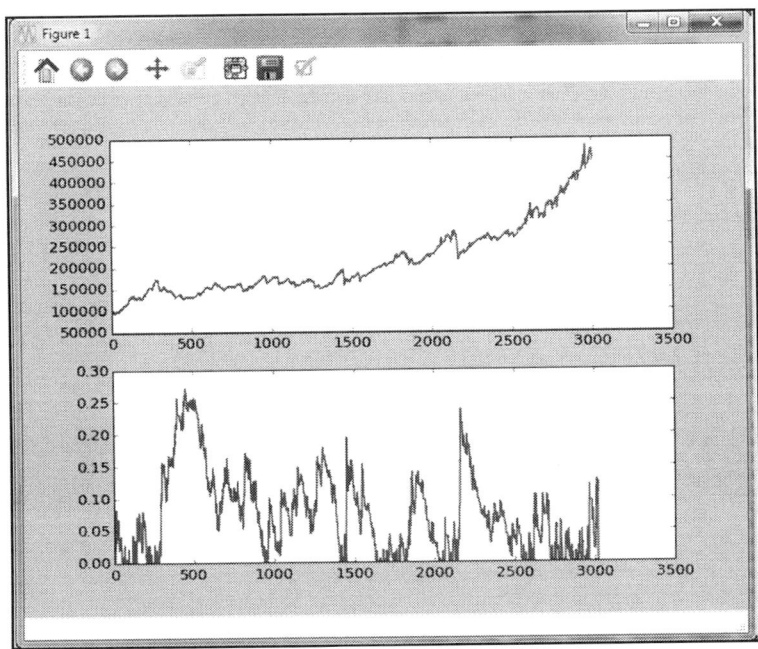

Figure 9.23 Equity curve and drawdown using safe-f. Update daily. 500 day moving window.

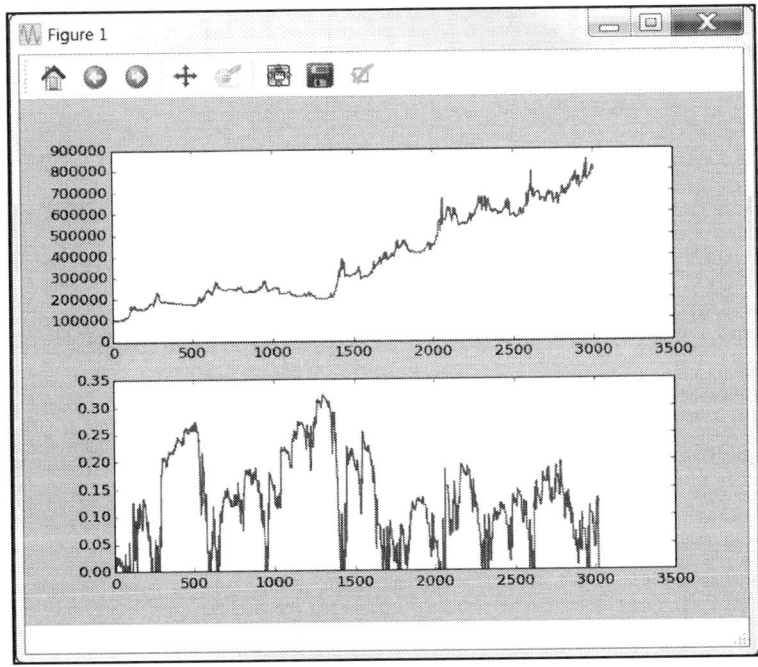

Figure 9.24 Equity curve and drawdown using safe-f. Update daily. 100 day moving window.

Almost Ready

You have some choices to make and some tuning to do.
- How often do you want to resynchronize the trading system?
- What is your risk tolerance?
- How often do you want to adjust your position size?
- Should you use leverage to take positions with fractions greater than 1.0?
- What other systems could be traded with these funds and what do their charts look like?

When you are satisfied with development and confident to use the program, the printed output will probably give you the best information. Figure 9.25 shows a few days at the end of 2014. Using the last day, December 31, as the example:
- The date is 2014-12-31
- The signal is 1—beLong
- The gainAhead is 0.0, because it is unknown.
- Two lines show intermediate calculations of the fraction. You may want to comment out the Python code that prints them.
- The final line shows safe-f is 1.72. If you do use leverage through margin, options, or ETFs with beta of 2X, the program recommends doing so for the next day. CAR25 is 13.5. Use this as the metric by which you compare alternative uses of the funds.

```
2014-12-29 00:00:00 -1 -0.004324636
   Fraction   1.0
   Fraction   1.98904853897
2.10738816065 18.6137569148
2014-12-30 00:00:00 1 -0.009989865
   Fraction   1.0
   Fraction   1.6391520165
1.77528496126 14.839979211
2014-12-31 00:00:00 1 0.0
   Fraction   1.0
   Fraction   1.48206688141
1.72269673884 13.5178962584
```

Figure 9.25 Text output from the dynamic position size program

Your Own Genie

You have tools and procedures to develop and manage trading systems quantitatively. You have your own genie. You tell her your risk tolerance and give her some suggestions for issues to trade. She works her magic and returns a chart of account growth for a system that operates within your tolerance.

Chapter 10

Summary and Random Thoughts

Abandon Financial Astrology

Maybe astrology helps with your personal relationships. But whenever some suggests that I incorporate Gann, Fibonacci, or moon phase, I ask for precise definitions that do not repaint, then require thorough testing. None of these have yet passed my filters.

Become a Competent Programmer

You must be able to design, program, debug, and operate your own programs. Do not rely on a black box or a consultant.

Best Estimate

If the data used to populate the best estimate set is badly biased, then augmented by realized trades, the distribution is a mixture of two different processes. The result is more uncertain than if the prior is assumed to be random.

Bad data is worse than no data.

Broad Principles

Think probabilistically.

Forecasts can change. They get better with experience and new information.

Data

If the data series fails the risk test, there is no model that works.

Degree of Belief

When a gambling analyst tells us that the probability of the ball landing in a red pocket of a fair roulette wheel is 18 out of 38, or 47.4%, that probability can be verified experimentally with repeated trials. As the number of trials grows very large and approaches infinity, the proportion of those trials where the outcome was red approaches 47.4%. This is a frequentist interpretation of probability.

When a political analyst predicts a 30% probability of a candidate winning, the 30% value is not the result of repeating an experiment many times and counting the proportion where she won. It is a statement of the degree of belief that she will win.

From the frequentist perspective, the data is seen as random with fixed parameters to be estimated. Sampling is infinite, and decision rules can be sharp. Studies can be repeated. There is no information prior to the specification of the model.

From the Bayesian perspective, the data is seen as given. The parameters are unknown and random, and are updated as additional data is observed. Studies cannot be repeated. Prior information is important and useful.

Use whichever tools are helpful in solving the problem or establishing the confidence you need.

Discard Harmful Biases

Nostalgia is fine for antique furniture. But not for techniques for trading.

Embrace Monte Carlo

Use Monte Carlo simulation and analysis to study relationships and alternatives.

Feature Engineering

A simple algorithm with refined data usually outperforms a complex algorithm with raw data.

Gambling

Trading systems are not like roulette. Roulette has no model that works.

Trading systems are like blackjack. There is a model that works under some conditions. We want to recognize the conditions and play correctly. Stand aside otherwise.

Impartial Goal

List all subjective constraints, planning to exclude any system that violates any of them.

Consider all remaining systems impartially. Normalize for risk, then use those that have the highest account growth.

Is It Broken?

Make certain you can tell when your system performance is deteriorating. Take drawdowns as early warnings to reduce position size.

Learn the Mathematics

You must understand the mathematics that is the foundation of both trading systems and trading management. You must be able to assess program operation and results.

Learning and Model Complexity

Training data
- Guide the learning
- In-sample

Testing data
- Test whether learning happened
- Out-of-sample

Learning
- The model fits the training data, and also gives accurate predictions for test and live data.

Overfitting
- The model fits the training data, but gives inaccurate predictions for out-of-sample data.
- Make the model less complex, or replace it.

Not learning
- The model does not fit the training data. (Hence, cannot be trusted no matter how it fits the out-of-sample data.)
- Make the model more complex, or replace it.

Model

The whole purpose of the model is to identify the signal.

Model and Data

We are fitting a model to data so we can use the model to make predictions. Our first prediction is the direction of price change. Our confidence in that prediction is expressed in the size of the position taken.

Nothing is Stationary

Nothing about financial data or trading systems is stationary.

Every tool and technique you use must deal with changes in relationships.

Physical Laws

There are no physical laws governing the behavior of financial markets. If there were, new information would not matter much, and there would be little profit opportunity.

Position Sizing

Given a trading system that issues buy and sell signals, the only tool available for managing trading of that system is trade by trade position sizing.

Position size cannot be a component of the trading system's model. Putting it there removes it from trading management, assumes it is stationary, and assumes systems never fail.

Prediction

Are we predicting? Yes! The model is identifying, in advance, profitable trading opportunities. It is predicting them.

Quantify Your Risk Tolerance

I am trading a $100,000 account, and forecasting two years. I want to hold the probability of a drawdown greater than 20% to a chance of 5%.

Use your risk tolerance to normalize results for comparison.

Read, Read, Read

This field is changing with astonishing speed. Subscribe to discussion forums, read research journals, watch lectures. Stay current. Your competition is.

Regime Switching

CAR25 is a universal objective function. It is the estimated growth rate of the trading system, normalized for risk. Absent reasons not related to the performance, CAR25 can be used to rank alternative systems in a regime switching *portfolio of systems*. (This is an interesting project, already ongoing, and profitable.)

Risk
- Personal
- Data
- System

Small safe-f

The value of safe-f is related to the expected drawdown in the entire balance of the account trading the system—both the portion in shares and the portion in ballast funds. If the recommended value of safe-f is small, drawdowns in the portion in shares will be much larger than your stated tolerance. This much larger: 1.00 / safe-f.

Stationarity

Nothing is stationary.
- Not prices.
- Not detrended prices.
- Not differenced prices.
- Not volatility.
- Not indicator signal frequency.
- Not trade frequency.
- Not trade profitability.
- Not position size.

Deal with the non-stationarity. Treating financial data and trading systems with tools that assume stationarity guarantees failure.

System Evaluation

The system results in an equity curve. Analysis of the equity curve determines the goodness of the system. That is, what is the terminal wealth and what is the drawdown.

Given two systems, compare them by normalizing the risk, then comparing the terminal wealth. Does anything else matter?

The Data Is What It Is

Financial data does not follow Normal distribution. Do not assume that it does, nor try to force it to be, nor naively use techniques that assume Normality.

ToDo List

There is much more that can be done. For example:
- Short / flat systems

- Pairs trading
- FOREX
- Futures
- Intra-day entries and exits
- Regime switching
- Consensus models
- Automated trading

Perhaps in the next book.

Use the Entire Distribution

Understand and use cumulative distribution functions and their charts.

When You Have Enough, Quit

No matter how profitable, consistent, and safe your system appears, there is always a non-zero probability of an account destroying black swan event.

Why This Is So Hard

You are competing one-on-one with Goldman Sachs. There are no handicaps and no mulligans.

Appendix 1
Bibliography

The bibliography is intended to be practical rather than encyclopedic. I have listed books and websites that I have found provide background and examples that are helpful in learning about and implementing trading system with the characteristics that have high probability of being profitable with low risk.

This list is heavy in machine learning, pattern recognition, probability, statistics, modeling, and simulation—because those topics are of primary importance in developing quantitative trading systems. It is light on traditional trading systems, indicators, and charting—because those topics are not very useful for systems that fit the trading profile most likely to be profitable.

Machine Learning, Data Analysis

Abu-Mostafa, Yaser, Malik Magdon-Ismail, and Hsuan-Tien Lin, *Learning from Data*, AML Books, 2012.

—, *Machine Learning*, California Institute of Technology, online course. https://work.caltech.edu/

Aronson, David, and Timothy Masters, *Statistically Sound Machine Learning for Algorithmic Trading of Financial Instruments: Developing Predictive-Model-Based Trading Systems Using TSSB*, Aronson, 2013.

Bishop, Christopher, *Pattern Recognition and Machine Learning*, Springer, 2007.

Bishop, Christopher, *Introduction to Bayesian Inference*, video lecture.
    `http://videolectures.net/mlss09uk_bishop_ibi/`

Box, George, and Friends, *Improving Almost Anything: Ideas and Essays*, Revised Edition, Wiley, 2006.

de Freitas, Nando, Machine Larning and Data Mining, University of British Columbia, video lectures.
    `http://www.cs.ubc.ca/~nando/340-2012/`

Downey, Allen, *Think Bayes*, O'Reilly, 2013.

—, *Think Stats*, O'Reilly, 2011.

Flach, Peter, *Machine Learning: The Art and Science of Algorithms that Make Sense of Data*, Cambridge, 2012.

Foreman, John, *Data Smart: Using Data Science to Transform Information into Insight*, Wiley, 2013.

Garreta, Raul, and Guillermo Moncechi, *Learning scikit-learn: Machine Learning in Python*, Packt, 2013.

Gigerenzer, Gerd, *Calculated Risks: How to Know When Numbers Deceive You*, Simon & Schuster, 2003.

Haigh, John, *Taking Chances: Winning with Probability*, Oxford, 2003.

Harrington, Peter, *Machine Learning in Action*, Manning, 2012.

Hastie, Trevor, Robert Tibshirani, and Jerome Friedman, *The Elements of Statistical Learning: Data Mining, Inference, and Prediction*, Second Edition, Springer, 2011.

Hubbard, Douglas, *How to Measure Anything: Finding the Value of Intangibles in Business*, Wiley, 2014.

Japkowicz, Nathalie, and Mohak Shah, *Evaluating Learning Algorithms: A Classification Perspective*, Cambridge, 2011.

Koller, Daphne, and Nir Friedman, *Probabilistic Graphical Models: Principles and Techniques*, MIT, 2009.

—, *Probabilistic Graphical Models*, Stanford University, Coursera online course.
    `https://www.coursera.org/course/pgm`

Kruschke, John, *Doing Bayesian Analysis, Second Edition*, Academic Press, 2014.

Marsland, Stephen, *Machine Learning: An Algorithm Perspective*, CRC, 2009.

Mauboussin, Michael, *More Than You Know: Finding Financial Wisdom in Unconventional Places*, Columbia, 2007.

—, *The Success Equation: Untangling Skill and Luck in Business, Sports, and Investing*, Harvard, 2012.

McGrayne, Sharon Bertsch, *The Theory that Would Not Die: How Bayes Rule Cracked the Enigma Code, Hunted Down Russian Submarines, and Emerged Triumphant from Two Centuries of Controversy*, Yale, 2011.

Miller, Thomas, *Modeling Techniques in Predictive Analytics: Business Problems and Solutions with R*, Pearson, 2013.

Miner, Gary, Robert Nisbet, and John Elder, *Handbook of Statistical Analysis and Data Mining Applications*, Academic Press, 2009.

Murphy, Kevin, *Machine Learning: A Probabilistic Perspective*, MIT Press, 2012.

Ng, Andrew, *Machine Learning*, Standford University Open Course. http://openclassroom.stanford.edu/MainFolder/CoursePage.php?course=MachineLearning

Pearl, Judea, *Causality: Models, Reasoning, and Inference*, Second Edition, Cambridge, 2009.

Pratt, John, Howard Raiffa, and Robert Schlaifer, *Introduction to Statistical Decision Theory*, MIT, 1995.

Provost, Foster, and Tom Fawcett, *Data Science for Business: What You Need to Know About Data Mining and Data-Analytic Thinking*, O'Reilly, 2013.

Pyle, Dorian, *Data Preparation for Data Mining*, Morgan Kaufmann, 1999.

Richert, Willi, and Luis Pedro Coelho, *Building Machine Learning Systems with Python*, Packt, 2013.

Russell, Stuart, and Peter Norvig, *Artificial Intelligence: A Modern Approach*, Pearson, 2010.

Schapire, Robert, and Yoav Freund, *Boosting: Foundations and Algorithms*, MIT, 2014.

Schutt, Rachell, and Cathy O'Neill, *Doing Data Science: Straight Talk from the Frontline*, O'Reilly, 2014.

Segaran, Toby, *Programming Collective Intelligence: Building Smart Web 2.0 Applications*, O'Reilly, 2007.

Siegel, Eric, and Thomas Davenport, *Predictive Analytics: The Power to Predict Who Will Click, Buy, Lie, or Die*, Wiley, 2013.

Silver, Nate, *The Signal and the Noise: Why So Many Predictions Fail - But Some Don't*, Penguin, 2012.

Stone, James, *Bayes Rule: A Tutorial Introduction to Bayesian Analysis*, Sebtel, 2013.

Weisberg, Herbert, *Willful Ignorance: The Mismeasure of Uncertainty*, Wiley, 2014.

Winston, Patrick, *Artificial Intelligence*, MIT Open Courseware.
http://ocw.mit.edu/courses/electrical-engineering-and-computer-science/6-034-artificial-intelligence-fall-2010/

Witten, Ian, Eibe Frank, and Mark Hall, *Data Mining: Practical Machine Learning Tools and Techniques*, Third Edition, Morgan Kaufmann, 2011.

Programming, Data Structures, Algorithms, Python

Bressert, Eli, *SciPy and NumPy: An Overview for Developers*, O'Reilly, 2013.

Brownlee, Jason, *Clever Algorithms: Nature-Inspired Programming Recipes*, Brownlee, 2012.

Cormen, Thomas, Charles Leiserson, Ronald Rivest, and Clifford Stein, *Introduction to Algorithms*, 3rd Edition, MIT, 2009.

Downey, Allen, *Think Python*, O'Reilly, 2012.

Hetland, Magnus Lie, *Python Algorithms: Mastering Basic Algorithms in the Python Language*, Second Edition, Apress - Springer, 2014.

McKinney, Wes, *Python for Data Analysis: Data Wrangling with Pandas, NumPy, and iPython*, O'Reilly, 2012.

Sedgewick, Robert, and Kevin Wayne, *Algorithms*, 4th Edition, Addison-Wesley, 2011.

Steiner, Christopher, *Automate This: How Algorithms Came to Rule Our World*, Portfolio / Penguin, 2012.

Wilson, Greg, et al, *Best Practices for Scientific Computing*, Cornell University, 2012.
http://arxiv.org/pdf/1210.0530v4.pdf

Psychology

Kahneman, Daniel, *Thinking, Fast and Slow*, Farrar, Straus, and Giroux, 2011.

Surowiecki, James, *The Wisdom of Crowds*, Random House, 2004.

Trading

Bandy, Howard, *Introduction to AmiBroker: Advanced Technical Analysis Software for Charting and Trading System Development*, Second Edition, Blue Owl Press, 2012. http://www.introductiontoamibroker.com/

—, *Mean Reversion Trading Systems: Practical Methods for Swing Trading*, Blue Owl Press, 2013.

—, *Modeling Trading System Performance: Monte Carlo Simulation, Position Sizing, Risk Management, and Statistics*, Blue Owl Press, 2011.

—, *Quantitative Trading Systems: Practical Methods for Design, Testing, and Validation*, Second Edition, Blue Owl Press, 2011.

Connors, Larry, and Cesar Alvarez, *High Probability ETF Trading: 7 Professional Strategies to Improve Your ETF Trading*, Connors, 2009.

—, *How Markets Really Work: A Quantitative Guide to Stock Market Behavior*, Second Edition, Bloomberg, 2012.

Rhoades, Russell, *Trading VIX Derivatives: Trading and Hedging Strategies Using VIX Futures, Options, and Exchange Traded Notes*, Wiley, 2011.

Miscellaneous

Peta, Joe, *Trading Bases: How a Wall Street Trader Made a Fortune Betting on Baseball*, New American Library, 2013.

Raschka, Sebastian, *Terms in Data Science Defined in One Paragraph*, https://github.com/rasbt/pattern_classification/blob/master/resources/data_glossary.md, 2014.

Appendix 2
Program Listings

Programs that have program or figure numbers, and are listed here, can be downloaded from the book's website. Short programs, code segments, and pseudo-code that do not have figure numbers do not have download files.

The programs are intended to be educational examples. Use them as templates from which you can develop your own thoroughly tested programs for your own use.

These examples may have errors. If / when errors are found, corrected versions of the programs will be posted in the download area replacing the erroneous versions.

For clarity in illustrating techniques, execution error handling has been omitted. You should add it.

Figure Number	Program Name and Description	Page
Program 2.1	Trading system to produce the trades and equity curve analyzed in Chapter 2	75
Figure 4.2	Write data series to a disk file—AmiBroker	114
Figure 4.3	Write trade list to a disk file—Ami Broker	116
Figure 4.4	Read price history from Yahoo—Python code	117
Figure 4.7	Read end-of-day data from Google Finance	119
Figure 4.9	Read intra-day data from Google Finance	120

Figure 4.11	Write csv file—Python code	122
Figure 4.12	Read csv file—Python code	122
Listing 5.1	Python code for the simulator that computes risk, determines maximum safe position size, and estimates profit potential	148
Figure 7.1	Program template for a trading system	204
Figure 7.2	Custom objective function	208
Figure 7.4	Fit sine cycle	214
Figure 7.6	RSI model listing	215
Figure 7.8	Z-score model listing	217
Figure 7.10	PIR model listing	220
Figure 7.12	DPO model listing	222
Figure 7.14	Create the diffusion index	225
Figure 7.16	Use the diffusion index	227
Figure 7.18	Looping code for profit target exit	232
Figure 7.21	Looping code for holding period exit	235
Figure 7.22	Chandelier trailing exit	238
Figure 7.23	Parabolic trailing exit	240
Figure 7.25	Maximum loss exit	244
Figure 7.26	Manual entry design program	247
Figure 7.42	Estimate close for moving average cross	264
Figure 8.2	Using dates to define a time period in Python	269
Figure 8.4	Copying a section of data using a date range	271
Figure 8.6	RSI model using impulse signals (AmiBroker)	274
Figure 8.10	RSI model using impulse signals (Python)	279
Figure 8.12	RSI model using state signals (Python)	285
Figure 8.17	Determine default directory	295
Figure 8.19	Read iris data	296
Figure 8.21	Plot iris data	297
Figure 8.23	Plot iris pairs data	299
Figure 8.26	Creating five cross validation partitions	303

Program Listings

Figure 8.28	Shuffle before partitioning	305
Figure 8.35	Using StratifiedShuffleSplit to create train and test sets	313
Figure 8.38	Ada Boost classification	320
Figure 8.40	Decision tree classification	322
Figure 8.42	Gradient Boost classification	324
Figure 8.44	Linear discriminant classification	326
Figure 8.46	Logistic regression classification	328
Figure 8.48	Naive Bayes - Gaussian	330
Figure 8.50	Naive Bayes - multinomial	332
Figure 8.52	Nearest neighbor	334
Figure 8.54	Passive aggressive	336
Figure 8.56	Perceptron	338
Figure 8.58	Quadratic discriminant classification	340
Figure 8.60	Random forest classification	342
Figure 8.62	Support vector classification - linear kernel	344
Figure 8.64	Support vector classification - polynomial kernel	346
Figure 8.66	Support vector classification - radial basis kernel	348
Figure 8.75	Python trading system template	366
Figure 8.79	Program to create a best estimate set of trades	375
Figure 9.11	Read csv file signal and shadow trade data	402
Figure 9.20	Dynamic position sizing	420

Index

200 day moving average 170-174
Abu-Mostafa, Yaser 319
account:
  growth 17
  size 52
accuracy
  classification 302, 352
  general 182, 249
ada boost 320-321, 358
AIG bankruptcy 225
Albert, Jim 388
AmiBroker:
  custom objective function 186
  databases 80-89
  development platform 203-266
  environment 77-89
  Introduction book, free 78
  Mean Reversion book 78
  Quantitative Trading Systems book 78
  trial, free 78-80
  TSDP 78
AmiQuote:
  AmiBroker data manager 82
  free data 82-85
Anaconda 92
Anderson, Edgar 293
anticipate signals 175-176
  indicator-based 261-266
  precompute 176
anti-Martingale see Martingale
auxiliary data 23, 188

backtest:
  change 16
  historical 187-189
  indicator-based 246-248
  procedure 187-189
bad stuff happens 49
bad tick 315
Bandy, Howard
  Introduction to AmiBroker book 78
  Mean Reversion Trading Systems book 78, 161, 215, 217, 318
  Modeling Trading System Performance book 30, 54, 58, 167, 395
  Quantitative Trading Systems book 78, 224
Bayes, machine learning algorithm:
  Gaussian 330-331
  multinomial 332-333
Bayesian: 388, 395, 420
  change 16
  position size 31
best estimate 18, 54, 146, 198, 362-363, 374-375, 381
bet sequencing 388-390
bias:
  stationary 26
  confidence 34
bankable equity 47
binning data 164-165
black swan 55, 138
blackjack 34, 389, 421

Bollinger band 25

bonds 15, 23

Box, George 38

breakdown 17

California, Univ at Irvine 293

CAR25:
    characteristics 187
    universal objective function 186
    use 306

Carroll, Lewis 35

casino 35

catastrophic forgetting 397

central limit theorem 224, 411

certainty 52-54

chart pattern 16, 19

Chenoweth, Mark 118

class membership 350

classification:
    category 28, 91, 184, 292-293, 301, 306
    costs 350
    example 320-349
    target 284, 363-364

classifier 393

cognitive dissonance 31

commission 188

commodities 15

competition 37

components of trading:
    development see development
    flowchart 18
    management see management

compound annual rate of return (CAR):
    calculate 127
    define 62, 138
    metric 62, 134
    objective function 138
    position size 141

computer:
    language see language

confidence:
    drawdown 41
    faith 33
    goal 16
    position size 387
    quantifiable 34
    risk as limitation 16
    subjective 200
    validation 33

confusion matrix:
    AmiBroker 351
    change 16
    objective function 184

Continuum Analytics Anaconda 92

csi 112

cumulative distribution function (CDF):
    inverse 56
    risk tolerance 53, 55

currencies 15

curve-fit 182

cycle frequency 229

data driven 16

data series:
    alignment 21, 23
    auxiliary 23
    backtest 188
    bars 22
    bid-ask 22
    close, as last price 22
    daily 22
    end-of-day 22
    high, unknown order 22
    historical 16
    in-sample 28
    intra-day 22
    low, unknown order 22
    master dates 23
    mining 28
    missing 23, 188
    non-price 23
    not interchangable 27
    open, high, low, close 22
    open, as first price 22
    out-of-sample 28
    patterns 16
    price 22

primary 21-23, 187, 201, 237-238, 243, 250, 263, 272, 314, 355-356, 374, 393
synchronization 26
tick 22
time series 22, 26
transformation 21
variation required 16
volume 22

data:
  bar types 159-160
  characteristics:
    desirable 107
    mandatory 107
  fundamental 108-110
  mining 124
  number of points 196
  over-the-counter 110
  read and write:
    AmiBroker 114-115
    Python 116-122
  simulated 108
  sources, development 109
  sources, free:
    Google 85, 112
    Interactive Brokers 113
    msn 85, 113
    nasdaq 113
    quandl 85
    US Treasury 113
    Yahoo 85, 87, 114
  sources, subscription:
    csi 112
    dtn.iq 112
    eoddata 112
    eSignal 112
    Norgate 88, 113
    quandl 88
  sources, trading 109
  surrogate 108
  visual inspection 297

date alignment 23, 188

date, pivot 359

decision tree 322-323:
  AmiBroker 351
  change 16

decisions 35

Derman, Emanuel 23

deterministic 16

development
  backtest 18
  best estimate 18
  data 18
  issue selection 18
  iterative process 29
  objective function 28
  model 18
  validation 18

difficult 15, 35-38, 155

dimensionality 189-192, 357-359

distribution:
  see also Cumulative Distribution Function
  change 16
  drawdown 67
  final equity 62
  next day return 52
  no assumptions 23
  price changes 385
  tail 55
  trade results:
    position size 20

double down 229-230

Downey, Allen 92

drawdown 17, 19, 29
  account growth 53
  defined 40
  depth 42
  holding period 53, 129-143
  issue selection 126-152
  length 42
  maximum risk 52
  multi-day 42
  not symmetric 41
  objective function 187
  position size 53, 58-59
  reasons: 32-33
    broken system 33
    out of sync 33
    position size wrong 33
  recovery time 40
  system broken 53
  system health 42
  synchronization 42
  trade accuracy 130-152

dtn.iq 112

dynamic 16

dynamic position sizing:
   implementation 20, 385-418
   safe-f 59
   trading management 31

efficient markets 17, 155

encyclopedic 15

end-of-day data 22

eoddata 112

Elliott wave 175

empirical Bayes 388, 395

Enron 50

Enthought Canopy 92, 93-100

entries 230-231
   price 230
   time 230

entropy 301

equations 16

equity curve:
   change 16
   example system 56
   new high 41
   position size 59

eSignal 112

estimator 394

ETF see exchange traded fund

evolutionary operation 192

exchange traded fund 15

exit technique: 231-246
   chandelier 238-240
   logic 29, 42, 231-232
   maximum loss 29, 42, 243-246
   no external rules 42
   parabolic 240-243
   profit target 29, 42, 232-235
   quantitative system 42
   subjective action 42
   time 29, 42, 235-237
   trailing exit 29, 42, 237-243

expectation 187

expectations 384

extended trading 176

faith 41

false positive 353, 398

feature selection 358

feedback 36

Fibonacci 175

filters 170

Fisher, Ronald 293

fitting 182-184

fixed fraction 54

Flach, Peter 319

flash crash 315

flowchart:
   trading components 18

forecast horizon 52-54, 64, 125-127, 147-152, 363, 397, 405-414

FOREX 15

Frean 397

frequency of action 41

frequentist 16, 165, 388, 420

full fraction 57

futures 15

Galileo 16, 157

gambling 388-390, 420

generalization 183

genie 385, 418

global optimum 191

goal 15, 16

Google:
   data 85
   Python 92, 104-106

gradient boost 324-325

handicap 37

Hanson 192

Harrington, Peter 319

health, system:
   drawdown 27
   monitoring 19, 29

synchronization 27
holding period 34
  drawdown 129-143
  minimum 42
  objective function 187
  position size 53
  trade accuracy 129-143
horizon see forecast horizon
Hubble 16
hyper-parameteres 319
idea driven 16
impossible things 35
impulse signals 52, 168-170, 283-289
independent 156
  event 389-390
  variable 230-231, 263, 291
indicator: 16, 19
  based development 22, 153, 203-266
    see also model development
  Bollinger band 25
  Elliott wave 175
  Fibonacci 175
  fuzzy 162-163
  ideal 161-162
  initialization 188
  interchangability 161
  realistic 163-165
  threshold 353
  z-score 25
  zig-zag 175
inefficiency 36
information content:
  direction 23
  distribution of trades 23, 24
  list of trades 23, 24
  mean 23
  moments of distribution 23, 24
  reality 23, 24
  set of trades 23, 24
information theory 388
in-sample:
  confusion matrix 354
  data mining 28
  define 28
  fit always good 195
  length of period 35
  results always good 37
  results of little value 195
  short as practical 195
  stationarity 193-196, 386
intra-day:
  data 22
  drawdown 47
  signal 176
Interactive Brokers 113
invisible prices 43, 45
iris data 293, 302
issue selection 123-152
  accuracy 125-152
  detectable patterns 124
  holding period 125-152
  profit potential 123
  risk 123, 124-143
iterative search 54
Janeczko, Tomasz 207
Japkowicz, Nathalie 312
joblib 362
judgement 77, 309, 398
Kahneman, Daniel 154
Kelly criteria 58
Kohavi, Ron 304
kurtosis:
  define 25
landings are manditory 201
language:
  computer:
    general purpose 20
    Python 20
learning:
  classification 28
  data requirement 28
  estimation 28
  generalization 27
  in-sample 28
  out-of-sample 28
  patterns 27
  system 16, 17

learning repository 293

leverage ETF 61, 143

libraries, function:
  numpy 20
  Pandas 20
  scikit-learn 20
  scipy 20

linear discriminant analysis 326-327, 358

linear regression 163

liquidity 135

local optimum 191

logistic regression 328-329

Lopes 388

lost opportunity 363, 398

machine learning: 16
  based development 22, 153, 267-3xxx
    see also model development
  environment 77

management:
  best estimate 18
  measurement 49
  objective function 20
  parameter 20
  position size 18, 19
  process 15
  risk 18, 19

market-on-close (MOC) 44

market-on-open (MOO) 43

market research 123-124

markets, efficient 17

mark-to-market:
  adverse excursion 45
  equivalence 51-52, 64-66
  impulse signals 52
  issue selection 125
  number data points 52
  serial correlation 66
  state signals 52
  subjective decisions 52
  test period distortion 52, 169-170

Martingale 389-390

mathematics:
  increasingly important 155, 157
  required skill 77

matplotlib 91
  model development 267

maximum adverse excursion 43
  accumulated 48
  drawdown 48
  multi-day trade 45
  risk 43
  series of trades 46-47

maximum favorable excursion:
  mark-to-market 48
  metric 25

McKinney, Wes 90, 92, 93

mean:
  define 25

measurement:
  management 49
  process 15

membership bias 224-225
  Norgate Premium Data 225

memorization 183

memory 389

meta-parameters 319

metric, performance 15, 19
  baseline 19
  CAR25 134
  single valued 20

misclassification 350

missing data 23, 188

model:
  all are wrong 38
  data alignment 21
  data preparation 21
  entry 18
  exit 18
  goal 157
  indicators 22
  input 22
  metrics 19
  output 22
  parameters 16
  pattern recognition 19
  performance 22

position sizing 22
rules 16
signals 16, 21
simplifications 23
synchronization 26
trading system 16
trend following 34
transformation 22
validation 19
verify 16

model airplanes 200-201

model development:
  indicator-based 203-266
    AmiBroker 203-266
      anticipating signals 261-266
      backtesting 246-248
      indicators 203
        chart patterns 228-229
        data series 212
        detrended price oscillator 222-224
        diffusion index 224-228
        highpass filter 222
        lookback length 212, 213
        oscillator 212
        oversold depth 212
        percent rank 219
        position in range 219-221
        RSI 215-217
        selection 213-229
        stochastic 219
        Williams %R 219
        z-score 217-219
      entries 230-231
      exits 231-246
      in-sample 249
      Janeczko, Tomasz 207
      long / flat 212-213
      mean reversion 204
      membership bias 224-225
      objective function 205-211
        accurate trading 207
        bars held 206
        CAR25 206
        consecutive losers 206
        custom backtester 207
        decathlon scoring 207
        frequent trading 207
        gain per trade 206
        holding period 207
        losing trades 206,207
        maximum drawdown 206
        percent winners 206
        trades per year 206
      optimization 248-249
      out-of-sample 249-251
      program template 203
      rules 203
      short / flat 213
      tradable systems 255-256
      validated systems 256-259
      walk forward 251-255
      z-score 205
  machine learning 267-384
    "A" array 309-312
    accuracy 302, 308
    algorithms 319-349
      ada boost 320-321
      decision tree 322-323
      gradient boost 324-325
      linear discriminant analysis 326-327
      logistic regression 328-329
      naive Bayes—Gaussian 330-331
      naive Bayes—multinomial 332-333
      nearest neighbor 334-335
      passive aggressive 336-337
      perceptron 338-339
      quadratic discriminant analysis 340-341
      random forests 342-343
      support vector machine—linear kernel 344-345
      support vector machine—polynomial kernel 346-347
      support vector machine—radial basis kernel 349-350
    AmiBroker 267
    balancing class membership 350-351
    classification 292
    class weight 351
    confusion matrix 306-312, 350
    cost matrix 309-312, 350-351
    cross validation 302-306
    data and dates 268-272
    data independence 290-292

data mining 290
data preparation 314-318
date alignment 315
diagonal 308-312
domain knowledge 309
element independence 314-315
false negative 307-312
false positive 307-312
future leak 315
generalities 290-292
in-sample 310
interpolation 315
iris example 293-349
lagged values 291
linear scaling 317
linearly separable 302
logistic transformation 317-318
matrix algebra 309
misclassification costs 350-351
missing data 315
model evaluation 312
model fitting 310-312
model prediction 311
Murphy, Kevin 267
neural network 317
normalization 317
off-diagonal 308-312
outliers 315-318
out-of-sample 311
positive class 306-312
percent rank 317
precision 308
prediction 306-312
predictor variables 291, 298
Python 267-
regression 292
replacement 312-313
sample weight 351
scikit-learn 316
sequential covering 301
signals 272-274, 283-289
sliding window 316-318
softmax 317-318
standardization 316
stratified cross validation 304-306
stratified shuffle split 310-314
supervised 290-292
support vector machine 316
target variable 290, 316
trading 355-357
transformation 316-318
train / test split 310
true negative 307-312
true positive 307-312
TSDP coordination 382-383
TSDP translation 274-283
trading 351-3xxxx
trading system simulator 278-283
Type I-IV errors 307-308
unbalanced classes 302
unsupervised 290
weight parameter 351
Winzorize 315
preliminaries 153-202
  best estimate 154
  constraints 176-182
  entries and exits 165-168
  indicators 161-165
  learning 154
  pattern recognition 158
  perfect bottoms 165-168
  prediction 183
  purpose 183
  simplification 157
  two paths 154
  two processes 155-156
    trading system 156
    trading management 156
  validation 154

manifold learning 358

Margineantu 308

metaparameter 356

model examples:
  200 day moving average 170-174
  moving average cross 176-182

monitor:
  performance 16

Monte Carlo analysis:
  best estimate 67
  change 16
  compare single value 20
  distributions 20
  drawdown forecast 54
  dynamic position sizing 67, 395-418
  issue selection 125-152
  performance 30

position size 31
risk management 67
moving horizon 388
msn:
    data 85, 113
Murphy, Kevin 267
mutual funds 15
naive Bayes:
    Gaussian 330-331
    multinomial 332-333
nasdaq 113
nearest neighbor 334-335
next day return 52
no guarantee 66
noise 27, 35, 157-158, 183
non-linear 16
Norgate Premium Data: 113, 225
    AmiBroker 81
    membership bias 225
normalization 356
numpy:
    library 20, 91
    model development 267
objective 16
objective function:
    CAR25 186
    define 28, 184-187
    construction 28
    custom 186
    development 29
    rank alternatives 29
    subjectivity 28, 29
    trader psychology 30
    trading management 29
    use 28
    universal 138, 186
offline 17
open market 15
optimum 191
optimization 189-192
    alternatives 189
    indicator-based 248-249

order placement 175
Ostermeier 192
outlier 315-317, 406-407
out-of-sample:
    confusion matrix 354
    define 28
    length of period 35, 195
    poor results 33, 195
    results important 37
    stationarity 193-196
    validation 28, 194-196
overfit 182
p greater than n 357-358
passive aggressive 336-337
Pandas:
    book 90
    dataframe 296, 356, 401
    library 20, 91
    McKinney 90
    model development 267
particle learning 388
patriotic 41
patterns:
    importance 26
    persistent 17
    precede trades 16, 22
    profitable 17
    recognize 16, 17
    signals 17
percentile 54
perceptron 338-339
perfection 192
performance:
    best estimate set of trades 30
    distribution 29
    estimates 29
    monitor 17
    Monte Carlo 30
    profit potential 29
    risk 29
    system health 29
pickle 362
pipeline 361
pivot date 359

population:
  distinguish 23
portfolio 143-144
position size:
  ballast funds 12
  Bayesian analysis 31
  CAR25 relationship 141
  computing 17, 19
  drawdown 19, 31, 58-59
  dynamic see dynamic position sizing
  fixed fraction 54
  fixed ratio 58
  fixed size 20, 58
  importance 16, 19, 31
  Kelly 58
  maximum safe 15
  model 19
  Monte Carlo 31
  not fixed size 31
  not stationary 31, 128, 156
  profit 19
  safe-f:
    defined 58-
  single contract 58
  synchronization 27
  trade-by-trade 17
  trading management 18, 19, 385-418
posterior distribution 388
precision:
  classification 308, 352
  general 182, 249
precompute 176
prediction:
  change 16
  purpose of system 16, 22, 183
predictor variable 356
price 15
principal component 358
prior distribution 388, 419, 420
probabilistic 16
probability density function (pdf):
  defined: 24
probability mass function (pmf):

defined 24
histogram 55
risk 55
process:
  control 388
  designing system 15
  modeling 16
  monitoring system 15
profit:
  oriented 16
  potential 124-144
  risk relationship 16
  synchronization 27
programming:
  environments 77-106
  required skill 77, 157
  machine learning 90-106
  Python 77, 90-106
  trading system development platform (TSDP) 77-89
prospecting 124
psychology:
  cognitive dissonance 31
  objective function 30, 187
  trader 30
p-value 16, 34
pyramiding 229-230
Pyle, Dorian 314
Python:
  see also model development
  Anaconda Spyder 267
  books 92
  environment 77, 90-106, 267-3xxxxx
  file directories 294-295
  library stack 91
  trading system 365-373
  tutorial 91, 106
quadratic discriminant analysis 340-341
quality control 388
Quandl 88, 113, 365-366
quantify subjectivity 185
quantitative techniques:
  technical analysis 15

Index

random forests 342-343, 358
Rawlings, James 388
reaction 16
recall:
   classification 308, 352-355, 373
recognize patterns 17, 22
regularization 358
repainting 174-175
reward:
   tradeoff 15, 16
rewards high 37
Richert, Willi 319
risk:
   acceptable 16, 17
   account growth 39
   accuracy 40
   control 42
   drawdown 39
   dynamic position sizing 39
   entries 39
   estimating 19
   exits 39
   holding period 40
   inherent in data 31
   issue selection 39, 40
   intra-trade 40
   limitation 16
   management 39
   maximum adverse excursion 43, 48
   measurement 39, 40
   normalized: 15
      best and worst trades 71-73
   oriented 16
   personal tolerance 39
   position sizing 39
   statement: 40
      account size 52
      CDF 53
      certainty 52
      example 52
      forecast horizon 52
      maximum drawdown 52
      personal 67
   synchronization 39
   system design 39
   tolerance 16, 17, 31, 39-76, 385
      issue selection 125-152
   tradeoff 15, 16
   trade selection 39
   trading account 39
risk free:
   alternative 16
robust 192, 255, 361, 366, 406
Robins 397
Rogers, Will 49
root finding 176
roulette 35, 389-390, 420
safe-f:
   CAR25 relationship 141
   define 59, 135
   issue selection 124, 135
   mark-to-market 64
   risk tolerance 59
   trade-by-trade 59
   trading management 31
sample:
   distinguish 23
   estimate 24
   subset 24
scikit-learn:
   classification 20
   library 20, 91
   model development 267
   pattern recognition 20
   transformation 316-317
scipy:
   library 20, 91
   model development 267
search:
   evolutionary operation 192
   exhaustive 191
   non-exhaustive 191-192
   space 189-192
self deception 154
sensitivity 308, 407
sequential covering 301, 363
sequential learning 388, 395
shadow trades 395-406
Shah, Mohak 313

Sharpe ratio 25, 187

Shigezumi 388

short positions 44
  risk 132-134

signals:
  anticipate 175-176
  generated 16
  impulse 52
  noise 27, 35, 157-158
  precede trades 16, 157
  patterns 17
  state 52

Silver, Nate 27, 158

skewness:
  define 25
  stationary 16

slippage 188

softmax 317-318

Sortino ratio 187

SPY 50

Spyder:
  Anaconda Python 101-103

standard deviation:
  define 25

standardization 356

state signals 52, 168-170, 283-289
  mark-to-market 168
  test period boundary 169

stationary:
  assumption of 26
  bias 26
  correlations are not 144
  define 26
  machine learning 359-360
  nothing is 194
  position size is not 128, 156
  synchronization 193-196
  theorems require 26
  time series is not 26, 35, 193
  trading difficulty 35, 193
  walk forward 200

statistical significance 53

Statisticat 388

stay the course 386

stocks 15

stop trading, reasons 31-33

stratified K fold 373-374

stratified shuffle split 373-374

subjective 16, 125
  quantifying 185

support vector machine 344-350, 358

synchronization:
  data and model 26
  drawdown 42
  importance 26
  position size 27
  profit 27
  stationarity 193-196
  system health 27

system, trading:
  auxiliary data 21
  breakdown 17, 49, 67
  confidence 16
  health see health
  indicators 22
  intermarket data 21
  long / flat 125
  managing 15
  model + data 21
  monitoring 15
  objective function 28
  parameters 16, 20-22
  performance 15
  prediction 16
  profitable 16
  purpose 16
  requirements 16
  rules 16
  signals 16
  single issue 125

table limit 389-390

tail risk 55, 57, 61, 138, 406, 408

takeoffs are optional 201

technical analysis:
  charts 77
  quantitative 77

terminal wealth relative (TWR):
  CAR, related 127
  define 60
  metric 61

objective function 187
position size 60
Vince, Ralph 60

threshold 353

time series data:
different 36
not stationary 26, 36

toxic trades 187, 363--365

tradeoff, risk reward 15

trade quality:
best trades 67
buy and hold 67
risk-normalized 71-73
sweet spot 129-137
worst trades 70

trading management: 385-418
dynamic position sizing 31, 67
integrated approach 15, 16
Monte Carlo 67
overview 31
safe-f 31
stop trading 31-33

trading system:
development:
integrated approach 15
platform (TSDP) 16, 203-266, 382-383
model 16
RSI2 example 67-73
equity 68
listing 75
safe-f 70
statistics 69
trades 70

trades:
independence 20

train / test 373-375

transformation, data 21

trend following 34, 36, 160

triangular weighting 397, 404, 411

TSDP see trading system

UCI learning repository 293

uncertainty 35

US Treasury data 113

utility of money 52

validation 197-200
best estimate trades 198
machine learning 357-361, 373
walk forward 197-200

van Rossum, Guido 90

variance:
define 25

verify:
learning 16

Vince, Ralph 60

visible prices 43, 45

volatility:
maximum allowed 16
minimum required 16

volume 15

walk forward:
best estimate trades 198
confidence 34
define 197-200
gold standard 197
indicator-based 251-255

weights:
diffusion index 224
moving window 396-397
objective function 184

White queen 35

Winzorize 315

Yahoo:
data 85, 114

z-score 25

zig-zag 175

Made in the USA
San Bernardino, CA
28 January 2015